Automata Theory and Formal Languages

Express Learning Series

Automata Theory and Formal Languages

Express Learning Series

Shyamalendu Kandar

Assistant Professor
Computer Science and Engineering
Haldia Institute of Technology, Haldia
and
Course Co-ordinator
HIT Center M.Tech- IT(CWE)
Jadavpur University

ISBN 978-81-317-6077-2

First Impression

Published by Dorling Kindersley (India) Pvt. Ltd., licensees of Pearson Education in South Asia.

Head Office: 7th Floor, Knowledge Boulevard, A-8 (A), Sector 62, NOIDA, 201 309, UP, India.
Registered Office: 11 Community Centre, Panchsheel Park, New Delhi 110 017, India.

Compositor: Chennai Publishing Services

Printer: Anubha Printers

Dedication

To my parents,

Arun Kumar Kandar and Hirabati Kandar,

who have shown me the light of the universe and light of knowledge

&

My GURU in the field of technical education

Professor C. T. Bhunia

who is an inspiration in every step of my life

About the Author

Shyamalendu Kandar is Assistant Professor of Computer Science and Engineering at the Haldia Institute of Technology, Haldia, West Bengal. He has passed B.Tech. in Computer Science from Vidyasagar University in 2004 and M.Tech. in Information Technology (Courseware Engineering) from Jadavpur University in 2006. His research interest is mainly in multimedia communication, image processing, and automata theory. He has published a number of research papers in international journals and presented papers in international conferences.

Contents

Foreword

The worth of a book is to be measured by what you can carry away from it.—James Bryce

In the history of science and technology, if any branch has ever changed the prospective face of the world, it is nothing else but Computer Science and Engineering known as CSE microscopically in this gradually becoming short and nano society(!) The subject of automata theory is an important component of CSE, among others. It is said that it is "the study of abstract machine and the problems which they are able to solve." Thus, it is by right a primary and core part of CSE.

Many books on automata theory are available in the market and all these books have obvious attractions as well as drawbacks. Any attempt to author a book with authority to please everyone is next to impossible. Even any academic exercise to attain the defined objectives and decisive targets deserves commendation and encouragement. Thus, so I think the current book authored by Shyamalendu Kandar is a definite scholastic exercise that I am sure will fulfill the aspirations of undergraduate students of CSE and those of related interdisciplinary subjects. The book is written in easily understandable and simple language and contains a large number of solved problems, MCQs and exercises.

I would like to congratulate Shyamalendu for this bold academic productivity. Shyamalendu feels that he is a student of mine and, therefore, as a teacher I feel proud of him. I wish him ever growing success in the days to come!

Last but not the least, I am a firm believer that "*Good* teachers are costly, but bad teachers cost more." Shyamalendu proves this by his present academic work that he belongs to the family of good teachers who are costly by their own right and choice.

Good friends, good books and a sleepy conscience: this is the ideal life.—Mark Twain

Prof. Chandan Tilak Bhunia, SMIEEE
Director, BITM, Bolpur, West Bengal, India
and
Senior Associate, ICTP, Italy

Foreword

Computer Science and Engineering is considered as a modern field of engineering education. It is an emerging field of technical education and the theory of computation is a core subject of computer science.

This book by Shyamalendu Kandar is written in a simple language, easily understood by undergraduate students. It contains a large number of figures and many solved problems, exercises and multiple choice questions with each chapter to help students in understanding and learning the subject. The main feature of this book is that it is written in an interactive way. When a student goes through the book he is in a classroom and a teacher is taking his/her class related to the subject matter. Difficult sections of the subject are also explained lucidly in this book.

I congratulate Shyamalendu for writing this book. Shyamalendu is a student of mine and now working as a lecturer in Computer Science Department of my institute. I am proud of him and wish him the best of success!

Prof. M.M. Bag
Director, Haldia Institute of Technology
Haldia, West Bengal

Preface

An engineer must ask ‘why’ not ‘how’. The Bachelor of Computer Science and Engineering is not only about learning some application software and some programming languages but also about learning how a programming language works, how a program is compiled and how input is converted to output from the machine hardware level. The theoretical part of Computer Science includes Complexity Analysis, Compiler Construction, verifying correctness of circuits and protocols etc. Automata Theory is one of the core courses in the curriculum of Bachelor of Technology of Computer Science or Information Technology under any university. It is said that Automata Theory is “the study of abstract machine and the problems which they are able to solve”. This book is a part of series named *Express Learning Series* which has a number of books designed as quick reference.

Students have to study the two parts subject in Automata Theory and Theory of Computation. Automata Theory contains Switching Theory, Machine Construction, Machine Checking and Minimization whereas the Theory of Computation includes different types of languages and grammars according to Chomsky Hierarchy. During my teaching career, I have felt that students need a complete book containing both the sections, a large number of solved problems, multiple choice questions and useful exercise to practice. This book is written to fullfill this requirement of students. It is written in simple language keeping in mind the level of undergraduate students . The theory part is described with suitable examples and useful diagrams. Solved problems are included to explain the theory. At the end of each chapter a number of multiple choice questions related to the topic are which will help students preparing themselves for competitive examinations like GATE, NET. The book contains 7 chapters.

Chapter 1 deals with finite state machine, machine construction, machine minimization which are the main parts of automata theory. Chapter 2 describes different types of languages and grammar according to the classification by Chomsky. This chapter is the root part of theory of computation. Chapter 3 deals with introduction of finite automata, deterministic and non-deterministic finite automata, mealy machine, Moore machine and minimization of finite automata. Chapter 4 describes regular expressions Arden’s Theorem, Pumping Lemma for Regular Expression. Chapter 5 deals with context free grammar, simplification of context free grammar, different normal form. Chapter 6 deals with push down automata, construction of push down automata directly from context free grammar. Chapter 7 describes the Turing Machine.

I will appreciate suggestions for further improvement of the book. My mail address is shyamalenduk@yahoo.com.

My dream in writing this book will be successful if the students are benefited from this book.

SHYAMALENDU KANDAR

Acknowledgements

My journey of writing started with a personal pain that has now manifested itself in the form of this book. For this, I wish to express thanks to my friend Madhumita in the words of Rabindranath Tagore, 'your hurt is the touch of you and a gift to my life'. I am also indebted to Professor C. T. Bhunia for inspiring me to write this book. When he left our institute on 3 November 2008, it was the saddest day of my life. He was always engaged in creative work despite his busy schedule and he is my guru in the field of technical education. This work is a small token of respect for the great man.

I want to express my gratitude to the Director of Haldia Institute of Technology, Professor M. M. Bag, and my colleagues especially Subhankar Joarder, Arindam Giri, Ramkrishna Das. I am also thankful to Milan Bera, Mrityunjay Maity, Tanuka Sinha and Bapida who are an integral part of the department. I wish to express my heartfelt gratitude to Munmun Sarkar for constantly encouraging me during the course of my writing. She regularly enquired about the progress of the book. I'm thankful to my friend Sabyasachi Samantha, who is a lecturer in information technology, for providing necessary information and support. Thanks are also due to my student Dipankar Dutta who helped me in selecting and solving the problems. I am grateful to Pradeep Banerjee who helped me realise my dream of publishing a book.

Finally, my parents Arun Kumar Kandar and Hirabati Kandar deserve special mention for their constant encouragement and support during the preparation of this book.

SHYAMALENDU KANDAR

1

Finite State Machine

1.1 BASICS OF AUTOMATA

Q. What do you mean by formal language and automata theory (FLAT)?

Ans. Automata have some typical pronounceable symmetry with Automatic. In a computer all processes appear to be done automatically. A given input is being processed in the CPU and an output is generated. We are not concerned about the internal operation in the CPU. We are only concerned about the given input and the received output. However, in reality the input is converted to '0' and '1' and assigned to the process for which the input was given. It then performs some internal operation in its electronics circuit and generates output in '0' and '1' format. The output generated in '0' and '1' format is converted to user understandable format and we get the output. From the discussion it is clear that CPU performs machine operations internally. In Automata we shall learn about how to design such machines.

The name of the subject is formal language and automata theory (FLAT). We have got a basic idea about Automata theory. Now what is Formal language? Let discuss what language is. Language is a communication medium through which two persons communicate. For each nation there is some language to communicate like Hindi, English, Bengali, etc. Similarly for communicating with a computer the user needs some language called programming language. C, C++, Java are some examples of programming language. The characteristics of these types of languages are similar to English language and easily understandable by user. However, computer does not understand English in statements. It only understands binary numbers. Hence, they have a compiler that checks the syntax and acts as a converter from English statement to binary numbers and vice versa. However, to design the compiler some logic is needed. The logic can be designed by use of mathematics. For each language there is a grammar, which is a constructor for any language. Similarly the languages that are used for computer programming rely on grammar to construct them. These rules and grammar and the process to convert such grammar and languages to machine format are the main objectives of this subject.

Q. Why FLAT is sometimes called "Theory of Computer Science"?

Ans. This subject is called "Theory of Computation" because it includes rules for constructing a computer language and converts into machine format; i.e. the theory of computer science. Basically formal language and automata theory and theory of computation are different names for a single subject that covers all the aspects of the theoretical part of Computer Science.

1.2 FINITE STATE MACHINE

Q. Define synchronous and asynchronous circuit.

Ans. Synchronization is usually achieved by some timing device, e.g. clock. A clock produces equally spaced pulses. These pulses are fed into a circuit in such a way that various operations of the circuit take place with the arrival of appropriate clock pulses. Generally the circuits, whose operations are controlled by clock pulses, are called Synchronous circuit.

The operation of asynchronous circuit does not depend on clock pulses. The operations in asynchronous circuit are controlled by a number of completion and initialization signals. Here completion of one operation is the initialization of the execution of next consecutive operation.

Q. Define combinational circuits and sequential circuits. In this respect describe the block diagram of synchronous sequential circuit.

Ans. The circuits where the output depends only on the present input, i.e. output is the function of only present input are called combinational circuits.

O/P = Func.(Present I/P).

The circuits where the output depends on the external input and the stored information at that time, i.e., output is the function of external input and present stored information are called sequential circuits.

O/P = Func.(External I/P and present stored information).

Block diagram

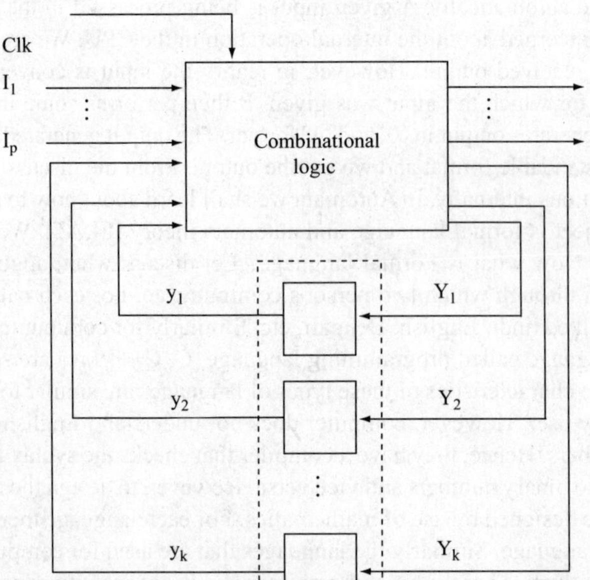

A synchronous sequential machine has finite number of inputs. If a machine has n number of input variables, the input set consists of 2^n distinct inputs called input alphabet I.

In the diagram the input alphabet is $I=\{I_1, I_2, \ldots\ldots, I_p\}$.

The number of outputs of a synchronous sequential machine is also finite.

Q. Design a sequential circuit which performs following.

A	B	O/P	Carry
0	0	0	0
0	1	1	0
1	0	1	0
1	1	0	1

The carry is added with the I/Ps in the next clock pulse.

Ans: Lets take two input strings X_1=0111 and X_2=0101.

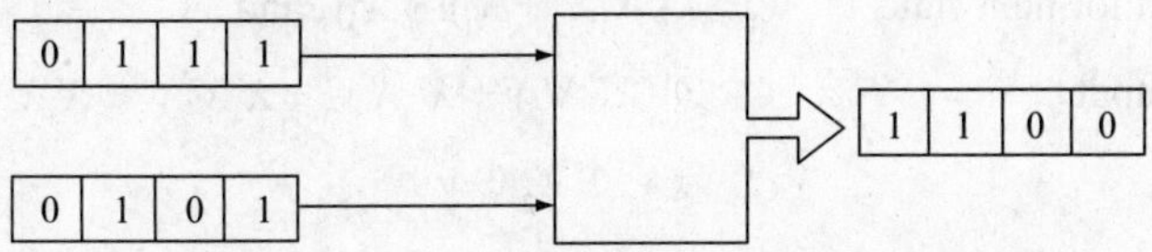

Here the output at time t_i is a function of the inputs X_1 and X_2 at the time t_i and of the carry generated for the input at $t_{i-1.}$

O/P =func.(I/P at t_i and carry generated for the input at t_{i-1}),
therefore, this is a sequential circuit.
The table above illustrates the two types of cases arisen. These are:

i. **Producing carry '0'**

ii. **Producing carry '1'**

We have to consider this as the O/P depends of the carry also.

Lets consider the cases as two states A for(i) and B for (ii). A table is constructed for the inputs X_1 and X_2. This is called state table.

Present state (PS)	Next state (NS), O/P(Z)			
	X_1X_2 00	01	11	10
A	A,0	A,1	B,0	A,1
B	A,1	B,0	B,1	B,0

This tabular form can be represented more clearly by a graphical notation. This is called state graph or state diagram

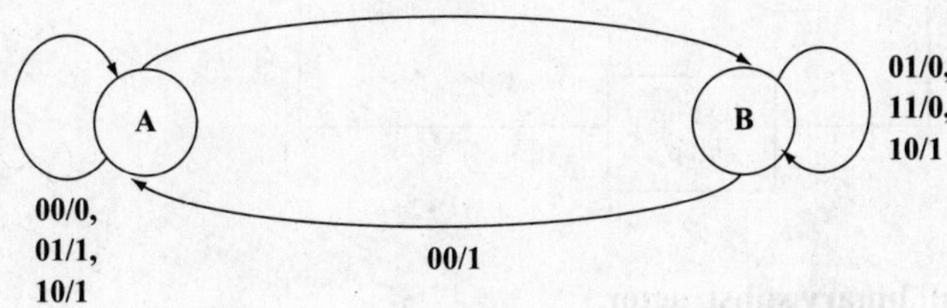

For designing a circuit we need only '0' and '1' i.e., boolean values. Hence the states A and B must be assigned boolean numbers. As there are only two states A and B so only one digit boolean value is sufficient. Lets assign A as '0' and B as '1'.

By assigning these boolean values to A and B the modified table become.

Present State(y)	Next State (Y) X_1X_2 00	01	11	10	Out put 00	01	11	10
0	0	0	1	1	0	1	0	1
1	0	1	1	1	1	0	1	0

Where the function for next state $Y = X_1X_2 + X_1y + X_2y$, and

the function for output $Z = X'_1X'_2y + X'_1X_2y' + X_1X'_2y' + X_1X_2y$

$= X_1 \oplus X_2 \oplus y.$

A digital circuit can easily be designed using the above functions. This is the circuit for full binary adder.

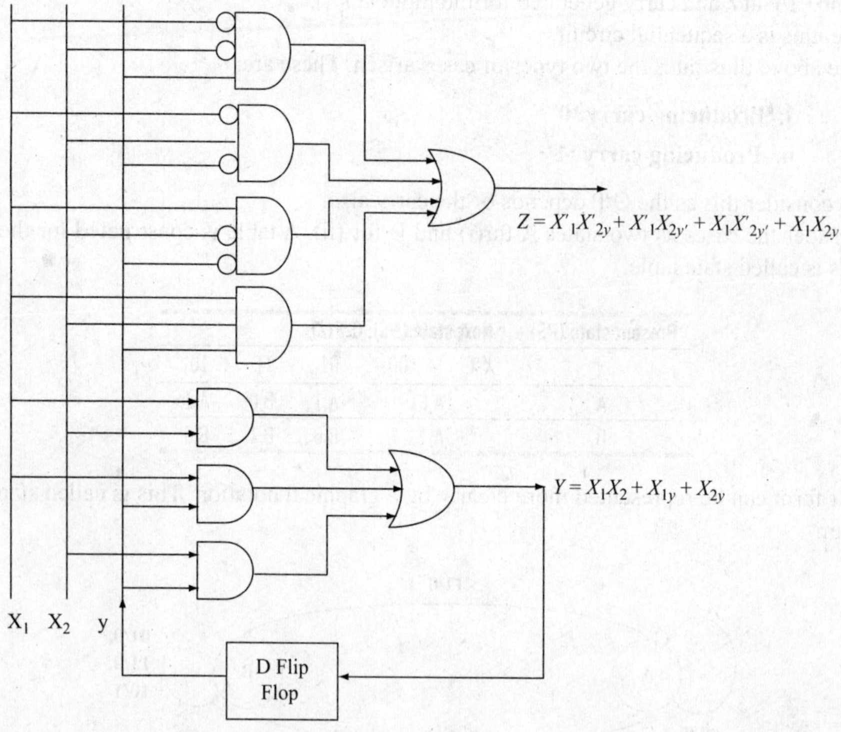

Q. Design a full binary substractor.

Ans. The truth table for a substractor is as follows:

A	B	O/P	Borrow
0	0	0	0
0	1	1	1
1	0	1	0
1	1	0	0

Lets assign two input strings X_1=1010 and X_2=0111.

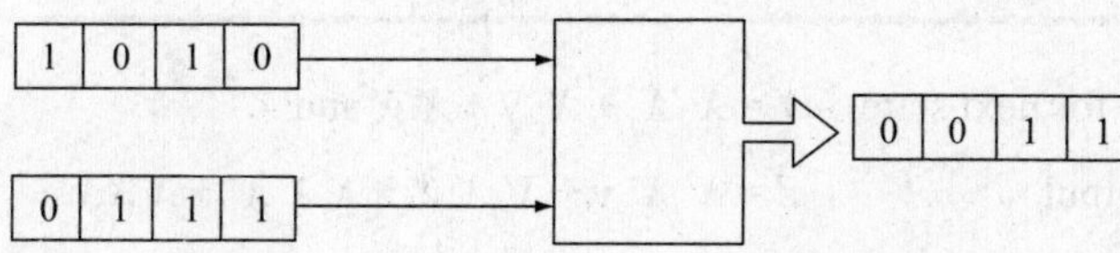

Here the output at time t_i is a function of the inputs X_1 and X_2 at the time t_i and the borrow generated for the input at t_{i-1}.

O/P=func.(I/P at t_i and carry generated for the input at t_{i-1}).

Therefore, this is a sequential circuit.

In the above table, two types of cases are arisen. These are:

i. **Producing Borrow '0'**

ii. **Producing Borrow '1'**

We have to consider the above as the O/P depends on the borrow too.

Lets consider the cases as two states S_1 for(i) and S_2 for (ii). The state table for the binary substractor is constructed for the inputs X_1 and X_2:

		NS (Y), O/P(Z)			
PS	X_1X_2	00	01	11	10
S_1		S_1,0	S_2,1	S_1,0	S_1,1
S_2		S_2,1	S_2,0	S_2,1	S_1,0

The state graph for binary substractor:

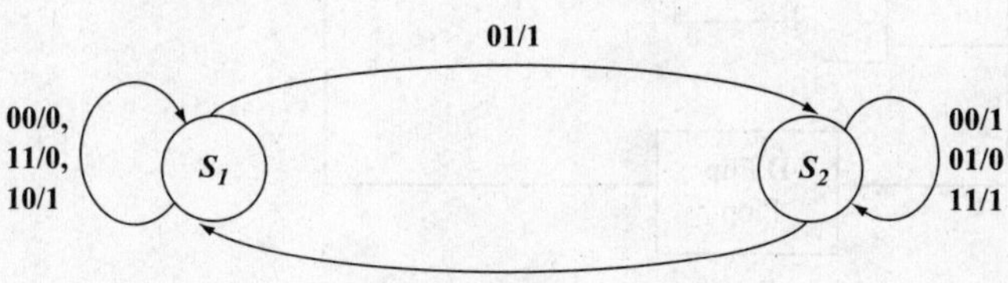

State assignments:

For designing a digital circuit, S_1 and S_2 are converted into some digital numbers. Since there are only two states, a 1 bit digital number which can produce two types of digital values – 0 or 1; is sufficient to represent S_1 and S_2.

Lets assign S_1 to 0 and S_2 to 1.
The modified state table is as follows:

	Next State (Y)				Out put			
Present State(y) X_1X_2	00	01	11	10	00	01	11	10
0	0	1	0	0	0	1	0	1
1	1	1	1	0	1	0	1	0

Where the function for next state $Y = X_1'X_2 + X_1'y + X_2y$, and

The function for output $Z = X'_1X'_2y + X'_1X_2y' + X_1X'_2y' + X_1X_2y$.

The digital circuit designed from the above functions is:

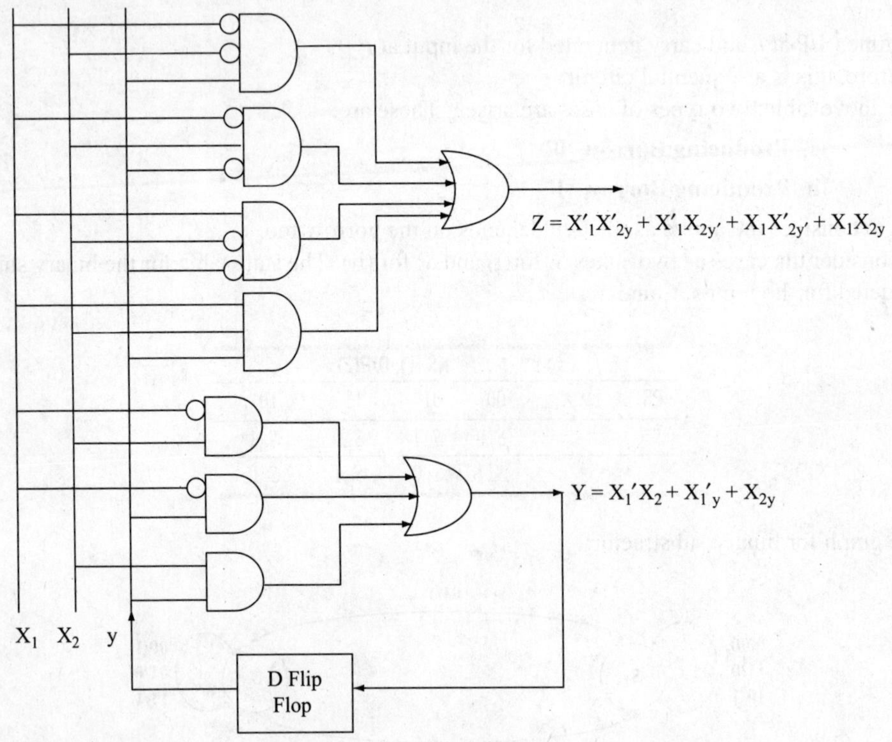

Sequence Detector

Q. Design a two input two output sequence detector which generates an output '1' every time the sequence 1001 is detected. And for all other cases output '0' is generated. Overlapping sequences are also counted.

Ans. Before designing this circuit some clarifications regarding sequence detector is needed. Lets assign the input string as 1001001.

We have to design the circuit in such a way that it will take one input at a time. The input can be either '0' or '1' (two types of input). The output will be also two types, either '0' or '1'. The circuit can store (memorize) the input string up to four clock pulses (t_{i-3} to t_i).

If the input string is placed according to clock pulses, the output is as follows:

	t_1	t_2	t_3	t_4	t_5	t_6	t_7
I/P	1	0	0	1	0	0	1
O/P	0	0	0	1	0	0	1

The first input at t_1 is 1 and as there is no input from t_{i-3} to t_i the input sequence does not equal to 1001. So the output will be 0. Similar cases occur for the inputs upto t_3.

However, at time t_4 the input from t_{i-3} to t_i becomes 1001, hence the output '1' is produced at time t_4. At time t_5 and t_6 the input string from t_{i-3} to t_i are 0010 and 0100, respectively. Therefore, the output '0' is produced. At t_7 clock pulse the input string is 1001, hence output '1' is produced. As the output '1' at t_4 is overlapped from t_1 to t_4 and from t_4 to t_7, this is called overlapping condition.

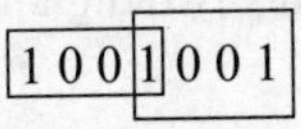

In this case the state diagram is to be drawn first according the following process:

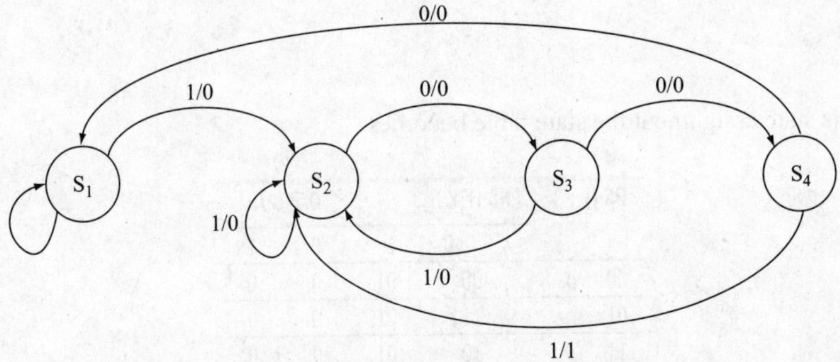

In state S_1, input may be either '0' or '1'. If given input '0', there is no chance to get 1001. Hence it loops on S_1 with output '0'. If the input is '1', there is a chance to get 1001 then machine moves to S_2 producing output '0'.

In S_2 again the input may be either '0' or '1'. If it is '1', the input becomes 11. There is no chance to get 1001 by taking previous inputs. But again there is a chance to get 1001 by considering the given input '1'. Hence it will be in state S_2. (If it goes to S_1 then there will be loss of clock pulse, i.e. from S_1 by taking input '1', again it has to come to S_2, i.e., one extra input, i.e. one clock pulse is needed and hence the output will not be in right pattern). If the input is '0', the input becomes 10 – by considering the previous input and there is chance to get 1001, so it will come to S_3.

In S_3 if it gets input '0', the input becomes 100 by considering the previous input and it has a chance to get 1001, so it can shift to S_4. But if it gets '0', it has no chance to get 1001 considering the previous input, but there is a chance to get 1001 by considering the given input '1'. So it will shift to S_2 as we know by getting '1' in S_1 the machine comes to S_2.

In S_4 if it gets '0', the input will become 1000, but it does not match with 1001. Therefore, it has to start from the beginning i.e., S_1. As overlapping condition is accepted, hence from the last '1' of 1001 if it gets 001 only, it will give an output '1'. Therefore it will go to S_2.

State table:

A state table can easily be constructed from the above state diagram.

PS	NS, O/P	
	X 0	1
S_1	S_1,0	S_2,0
S_2	S_3,0	S_2,0
S_3	S_4,0	S_2,0
S_4	S_1,0	S_2,1

State assignment:

The states must be assigned to some binary numbers to make a digital circuit. This is called state assignment. As the number of states is four, only two digit number is sufficient to represent the four states (2^2=4).

Lets assign
S_1 to 00,
S_2 to 01,
S_3 to 11,
S_4 to 10.

After doing this state assignment the state table becomes

PS (y_1y_2)	NS (Y_1Y_2)		O/P (z)	
	X 0	1	0	1
00	00	01	0	0
01	11	01	0	0
11	10	01	0	0
10	00	01	0	1

The digital function can easily be derived from this state assignment table:

Y_1

y_1y_2 \ X	0	1
00	0	0
01	1	0
11	1	0
10	0	0

Y_2

y_1y_2 \ X	0	1
00	0	1
01	1	1
11	0	1
10	0	1

z

y_1y_2 \ X	0	1
00	0	0
01	0	0
11	0	0
10	0	1

$Y_1 = X'y_2$
$Y_2 = X + y_1'y_2$
$z = Xy_1y_2'$

Y_1 and Y_2 are next states, which are the memory elements. These will be fed back to the input as state y_1 and y_2 with some delay by D flip flop.

The circuit diagram for this sequence detector will be

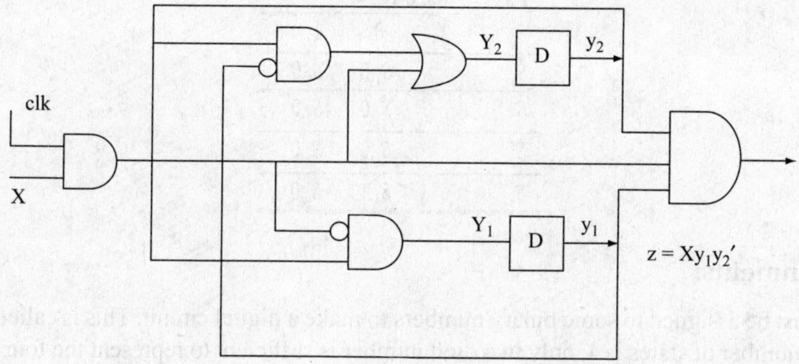

Q. Design a two input two output sequence detector which generates an output '1' every time the sequence 1010 is detected. And for all other cases output '0' is generated. Overlapping sequences are also counted.

Ans. The input string 1010100 is placed according to clock pulses as given below

	t_1	t_2	t_3	t_4	t_5	t_6	t_7
I/P	1	0	1	0	1	0	0
O/P	0	0	0	1	0	1	0

And the state diagram for the output is as follows:

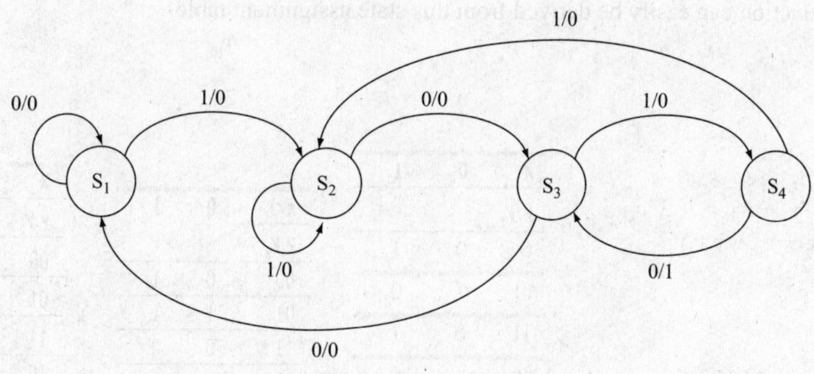

State table:

A state table constructed from the above state diagram:

PS	NS, O/P	
	X 0	1
S_1	S_1,0	S_2,0
S_2	S_3,0	S_2,0
S_3	S_1,0	S_4,0
S_4	S_3,1	S_2,0

State assignments:

The states must be assigned to some binary numbers to make a digital circuit. This is called state assignment. As the number of states is 4, only two digit number is sufficient to represent the four states (2^2=4).

Lets assign

S_1 to 00,
S_2 to 01,
S_3 to 11,
S_4 to 10.

The state table after this state assignment

PS (y_1y_2)	NS (Y_1Y_2)		O/P (z)	
	X 0	1	0	1
00	00	01	0	0
01	11	01	0	0
11	00	10	0	0
10	11	01	1	0

The digital function can easily be derived from this state assignment table.

Y_1

X	0	1
y_1y_2		
00	0	1
01	1	0
11	0	1
10	1	0

Y_2

X	0	1
y_1y_2		
00	0	1
01	1	1
11	0	0
10	1	1

z

X	0	1
y_1y_2		
00	0	0
01	0	0
11	0	0
10	1	0

$Y_1 = X'y_1'y_2 + Xy_1y_2 + X'y_1y_2'$
$Y_2 = y_1'y_2 + y_1'X + y_1y_2'$
$z = X'y_1y_2'$

The next states, Y_1 and Y_2, are the memory elements. These will be fed back to the input as state y_1 and y_2 with some delay by D flip flop

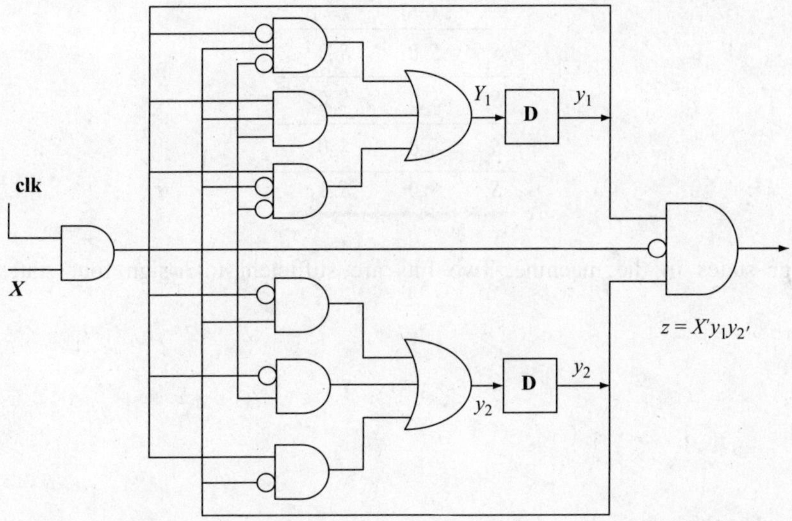

Binary Counter

Q. Design a Modulo 3 binary counter

Ans. The Modulo 3 Binary counter can count upto three. Binary representation of three is 11. It can count 00, 01, 10, and 11. There will be an external input *x*, which will act as a control variable and determine when the count should proceed. After counting three if it has to proceed, then it will come back to 00 again.

The state diagram for Mod 3 binary counter:

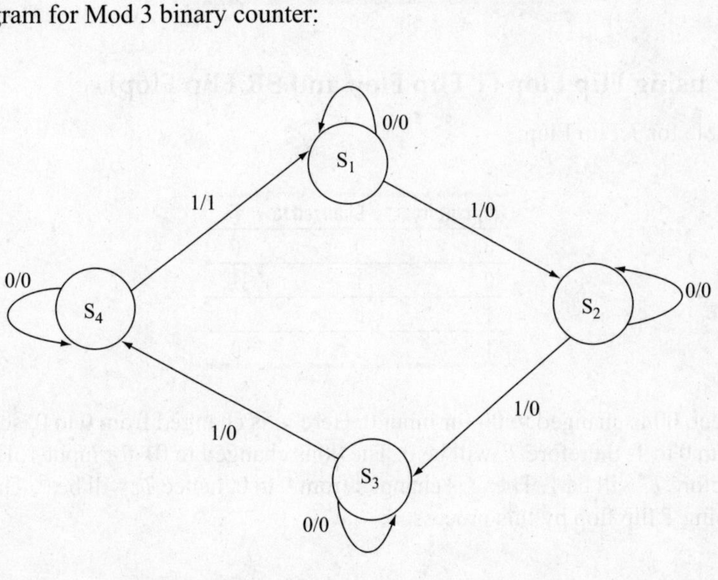

The state table for Mod 3 binary counter:

PS	NS, O/P	
	$X=0$	$X=1$
S_1	S_1,0	S_2,0
S_2	S_2,0	S_3,0
S_3	S_3,0	S_4,0
S_4	S_4,0	S_1,1

There are four states in the machine. Two bits are sufficient to assign four states into binary number.

Lets assign
S_1 to 00,
S_2 to 01,
S_3 to 10,
S_4 to 11.

The state table after this state assignment:

PS (y_2y_1)	NS (Y_1Y_2)		O/P (z)	
X	0	1	0	1
00	00	01	0	0
01	01	10	0	0
10	01	11	0	0
11	11	00	0	1

Designing By using Flip Flop (T Flip Flop and SR Flip Flop)

The excitation table for T Flip Flop:

Circuit from	Changed to	T
0	0	0
0	1	1
1	0	1
1	1	0

In state assignment, 00 is changed to 00 for input 0. Here y_1 is changed from 0 to 0, so T_1 will be 0. The y_2 is changed from 0 to 1, therefore T_1 will be 0. The 00 is changed to 01 for input 1. Here y_1 is changed from 0 to 1, therefore T_1 will be 1. The y_2 is changed from 0 to 0, hence T_1 will be 0. The excitation table of the counter using T flip flop by this process:

PS (y_2y_1)	T_2T_1	
	$X=0$	$X=1$
00	00	01
01	00	11
10	00	01
11	00	11

$T_1=X,$
$T_2=Xy_1,$
$z=Xy_1y_2.$

The circuit diagram for the above:

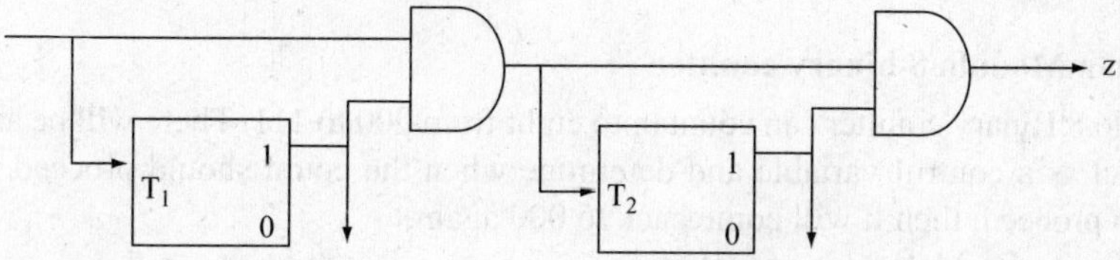

The excitation table for SR Flip Flop:

Circuit from	Changed to	S	R
0	0	0	--
0	1	1	0
1	0	0	1
1	1	--	0

In state assignment, the 00 is changed to 00 for input 0. Here y_1 is changed from 0 to 0, hence R_1 will be don't care and S_1 will be 0. The y_2 is changed from 0 to 0, hence R_2 will be don't care and S_2 will be 0. In state assignment table, 00 is changed to 01 for input 1. Here y_1 is changed from 0 to 1, therefore R_1 will be 0 and S_1 will be 1. The y_2 is changed from 0 to 0, hence R_2 will be don't care and S_2 will be 0. The excitation table of the counter using SR flip flop:

PS (y_2y_1)	$X=0$		$X=1$	
	S_1R_1	S_2R_2	S_1R_1	S_2R_2
00	0 --	0 --	1 0	0 --
01	-- 0	0 --	0 1	1 0
10	0 --	-- 0	1 0	-- 0
11	-- 0	-- 0	0 1	0 1

$S1=Xy1',\quad R1=Xy1,$
$S2=Xy1y2',\quad R2=Xy1y2.$

The circuit diagram for the above:

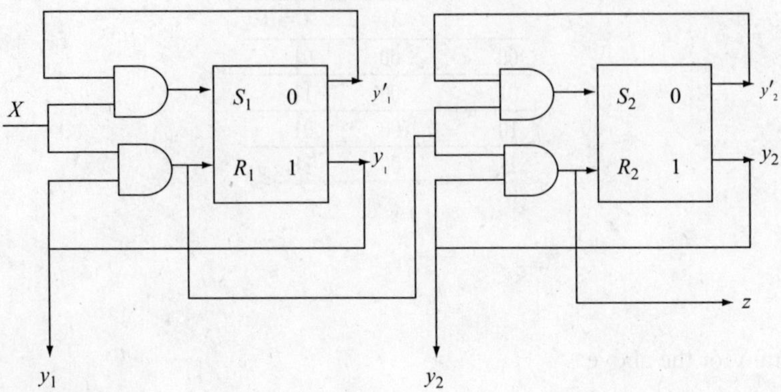

Q. Design a Modulo 8 binary counter.

Ans. Modulo 8 Binary counter can count upto eight from 000 to 111. There will be an external input x, which will act as a control variable and determine when the count should proceed. After counting eight if it has to proceed, then it will come back to 000 again.

The state diagram for Mod 8 binary counter:

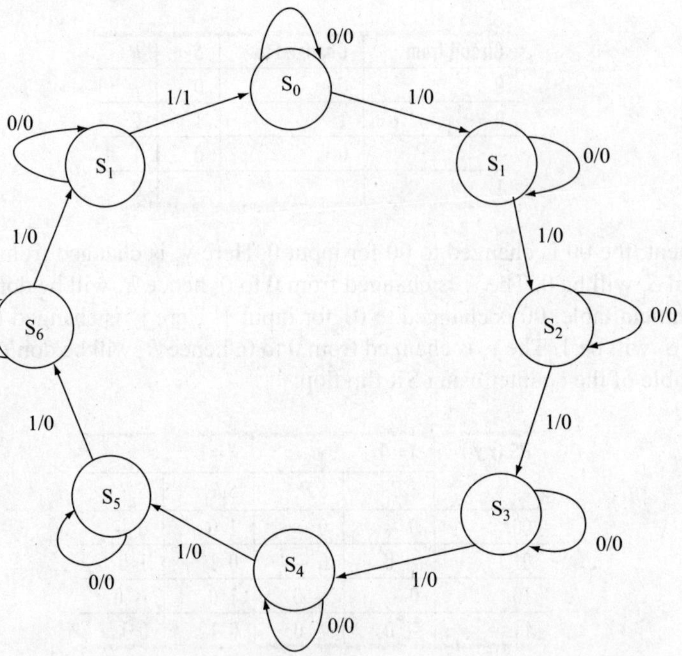

The state table for Mod 8 binary counter:

PS	NS, O/P	
	$X = 0$	$X = 1$
S_0	S_0,0	S_1,0
S_1	S_1,0	S_2,0
S_2	S_2,0	S_3,0
S_3	S_3,0	S_4,0
S_4	S_4,0	S_5,0
S_5	S_5,0	S_6,0
S_6	S_6,0	S_7,0
S_7	S_7,0	S_0,1

State assignment:

There are eight states in the machine. The three bits are sufficient to assign eight states into binary number (2^3=8).

Lets assign S_1 to 000, S_2 to 001, S_3 to 010, S_4 to 011, S_5 to 100, S_6 to 101, S_7 to 101, S_8 to 111.

PS($y_3y_2y_1$)	NS (Y_1Y_2)		O/P (z)	
X	0	1	0	1
000	000	001	0	0
001	001	010	0	0
010	010	011	0	0
011	011	100	0	0
100	100	101	0	0
101	101	101	0	0
101	101	111	0	0
111	111	000	0	1

The excitation table of the counter using T flip flop:

PS($y_3y_2y_1$)	$T_3T_2T_1$	
	$X = 0$	$X = 1$
000	000	001
001	000	011
010	000	001
011	000	111
100	000	001
101	000	011
101	000	001
111	000	111

$T_1 = X, T_2 = Xy_1, T_3 = Xy_1y_2, z = Xy_1y_2y_3.$

The circuit diagram for the above:

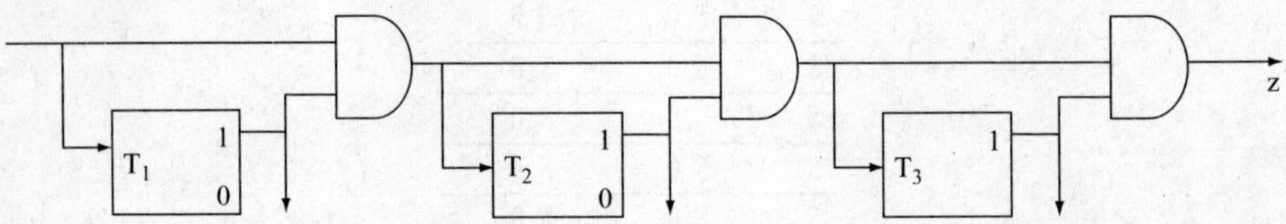

The excitation table of the counter using SR flip flop:

PS($y_3y_2y_1$)	X=0			X=1		
	S_1R_1	S_2R_2	S_3R_3	S_1R_1	S_2R_2	S_3R_3
000	0 –	0 –	0 –	1 0	0 –	0 –
001	– 0	0 –	0 –	0 1	1 0	0 –
010	0 –	– 0	0 –	1 0	– 0	0 –
011	– 0	– 0	0 –	0 1	0 1	1 0
100	0 –	0 –	– 0	1 0	0 –	– 0
101	– 0	0 –	– 0	0 1	1 0	– 0
110	0 –	– 0	– 0	1 0	– 0	– 0
111	– 0	– 0	– 0	0 1	0 1	0 1

$S_1 = Xy_1'$, $R_1 = Xy_1$,

$S_2 = Xy_1y_2'$, $R_2 = Xy_1y_2$,

$S_3 = Xy_1y_2y_3'$, $R_3 = Xy_1y_2y_3$.

The circuit diagram for the above:

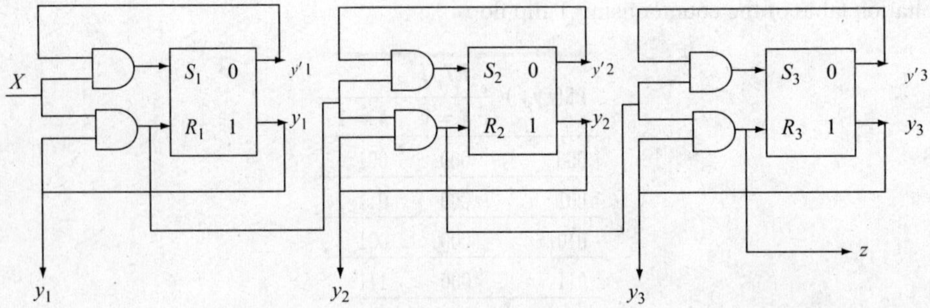

Q. What do you mean by finite state machine?

Ans. Finite state machine can be defined as a type of machine whose past histories can affect its future behavior in a finite number of ways. To clarify, consider for example of binary full adder. Its output depends on the present input and the carry generated from the previous input.

It may have a large number of previous input histories but they can be divided into two types: (i) Input combination that produces carry; (ii) Input combination that produces no carry.

Implying the past histories can affect the future behavior in a finite number of ways (here 2).

Q. What are the capabilities and limitations of finite-state machine?

Ans. Let a finite state machine have n states. Let a long sequence of input be given to the machine. The machine will progress starting from its beginning state to the next states according to the state transitions. However, after some time the input string may be longer than n, the number of states. As there are only n states in the machine, it must come to a state it was previously been in and from this phase if the input remains the same the machine will function in a periodically repeating fashion. From here a conclusion that 'for a n state machine the output will become periodic after a number of clock pulses less than equal to n' can be drawn.

States are memory elements. As for a finite state machine the number of states is finite, so finite number of memory elements are required to design a finite state machine.

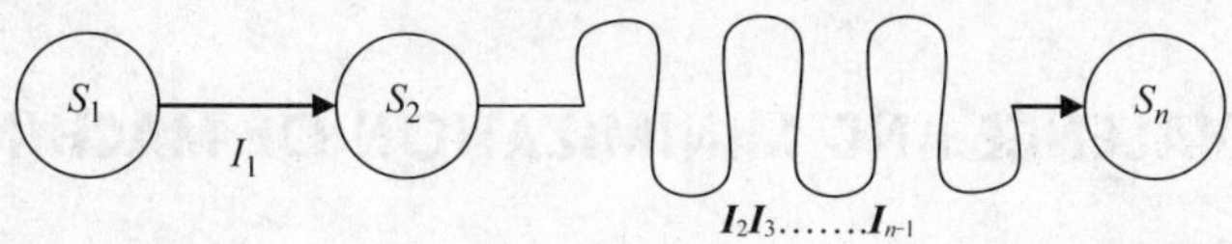

Limitations:

(a) No finite state machine can be produced for an infinite sequence.

Lets consider the design of a finite state machine which receives a long sequence of 1. The machine will produce an output 1, when the input string length will be equal to $[p(p+1)]/2$, where p=1,2,3,…, and 0 for all other cases.

Therefore for $p = 1$, $[p(p + 1)]/2 = 1$. In first place there will be o/p 1.

For $p = 2$, $[p(p + 1)]/2 = 3$. In third place there will be o/p 1.

For $p = 3$, $[p(p + 1)]/2 = 6$. In sixth place there will be o/p 1.

For this type of machine the input output form is as follows:

Time	t_1	t_2	t_3	t_4	t_5	t_6	t_7	t_8	t_9	t_{10}	t_{11}	t_{12}	t_{13}	t_{14}	t_{15}
I/P	1	1	1	1	1	1	1	1	1	1	1	1	1	1	1
O/P	1	0	1	0	0	1	0	0	0	1	0	0	0	0	1

Here the output does not become eventually periodic after a certain number of clock pulses. Hence from this type of sequence no finite state machine can be produced.

(b) No finite state machine can multiply two arbitrary large binary numbers.

Lets consider multiplying two binary numbers given that are input serially to a finite state machine for multiplication. The inputs are given to the machine with least significant bit (LSB) first then the other bits. Suppose, to multiply 2^m ′ 2^m, where m>n (n is the number of states of the Machine), the result will be 2^{2m}.

The 2^m is represented by one 1 followed by m number of '0's (Simlarly 2^3=1000). Hence the inputs are given to the machine from t_1 to t_{m+1} time. Throughout the time the machine produces '0'. At t_{m+2} times the input stops and the machine produce output 0 followed by 1 from t_{m+2} to t_{2m} time.

In the time period t_{m+1} to t_{2m}, no input is given to the machine, but the machine produces outputs. As $m > n$, according to the definition of Finite State machine the output must be periodic and the period must be $< m$. As we are not getting any repeating output sequence, therefore Binary Multiplication of two arbitrary large binary numbers is not possible to design by using finite state machine.

t_{2m+1}	t_{2m}	...	t_{m+1}	t_m	...	t_2	t_1	time
			1	0		0	0	First number
			1	0		0	0	Second number
1	0	...	0	0	...	0	0	Result

1.3 STATE EQUIVALENCE AND MINIMIZATION OF MACHINE

Q. What do you mean by state equivalence and state distinguishable? Give an example to clarify this.

Ans. Two states S_i and S_j of machine M are said to be equivalent if they produce same output sequences for all input string applied to the machine M, considering S_i and S_j as initial states.

Two states S_i and S_j of machine M are said to be distinguishable if there exists a minimum length input sequence which when applied to the machine M, considering S_i and S_j as the initial states, produce different output sequence. (Input string is always applied on initial state)

The sequence that distinguishes those two states is called distinguishing sequence for the pair S_i and S_j.

If two states S_i and S_j are distinguished for the input string of length k, then S_i and S_j are called k distinguishable. The k is the minimum number of the length of the string for which the states produce different output. If two states are k distinguishable then they are (k–1) equivalent for k=k to 1.

The table given below elucidates the concept

PS	NS, z	
	x=0	x=1
A	E,0	C,0
B	F,0	C,1
C	E,0	A,0
D	F,0	A,1
E	A,0	D,0
F	D,0	E,1

Consider the previous example.

The states A and C give same output (here 0) for the input string of length 1 (Either 0 or 1). Hence A and C are 1 Equivalent.

States A and B give different output for input string of length 1 (For input string length 0, means for no input – outputs are same; but for length 1, in case of input 1 they produce different outputs). Therefore, A and B are 1 distinguishable.

Let check for string length 2. String length 2 means it gives four types of combinations 00, 01, 11 and 10.

PS	00	01	11	10
A	00(A)	00(A)	00(A)	00(E)
B	00(D)	01(E)	10(A)	10(A)
C	00(E)	00(D)	00(C)	00(E)
D	00(D)	01(E)	10(C)	10(C)
E	00(E)	00(C)	01(A)	00(F)
F	00(D)	01(A)	10(D)	10(A)

The A and E are 2 distinguishable, since they produce different output for 11. Distinguishing sequence for A and E is 11.

Q. Define equivalent partition. Prove that equivalent partition is unique.

Ans. Equivalent partition of a machine M can be defined as a set of maximum number subsets of states where states which reside in same subset are equivalent for any input given to the states. The states which reside in different subsets are distinguishable for some input.

Proof:
Suppose for a machine M there exist two equivalent partitions P_1 and P_2, where $P_1 \neq P_2$. As $P_1 \neq P_2$, there must exist atleast two states S_i and S_j, which are in the same block of one partition (Let P_1) and different blocks in other partition(Let P_2). As they are in different blocks in P_2, there must exist an input sequence which distinguishes S_i and S_j. Hence they cannot be in the same block of P_1. Therefore, our assumption is wrong. For a single machine here cannot exist two equivalent partitions.

Hence, from here we can conclude that Equivalent partition is unique, i.e. $P_1 \equiv P_2$.

Q. Find the equivalent partition for the machine given below. From here minimize the above machine.

PS	NS, z	
	x=0	x=1
A	E,0	C,0
B	F,0	C,1
C	E,0	A,0
D	F,0	A,1
E	A,0	D,0
F	D,0	E,1

Ans. For string length 0 (i.e. for no input) there is no output, Hence all the states are equivalent.

P_0 = (ABCDEF).

Consider for string length 1 (i.e. two inputs 0 or 1). For 0, for all states output is 0. For 1 we get different output for (ACE) and (BDF). States A and B are 1 distinguishable. The A and C are 1 equivalent.

Therefore,

P_1=[(ACE) (BDF)].

Consider for string length 2 (i.e. four types of input 00, 01, 11, and 10)

PS	00	01	11	10
A	00(A)	00(A)	00(A)	00(E)
C	00(E)	00(D)	00(C)	00(E)
E	00(E)	00(C)	01(A)	00(F)
B	00(D)	01(E)	10(A)	10(A)
D	00(D)	01(E)	10(C)	10(C)
F	00(D)	01(A)	10(D)	10(A)

For A and C, outputs are same for 00, 01, 11, and 10. However, E has different output for 11. For B, D, and F outputs are same for all inputs.

P_2= [(AC)(E)(BDF)].

Consider for string length 3 [i.e. eight types of input combinations]. Hence it will be difficult to find output sequences and the equivalent partitions, as the length of input string increases.

It will be easier to check for the next states.

We know P_1 = [(ACE) (BDF)].

Lets rename (ACE) as set S_1 and (BDF) as set S_2.

For ACE with input 0, the next states are (EEA). Both A and E belong to set S_1. For input 1, the next states are (CAD). Here A and C belong to set S_1, but D belongs to set S_2. Therefore, the set (ACE) will be divided as (AC) and (E) for input string length 2.

For (BDF) with input 0, the next states are (FFD). Both F and D belong to same set S_2. For input 1, the next states are (CAE). All of these belong to same set S_1. So (BDF) cannot be divided for input string length 2.

The partition of states becomes:

P_2=(AC)(E)(BDF) (Same result obtained with considering output).

Lets check for input string length 3.

For (AC) with input 0, the next states are (EE). Both the next states belong to single set. For input 1, the next states are (AC). Both the next states belong to single set. So (AC) cannot be divided for input string length 3.

(E) is a set of single state. So (E) cannot be divided.

For (BDF) with input 0, the next states are (FFD). All of them belong to single set. With input 1, the next states are (CAE). The C and A belong to one set in P_2 and E belongs to another set in P_2. Hence

(BDF) will be divided as (BD) and (F) for input string length 3.

The partition of states becomes:

P_3 = (AC)(E)(BD)(F).

Lets check for input string length 4.

For (AC) with input 0, the next states are (EE), belong to single set. For input 1, the next states are (AC), belong to single set. Hence (AC) cannot be divided for input string length 4.

The (E) is a set of single state. Hence (E) cannot be divided.

For (BD) with input 0 and 1, the next states are (FF) and (AC), respectively. (FF) belong to a single set and (AC) also belong to a single set. Hence (BD) cannot be divided. As (F) is a single state, it cannot be divided.

The partition of states becomes

P_4 = (AC)(E)(BD)(F).

As P_3 and P_4 consist of same partitions, P_3 = (AC)(E)(BD)(F) is the equivalent partition for the machine M.

Minimization:

We know that equivalent partition is unique. So P_3 = (AC)(E)(BD)(F) is the unique combination. Here each single set represents one state of the minimized machine.

Lets rename these partitions for simplification.

Rename (AC) as S_1, (E) as S_2, (BD) as S_3, and (F) as S_4.

The AC with input 0, goes to (EE) with output 0, hence there will be a transaction from S_1 to S_2 with output 0. E with input 0, goes to A producing output 0. A belongs to set S_1 in the minimized machine, Hence there will be a transaction from S_2 to S_1 with output 0. By this process, the whole table of the minimized machine is constructed.

The minimized machine is as follows:

PS	NS, z	
	$x = 0$	$x = 1$
S_1(AC)	S_2,0	S_1,0
S_2(E)	S_1,0	S_3,0
S_3(BD)	S_4,0	S_1,1
S_4(F)	S_3,0	S_2,1

Q. Find the equivalent partition for the machine given below. From here minimize the above machine.

PS	NS, z	
	$x = 0$	$x = 1$
A	B,0	H,1

B	C,0	G,1
C	B,0	F,1
D	F,1	C,1
E	B,1	C,1
F	B,1	B,1
G	C,1	B,1
H	D,1	A,1

Ans. For string length 0 (i.e. for no input) there is no output, hence all the states are equivalent. It is called 0-equivalent. Expressed as

P_0 = (ABCDEFGH).

For string length 1, there are two types of inputs — 0 and 1. The states A, B, and C give output 0 for input 0 and states D, E, F, G, and H give output 1 for input 0. All the states give output 1 for input 1.

Therefore, the states in the set P_0 is divided into (ABC) and (D, E, F, G, and H). Written as

P_1 = [(ABC) (DEFGH)].

Here A and F are 1 distinguishable because they produce different outputs for input string length 1. For input string length 2, check the distinguishability by next state combination. The states A, B, and C for input 0 produce next states B, C, and B, respectively, and produce next states H, G, and F for input 1. BCB belong to same set, and HGF also belong to same set. Hence ABC cannot be partitioned for input string length 2.

The states DEFGH for input 0, produce next states F, B, B, C, and D, respectively, and produce next states C, C, B, B, and A for input 1. The B, B, and C belong to same set but F and D belong to different sets. Hence the set (DEFGH) is portioned into (DH) and (EFG). The new partition becomes

P_2 = {(ABC)[(DH)(EFG)]}.

The states D and G are 2 distinguishable, because they produce different outputs for input string length 2.

The states A,B, and C for input 0 produce next states B,C, and B respectively and produce next states H,G,F for input 1. BCB belong to same set, but H and G, F belong to different set. Hence the set (ABC) is partitioned into (A) and (BC).

The states B and H produce next states C and D, respectively for input 0 and produce next states G and A for input 1. C and D belong to different sets hence the set (BH) is divided to (B) and (H).

The states E, F, and G produce next states B, B and C for input 0 and next states C, B, and B for input 1. Both B and C belong to same set, so the set (EFG) cannot be partitioned.

The new partition becomes

P_3 = {[(A)(BC)]{[(D) (H)] (EFG)}}.

Here A and B are 3 distinguishable, because they produce different outputs for input string length 3.

By this process we will get P_4 also as

P_4 = {[(A)(BC)] {[(D)(H)] (EFG)}}.

As P_3 and P_4 consist of same partitions, therefore P_3={[(A)(BC)]{[(D)(H)](EFG)}} is the equivalent partition for the machine M.

Minimization:

We know that equivalent partition is unique. Therefore $P_3 = \{[(A)(BC)]\{[(D)(H)] (EFG)\}\}$ is the unique combination. Here each single set represents one state of the minimized machine.

Lets rename these partitions for simplification.

Rename (A) as S_1, (BC) as S_2, (D) as S_3 (H) as S_4 and (EFG) as S_5.

State (A) with input 0 goes to (B), Hence there will be transaction from S_1 to S_2 with input 0. The (A) with input 1 goes to (H), hence there will be transaction from S_1 to S_4 with input 1. The (BC) with input 0 goes to (BC) for input 0. There will be a transaction from S_2 to S_2 for input 0. State (BC) with input 1 goes to (FG). There will be transaction from S_2 to S_5 for input 1.

By this process the whole table of the minimized machine is constructed.

The minimized machine becomes

PS	NS, z	
	x=0	x=1
S_1(A)	S_2, 0	S_4, 1
S_2(BC)	S_2, 0	S_5, 1
S_3(D)	S_5, 1	S_2, 1
S_4(H)	S_3, 1	S_1, 1
S_5(EFG)	S_2, 1	S_2, 1

1.4 INCOMPLETELY SPECIFIED MACHINE AND MINIMAL MACHINE

Q. Define incompletely specified machine? How an incompletely specified machine can be simplified? Simplify the following incompletely specified machine.

PS	00	01	11	10
A	_,_	B,0	C,1	_,_
B	A,0	B,1	_,0	C,_
C	D,1	A,_	B,0	D,1
D	_,0	_,_	C,0	B,1

Ans. In real life, for all states for all inputs, the next state or outputs or both are not mentioned. For such types of machines, where for all states for all inputs the next state, or output or both are not mentioned, those types of machines are called incompletely specified machine.

In the previous machine for state A for 00 input no next state and outputs are specified. Hence the previous machine is an example of incompletely specified machine.

Simplification:

An incompletely specified machine can be simplified by the following steps:

(a) If next state is not mentioned for a state, for a given input, put a temporary state T in that place.
(b) If output is not mentioned, make it blank.
(c) If next state and output are not mentioned, put a temporary state T in next state place and nothing in output place.
(d) Add the temporary state T in the present state column, putting T as next state and no output for all inputs.

By following the previous steps, the simplification of the previous incompletely specified machine is as follows:

PS	NS, Z			
	00	01	11	10
A	T, _	B,0	C,1	T, _
B	A,0	B,1	T,0	C,_
C	D,1	A,_	B,0	D,1
D	T,0	T, _	C,0	B,1
T	T,_	T,_	T,_	T,_

Q. Simplify the following incompletely specified machine.

PS	NS, Z		
	I_1	I_2	I_3
A	C,0	E,1	_ _
B	C,0	E,_	
C	B, _	C,0	A,_
D	B,0	C, _	E,_
E	_ _	E,0	A,_

Ans. Put a temporary state T in the next state place, where next states are not specified. If the output is not mentioned, need to put any output.

As a temporary state T is considered, so T is put in the present state column with next states T for all inputs with no output.

The simplified machine becomes

PS	NS, Z		
	I_1	I_2	I_3
A	C,0	E,1	T,_
B	C,0	E,_	T,_

C	B,_	C,0	A,_
D	B,0	C,_	E,_
E	T,_	E,0	A,_
T	T,_	T,_	T,_

Q. Define Minimal machine. What is the difference with it with minimum machine? Give an example.

Ans. Minimal machine is the minimum of the machines obtained by minimizing an incompletely specified machine.

In an incompletely specified machine, for all states and for all inputs, the next state, or output or both are not mentioned. At the time of minimizing the incompletely specified machine different persons can take the not mentioned next states or outputs according to their choice. Therefore there is a great possibility to get different equivalent partitions for a single machine. But we know equivalent partition is unique for a given machine. It is not possible to find a unique minimized machine for a given incompletely specified machine most of the times. Therefore our aim must be to find a reduced machine which not only covers the original machine but also has a minimal (least of the minimum) number of states. This type of machine is called minimal machine, i.e. it is the minimum of the machines obtained by minimizing an incompletely specified machine.

Example: Lets consider the following incompletely specified machine:

PS	NS, z	
	$x=0$	$x=1$
A	E,1	D,0
B	E,0	C,1
C	A,0	B,_
D	A,0	D,1
E	A,_	B,0

In this machine C with input 1 output is not specified and same for E with input 0. There are two types of outputs occur in the machine. Hence the unspecified outputs can be any of the followings: (a) (B, 0 A, 0); (b) (B, 0 A, 1); (c) (B, 1 A, 1); (d) (B, 1 A, 0).

For (a) the machine and its equivalent partition is

PS	NS, z		
	$x = 0$	$x = 1$	
A	E,1	D,0	P_0=(ABCDE)
B	E,0	C,1	P_1=(ABD) (CE)
C	A,0	B,0	P_2=(A)(B)(D)(CE)
D	A,0	D,1	
E	A,0	B,0	

For (b) the machine and its equivalent partition is

PS	NS, z		
	$x = 0$	$x = 1$	$P_0 = (ABCDE)$
A	E,1	D,0	$P_1 = (AE)(BD)(C)$
B	E,0	C,1	$P_2 = (AE)(B)(D)(C)$
C	A,0	B,0	$P_3 = (A)(E)(B)(D)(C)$
D	A,0	D,1	
E	A,1	B,0	

For (c) the machine and its equivalent partition is

PS	NS, z		
	$x = 0$	$x = 1$	
A	E,1	D,0	$P_0 = (ABCDE)$
B	E,0	C,1	$P_1 = (AE)(BCD)$
C	A,0	B,1	
D	A,0	D,1	
E	A,1	B,0	

For (d) the machine and its equivalent partition is

PS	NS, z		
	$x = 0$	$x = 1$	$P_0 = (ABCDE)$
A	E,1	D,0	$P_1 = (A)(BCD)(E)$
B	E,0	C,1	$P_2 = (A)(B)(CD)(E)$
C	A,0	B,1	$P_3 = (A)(B)(C)(D)(E)$
D	A,0	D,1	
E	A,0	B,0	

In cases (b) and (d), the number of equivalent partitions are 5, equals to the number of states of the machine, i.e. machine constructed from the equivalent partitioned obtained in cases (b) and (d) and the original machines for cases (b) and (d) are the same.

1.5 MERGER GRAPH AND COMPATIBILITY GRAPH

Q. What is Merger graph?

Ans. Merger graph of a machine M of n states is an undirected graph defined as follows.

1. Merger graph consists of n number of vertices, where n is the number of states of the machine. That is in other words each states of the machine represent one vertex.
2. There is an undirected arc between a pair of vertices (states) if the outputs do not conflict for those pair of states.
   (a) The arc will be an uninterrupted arc if the next states of the two states [Vertices] do not conflict.
   (b) The arc will be an interrupted arc if the next states of the states [Vertices] conflict. The conflicting next states will be placed in the interrupted portions.
3. There will be no arc between the two vertices if the outputs of the pair of states conflict.

Q. Develop the Merger graph for the following machine.

PS	NS, z			
	I_1	I_2	I_3	I_4
A	E,1	B, 0	_,_	E, 0
B	_,_	_,_	_,_	C, 0
C	D, 1	F, 0	A, 0	_,_
D	_,_	B, 1	_,_	_,_
E	_,_	_,_	A, 1	A, 0
F	B, 1	C, 1	E, 1	_,_

Ans. In the above machine there are six states. Therefore, number of vertices of the Merger Graph is six, namely A, B, C, D, E, and F.

Lets consider two vertices A and B. In the state table for A and B for input I_1, outputs are 1 and don't care. It is treated as same output (Don't care can be either 0 or 1). Same for I_2, I_3, and I_4 the outputs do not conflict. (If the outputs are don't care, consider it same with the other) Therefore, an undirected arc is drawn between A and B.

For input I_4, A produces next state E and B produces next state C. Hence the undirected arc between A and B is an interrupted arc and EC is placed in the interrupted portion.

Consider A and C. The outputs do not conflict for inputs I_1, I_2, I_3, and I_4. An undirected arc is drawn between A and C. The next states produced by A and C for input I_1 are D and E, i.e. conflicting. For input I_2 the next states are B and F – also conflicting. The arc is an interrupted arc and (BF) and (DE) is placed in the interrupted portion.

Consider A and D. For input I_2, A and D produce conflicting outputs – 0 for A and 1 for B. So no arc can be drawn between A and D.

Consider A and E. For all the inputs they produce same outputs. An undirected arc is drawn between A and E. The A and E produce next states E and A, respectively, for input I_4. Hence the arc is an interrupted arc and (EA) is placed in the interrupted portion.

Consider A and F. The A and F produce conflicting outputs (0 for A, 1 for F) for input I_2. Hence no arc can be drawn between A and F.

By this process, an uninterrupted arc is drawn between B and C.
An uninterrupted arc is drawn between B and D.
An interrupted arc is drawn between B and E and AC is placed in the interrupted portion.
An uninterrupted arc is drawn between B and F.

For input I_2, C and D produce conflicting outputs. No arc can be drawn between C and D.
For input I_3, C and E produce conflicting outputs. No arc can be drawn between C and E.
For input I_3, C and F produce conflicting outputs. No arc can be drawn between C and F.

The D and E produce same outputs and same next states for all the inputs. An uninterrupted arc is drawn between D and E.

The D and F produce same outputs for all the inputs but conflicting next states (B and C) for input I_2. An interrupted arc is drawn between D and F and BC is placed in the interrupted portion.

The E and F produce same output for all the inputs but conflicting next states (A and E) for input I_3. An interrupted arc is drawn between E and F and AE is placed in the interrupted portion.

The final Merger graph is

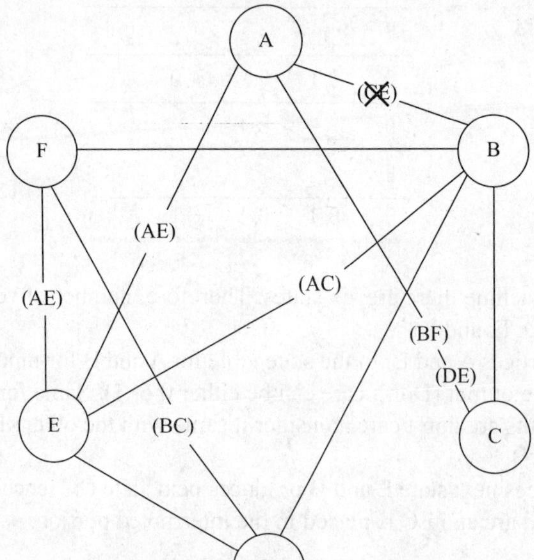

The A and B are connected by an uninterrupted, undirected arc. In the interrupted portion CE is placed. The connection between A and B will be uninterrupted if C and E are connected by uninterrupted arc. But there is no arc between C and E. So there will be no arc between A and B. CE is crossed therefore.

The A and C are connected by uninterrupted undirected arc. In the interrupted portion DE and BF are placed. The A and C will be connected by uninterrupted arc if B, F and D, E are connected.

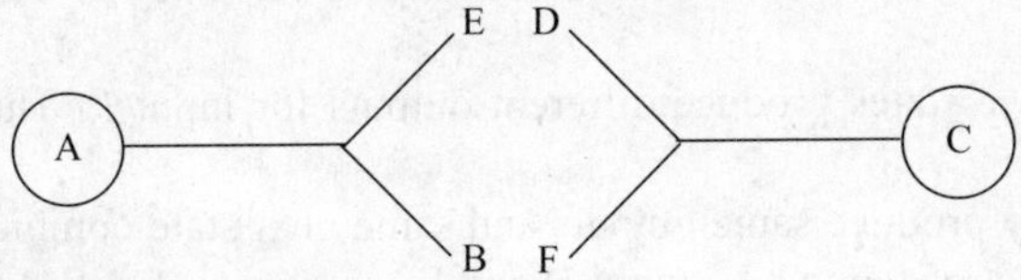

If either ED or BF is not connected, there will be no arc between A and C. But here ED and BF are connected.

Q. Develop the Merger graph for the following machine.

PS	NS, z		
	I_1	I_2	I_3
A	E, 0	B, _	C, _
B	_, _	D,_	B, 0
C	E, _	D, _	C, 0
D	C, 0	_, _	B, 1
E	C, 0	_, _	B, 1

Ans. Number of states of the machine is 5. So number of vertices of the Merger graph is 5. Let name them in the name of the states.

Consider two vertices A and B. The states A and B produce same outputs for all the inputs but different next states for input I_2 (conflicting states BD) and for input I_3 (conflicting states BC). Hence an interrupted undirected arc is drawn between A and B and (BC), (BD) is placed in the interrupted portion.

Consider A and C. The two states produce same outputs for all the inputs. However, A and C produce conflicting next states (BD) for input I_2. Therefore, between A and C an undirected interrupted arc is drawn and (BD) is placed in the interrupted portion.

Consider A and D. The states produce same outputs for all the inputs. But they produce conflicting next states (BC) and (EC) for inputs I_1 and I_3, respectively. Therefore an undirected interrupted arc is drawn between A and D and (BC)(EC) is placed in the interrupted portion.

Consider A and E. The states produce same outputs for all the inputs. But they produce conflicting next states for input I_1 and I_3. The conflicting next states are (CE) and (BC). An interrupter arc is drawn between A and E and (CE)(BC) is placed in the interrupted portion.

Consider B and C. They produce same outputs for all the inputs but conflicting next state pair (BC) for input I_3. Hence an interrupted arc is drawn between B and C placing (BC) in the interrupted portion.

Consider B and D. No arc is drawn between B and D as they produce different outputs for input I_3.

Consider B and E. No arc is drawn between B and E as they produce different outputs for input I_3.

Consider C and D. These states produce different outputs for input I_3. Therefore no arc is drawn between C and D.

Consider C and E. These states produce different outputs for input I_3. Therefore no arc is drawn between C and E.

Consider D and E. They produce same outputs and same next state combination for all the inputs. Therefore an uninterrupted arc is drawn between D and E.

The Merger graph for the above machine:

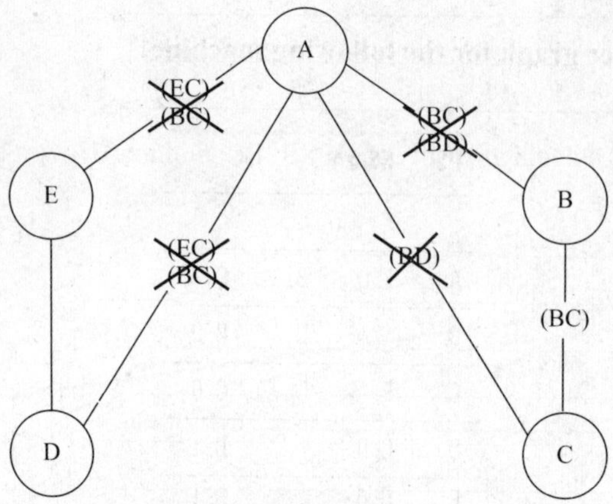

Between C and E there is no arc. Hence the combinations (EC)(BC), placed between A,D and A,E is crossed off. Now there is no connection between A and E, and A and D. There is no arc between B and D. Hence the next state combination (BC)(BD) and (BD),placed between A,B and A,C, respectively is crossed off.

Q. Define compatible pair and implied pair. What do you mean by a compatibility graph?

Ans.

Compatible Pair: Two states say S_i and S_j are said to be compatible, if both of them give same output strings for all input strings applied to the machine separately, considering S_i and S_j as the initial states.

(In the sense of Merger Graph, two states are said to be compatible if there exists an uninterrupted arc between the two states.)

Implied Pair: Two states S_i and S_j are said to be implied on S_p and S_q, if and only if (S_p, S_q) is compatible then only (S_i, S_j) is compatible. (S_p, S_q) is said to be the implied pair of (S_i, S_j).

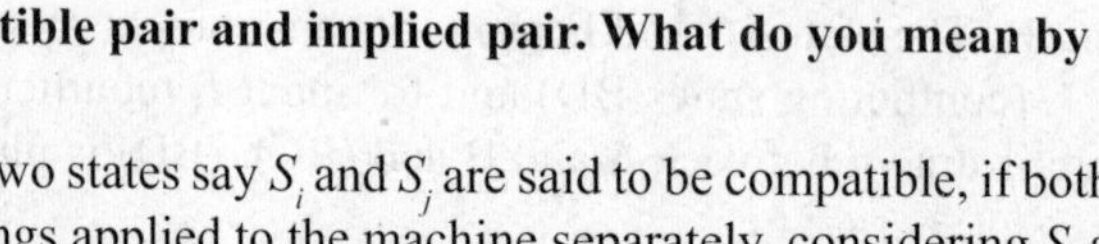

Compatibility Graph: Compatibility graph is a directed graph constructed as follows:

(1) Number of vertices of the compatibility graph corresponds to the number of compatible pairs obtained from the machine.

(2) A directed arc is drawn between two compatible pairs (vertices) say from (S_i, S_j) to (S_p, S_q) [Where $(S_i, S_j) \neq (S_p, S_q)$], if (S_p, S_q) is the implied pair for (S_i, S_j).

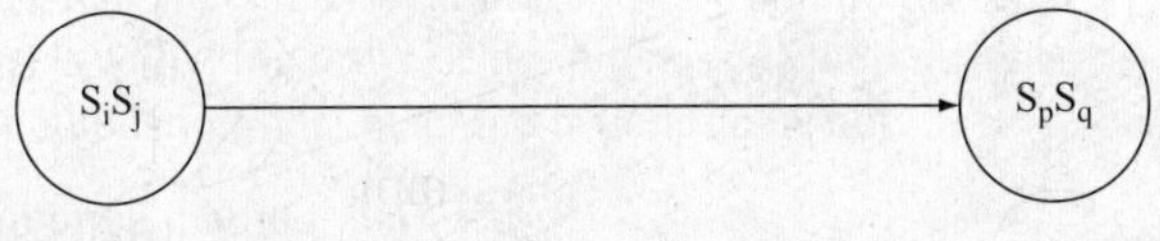

Q. Define closed compatibles and closed covering. How to find a minimal machine from a given compatibility graph of a machine?

Ans. A Subgraph of a compatibility graph is called closed, if for every vertex in the subgraph, all outgoing arcs and the terminal vertices of the arcs also belong to the subgraph. The pair of states belongs to the subgraph as terminal vertices are called closed compatible. If a subgraph is closed, and if every state of the machine is covered by atleast one vertex of the subgraph of a compatibility graph, then the subgraph forms a closed covering of the machine.

To find a minimal machine we need to find the subgraphs that closed cover the machine. Then we need to find the subgraph that contains less number of vertices and, which can generate a simpler machine. The states of the minimal machine are the vertices of the subgraph. From these states the transition functions are constructed. By this process a minimal machine of the given machine is constructed. [There is no easy method to find minimal closed covering. It will be choose manually]

Q. Draw a compatible graph for the following machine. Hence find the minimal machine.

PS	NS, z			
	I_1	I_2	I_3	I_4
A	E, 1	C, 1	_, _	B, 1
B	_, _	_, _	D, 0	D, 1
C	_, _	_, _	E, 0	_, _
D	C, 0	B, 1	B, 0	_, _
E	A, 0	F, 1	_, _	D, 0
F	C, 1	_, _	_, _	_, _

Ans: To find the Compatible pairs we need to construct the Merger graph of the machine first. The Merger graph of the machine:

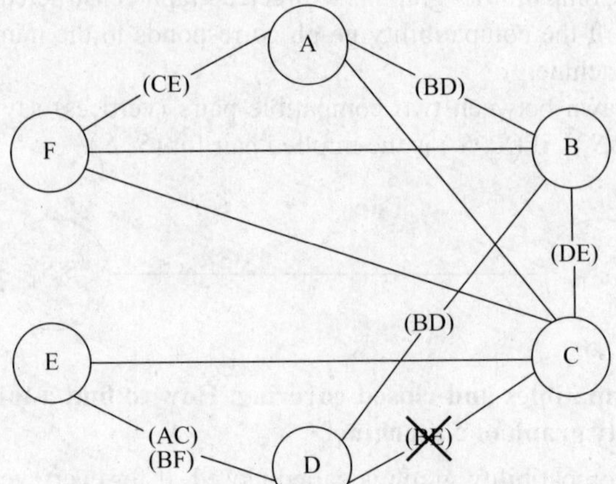

The pair of states which are connected by undirected arcs (Not Crossed in the interrupted portion) are compatible pairs. The compatible pairs of the given machine are (AB), (AC), (AF), (BC), (BD), (BF), (CE), (CF), and (DE). Therefore in the compatibility graph there are nine vertices.

In the given machine,
The (BD) is implied pair for (AB). Hence a directed arc is drawn from (AB) to (BD).
The (CE) is implied pair for (AF). Hence a directed arc is drawn from (AF) to (CE).
The (DE) is implied pair for (BC). Hence a directed arc is drawn from (BC) to (DE).
The (BD) is implied pair for (BD). As $(S_i, S_j) \neq (S_p, S_q)$, no arc is drawn from (BD) to (BD)
The (AC) and (BF) are implied pair for (DE). The two directed arcs are drawn from (DE) to (AC) and (BF).
The compatibility graph for the given machine:

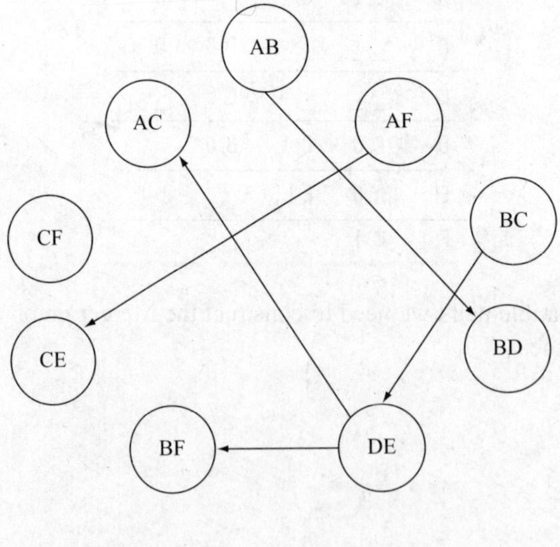

Minimal machine:

The subgraph (AC), (DE), (BF) or (AB), (BD), (AF), (CE) or (AF), (CE), (BC), and (DE) are closed subgraphs of the compatibility graph and forms a closed cover of the machine (Here every state of the machine is covered by atleast one vertex of the subgraph). Among them, the subgraph (AC), (DE), and (BF) contains less number of vertices. In the minimal machine the states are (AC), (BF), and (DE). Let rename them as S_1, S_2, and S_3, respectively. The minimal machine becomes

PS	NS, z			
	I_1	I_2	I_3	I_4
S_1(AC)	S_3, 1	S_1, 1	S_3, 0	S_2, 1
S_2 (BF)	S_1, 1	_, _	S_3, 0	S_3, 1
S_3 (DE)	S_1, 0	S_2, 1	S_2, 0	S_3, 0

Q. Draw a compatible graph for the following machine. Hence find the minimal machine.

PS	NS, z			
	I_1	I_2	I_3	I_4
A	_, _	D, 0	D, 0	C, _
B	A, 1	_, _	_, _	D, _
C	B, 1	C, 0	E, 0	_, _
D	E, 1	C, 0	_, _	D, 0
E	_, _	_, _	_, _	A, 1

Ans: To find the compatible pairs of a machine, we need to construct the Merger the graph first. According to the rules of the construction of Merger Graph the following graph is constructed.

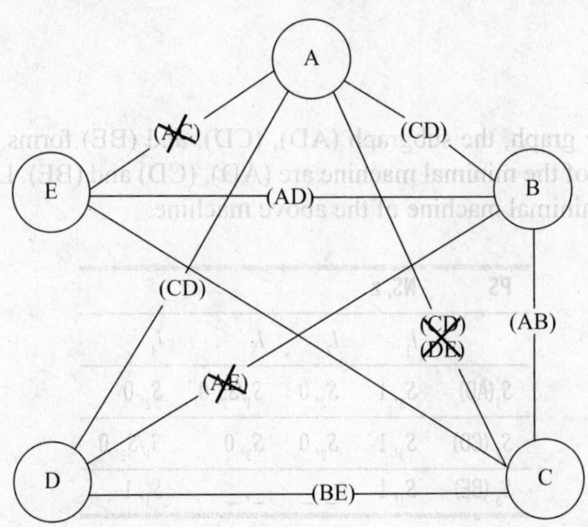

The pair of states which are connected by undirected arcs (Not crossed in the interrupted portion) are compatible pairs. The compatible pairs of the given machine are (AB), (AD), (BC), (BE), (CD) and (CE). Therefore in the compatibility graph of the above machine there are nine vertices.

The (CD) is implied pair for (AB). A directed arc is drawn from (AB) to (CD).
The (CD) is implied pair for (AD). A directed arc is drawn from (AD) to (CD).
The (AB) is implied pair for (BC). A directed arc is drawn from (BC) to (AB).
The (AD) is implied pair for (BE). A directed arc is drawn from (BE) to (AD).
The (BE) is implied pair for (CD). A directed arc is drawn from (CD) to (BE).
The compatibility graph is

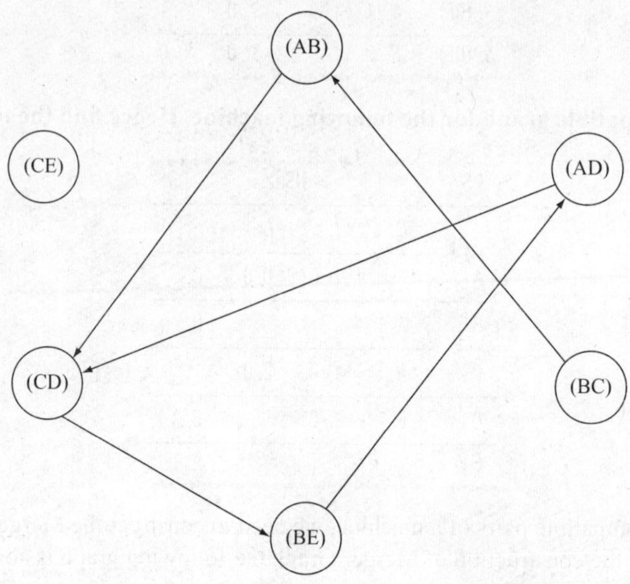

Minimal Machine:

In the above compatibility graph, the subgraph (AD), (CD), and (BE) forms a closed covering of the given machine. The states of the minimal machine are (AD), (CD) and (BE). Let rename them as S_1, S_2, and S_3, respectively. The minimal machine of the above machine:

PS	NS, z			
	I_1	I_2	I_3	I_4
S_1(AD)	S_3, 1	S_2, 0	S_1/S_2, 0	S_2, 0
S_2 (CD)	S_3, 1	S_2, 0	S_3, 0	S_1/S_2, 0
S_3 (BE)	S_1, 1	_, _	_, _	S_1, 1

Q. What is Merger table? Why Merger table is used? How is a Merger table is constructed?

Ans. Merger table is a substitute application of Merger graph. From a Merger graph we can get the compatible pairs and implied pairs.

If number of states of a machine increases, number of combination pair increases. For a machine of n states, number of two state combinations are ${}^{n}C_{2}$ i.e. $n(n-1)/2$. If $n=(n-1)$, number of combinations are $(n-1)(n-2)/2$. Number of combination increases to $(n-1)$ if number of states increases from $(n-1)$ to n. It is difficult to connect two states by arcs in a merger graph, if number of states increase. Hence a Merger table is an easier process to find compatible pairs and implied pairs.

Process of construction:

A Merger table can be constructed as follows:

1. Make a table of $(n-1) \times (n-1)$ where left-hand-side is labeled by second state to n^{th} state and right-hand-side is labeled by first state to $(n-1)^{th}$ state.
2. Each box represents a pair of states combination.
3. Put a cross in the box if the output conflict for the pair of states.
4. Put a right sign in the box if the outputs as well as next states do not conflict for the pair of states.
5. If the outputs do not conflict but the next states conflict for the pair of states, put the conflicting next states in the box.

Q. Construct Merger table of the following machine and find the compatible pairs.

PS	NS, z		
	I_1	I_2	I_3
A	E, 0	B, _	C, _
B	_, _	D, _	B, 0
C	E, _	D, _	C, 0
D	C, 0	_, _	B, 1
E	C, 0	_, _	B, _

Ans: Make a table like the following

B				
C				
D				
E				
	A	**B**	**C**	**D**

Consider the state combination (AB). Here outputs do not conflict but the next states for I_2 and I_3 conflict. Hence conflicting next state combination, (BD) and (BC) are placed in the box labeled (AB).

Consider the state combination (AC). Here outputs do not conflict but the next states for I_2 conflict. Hence conflicting next state combination, (BD) is placed in the box labeled (AC).

Consider the state combination (AD). Outputs do not conflict, but the next states for I_1 and I_3 conflict. Conflicting next state combinations (CE) and (BC) are placed in the box labeled (AD).

Consider state combination (AE). The outputs for the states do not conflict, but the next states for input I_1 and I_3 conflict. The (CE) and (BC) are placed in the box labeled (AE).

Consider state combination (BD). Here outputs for input I_3 conflict. There will be a '' (cross) in the box labeled (BD).

Consider state combination (DE). Here both the outputs and next state combination are same for all the inputs. Hence a '√' (tick) is placed in the box labeled (DE).

By this process the Constructed Merger Table is:

B	(BD) (BC)			
C	(BD)	(BC)		
D	(CE) (BC)	√	×	
E	(CE) (BC)	√	(CE) (BC)	√
	A	B	C	D

The boxes which are not crossed are compatible pairs. Hence, the compatible pairs are (AB), (AC), (AD), (AE), (BC), (BD), (BE), (CD), and (DE).

Q. Construct Merger table of the following machine and find the compatible pairs.

PS	NS, z			
	I_1	I_2	I_3	I_4
A	C, _	_, _	_, _	_, _
B	_, _	C, _	D, _	E, _
C	_, _	F, 0	B, _	_, _
D	E, _	_, 1	_, _	A, _
E	_, _	B, _	_, _	C, _
F	B, _	_, _	E, _	_, _

Ans: For the states AB, for all the inputs, next states and output do not conflict. Hence a √ (tick) is placed in the box labeled AB. For states AC, next states and outputs do not conflict for all the inputs.

Hence a √ (tick) is placed in the box labeled AC. For states AD, the outputs do not conflict, but the next states for input I_1 conflict. So the conflicting next state pair (CE) is placed in the box labeled AD.

In the box labeled (AE) a √ (tick) is placed.
In the box (AF), conflicting next state pair (BC) is placed.
In the box (BC), conflicting next state pair (CF) and (BD) is placed.
In the box (BD), conflicting next state pair (AE) is placed.
In the box (BE), conflicting next state pair (BC) and (CE) is placed.
In the box (BF), conflicting next state pair (DE) is placed.
The outputs for I_2 for state (CD), conflict. Hence a ′ (cross) is placed in the box (CD).
In the box (CE), conflicting next state pair (BF) is placed.
In the box (CF), conflicting next state pair (BE) is placed.
By this process the constructed Merger table

B	√				
C	√	(CF) (BD)			
D	(CE)	(AE)	×		
E	√	(BC) (CE)	(BF)	(AC)	
F	(BC)	(DE)	(BE)	(BE)	√
	A	B	C	D	E

The compatible pairs are (AB), (AC), (AD), (AE), (AF), (BC), (BD), (DE), (DF), (CE), (CF), (DE), (DF), and (EF).

Q. Construct Merger Table of the following machine and find the compatible pairs.

PS	NS, z			
	I_1	I_2	I_3	I_4
A	_, _	D, 0	D, 0	C, _
B	A, 1	_, _	_, _	D, _
C	B, 1	C, 0	E, 0	_, _
D	E, 1	C, 0	_, _	D, 0
E	_, _	_, _	_, _	A, 1

Ans. The Merger Table for the above machine is:

B	(CD)			
C	(CD) (DE)	(AB)		
D	(CD)	(AE)	(BE)	
E	(AC)	(AD)	√	×
	A	B	C	D

Here (DE) is crossed, hence (AC) will be crossed. As (AC) is crossed, (AE) will be crossed. As (AE) is crossed, (BD) will be crossed. The final Merger graph:

B	(CD)			
C	(CD) (DE)	(AB)		
D	(CD) ✗	(AE)	(BE)	
E	(AC)	(AD) ✗	√	×
	A ✗	B	C	D

The compatible pairs of the given machine are (AB), (AD), (BC), (BE), (CD) and (CE).

1.6 FINITE MEMORY AND DEFINITE MEMORY MACHINE

Q. Define finite memory machine. What are the processes of testing whether a machine is finite or not?

Ans.

Finite memory machine:

A finite state machine M is called finite memory machine of order μ if μ is the least integer so that the present state of the machine M can be obtained uniquely from the knowledge of last μ number of inputs and the corresponding μ number of outputs. There are two methods to find a machine is finite or not:

1. Testing table and testing Graph for finite memory
2. Vanishing connection Matrix.

1. Testing table and testing Graph for finite memory method

The testing table for finite memory is divided into two halves. Upper half contains single state input-output combination. If in a machine there are two types of inputs and two types of outputs let 0 and 1, the input-output combinations are 0/0, 0/1, 1/0, and 1/1. Here 0/0 means 0 input and 0 outputs, i.e. for the cases we are getting output 0 for input 0, 0/1 means 0 input and 1 output, i.e. for the cases we are getting output 1 for input 0. Lower half of the table contains all combination of present states taking two into combination. For four present states (Let A, B, C, and D) there are ${}^4C_2$ means 6 combinations. AB, AC, AD, BC, BD, and CD. Table is constructed according to the machine given. Pair of present state combination is called uncertainty pair. And its successor is called implied pair.

In the testing graph for finite memory

1. Number of nodes will be number of present states combination taking two into account.
2. There will be an directed arc with label of input output combination, from S_iS_j $(i \neq j)$ to S_pS_q $(p \neq q)$ if S_pS_q is the implied pair of S_iS_j.

If the testing graph is of loop free, the machine is of finite memory. The order of finiteness is the length of the longest path in the testing graph (l)+1, i.e. $\mu=l+1$.

2. Vanishing connection matrix method

If the number of states increases then it becomes difficult to find the longest path in the testing graph for finite memory. There is an easy method to determine whether a machine is finite or not, and if finite, to find its order of finiteness. The process is called vanishing connection matrix method.

Constructing method of connection matrix.

1. Number of Rows will be equal to number of columns ($p \times p$ matrix).
2. The rows and columns will be labeled with the pair of present state combinations. The labels associated with corresponding rows and columns will be identical.
3. In the matrix (i,j)th entry will be 1 if there is an entry in (S_aS_b) and (S_pS_q) combination in the corresponding testing table. Otherwise the entry will be 0.

Vanishing of connection matrix

1. Delete all rows having 0s in all positions and delete the corresponding columns also.
2. Repeat this step until one of the following steps achieved:
   (i) No row left with having 0's in all positions.
   (ii) The matrix vanish that means no rows and no columns left.

If the condition 2(i) arrives the machine is not of finite memory.

If the condition 2(ii) arrives the machine is of finite memory and the number of steps requires to vanish the matrix is the order of finiteness of the machine.

Q. Test whether the following machine is of finite memory or not by using testing table–testing graph and vanishing matrix method.

PS	NS, z	
	$x = 0$	$x = 1$
A	D,0	A,1
B	D,1	A,1
C	B,1	B,1
D	A,1	C,1

Ans. A table which is divided into two halves is made. The machine has two inputs and two outputs. There are four input–output combinations namely 0/0, 0/1, 1/0, 1/1. The upper half of the machine contains single state input output combination and lower half contain two state input output combinations. There are four states, so six combination pairs are made. The testing table becomes

PS	0/0	0/1	1/0	1/1
A	D	—	—	A
B	—	D	—	A
C	—	B	—	B
D	—	A	—	C
AB	—	—	—	AA
AC	—	—	—	AB
AD	—	—	—	AC
BC	—	BD	—	AB
BD	—	AD	—	AC
CD	—	AB	—	BC

In Testing Table there are six present states combinations. So, in the testing table there are six nodes. There is a directed arc with label of input output combination, from S_iS_j $(i \neq j)$ to S_pS_q $(p \neq q)$ if S_pS_q is the implied pair of S_iS_j. The testing graph for finite memory:

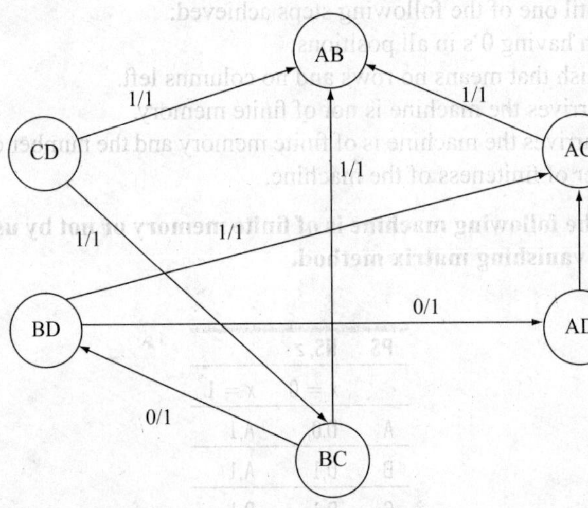

(AB to AA there will be no arc as in AA, both are the repetition of same state).

The longest path in the Testing graph is 5 [CD → BC → BD → AD → AC → AB], so the order of definiteness μ = 5+1 =6.

Vanishing connection matrix method

According to the rule of the construction of Connection Matrix a table is constructed with six rows and six columns labeled with the present state combinations. In the testing table, (AB) is the next state combination for (AC) for input 1/1. So an entry 1 is placed in the box labeled (AC)(AB).[i.e.{Label of Row] [Label of Column]} All the other entries are 0.

By this process the following vanishing connection matrix is generated.

	AB	AC	AD	BC	BD	CD
AB	0	0	0	0	0	0
AC	1	0	0	0	0	0
AD	0	1	0	0	0	0
BC	1	0	0	0	1	0
BD	0	1	1	0	0	0
CD	1	0	0	1	0	0

The row labeled AB contains all entry '0'. So the row labeled AB and the corresponding column is crossed.

	AB	AC	AD	BC	BD	CD
AB	0	0	0	0	0	0
AC	1	0	0	0	0	0
AD	0	1	0	0	0	0
BC	1	0	0	0	1	0
BD	0	1	1	0	0	0
CD	1	0	0	1	0	0

Now the table does not contain the row and column labeled AB. The row labeled AC contains all '0'. So the row labeled AC and the corresponding column is crossed.

	AC	AD	BC	BD	CD
AC	0	0	0	0	0
AD	1	0	0	0	0
BC	0	0	0	1	0
BD	1	1	0	0	0
CD	0	0	1	0	0

Now the table does not contain the row and column labeled AC. The row labeled AD contains all '0'. So the row labeled AD and the corresponding column is crossed.

	AD	BC	BD	CD
AD	0	0	0	0
BC	0	0	1	0
BD	1	0	0	0
CD	0	1	0	0

The table does not contain the row and column labeled AD. The row labeled BD contains all '0'. So the row labeled BD and the corresponding column is crossed.

	BC	BD	CD
BC	0	1	0
BD	0	0	0
CD	1	0	0

The table does not contain the row and column labeled BD. The row labeled BC contains all '0'. So the row labeled BC and the corresponding column is crossed.

	BC	CD
BC	0	0
CD	1	0

The table does not contain the row and column labeled BC. The row labeled CD contains all '0'. So the row labeled CD and the corresponding column is crossed, means the matrix vanishes.

	CD
CD	0

Number of steps required to vanish the matrix is six. Hence order of finiteness μ=6.

Q. Check whether the following machine is of Finite Memory or not by vanishing Connection Matrix Method.

PS	NS, z	
	$x = 0$	$x = 1$
A	B,0	C,0
B	D,0	E,1
C	A,0	A,1
D	E,1	E,1
E	E,1	C,0

Ans: To construct the connection matrix we need to first construct the testing table.
The testing table

PS	0/0	0/1	1/0	1/1
A	B	—	C	—
B	D	—	—	E

C	A	—	—	A
D	—	E	—	E
E	—	E	C	—

AB	BD	—	—	—
AC	AB	—	—	—
AD	—	—	—	—
AE	—	—	CC	—
BC	AD	—	—	AE
BD	—	—	—	EE
BE	—	—	—	—
CD	—	—	—	AE
CE	—	—	—	—
DE	—	EE	—	—

According to the rule of the construction of connection matrix a table is constructed with 10 rows and 10 columns labeled with the present state combinations. In the testing table there is an entry BD for AB for input 0/0. Hence a '1' is placed in AB row BD column entry. All the other entries are '0'. By this process the constructed connection matrix:

	AB	AC	AD	AE	BC	BD	BE	CD	CE	DE
AB	0	0	0	0	0	1	0	0	0	0
AC	1	0	0	0	0	0	0	0	0	0
AD	0	0	0	0	0	0	0	0	0	0
AE	0	0	0	0	0	0	0	0	0	0
BC	0	0	1	1	0	0	0	0	0	0
BD	0	0	0	0	0	0	0	0	0	0
BE	0	0	0	0	0	0	0	0	0	0
CD	0	0	0	1	0	0	0	0	0	0
CE	0	0	0	0	0	0	0	0	0	0
DE	0	0	0	0	0	0	0	0	0	0

In the matrix the rows labeled AD, AE, BD, BE, CE, and DE contain all 0 entries. These rows with the corresponding columns are crossed off.

	AB	AC	AD	AE	BC	BD	BE	CD	CE	DE
AB	0	0	0	0	0	1	0	0	0	0
AC	1	0	0	0	0	0	0	0	0	0
AD	0	0	0	0	0	0	0	0	0	0
AE	0	0	0	0	0	0	0	0	0	0
BC	0	0	1	1	0	0	0	0	0	0
BD	0	0	0	0	0	0	0	0	0	0
BE	0	0	0	0	0	0	0	0	0	0
CD	0	0	0	0	0	0	0	0	0	0
CE	0	0	0	0	0	0	0	0	0	0
DE	0	0	0	0	0	0	0	0	0	0

In the Matrix there is no row and columns labeled AC, AD, AE, BD, BE, DE. In the modified matrix all the rows contain '0', so all the rows and corresponding columns are crossed.

	AB	BC	CD	CE
AB	0	0	0	0
BC	0	0	0	0
CD	0	0	0	0
CE	0	0	0	0

The matrix vanishes. Number of steps required to vanish the matrix is 2. Hence order of finiteness of the machine $\mu = 2$.

Q. Check whether the following machine is of Finite Memory or not by Testing table –Testing graph and vanishing connection matrix method.

PS	NS, z	
	x=0	x=1
A	B,1	D,0
B	A,1	C,1
C	D,1	A,0
D	B,1	A,1

Ans. A table that is divided into two halves is made. The machine has two inputs and two outputs. There are four input–output combinations namely 0/0, 0/1, 1/0, 1/1. The upper half of the machine contains single-state input–output combination and lower half contain two-state input–output combinations. There are four states, so six combination pairs are made. The testing table becomes:

PS	0/0	0/1	1/0	1/1
A	—	B	D	—
B		A		C
C	—	D	A	—
D	—	B	—	A
AB	—	AB		—
AC	—	BD	AD	—
AD		BB	—	—
BC	—	AD	—	—
BD	—	AB	—	AC
CD	—	BD	—	—

In testing table there are six present states combinations. Hence, in the testing table there are six nodes. There is a directed arc with label of input–output combination, from S_iS_j (i ≠ j) to S_pS_q (p ≠ q) if S_pS_q is the implied pair of S_iS_j. The testing graph for finite memory:

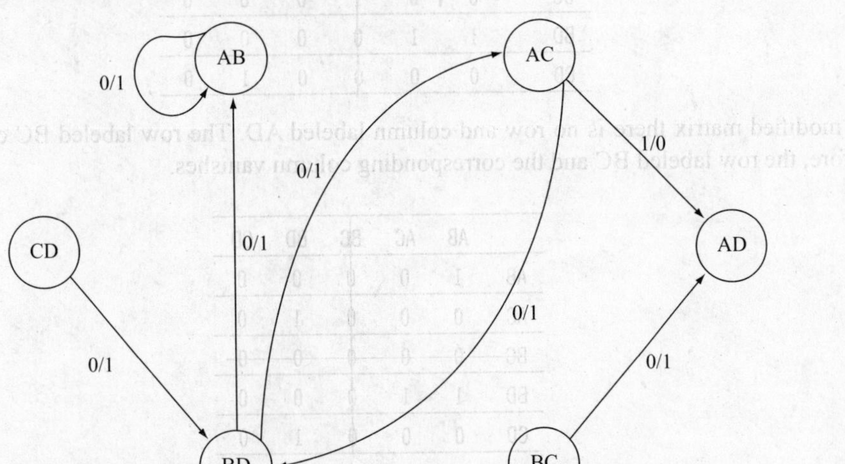

The testing graph for finite memory contain two loops AB to AB with label 0/1 and AC to BD with label 0/1, BD to AC with label 0/1. As the testing graph is not loop free the machine is not of finite memory.

Test by vanishing connection matrix method:

In the testing table, six present state pairs are formed. Therefore the connection matrix consists of six rows and six columns. The rows and columns are labeled with pair of present state combinations. In the matrix (i,j)th entry will be 1 if there is an entry in (S_aS_b) $(a \neq b)$ and (S_pS_q) $(p \neq q)$ combination in the corresponding testing table. Otherwise the entry will be 0. The connection matrix of the above machine is as follows:

	AB	AC	AD	BC	BD	CD
AB	1	0	0	0	0	0
AC	0	0	1	0	1	0
AD	0	0	0	0	0	0
BC	0	0	1	0	0	0
BD	1	1	0	0	0	0
CD	0	0	0	0	1	0

In the above matrix the row AD contains all '0'. Hence the row labeled AD and the corresponding column vanishes.

	AB	AC	AD	BC	BD	CD
AB	1	0	0	0	0	0
AC	0	0	1	0	1	0
AD	0	0	0	0	0	0
BC	0	0	1	0	0	0
BD	1	1	0	0	0	0
CD	0	0	0	0	1	0

In the modified matrix there is no row and column labeled AD. The row labeled BC contains all '0'. Therefore, the row labeled BC and the corresponding column vanishes.

	AB	AC	BC	BD	CD
AB	1	0	0	0	0
AC	0	0	0	1	0
BC	0	0	0	0	0
BD	1	1	0	0	0
CD	0	0	0	1	0

In the modified matrix there is no row and column labeled BC. The modified matrix becomes

	AB	AC	BD	CD
AB	1	0	0	0
AC	0	0	1	0
BD	1	1	0	0
CD	0	0	1	0

The matrix does not contain any row containing all '0'. So the matrix does not vanish. Therefore the machine is not of finite memory.

Q. Define definite machine. What are the processes of testing whether a machine is definite or not?

Ans. Definite Machine: A sequential machine M is called definite if there exist a least integer μ, so that the present state of the machine M can be uniquely obtained from the past μ number of inputs to the machine M. Hence μ is called the order of definiteness of the machine.

There are three methods to find a machine is definite or not.

1. Synchronizing tree method
2. Contracted table method
3. Testing table-testing graph for definiteness method.

1. Synchronizing tree method:

For a machine with definite memory only inputs play a role. There is no role of outputs. So, the present state combinations can be divided into two parts for two types of inputs, 0 and 1. Those divided combinations of states can again be divided for input 0 and 1.

If the leaf nodes are of single state, stop constructing the tree. The order of definiteness is the maximum label of the synchronizing tree. Else the machine is not of definite memory.

2. Contracted table method:

(a) Find those present states whose next states are identical.

(b) Represent those present states as single states (Those present states are equivalent).

(c) Obtain the contracted table by replacing only one of the present states from the equivalent state set and modify the table according to it.

(d) Repeat steps from (a) to (c) until new contraction are possible.

By this process if at last a machine with single state is received, then the machine is definite. Its order is the number of steps required to obtain the single state machine. Else the machine is not definite.

3. Testing table–testing graph for definiteness method.

The Testing Table for definiteness is divided into two halves. The upper half contains input and next state combination. Lower half of the table contains all combination of present states taking two into combination. For four present states (Let A, B, C, and D) there are ${}^4C_2$, i.e. six combinations. AB, AC, AD, BC, BD, and CD.

Table is constructed according to the machine given. For these present state combinations find the next state combinations for input 0 and input 1. Pair of present state combination is called uncertainty pair. And its successor is called implied pair.

In the testing graph for definite memory,

1. Number of nodes will be number of present states combination taking two into account.
2. There will be an directed arc with label of input output combination, from S_iS_j $(i \neq j)$ to S_pS_q $(p \neq q)$ if S_pS_q is the implied pair of S_iS_j.

If the testing graph is loop-free, the machine is of definite memory. The order of definiteness is the length of the longest path in the testing graph (l)+1, i.e. $\mu=l+1$.

Q. Test whether the following machine is definite or not by any of the method. If definite find the order of definiteness.

PS	NS	
	$X = 0$	$X = 1$
A	C	B
B	A	D
C	C	B
D	C	D

Ans. Synchronizing Tree Method: The present state combination of the machine is (ABCD). It has two types of inputs 0 and 1. The (ABCD) with input 0 produce next state combination (CACC). It can be grouped into two distinct states (AC). The (ABCD) with input 1 produce next state combination (BDBD) which can be grouped into (BD).

In the next level, (AC) with input 0 produces a single next state C. With input 1, (AC) produces single next state B. As C and B are single states, no need to approach further to next level. The state combination (BD) with input 0 produces next state combination (AC). With input 1, state combination (BD) produces single state D. In the next level state combination (AC) produces C and B, respectively for input 0 and 1.

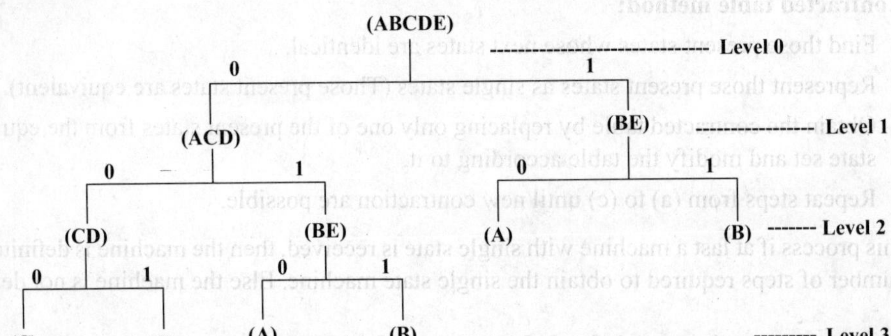

As the leaf nodes are of single state, stop constructing the tree. The order of definiteness is the maximum label of the synchronizing tree. In this case order is 3.

Contracted table method

PS	NS	
	$X = 0$	$X = 1$
A	C	B
B	A	D
C	C	B
D	C	D

In the previous machine A and C have same next state combination (both cases C and B). Therefore, A and C are equivalent states. Among A and C let take only A, i.e. all the C in the state table are replaced by A. The contracted table is

PS	NS	
	$x = 0$	$x = 1$
A	A	B
B	A	D
D	A	D

In the table, B and D produce same next state combination for input 0 and 1. Therefore, B and D are equivalent states. D is replaced by B. The contracted table becomes

PS	NS	
	$x = 0$	$x = 1$
A	A	B
B	A	B

The table contains two states A and B with same next states combination for input 0 and 1. So they are equivalent states. B is replaced by A. The contracted table becomes

PS	NS	
	$x=0$	$x=1$
A	A	A

A machine with single state is received, the machine is definite. Its order is the number of steps required to obtain the single state machine (here 3).

Testing table testing graph method:

A table with two halves is made. The upper half contains input and next state combination. Lower half of the table contains all combination of present states taking two into combination. Here for four present states (Let A, B, C, and D) there are $^4C_2$ means six combinations. AB, AC, AD, BC, BD, and CD. The table:

PS	0	1
A	C	B
B	A	D
C	C	B
D	C	D

AB	AC	BD
AC	CC	BB
AD	CC	BD
BC	AC	BD
BD	AC	DD
CD	CC	BD

The lower half of the testing table contains six present state combination pairs. The testing graph:

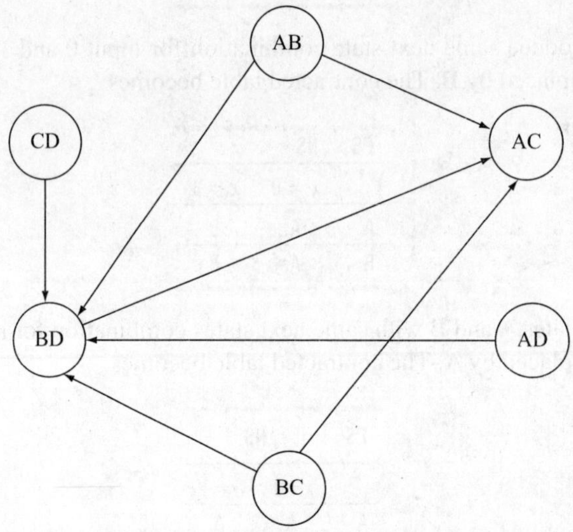

The testing graph is loop-free. So the machine is of definite memory. The longest path of the testing graph is 2 [AB → BD → AC or AD →BD → AC]. So order of definiteness of the machine is 2+1 = 3.

Q. Test whether the following machine is definite or not by any of the method (synchronizing tree or contracted table). If definite, find the order of definiteness.

PS	NS	
	$x = 0$	$x = 1$
A	D	E
B	A	B
C	C	B
D	C	B
E	A	B

Ans. Synchronizing Tree Method:

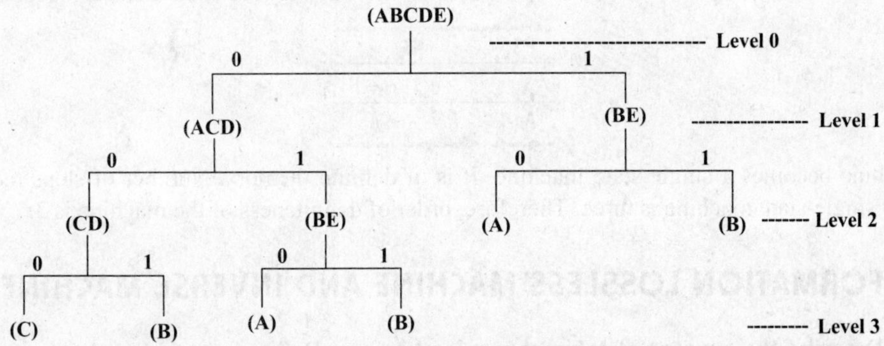

The synchronizing tree thus obtained contains leaf nodes of single state. Hence the machine is of definite memory. Number of level of the tree is 3. Therefore, order of definiteness of the machine is 3.

Contracted table method:

PS	NS	
	$x = 0$	$x = 1$
A	D	E
B	A	B
C	C	B
D	C	B
E	A	B

States B and E are producing same next state combination for input 0 and 1. Hence they are equivalent. The E is replaced by B, C and D is producing same next state combination, D is replaced by C. The contracted table becomes

PS	NS	
	$x = 0$	$x = 1$
A	C	B
B	A	B
C	C	B

State A and C are producing same next state combination for input 0 and 1. Hence A and C are equivalent, C is replaced by A. The contracted table becomes

PS	NS	
	$x = 0$	$x = 1$
A	A	B
B	A	B

Both of the states are producing same next state combination, so they are equivalent. B is replaced by A.

PS	NS	
	X = 0	X = 1
A	A	A

The machine becomes a single-state machine. It is of definite memory. Number of steps required to make it a single-state machine is three. Therefore, order of definiteness of the machine is 3.

1.7 INFORMATION LOSSLESS MACHINE AND INVERSE MACHINE

Q. Describe the concept of information losslessness. Define information lossless machine. Justify your definition with an example.

Ans. The main problem of coding and information transmission theory is to determine the conditions for which it is possible to regenerate the input sequence given to a machine from the achieved output sequence.Let information be given to a machine, used for coding device. Input and the output achieved is the coded message and let the initial and final states be known. It this case information losslessness of the machine guarantees that the coded message (output) can always be deciphered.

A machine is called information lossless if its initial state, final state, and output string is sufficient to determine uniquely the input string.

A machine is said to be (information) lossless of order μ (ILF-μ) if the knowledge of the initial state and the first μ output symbols is sufficient to determine uniquely the first input symbol.

Example:

Let take a machine M as follows

PS	NS, z	
	$x = 0$	$x = 1$
A	A, 1	B, 0
B	B, 0	A, 1

Let the initial state of the machine be A, final state achieved is A, and coded message (output) is 01. We have to find the information given as input. A as a next state is produced for two cases A as a present state for input 0 and B as a present state for input 1. By this process the output successor table is constructed.

Now we construct the machine according to the output achieved.

NS	PS, i/p	
	$z = 0$	$z = 1$
A	--	A, 0 B, 1
B	A, 1 B, 0	--

Output 01 implies that when reversed it is 10. Initial state is A and final state is A. Hence the diagram will become

Output 1 with next state A is produced for two cases – Previous state A with input 0 or previous state B with input 1.

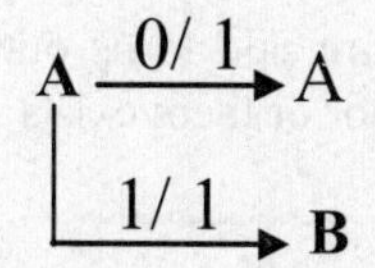

Output 0 with next state A is produced for no cases. Output 0 with next state B is produced for two cases – previous state A with input 1 and previous state B with input 0.

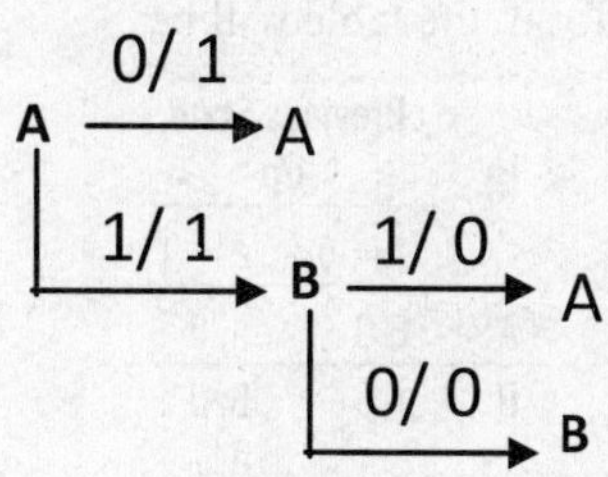

The initial state is A. In the previous case A is produced for input 11. Therefore, the input is 11.

Q. What is lossy machine? Describe with an example. What is the condition for a machine to be a lossy?

Ans: A machine which is not lossless is called lossy.

PS	NS, z	
	$x = 0$	$x = 1$
A	A, 1	B, 0
B	B, 1	A, 1

If the testing table obtained from the given machine contains repeated entry of states, the machine is lossy. As an example for the previous machine the testing table is as follows

PS	NS	
	z = 0	z = 1
A	B	A
B	–	AB
AB	–	AA, AB

The testing table contains repeated entry of states in the form of AA. So the machine is lossy.

Q. What do you mean by output compatible pair and its implied pair?

Ans. Two states S_i S_j of a machine M are said to be output compatible if there exist some state S_p, such that both S_i and S_j are its O_k successor or there exists a compatible pair of states S_a S_b such that S_i S_j are its O_k successor.

PS	NS, z	
	x = 0	x = 1
A	A, 1	B, 0
B	B, 1	A, 1

If we construct output successor table for it, the table will be

NS	Previous State, i/p	
	z = 0	z = 1
A	B, 1	A, 0
B	–	B, 0 A, 1

Let apply input 1 and 0 on states B and A, respectively. The next state will be A for both the cases and the output will be 1 for both the cases. Therefore, we can say A and B are output compatible as there exist a state A such that both A and B are its 1 successor.

Q. What is the process of testing an information lossless machine? How to determine the order of lossnessness?

Ans. The process of testing a machine is information lossless or not, is to construct a testing table and testing graph. The testing table is constructed in the following way.

i. **The testing table for checking information losslessness is divided into two halves. The upper half contains present states and its output successors.**

ii. **The lower half of the table is constructed in the following way**

(a) Every compatible pair appearing in the output successor table is taken into present state column. The successors of these pairs are constructed from the original table. Here if any compatible pair appears, then that pair is called the implied pair for the compatible pair in the present state column.

(b) That new pair is again taken in the present state column if it is not taken.
(c) The process terminates when all compatible pairs have been taken in the present state column.

The machine is information lossless if and only if its testing table does not contain any compatible pair consisting of repeated entry. From the testing table, testing graph is constructed. The testing graph is constructed in the following way.

(1) Number of vertices of the testing graph is equal to number of output compatible pairs taken in the lower half of the testing table. The labels of the vertices are the compatible pairs in the lower half of the testing table.
(2) A directed arc is drawn from vertex S_iS_j to vertex S_pS_q $(p'q)$ if S_pS_q is implied pair for S_iS_j.

The machine is information lossless if the testing graph is loop free and its order m = 1 + 2, where l is the length of the longest path of the testing graph.

Q. Test whether the following machine is information lossless or not. If lossless find its order.

PS	NS, z	
	X = 0	X = 1
A	C,1	D,1
B	A,1	B,1
C	B,0	A,0
D	D,0	C,0

Ans. First step to test whether a machine is lossless or not is to construct a testing table. The testing table is divided into two halves.

PS	z = 0	z = 1
A	—	CD
B	—	AB
C	AB	—
D	CD	—
AB	—	(AC)(BC) (AD)(BD)
CD	(BD)(BC) (AD)(AC)	—
AC	—	—
AD	—	—
BC	—	—
BD	—	—

Testing graph consists of six vertices.

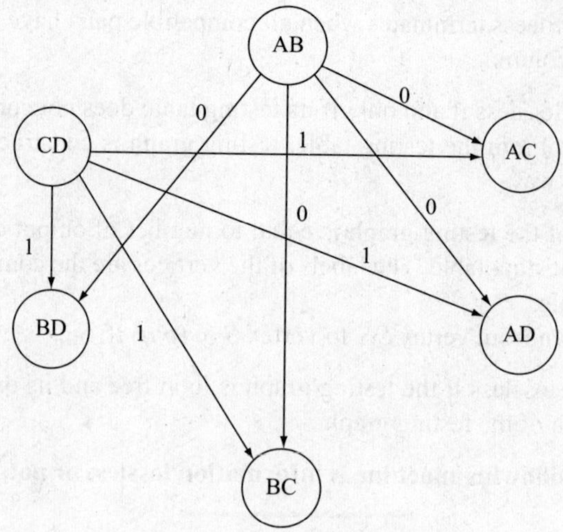

The testing table does not contain any repeated entry. The machine is lossless machine. The testing graph does not contain any loop. The order of losslessness is $\mu = 1 + 2 = 3$. The length of the longest path of the graph is 1.

Q. Find the input string which is applied on state 'A' producing output string 00011 and final state 'B' for the machine given below.

PS	NS, z	
	$x = 0$	$x = 1$
A	A,0	B,0
B	C,0	D,0
C	D,1	C,1
D	B,1	A,1

Ans. First we need to prove the machine is information lossless. For this we need to construct a testing table for information lossless.

PS	$z = 0$	$z = 1$
A	AB	—
B	CD	—
C	—	CD
D	—	AB
AB	(AC)(BC) (AD)(BD)	—

CD	—	(AC)(BC) (AD)(BD)
AC	—	—
AD	—	—
BC	—	—
BD	—	—

The testing table does not contain any repeated entry. So the machine is information lossless.

We need to first construct the output successor table

PS	$z = 0$	$z = 1$
A	A/0, B/1	—
B	C/0, D/1	—
C	—	C/1, D/0
D	—	A/1, B/0

The input string is applied on state A and has produced output 0. From the output successor table it is clear that the next states are A or B. By this process the transition is like the following:

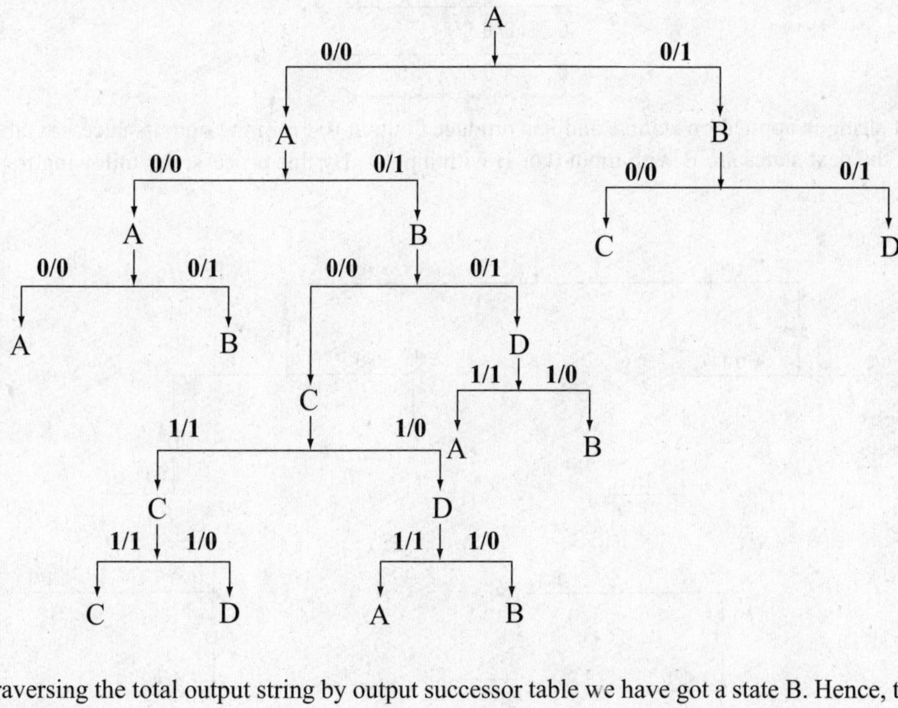

After traversing the total output string by output successor table we have got a state B. Hence, the input string is 01000.

(Input string retrieval is only possible for information lossless machine. This can be illustrated in the following example)

Q. Find the input string which is applied on state 'A' producing output string 00101 and final state 'C' for the machine given below.

PS	NS, z	
	x = 0	x = 1
A	B, 0	B, 0
B	C, 0	D, 0
C	D, 0	C, 0
D	A, 0	C, 1

Ans. The machine is not information lossless as in the testing table for information losslessness contains a repeated entry BB for the state 'A' and output '0'. Yet, again try to find the input sequence by constructing the output successor table.

The output successor table for the given machine is

PS	z = 0	z = 1
A	B/ 0, B/ 1	—
B	C/ 0, D/ 1	—
C	D/ 0, C/ 1	—
D	A/ 0	C/1

The input string is applied on state A and has produced output 0. From the output successor table it is clear that the next states are B with input 0 or B with input 1. By this process, the following transition is obtained:

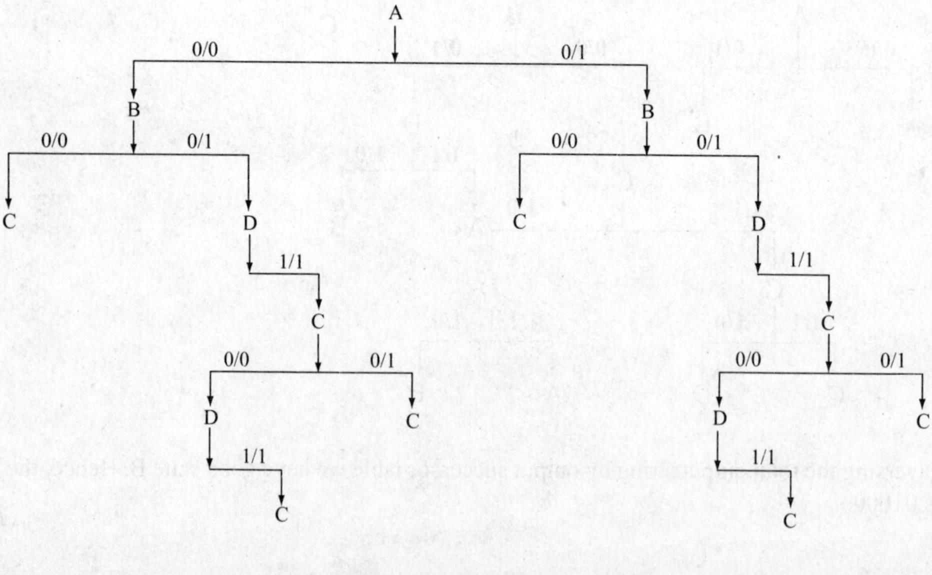

We are getting C as final state for two input sequences 01101 and 11101. Hence we cannot uniquely determine the input string. We can conclude that input string retrieval is not possible for information lossy machine.

Q. Test whether the following machine is information lossless or not. If lossless find its order.

PS	NS, z	
	$x = 0$	$x = 1$
A	B, 0	C, 0
B	D, 0	E, 1
C	A, 1	E, 0
D	E, 0	D, 0
E	A, 1	E, 1

Ans. First step to test whether a machine is lossless or not is to construct a testing table. The testing table is divided into two halves.

PS	$z = 0$	$z = 1$
A	BC	—
B	D	E
C	E	A
D	DE	—
E	—	AE
BC	DE	AE
DE	—	—
AE	—	

The testing table does not contain any repeated entry. The machine is information lossless machine. The testing graph for the machine:

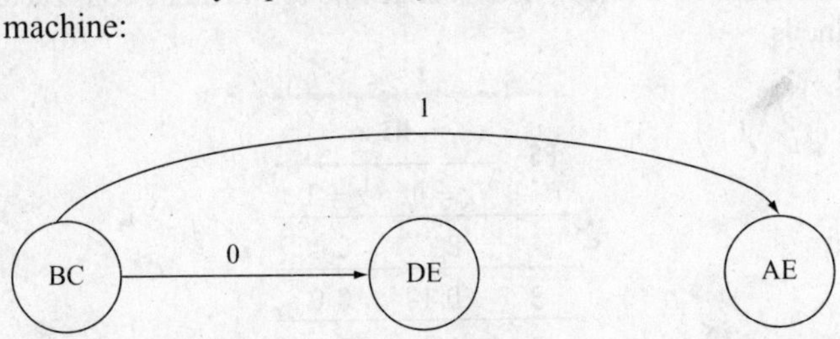

The testing graph for information losslessness is loop-free. The order of losslessness is μ=1+2=3. The length of the longest path of the graph is 1.

1.8 INVERSE MACHINE

Q. Define inverse machine. What is the necessary condition for constructing an inverse machine from a given machine? Construct an inverse machine of the following machine.

PS	NS, z	
	x = 0	x = 1
A	B, 0	C, 1
B	C, 1	D, 0
C	A, 0	D, 1
D	A, 1	C, 0

Ans. An inverse machine M^i is a machine which is developed from the given machine M with its output sequence and produces the input sequence given to machine M, after at most a finite delay. A deterministic inverse machine can be constructed if and only if the given machine is lossless. The machine can produce the input sequence applied to the original machine after at most a finite delay if and only if M is lossless of finite order.

Inverse Machine of the given machine

Before constructing the inverse machine we need to test whether the machine is information lossless or not. The testing table for information lossless:

PS		
	z = 0	z = 1
A	B	C
B	D	C
C	A	D
D	C	A

This is information lossless of first order, as here first input symbol can be determined from the knowledge of the initial state and the first output symbol.

As the machine is information lossless, inverse machine for it can be constructed.

The inverse machine is

PS	NS, x	
	z = 0	z = 1
A	B, 0	C, 1
B	D, 1	C, 0
C	A, 0	D, 1
D	C, 1	A, 0

Q. Define minimal inverse machine. Construct a minimal inverse machine for the machine given below.

PS	NS, z	
	$x = 0$	$x = 1$
A	A, 0	B, 0
B	C, 1	D, 1
C	B, 0	A, 1
D	A, 0	B, 1

Ans. Inverse machine is only possible if the machine is lossless. First we have to check if the machine is lossless or not.

PS	NS, z	
	$z = 0$	$z = 1$
A	AB	—
B	—	CD
C	B	A
D	A	B
AB	—	—
CD	AB	AB

The machine is lossless as the testing table does not contain any entry of repeated states. The testing graph for the information lossless machine:

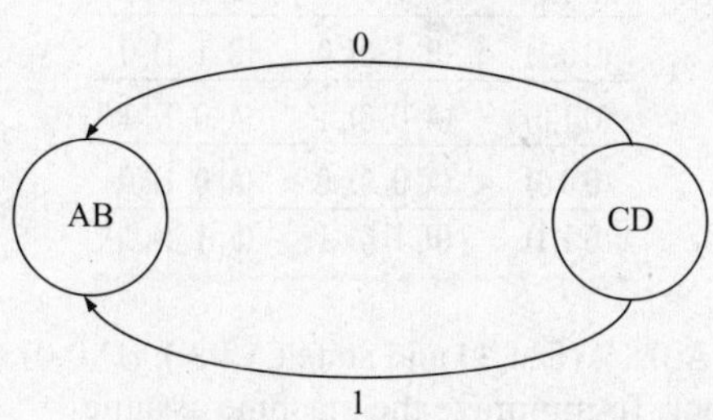

The order of losslessness of the machine is 3. Let us define a set of triple denoted ($S(t)$, $z(t+1)$, $z(t+2)$).

Where $S(t)$ is the initial state of the machine, $z(t + 1)$ is the one of the output symbols that can be produced by single transition from this state, $z(t+2)$ is another output symbol that can follow this initial state and the first output symbol.

For the given machine the possible triples are

(A, 0, 0) (B, 1, 0) (C, 0, 1) (D, 0, 0)
(A, 0, 1) (B, 1, 1) (C, 1, 0) (D, 1, 1).

[Let take B. The state B has outputs '1' for both input '0' and '1'. So make a combinations (B,1,) and (B, 1,). Next states of B are C and D. C produces outputs '0' and '1' and D produces outputs '0' and '1'. So the triples are (B, 1, 0) and (B, 1, 1)]

The minimal inverse machine is constructed by the following rule.

i. **Present states are the triples obtained from the given machine.**
ii. **The first member is the state to which the machine goes when it is initially in the state that is the first member of the present inverse state, and when it is supplied with the first input symbol.**
iii. **The second member is the third member of the corresponding present state.**
iv. **The third member is the present output of the constructing minimal inverse machine.**
v. **The output of constructing minimal inverse machine is equal to input at (t–2) to the given information lossless machine. (As an example : From B we get D for input 1 and C for input 0. So for the third row the outputs are 1 and 0, respectively)**

The Minimal inverse machine:

Present State	Next State, x	
	$z = 0$	$z = 1$
(A,0,0)	(A, 0, 0), 0	(A, 0, 1), 0
(A,0,1)	(B, 1, 0), 1	(B, 1, 1), 1
(B,1,0)	(D, 0, 0), 1	(C, 0, 1), 0
(B,1,1)	(C, 1, 0), 0	(D, 1, 1), 1
(C,0,1)	(B, 1, 0), 0	(B, 1, 1), 0
(C,1,0)	(A, 0, 0), 1	(A, 0, 1), 1
(D,0,0)	(A, 0, 0), 0	(A, 0, 1), 0
(D,1,1)	(B, 1, 0), 1	(B, 1, 1), 1

In the previous machine state (A,0,1), (D,1,1) and state (A,0,0), (D,0,0) are equivalent as they produce same next states and same output. To minimize the machine assume

(A, 0, 0) as S_1, (A, 0, 1) as S_2
(B, 1, 0) as S_3 (B, 1, 1) as S_4
(C, 0, 1) as S_5 (C, 1, 0) as S_6

No need to name (D, 0, 0) and (D, 1, 1) as they are equivalent with S_1 and S_2 respectively.

The minimized machine:

PS	NS, x	
	$z = 0$	$z = 1$
S_1	S_1, 0	S_2, 0
S_2	S_3, 1	S_4, 1
S_3	S_1, 1	S_5, 0
S_4	S_6, 0	S_2, 1
S_5	S_3, 0	S_4, 0
S_6	S_1, 1	S_2, 1

WHAT WE HAVE LEARNED SO FAR

1. Formal language and automata theory and theory of computation are different names for a single subject that covers all the aspects of the theoretical part of Computer Science.
2. The circuits, whose operations are controlled by clock pulses, are called synchronous circuit. The operations in asynchronous circuit are controlled by a number of completion and initialization signals. Here completion of one operation is the initialization of the execution of next consecutive operation.
3. In combinational circuit output depends on present state only.

   i.e. O/P = Func.(Present I/P).

   In sequential circuit output is the function of external input and present stored information.

   i.e. O/P = Func.(External I/P and Present stored information).
4. Finite state machine can be defined as a type of machine whose past histories can affect its future behavior in a finite number of ways. Finite state machine has finite number of states.
5. No Finite state machine can be designed for an infinite sequence. No finite state machine can multiply two arbitrary large binary numbers.
6. Two states of a machine are called equivalent if they produce same output sequence for an input sequence applied to the states separately considering those two states as initial states.
7. Equivalent partition of a machine M can be defined as a set of maximum number subsets of states where states which reside in same subset are equivalent for any input given to the states.
8. Equivalent partition is unique.
9. The machines where for all states for all inputs, the next state or outputs or both are not mentioned are called incompletely specified machine.
10. Minimal machine is the minimum of the machines obtained by minimizing an incompletely specified machine.
11. Merger graph is an undirected graph where as compatible graph is a directed graph.
12. Merger table is a substitution of Merger graph.

13. A finite state machine M is called finite memory machine of order μ if μ is the least integer so that the present state of the machine M can be obtained uniquely from the knowledge of last μ number of inputs and the corresponding μ number of outputs.
14. A sequential machine M is called definite if there exist a least integer μ, so that the present state of the machine M can be uniquely obtained from the past μ number of inputs to the machine M. Here μ is called the order of definiteness of the machine.
15. A machine is called information lossless if its initial state, final state and output string is sufficient to determine uniquely the input string.
16. A machine which is not lossless is called lossy.

SOLVED PROBLEMS

1. Design a two input two output sequence detector which generates an output '1' every time the sequence 1011 is detected. And for all other cases output '0' is generated. Overlapping sequences are also counted. Draw only state table and state diagram.

Ans. The sequence is 1011. We have to start from S_1. If we get input 0, then there is no chance to get 1011, so it is confined in S_1 producing output 0. If we get input 1 then there is a chance to get 1011, so the control moves to S_2 producing output 0 (As we have not till got 1011 as input). In S_2 if we get 0, then there is a chance to get 1011, so the control moves to S_3 producing output 0. In S_2 if we get input 1 then there is a chance to get 1011 considering the last 1. So the control will be confined in S_2, producing output 0.

In S_3 if we get input 0, then there is no chance to get 1011. In this case we have to start again from the beginning i.e. from S_1. So the control moves to S_1 producing output 0. In state S_3 if we get input 0 then there is no chance to get 1011 considering any of the fourth or third and fourth or second, third and fourth or first, second, third and fourth input combination. . In this case we have to start again from the beginning i.e. from S_1. So the control moves to S_1 producing output 0. If we get input 1, then the string 1011 is achieved, so output 1 is produced. As overlapping sequence is also accepted, the control moves to S_2 so that by getting 011, the sequence detector can produce 1.

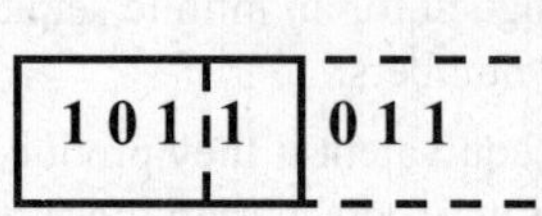

The state diagram is given.

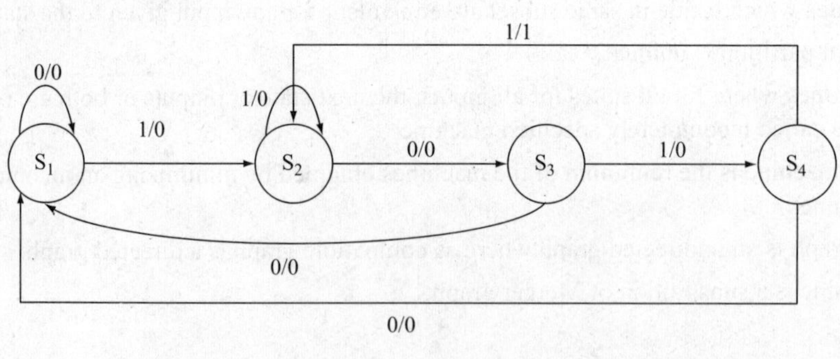

The state table for the sequence detector is

PS	NS, O/P	
X	0	1
S_1	S_1,0	S_2,0
S_2	S_3,0	S_2,0
S_3	S_1,0	S_4,0
S_4	S_1,0	S_2,1

2. Design a two input two output sequence detector which generates an output '1' every time the sequence 10101 is detected. And for all other cases output '0' is generated. Overlapping sequences are also counted. Draw only state table and state diagram and make state assignment.

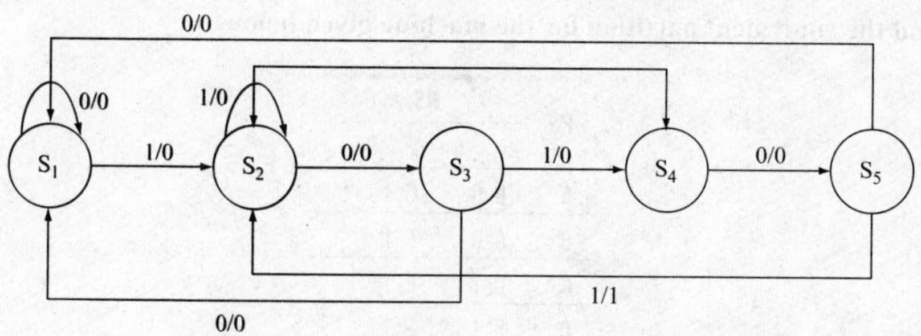

Ans. The state diagram is constructed above. Here the overlapping sequence is 101.

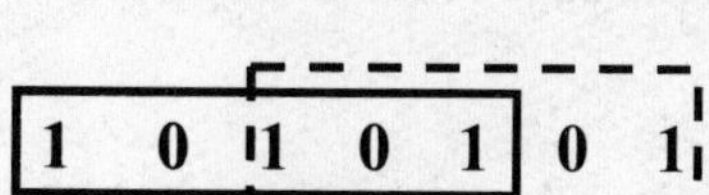

The state table for the sequence detector is

PS	NS, O/P	
	X 0	1
S_1	S_1,0	S_2,0
S_2	S_3,0	S_2,0
S_3	S_4,0	S_1,0
S_4	S_5,0	S_2,0
S_5	S_1,0	S_2,1

For doing state assignment we have to assign the states to some binary numbers. Here are 5 states so we have to take binary string of length three because $2^3 = 8 > 5$.

Let assign

000 as S_1, 001 as S_2, 011 as S_3, 010 as S_4, 100 as S_5.

After doing the state assignment, the state table become

PS ($y_2 y_1$)	NS ($Y_1 Y_2$)		O/P (z)	
X	0	1	0	1
000	000	001	0	0
011	011	001	0	0
011	010	000	0	0
010	100	001	0	0
100	000	001	0	1

3. Find the equivalent partition for the machine given below.

PS	NS, z	
	$x = 0$	$x = 1$
A	B, 0	C, 1
B	A, 0	E, 1
C	D, 1	E, 1
D	E, 1	B, 1
E	D, 1	B, 1

Ans. For string length 0 (i.e. for no input) there is no output, Hence all the states are equivalent. It is called 0-equivalent. Written as:

$P_0 =$ (ABCDE).

For string length 1, there are two types of inputs – 0 and 1. The states A and B give output 0 for input 0 and states C, D, and E give output 1 for input 0. All of the states give output 1 for input 1. Hence the states in the set P_0 is divided into (AB) and (C, D, and E). Written as:

$P_1 =$ [(AB)(CDE)].

Here A and E are 1 distinguishable because they produce different outputs for input string length 1.

For input string length 2, check the distinguishability by next state combination.

The states A and B for input 0 produce next states B and A, respectively and produce next states C and E for input 1. B and A belong to same set, and C and E also belong to same set. Hence AB cannot be partitioned for input string length 2.

The states CDE for input 0, produce next states D,E, and D, respectively and produce next states E,B, and B for input 1. D and E belong to same set but B and E belong to different sets. Hence the set (CDE) is portioned into (C) and (DE). The new partition becomes

$P_2 =$ {(AB)[(C)(DE)]}.

For input string length 3, we have to perform similar to string length 2. The states A,B for input 0 produce next states B and A, respectively and produce next states C and E for input 1. The B and A belong to same set, but C and E belong to different set. So the set (AB) is partitioned into (A) and (B). C is a single state and cannot be partitioned further.

The state D and E produce next states E and D, respectively for input 0 and produce next states B for each of the states for input 1. D and E belong to same set. Therefore, D and E cannot be divided. The new partition becomes

P_3 = (A)(B)(C)(DE).

Next we have to check for input string length 4. Three subsets contains single state – A, B, C and cannot be partitioned further.

The state D and E produce next state E and D, respectively for input 0 and next state B for each for input 1. D and E belong to same set, hence D and E cannot be partitioned further. The partition is same as P_3. So the partition P_3 is the equivalent partition of the machine.

Minimization:

We know that Equivalent Partition is unique. Therefore,

P_3 = (A)(B)(C)(DE) is the unique combination. Here each single set represents one state of the minimized machine.

Let rename these partitions for simplification.

Rename (A) as S_1, (B) as S_2, (C) as S_3 (DE) as S_4.

The minimized machine becomes

PS	NS, z	
	x = 0	x = 1
S_1(A)	S_2, 0	S_3, 1
S_2(B)	S_1, 0	S_4, 1
S_3(C)	S_4, 1	S_4, 1
S_4(DE)	S_4, 1	S_2, 1

4. Find the equivalent partition for the machine given below.

PS	NS, z	
	x = 0	x = 1
A	E, 1	D, 1
B	C, 1	D, 1
C	B, 1	E, 1
D	G, 1	C, 1
E	A, 1	E, 1
F	G, 1	A, 1
G	F, 0	B, 1

Ans. The partitions are:

P_0 = (ABCDEFG),

P_1 = (ABCDEF)(G),

P_2 = (ABCE)(DF)(G),

P_3 = (AB)(CE)(DF)(G),

P_4 = (AB)(CE)(D)(F)(G),

P_5 = (AB)(CE)(D)(F)(G).

As P_4 and P_5 are similar, P_4 is the equivalent partition.

Minimization:

We know that equivalent partition is unique. Hence,

P_4 = (AB)(CE)(D)(F)(G) is the unique combination. Here each single set represents one state of the minimized machine. Let rename these partitions for simplification.

Rename (AB) as S_1, (CE) as S_2, (D) as S_3, (F) as S_4 and (G) as S_5.

The minimized machine becomes

PS	NS, z	
	x = 0	x = 1
S_1(AB)	S_2, 1	S_3, 1
S_2(CE)	S_1, 1	S_2, 1
S_3(D)	S_5, 1	S_2, 1
S_4(F)	S_5, 1	S_1, 1
S_5(G)	S_4, 0	S_1, 1

5. Find the equivalent partition of the machine given below.

PS	NS, z	
	x = 0	x = 1
A	B, 0	D, 1
B	D, 1	F, 1
C	F, 1	B, 1
D	F, 0	A, 1
E	C, 0	A, 1
F	C, 1	B, 1

Ans. The partitions are:

P_0 = (ABCDEF).

P_1 = (ADE)(BCF) [Depending on o/p for i/p 0].

P_2 = (ADE)(B)(CF) [For i/p 0 next state of B goes to another set].

P_3 = (A)(DE)(B)(CF) [For i/p 0 next state of A goes to another set].

P_4 = (A)(DE)(B)(CF).

As P_3 and P_4 are same so P_3 is the equivalent partition.

Minimization:

We know that Equivalent Partition is unique. Therefore,

P_4 = (A)(DE)(B)(CF) is the unique combination. Here each single set represents one state of the minimized machine. Let rename these partitions for simplification.

Rename (A) as S_1, (B) as S_2, (DE) as S_3 and (CF) as S_4.

The minimized machine becomes

PS	NS, z	
	$x = 0$	$x = 1$
S_1(A)	S_2, 0	S_3, 1
S_2(B)	S_3, 1	S_4, 1
S_3(DE)	S_4, 0	S_1, 1
S_4(CF)	S_4, 1	S_2, 1

6. Find the equivalent partition of the machine given below.

PS	NS, z	
	$x = 0$	$x = 1$
A	C, 1	D, 0
B	D, 1	E, 0
C	B, 1	E, 1
D	B, 1	A, 0
E	D, 1	B, 1

Ans. The partitions are:

P_0 = (ABCDEF).

P_1 = (AD)(BCE) [Depending on o/p for i/p 1].

P_2 = (AD)(BE)(C) [For i/p 0 next state of C goes to another set].

P_3 = (A)(D)(BE)(C) [For i/p 0 next state of A and D goes to different set].

P_4 = (A)(D)(BE)(C).

As P_3 and P_4 are similar, P_3 is the equivalent partition.

Minimization:

We know that equivalent partition is unique. Therefore, P_4=(A)(D)(BE)(C) is the unique combination. Here each single set represents one state of the minimized machine.

Let rename these partitions for simplification.

Rename (A) as S_1, (BE) as S_2, (C) as S_3, and (D) as S_4.

The minimized machine becomes

PS	NS, z	
	$x = 0$	$x = 1$
S_1(A)	S_3, 1	S_4, 0
S_2(BE)	S_4, 1	S_2, 1
S_3(C)	S_2, 1	S_2, 1
S_4(D)	S_2, 1	S_1, 0

7. Simplify the following incompletely specified machine.

PS	NS, Z		
	I_1	I_2	I_3
A	D,1	E,1	_ _
B	B,0	E, _	C, _
C	C, _	C,0	B, _
D	B,0	D, _	E, _
E	_ _	B,0	A, _

Ans. Put a temporary state T in the next state place, where next states are not specified. If the output is not mentioned, need to put any output. As a temporary state T is considered, so T is put in the present state column with next states T for all inputs with no output.

The simplified machine becomes

PS	NS, Z		
	I_1	I_2	I_3
A	D,1	E,1	T, _
B	B,0	E, _	C, _
C	C, _	C,0	B, _
D	B,0	D, _	E, _
E	T,_	B,0	A, _
T	T, 0	T, 0	T, 0

8. Minimize the following incompletely specified machine.

PS	NS, Z		
	I_1	I_2	I_3
A	A, 1	D, _	C, _
B	A, _	D, _	E, _
C	E, 0	A, 1	_, _
D	E, _	A, 1	_, _
E	E, 0	_, _	C, _

Ans. In an incompletely specified machine, all the next states or all the output or both are not mentioned. We can minimize an incompletely specified machine by using Merger graph and compatible graph method. From the merger graph we have to find compatible pair and from that compatible pair and implied pair we have to construct compatible graph. From compatible graph we have to find closed partition. And the closed partitions are the minimized states of the machine.

Merger Graph:

The machine consists of 5 states. So the merger graph consists of 5 nodes, named A, B, C, D and E. The outputs of A and B does not differ, hence there is an arc between A and B. For input I_3, the next state conflicts – so the arc is an interrupted arc and in the interrupted portion conflicting next state pair (CE) is placed.

For state A and C the output conflicts, hence there is no arc between A and C.

For the states C and D the output as well as next states do not conflict. So an uninterrupted arc is placed between C and D. By this process the merger graph is constructed. The merger is as follows:

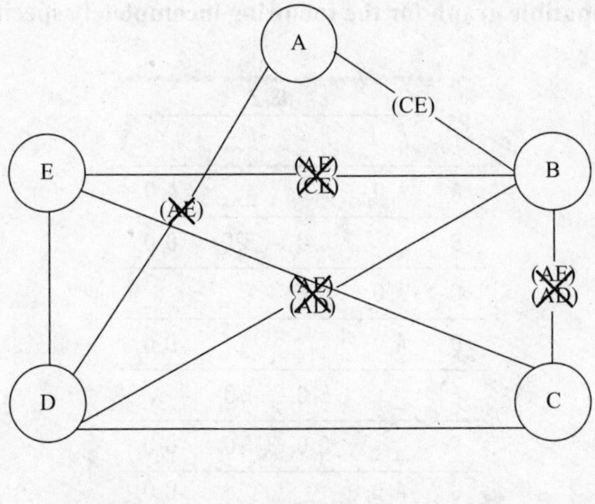

As there is no arc between A and E, the arc between (AD), (BE), (BD), and (BC) are also crossed.

Compatible graph:

The (CE) is the implied pair for (AB). A directed arc is drawn from (AB) to (CE). The compatible graph consists of four vertices (AB), (CD), (DE) and (CE).

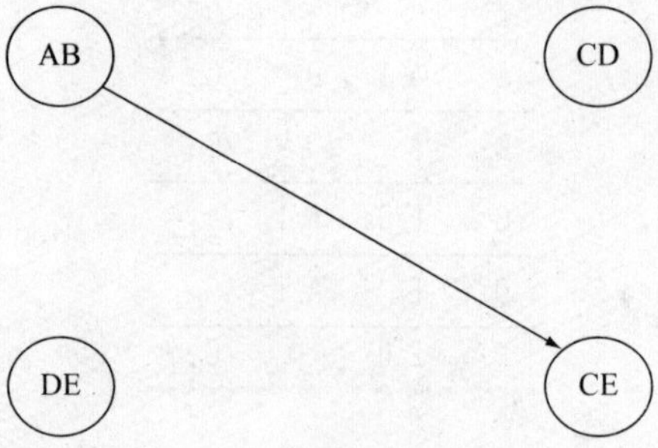

A subgraph of a compatibility graph is said to be closed cover for the machine if for every vertex in the subgraph, all outgoing edges and their terminal vertices also belong to the subgraph and every state of the machine is covered by at least one vertex of the subgraph.

For the constructed compatible graph (AB), (CD) and (CE) forms a closed covering. The states of the minimized machine are (AB) and (CDE). Rename (AB) as S_1 and (CDE) as S_2.

The minimized machine is

PS	NS, Z		
	I_1	I_2	I_3
S_1	S_1, 1	S_2, _	S_2, _
S_2	S_2, 0	S_1, 1	S_2, _

9. Construct Compatible graph for the following incompletely specified machine.

PS	NS, Z			
	I_1	I_2	I_3	I_4
A	A, 0_1	E, 0_2	_, _	A, 0_2
B	_, _	C, 0_3	B, 0_1	D, 0_4
C	A, 0_1	C, 0_3	_, _	_, _
D	A, 0_1	_, _	_, _	D, 0_4
E	_, _	E, 0_2	F, 0_1	_, _
F	_, _	G, 0_3	F, 0_1	G, 0_4
G	A, 0_1	_, _	_, _	G, 0_4

Ans. To construct compatible graph we have to first find compatible pairs. To find compatible pairs we need to construct Merger graph. Since this machine has 7 states, it is difficult to construct a Merger graph – hence we have to construct Merger table to find compatible pairs.

Merger table

B	X					
C	X	√				
D	X	√	√			
E	√	X	X	√		
F	X	(CG)(DG)	(CG)	(DG)	X	
G	X	(DG)	√	√	√	√
	A	B	C	D	E	F

Compatible pairs are (AE), (BC). (BD), (CD). (CG), (DE), (DG), (EG), (GF) and

If (CG) and (DG) are compatible, then (BF) is compatible; If (DG) is compatible, then (BG) is compatible; If (CG) is compatible, then (CF) is compatible; If (DG) is compatible, then (DF) is compatible.

Compatible graph:

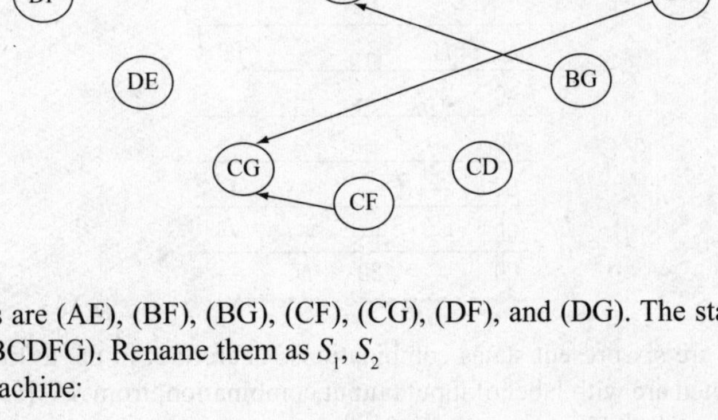

The closed partitions are (AE), (BF), (BG), (CF), (CG), (DF), and (DG). The states of the minimized machine are (AE), (BCDFG). Rename them as S_1, S_2

The minimized machine:

PS	NS, Z			
	I_1	I_2	I_3	I_4
S_1	$S_1, 0_1$	$S_1, 0_2$	$S_2, 0_1$	$S_1, 0_2$
S_2	$S_1, 0_1$	$S_2, 0_3$	$S_2, 0_1$	$S_2, 0_4$

10. Test whether the following machine is finite or not.

PS	NS, o/p	
	$x = 0$	$x = 1$
A	A, 0	B, 1
B	C, 0	D, 1
C	B, 1	A, 0
D	D, 1	C, 0

Ans.

Testing table–testing graph method

A table which is divided into two halves is made. The machine has two inputs and two outputs. There are four input–output combinations namely 0/0, 0/1, 1/0, and 1/1. The upper half of the machine contains single-state input–output combination and lower half contain two-state input–output combinations. There are four states, hence six combination pairs are made. The testing table is as follows:

PS	0/0	0/1	1/0	1/1
A	A	—	—	B
B	C	—	—	D
C	—	B	A	—
D	—	D	C	—
AB	AC	—	—	BD
AC	—	—	—	—
AD	—	—	—	—
BC	—	—	—	—
BD	—	—	—	—
CD	—	BD	AC	—

In testing table, there are six present states combinations. Therefore, in the testing table there are six nodes. There is a directed arc with label of input output combination, from S_iS_j $[i \neq j]$ to S_pS_q $[p \neq q]$ if S_pS_q is the implied pair of S_iS_j. The testing graph for finite memory:

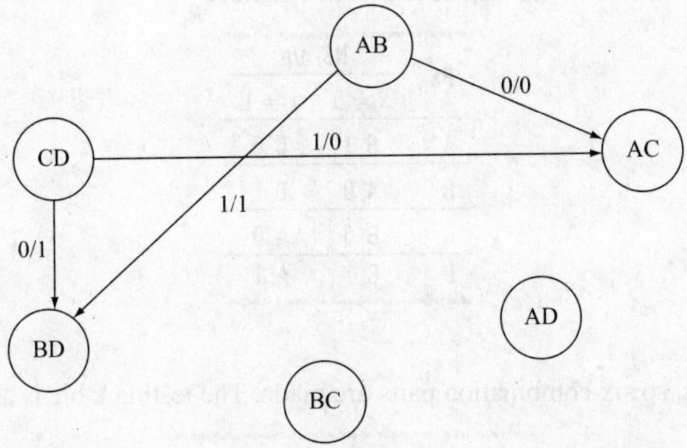

The testing graph is loop-free. Therefore, the machine is finite. The longest path in the testing graph is 1. The order of finiteness of the machine μ=1+1=2. This can be proved by vanishing connection matrix method.

In the testing table, six present state pairs are formed. Therefore, the connection matrix consists of six rows and six columns. The rows and columns are labeled with pair of present state combinations.

In the matrix, (i,j)th entry will be 1 if there is an entry in (S_aS_b) $(a \neq b)$and $(S_pS_q)(p \neq q)$ combination in the corresponding testing table. Otherwise the entry will be 0.

The connection matrix of the above machine is as follows.

	AB	AC	AD	BC	BD	CD
AB	0	1	0	0	1	0
AC	0	0	0	0	0	0
AD	0	0	0	0	0	0
BC	0	0	0	0	0	0
BD	0	0	0	0	0	0
CD	0	1	0	0	1	0

In the above matrix the rows AC, AD, BC and BD all contain 0s. Therefore the row labeled AC, AD, BC, and BD with the corresponding columns vanishes.

The remaining matrix becomes

	AB	CD
AB	0	0
CD	0	0

In the above matrix the row AB and CD contains all '0'. Therefore the rows labeled AB and CD with the corresponding columns vanish. The matrix vanishes. Number of steps required to vanish the matrix is 2. So order of finiteness of the machine $\mu = 2$.

11. Test whether the following machine is finite or not.

PS	NS, o/p	
	$x = 0$	$x = 1$
A	B, 1	C, 0
B	A, 0	D, 1
C	B, 0	A, 0
D	C, 1	A, 1

Ans.

There are four states, so six combination pairs are made. The testing table is as follows:

PS	0/0	0/1	1/0	1/1
A	—	B	C	—
B	A	—	—	D
C	B	—	A	—
D	—	C	—	A
AB	—	—	—	—
AC	—	—	AC	—
AD	—	BC	—	—
BC	AB	—	—	—
BD	—	—	—	AD
CD	—	—	—	—

In testing table there are six present states combinations. Therefore, in the testing table there are six nodes. There is a directed arc with label of input–output combination, from S_iS_j $(i \neq j)$ to S_pS_q $(p \neq q)$ if S_pS_q is the implied pair of S_iS_j. The testing graph for finite memory:

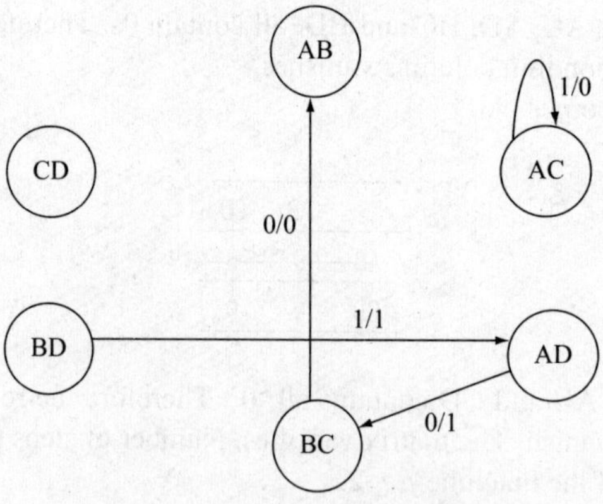

In the testing graph there is a loop from AC to AC with label 1/0. The testing graph is not loop-free. Therefore, the machine is not of finite memory. This can be proved by vanishing connection matrix method. In the testing table, six present state pairs are formed. Therefore the connection matrix consists of six rows and six columns. The rows and columns are labeled with pair of present state combinations. The connection matrix of the above machine is as follows:

	AB	AC	AD	BC	BD	CD
AB	0	0	0	0	0	0
AC	0	1	0	0	0	0
AD	0	0	0	1	0	0
BC	1	0	0	0	0	0
BD	0	0	1	0	0	0
CD	0	0	0	0	0	0

In the above matrix the row AB and CD contains all '0'. Hence the row labeled AB and CD and the corresponding column vanishes. The remaining matrix becomes:

	AC	AD	BC	BD
AC	1	0	0	0
AD	0	0	1	0
BC	0	0	0	0
BD	0	1	0	0

In the above matrix the row AD contains all '0'. Hence the row labeled AD and the corresponding column vanishes. The remaining matrix becomes:

	AC	BC	BD
AC	1	0	0
BC	0	0	0
BD	0	0	0

In the above matrix the row BC and BD contains all '0'. Hence the row labeled BC and BD and the corresponding column vanishes. The remaining matrix becomes:

	AC
AC	1

The matrix does not vanish. Therefore, the machine is not of finite memory.

12. Test whether the following machine is finite or not.

PS	NS, o/p	
	$x = 0$	$x = 1$
A	B, 0	A, 1
B	D, 1	C, 0
C	C, 0	D, 1
D	A, 1	B, 0

Ans. There are four states, hence six combination pairs are made. The testing table is as follows:

PS	0/0	0/1	1/0	1/1
A	B	—	—	A
B	—	D	C	—
C	C	—	—	D
D	—	A	B	—
AB	—	—	—	—
AC	(BC)	—	—	(AD)
AD	—	—	—	—
BC	—	—	—	—
BD	—	(AD)	(BC)	—
CD	—	—	—	—

In testing table there are six present states combinations. Therefore, in the testing table there are six nodes. The testing graph for finite memory:

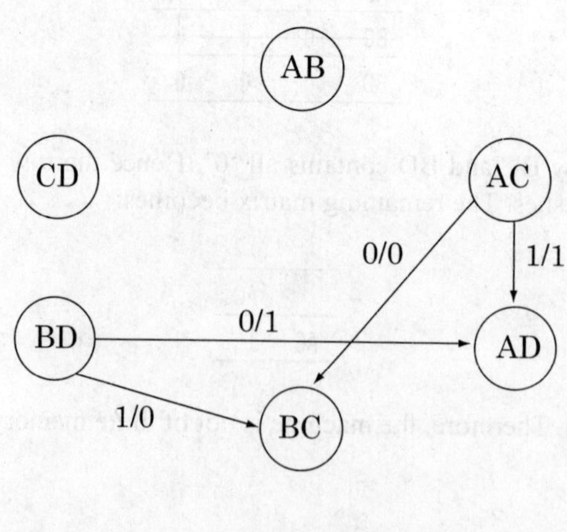

The testing graph is loop-free. Therefore, the machine is finite. The longest path in the testing graph is 1. The order of finiteness of the machine $\mu = 1 + 1 = 2$.

Proof by Vanishing Connection Matrix

In the testing table, six present state pairs are formed. Therefore the connection matrix consists of six rows and six columns. The rows and columns are labeled with pair of present state combinations. The connection matrix of the above machine is as follows:

	AB	AC	AD	BC	BD	CD
AB	0	0	0	0	0	0
AC	0	0	1	1	0	0
AD	0	0	0	0	0	0
BC	0	0	0	0	0	0
BD	0	0	1	1	0	0
CD	0	0	0	0	0	0

In the above matrix the rows AB, AD, BC and CD contains all '0's. Therefore, the row labeled AB, AD, BC, and CD and the corresponding columns vanish.

The remaining matrix becomes:

	AC	BD
AC	0	0
BD	0	0

The matrix vanishes. Hence the machine is of finite memory. The connection matrix vanishes in two steps. Therefore the order of finiteness of the machine $\mu = 2$.

13. Find whether the following machine is definite or not.

PS	NS, o/p	
	$x = 0$	$x = 1$
A	D	E
B	A	B
C	C	B
D	C	B
E	A	B

Ans. Whether a machine is definite or not definite can be checked by three methods: (a) synchronizing tree method, (b) contracted table method, and (c) testing table–testing graph method.

Synchronizing tree method: The present state combination of the machine is (ABCDE). It has two types of inputs 0 and 1. The (ABCDE) with input 0 produce next state combination (DACCA). It can be grouped into two distinct states (ACD). The (ABCDE) with input 1 produce next state combination (EBBBB) which can be grouped into (BE). In the next level, (ACD) with input 0 produces the next state combination (CD). With input 1, (ACD) produce next state combination (BE). The state combination (BE) with input 0 produces a single next state (A). With input 1, state combination (BE) produces single state B. As A and B are single state, it need not to be derived again. By this process (CD) and (BE) are also derived for input 0 and 1. The synchronizing tree:

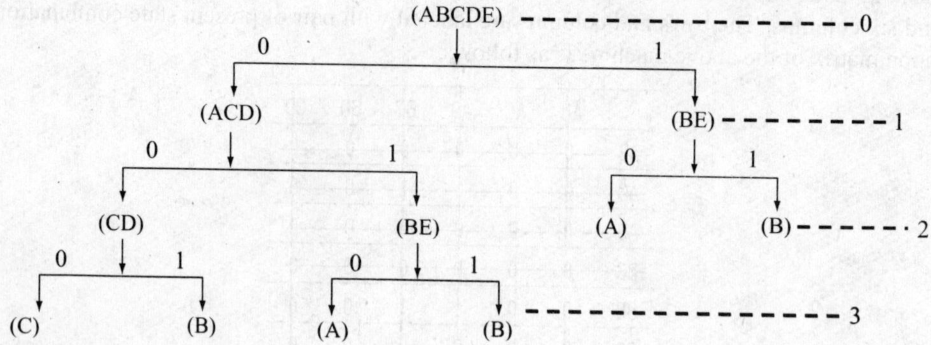

As the leaf nodes are of single state, stop constructing the tree. The order of definiteness is the maximum label of the synchronizing tree. In this case order is 3.

Contracted table method:

In the previous machine C and D have same next state combination (both cases C and B). The B and E also have same next state combination (both cases C and B). Therefore, C and D are equivalent states and B and E are also equivalent state. Among C and D lets consider only C and among B and E lets consider B. This implies all the D in the state table are replaced by C and all the E in the state table are replaced by B. The original and contracted table:

P.S	NS, o/p	
	$x = 0$	$x = 1$
A	D	E
B	A	B
C	C	B
D	C	B
E	A	B

⇩

P.S	NS, o/p	
	$x = 0$	$x = 1$
A	C	B
B	A	B
C	C	B

In the previous machine A and C have same next state combination (both cases C and B). Therefore, A and C are equivalent states. Among A and C let take only A. Implies all the C in the state table are replaced by A. The contracted table becomes:

P.S	NS, o/p	
	$x = 0$	$x = 1$
A	A	B
B	A	B

In the previous machine A and B have same next state combination (both cases A and B). Therefore, A and B are equivalent states. Among A and B lets consider only A. Implies all the B in the state table are replaced by A. The contracted table becomes:

P.S	NS, o/p	
	$x = 0$	$x = 1$
A	A	A

The obtained table is consists of single row. Therefore, the machine is definite. Its order is the number of steps required to obtain the single state machine, here 3.

Testing table–testing graph method:

A table with two halves is made. The upper half contains input and next state combination. Lower half of the table contains all combination of present states taking two into combination. Here for five present states (A, B, C, D, and E) there are $^5C_2$ means 10 combinations. The table:

PS	0	1
A	D	E
B	A	B
C	C	B
D	C	B
E	A	B
AB	AD	BE
AC	CD	BE
AD	CD	BE
AE	AD	BE
BC	AC	BB
BD	AC	BB
BE	AA	BB
CD	CC	BB
CE	AC	BB
DE	AC	BB

The testing graph:

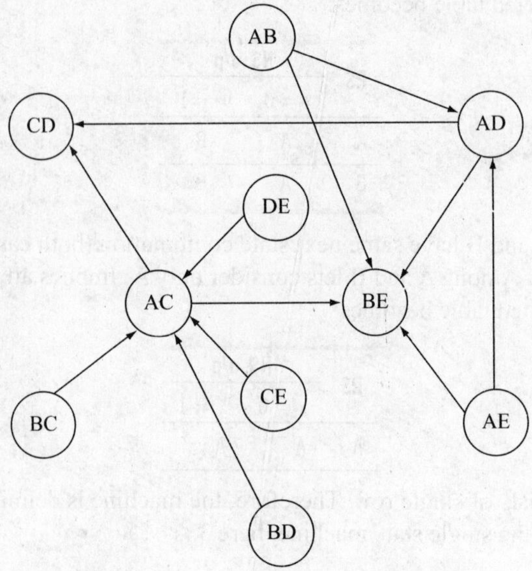

The testing graph is loop-free. So the machine is of definite memory. The longest path of the testing graph is 2 (AE → AD → BE or AB → AD → BE). Therefore order of definiteness of the machine is 2 + 1 = 3.

(*We can use any of the methods to check definiteness of the machine. Among them contracted table method is the best. Synchronizing tree method good, but if the machine is not definite the leaf nodes of the synchronizing tree will not become single state. And the construction will be an endless process. If number of states of the machine is large then number of nodes will also be large. It will be difficult to construct testing table and testing graph.*)

14. Find whether the following machine is definite or not.

P.S	NS, o/p	
	$x = 0$	$x = 1$
A	C	B
B	E	F
C	A	F
D	E	B
E	C	D
F	E	F

Ans. A machine is definite or not can be checked by three ways. But among them contracted table method is the best.

In the above machine B and F produce same next state (Both cases E and F). Therefore, B and F are equivalent state. Consider any of them e.g., B, implies all F in the state table is replaced by B. The contracted table from the original one:

P.S	NS, o/p	
	$x = 0$	$x = 1$
A	C	B
B	E	F
C	A	F
D	E	B
E	C	D
F	E	F

⇩

PS	NS, o/p	
	$x = 0$	$x = 1$
A	C	B
B	E	B
C	A	B
D	E	B
E	C	D

In the previous state table, B and D produce same next states (both cases E and B). Therefore they are equivalent states. Lets consider only B and replace all occurrences of D by B. The contracted table becomes:

P.S	NS, o/p	
	$x = 0$	$x = 1$
A	C	B
B	E	B
C	A	B
E	C	B

In the previous state table, A and E are equivalent states as they produce same next state combination (both cases C and B). Lets consider only A and replace all occurrences of E in the table by A. The contracted table:

P.S	NS, o/p	
	$x = 0$	$x = 1$
A	C	B
B	A	B
C	A	B

In the state table above B and C are equivalent states as they produce same next state combination for input 0 and 1. Let take only B and replace all occurrences of C in the table by B. The contracted table becomes:

P.S	NS, o/p	
	$x = 0$	$x = 1$
A	B	B
B	A	B

The state table does not become a single row table. Hence the machine is not definite.

15. Find whether the following machine is definite or not.

P.S	NS, o/p	
	$x = 0$	$x = 1$
A	B	C
B	D	A
C	B	E
D	D	E
E	B	E
F	B	C

Ans. Contracted table method is used to check whether the given machine is definite or not. In the above machine present state C and E produce same next state combination for input 0 and 1. Same way A and F also produce same next state combination (both cases B and C). Therefore C and E are equivalent state and, A and F are equivalent states. Keep C and remove E from the present state column and replace all occurrences of E in the next state column by C. Similarly, keep A and remove F from the present state column and replace all occurrences of F in the next state column by A. The contracted table becomes:

P.S	NS, o/p	
	$x = 0$	$x = 1$
A	B	C
B	D	A
C	B	C
D	D	C

In the previous table A and C are equivalent states as they produce same next state combination for input 0 and 1. Remove C from present state column and replace all occurrences of C in the next state portion by A. The contracted table becomes:

P.S	NS, o/p	
	x = 0	x = 1
A	B	A
B	D	A
D	D	A

In the above state table B and D are equivalent state as they produce same next state combination for input 0 and 1. Consider B, remove D and replace all occurrences of D in the next state portion by B. The contracted table becomes:

P.S	NS, o/p	
	x = 0	x = 1
A	B	A
B	B	A

In the above state table A and B are equivalent states as they produce same next state combination for input 0 and 1. Replace B by A and remove B as a present state. The contracted table:

P.S	NS, o/p	
	x = 0	x = 1
A	A	A

The obtained table is consists of single row. Therefore, the machine is definite. Its order is the number of steps required to obtain the single state machine, here 4.

16. Test whether the following machine is information lossless or not. If lossless find its order.

PS	NS, o/p	
	x = 0	x = 1
A	B, 1	A, 1
B	D, 0	B, 0
C	D, 0	B, 1
D	E, 1	C, 1
E	A, 1	B, 0

Ans. First step to test whether a machine is lossless or not, is to construct a testing table. The testing table is divided into two halves.

P.S	NS	
	z = 0	z = 1
A	—	(AB)
B	(BD)	—
C	D	B
D	—	(CE)
E	B	A
(AB)	—	—
(BD)	—	—
(CE)	(BD)	(AB)

The testing table does not contain any repeated entry. The machine is information lossless machine.

The testing graph for the machine:

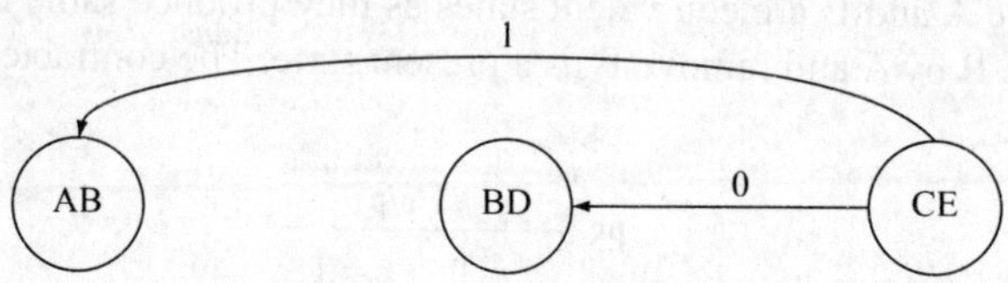

The testing graph for information losslessness is loop-free. The order of losslessness is $\mu = 1 + 2 = 3$. The length of the longest path of the graph is 1.

16. Test whether the following machine is information lossless or not. If lossless find its order.

P.S	NS, o/p	
	x = 0	x = 1
A	B, 1	C, 1
B	D, 0	E, 0
C	A, 1	F, 1
D	C, 0	B, 0
E	F, 1	A, 1
F	E, 0	D, 0

Ans. First we have to construct a testing table for information losslessness for testing whether the machine is information lossless or not. The testing table is divided into two halves.

P.S	NS	
	$z = 0$	$z = 1$
A	—	BC
B	DE	—
C	—	AF
D	BC	—
E	—	AF
F	DE	—
AF	—	—
BC	—	—
DE	—	—

The testing table does not contain any repeated entry. The machine is information lossless machine.

The testing graph for the machine:

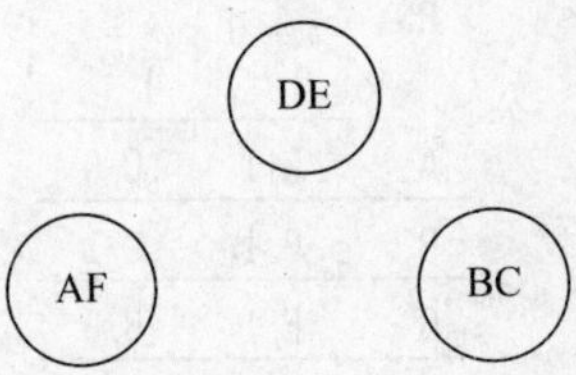

The testing graph for information losslessness is loop-free. The order of losslessness is m=0+2=2. The length of the longest path of the graph is 0.

17. Test whether the following machine is information lossless or not. If lossless find its order.

P.S	NS, o/p	
	$x = 0$	$x = 1$
A	B, 0	E, 0
B	E, 0	D, 0
C	D, 1	A, 0
D	C, 1	E, 0
E	B, 0	D, 0

Ans. First we have to construct a testing table for information losslessness for testing whether the machine is information lossless or not. The testing table is divided into two halves.

	z = 0	z = 1
A	BE	—
B	DE	—
C	A	D
D	E	C
E	BD	—
BD	(DE)(EE)	—
BE	(BD)(DE)	—
DE	(BE)(DE)	—

The testing table contains repeated entry (EE). The machine is lossy machine.

18. Test whether the following machine is information lossless or not. If lossless find its order.

P.S	NS, o/p	
	x = 0	x = 1
A	B, 1	C, 0
B	B, 1	D, 1
C	E, 1	B, 0
D	A, 0	E, 0
E	F, 0	D, 1
F	A, 1	D, 0

Ans. First we have to construct a testing table for information losslessness for testing whether the machine is information lossless or not. The testing table is divided into two halves.

P.S	NS	
	z = 0	z = 1
A	C	B
B	—	(BD)
C	B	E
D	(AE)	—
E	F	D
F	D	A

AE	CF	BD
BD	—	—
CF	BD	AE

The testing table does not contain any repeated entry. The machine is information lossless machine. The testing graph for the machine:

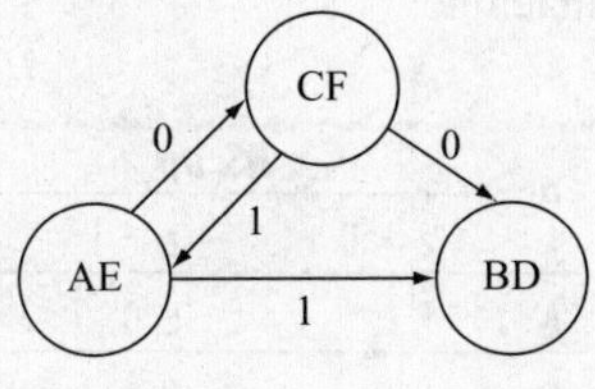

The testing graph contains loop. Hence the machine is not information lossless of finite order.

19. Find the input string which is applied on state 'C' producing output string 1110000010 and final state 'B' for the machine given below.

PS	NS,z	
	$x = 0$	$x = 1$
A	E, 1	F, 0
B	D, 0	C, 1
C	F, 1	A, 0
D	C, 0	E, 0
E	B, 0	D, 1
F	D, 1	F, 1

Ans. First, we need to prove the machine is information lossless. For this we need to construct a testing table for information lossless. If the machine is information lossless then and only a single input string can be found for a single beginning state and single final state.

The testing table for information lossless:

PS	NS	
	$z=0$	$z=1$
A	F	E
B	D	C
C	A	F
D	(CE)	—

E	B	D
F	—	(DF)
CE	AB	DF
AB	DF	CE
DF	—	—

The testing table does not contain any repeated entry. The machine is information lossless machine. The output successor table for the given machine:

PS	NS, i/p	
	z = 0	z = 1
A	F, 1	E, 0
B	D, 0	C, 1
C	A, 1	F, 0
D	(C, 0) (E, 1)	—
E	B, 0	D, 1
F	—	(D, 0) (F, 1)

The input string is applied on state C and has produced output 1. From the output successor table it is clear that the next states are F with input 0. By this process the transition is as follows:

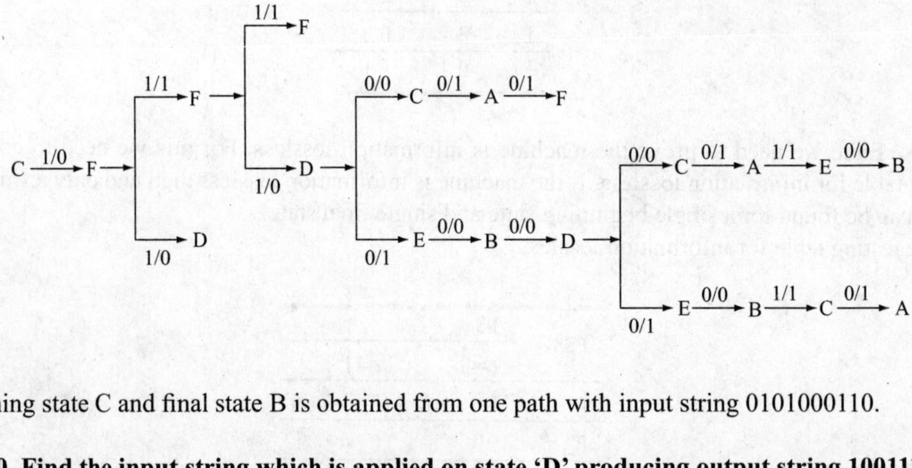

Beginning state C and final state B is obtained from one path with input string 0101000110.

20. Find the input string which is applied on state 'D' producing output string 10011110 and final state 'D' for the machine given below.

PS	NS, z	
	$x = 0$	$x = 1$
A	A, 1	C, 1
B	E, 0	B, 1
C	D, 0	A, 0
D	C, 0	B, 0
E	B, 1	A, 0

Ans. First we need to prove the machine is information lossless. For this we need to construct a testing table for information lossless. If the machine is information lossless then and only a single input string can be found for a single beginning state and single final state.

The testing table for information lossless:

PS	NS	
	$z = 0$	$z = 1$
A	—	(AC)
B	E	B
C	(AD)	—
D	(BC)	—
E	A	B
AC	—	—
AD	—	—
BC	(AE)(DE)	—
AE	—	(AB)(BC)
DE	(AB)(AC)	—
AB	—	(AB)(BC)

The testing table does not contain any repeated entry. The machine is information lossless machine. The output successor table for the given machine:

PS	NS, i/p	
	$z = 0$	$z = 1$
A	—	(A, 0), (C, 1)
B	E, 0	B, 1
C	(D, 0), (A, 1)	—
D	(C, 0), (B, 1)	—
E	A, 1	B, 0

Transition is as follows:

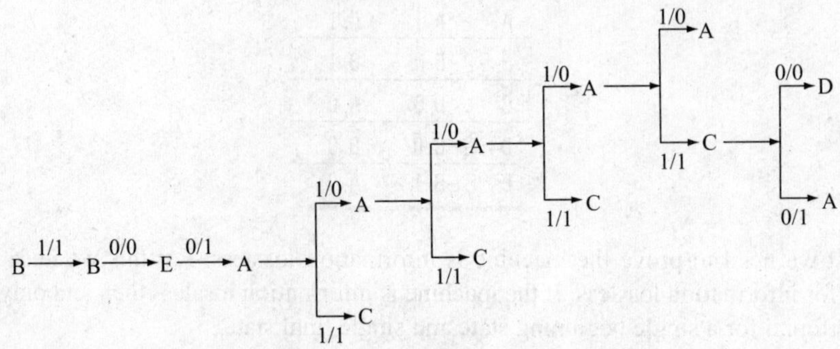

Beginning state B and final state D is obtained from one path with input string 10100010.

MULTIPLE CHOICE QUESTIONS

1. Operation of Synchronous circuits are controlled by
   (a) Input (b) State (c) Output (d) Clock pulses.
2. Output of Combinational circuit depends on
   (a) Present state (b) Past input
   (c) Present input (d) Present stored information and present input.
3. Output of sequential circuit depends on
   (a) Present state (b) Past input
   (c) Present input (d) Present stored information and present input.
4. For which of the following Finite state machine cannot be designed
   (a) Addition of two binary numbers (b) Subtraction of two binary numbers
   (c) Multiplication of two binary numbers (d) All of these
5. Two states are called 1 equivalent if
   (a) Both of the states produce 1.
   (b) If both of the states produce same output for string length 1.
   (c) If both of the states produce same output for same input.
   (d) If both of the states produce same output for input 1.
6. Which is true for incompletely specified machine?
   (a) All Next states are not mentioned (b) All outputs are not mentioned
   (c) All inputs are not mentioned (d) Both a and b.
7. Compatible pairs are obtained from
   (a) Merger graph (b) Compatible graph (c) Testing table (d) Testing graph.
8. Number of vertices of a Merger graph is
   (a) The number of states of the machine (b) Number of compatible pairs
   (c) Number of states combinations (d) None of these.

9. Number of vertices of a Compatible graph is
   (a) The number of states of the machine
   (b) Number of compatible pairs
   (c) Number of states combinations
   (d) None of these.
10. Merger Table is a substitution for
   (a) Merger graph
   (b) Compatible graph
   (c) Testing graph
   (d) Testing table.
11. A finite state machine M is called finite memory machine of order μ if present state of the machine M can be obtained from
   (a) last μ number of inputs and corresponding μ number of next states
   (b) last μ number of inputs and corresponding μ number of outputs
   (c) last μ number of next states and corresponding μ number of outputs
   (d) last μ number of inputs.
12. A sequential machine M is called definite if there exist a least integer μ, so that the present state of the machine M can be uniquely obtained from the
   (a) Past μ number of inputs
   (b) Past μ number of outputs
   (c) Past μ number of next states
   (d) Past μ number of inputs, outputs and next states.
13. Which is sufficient to find the initial state of an information lossless machine from the input string?
   (a) Next state and output string
   (b) Final state and Next state
   (c) Final state and output string
   (d) Final state, next state and output string.
14. Which is true of the followings?
   (a) All information lossless machines are of finite order
   (b) Some information lossless machines are of finite order
   (c) Those machines which are not lossless of finite order are lossy.
   (d) None of the above.

Ans. 1. d 2. c 3. d 4. c 5. b 6. d 7. a 8. a 9. b 10. a 11. b 12. a 13. c 14. b.

EXERCISES

1. Design a two input two output sequence detector which generates an output '1' every time the sequence 0101 is detected. And for all other cases output '0' is generated. Overlapping sequences are also counted.
2. Design a two input two output sequence detector which generates an output '1' every time the sequence 1101 is detected. And for all other cases output '0' is generated. Overlapping sequences are also counted.
3. Design a Modulo 8 binary counter using JK flip flop.

4. Find the Equivalent Partition for the machine given below

PS	NS, o/p	
	$x = 0$	$x = 1$
A	E,0	G,0
B	G,0	F,0
C	H,0	B,1
D	G,0	A,1
E	A,0	G,0
F	A,0	A,0
G	F,0	A,0
H	C,1	A,1

From here minimize the machine.

5. Find the Equivalent Partition for the machine given below

PS	NS, o/p	
	$x = 0$	$x = 1$
A	E,0	D,1
B	F,0	D,0
C	E,0	B,1
D	F,0	B,0
E	C,0	F,1
F	B,0	C,0

Find the shortest input sequence that distinguishes state A with state E. From here minimize the machine.

6. Simplify the following incompletely specified machine:

PS	NS, o/p	
	$x = 0$	$x=1$
A	B, 1	C, 0
B	A, 1	_, 1
C	_, _	B, 0

7. Simplify the following incompletely specified machine:

PS	NS, z	
	$x = 0$	$x = 1$
A	E,1	D,0
B	E,0	_,_
C	__,0	B,_
D	A,0	D,1
E	A,_	B,0

8. Find a minimal machine from the minimum machines for the machine given below considering the unspecified outputs as '0' or '1'.

PS	NS, o/p	
	$x = 0$	$x = 1$
A	B, 1	C,_
B	A ,_	C, 0
C	A, 1	B, 0

9. Develop a Merger Graph for the following incompletely specified machine. From there find the compatible pairs.

PS	NS, Z			
	I_1	I_2	I_3	I_4
A	D, 1	C, _	_,_	D, 1
B	_,_	D, _	A, 0	_,_
C	E, 1	_,_	B, 0	C, 1
D	_,_	D, 1	E, 0	C, 1
E	_,_	A, 0	_,_	_,_

10. For the machine given above develop compatible graph and from there develop the minimal machine.

11. Develop Merger graph from the machine given below.

PS	NS, Z		
	I_1	I_2	I_3
A	C, 0	E, 1	_, _
B	C, 0	E, _	_, _
C	B, _	C, 0	A, _
D	B, 0	C, _	E, _
E	_, _	E, 0	A, _

From there find the compatible pairs. Check either same compatible pairs are obtained or not from the Merger table constructed from the above machine
From the compatible pairs develop compatible graph and hence find the minimal machine.

12. Find whether the following machines are of finite memory or not by testing table–testing Graph and vanishing connection matrix method. If Finite find its order.

PS	NS, o/p	
	$x = 0$	$x = 1$
A	E,0	G,0
B	G,0	F,0
C	H,0	B,1
D	G,0	A,1
E	A,0	G,0
F	A,0	A,0
G	F,0	A,0
H	C,1	A,1

PS	NS, o/p	
	$x = 0$	$x = 1$
A	D,0	C,0
B	A, 0	E, 0
C	E, 0	B, 0
D	C, 0	D, 0
E	E, 0	B, 1

PS	NS, o/p	
	$x = 0$	$x = 1$
A	B, 0	D, 0
B	C, 0	C, 0
C	D, 0	A, 0
D	D, 0	A, 1

13. Test whether the following machines are definite or not by using synchronizing tree, contracted table and testing table–testing graph method. If definite find its order.

PS	NS	
	$x = 0$	$x = 1$
A	B	C
B	A	D
C	B	A
D	C	A

PS	NS	
	$x = 0$	$x = 1$
A	D	A
B	B	B
C	A	A
D	C	B

PS	NS	
	$x = 0$	$x = 1$
A	A	B
B	E	B
C	E	F
D	E	F
E	A	D
F	E	B

14. Find whether the following machines are information lossless or not. If lossless of definite order, find the order of losslessness.

PS	NS, o/p	
	$x = 0$	$x = 1$
A	A, 1	C, 1
B	E, 0	B, 1
C	D, 0	A, 0
D	C, 0	B, 0
E	B, 1	A, 0

PS	NS, o/p	
	$x = 0$	$x = 1$
A	D, 1	E, 0
B	A, 0	B, 1
C	C, 0	B, 0
D	C, 1	B, 1
E	A, 0	B, 0

15. Find the input string applied to state A of the machine given below where final state is B and output string is 00011.

PS	NS, z	
	$x = 0$	$x = 1$
A	A, 0	B, 0
B	C, 0	D, 0
C	D, 1	C, 1
D	B, 1	A, 1

FILL IN THE BLANKS

1. Synchronous Circuit is controlled by __________.
2. The operations in asynchronous circuit are controlled by a number of __________.
3. The output of Combinational Circuits is a function of __________.
4. The output of Sequential Circuits is a function of __________.
5. Binary adder is a __________.
6. Modulo 3 binary counter has __________ states.
7. Finite state machine can be defined as a type of machine whose past histories can affect its __________ in a __________ of ways.
8. Two states Si & Sj of machine M are said to be equivalent if they produce same __________. for an __________ applied to the machine M, considering Si and Sj as initial states.
9. If two states are k distinguishable then they are __________ equivalent for k = k to 1
10. Equivalent partition is __________.
11. Incompletely specified machines are those machine where for all states for all inputs the __________ or __________ or both are not mentioned
12. Minimal machine is the __________ of the machines obtained by minimizing an incompletely specified machine.
13. Merger graph of a machine M of n states is an __________ graph.
14. In a merger graph there will be an __________ arc if the next states of the two states [Vertices] do not conflict.
15. In a Merger Graph there will be no arc between the two vertices if the __________ of the pair of states conflict.
16. Two states say Si & Sj are said to be compatible, if both of them give same __________ strings for all __________ strings applied to the machine separately, considering Si & Sj as the initial states.
17. Compatibility graph is a __________ graph
18. A Subgraph of a Compatibility Graph is called __________ if for every vertex in the subgraph, all outgoing arcs and the terminal vertices of the arcs also belong to the subgraph.
19. Merger Table is a substitute application of __________.
20. From a Merger Graph we can get the compatible pairs and __________.
21. Vanishing connection Matrix is used to find whether a machine is __________ or not.
22. Synchronizing Tree Method is used to find whether a machine is __________ or not.
23. Contracted Table Method is used to find whether a machine is __________ or not.

24. The order of definiteness μ = ____________ if the length of the longest path in the Testing Graph is l.

25. The order of definiteness of a machine is the ____________ of the synchronizing tree.

26. A machine is called information lossless if its ____________ state, ____________ state & ____________ string is sufficient to determine uniquely the input string.

27. A machine which is not lossless is called ____________

ANSWERS

1. Clock Pulses	2. completion and initialization	3. Present I/P signals
4. External I/P & Present stored information	5. Sequential Circuit	6. Three
7. future behavior, finite number	8. output sequences, input string	9. k-1
10. Unique	11. Next State, output	12. Minimum
13. undirected	14. Uninterrupted	15. Outputs
16. Output, input	17. Directed	18. Closed
19. Merger Graph	20. implied pairs.	21. finite
22. definite	23. definite	24. l+1
25. Maximum Label	26. Initial, final, output	27. lossy

2

Language and Grammar

2.1 BASIC TERMINOLOGY AND DEFINITIONS

Q. Define symbol, alphabet and string.

Ans. Symbol: A symbol is a user-defined entity.

Alphabet: An alphabet is a finite set of symbols denoted by Σ in automata. Alphabets are a set of symbols used to construct a language. Example, $\{0, 1\}$ is binary alphabet, $\{A\ldots, Z, a\ldots z\}$ is the alphabet set for the English language.

String: A string is defined as a sequence of symbols of finite length. A string is denoted by w in automata. Example, 000111 is a binary string.

(Length of a string w is denoted by $|w|$. For the previous case, $|w| = |000111| = 6$).

Q. Define Prefix, proper Prefix, Suffix, proper Suffix, and substring in relation to a string.

Ans. Prefix: The prefix of a string is the string formed by taking any number of symbols from the start of the string. Example, let us take a string $w = 0111$. For the particular string $\in$, 0, 01, 011, 0111 are prefixes of the string 0111. For a string of length n, there are $n + 1$ number of prefixes.

Proper prefix: For a string, any prefix of the string other than the string itself is called the proper prefix of the string. Example: For the string $w = 0111$, the proper prefixes are $\in$, 0, 01, 011.

Suffix: The suffix of a string is formed by taking any number of symbols from the last of the string.

Example, let us take a string $w = 0110$. For the particular string $\in$, 0, 10, 110, 0110 are suffixes of the string 0110. For a string of length n, there are $n + 1$ number of suffixes.

Proper suffix: For a string, any suffix of the string other than the string itself is called the proper suffix of the string. Example: For the string $w = 0110$, the proper suffixes are $\in$, 0, 10, 110.

Substring: A substring of a string is defined as a string formed by taking any number symbols of the string. Example: For the string $w = 012$, the substrings are $\in$, 0, 1, 2, 01, 12 and 012.

Q. Define set and describe with an example.

Ans. Set: A set is a well-defined collection of objects. Objects constructing a set are called elements or members of the set.

Example, $L = \{2, 4, 6, 8\}$ is a set, where 2, 4, 6 and 8 are elements or the members of the set.

Q. Define union, intersection, difference, Cartesian product, power set, concatenation in relation to set and describe each of these with examples.

Ans. Union: If there are two sets A and B, then their union is denoted by $A \cup B$. Let $A = \{2, 3, 4\}$ and $B = \{3, 5, 6\}$, then $A \cup B = \{2, 3, 4, 5, 6\}$. In general, $A \cup B = \{x|x \in A \text{ or } x \in B\}$.

Intersection: If there are two sets A and B, then their intersection is denoted by $A \cap B$. Let $A = \{2, 3, 4\}$ and $B = \{3, 4, 5, 6\}$, then $A \cap B = \{3, 4\}$. In general, $A \cap B = \{x|x \in A \text{ and } x \in B\}$.

Difference: If there are two sets A and B, then their difference is denoted by $A - B$. Let $A = \{2, 3, 4, 5\}$ and $B = \{3, 4\}$, then $A - B = \{2, 5\}$. In general, $A - B = \{x|x \in A \text{ and } x \notin B\}$.

Cartesian product: If there are two sets A and B, then their Cartesian product is denoted by $A \times B$. $A = \{2, 3, 4, 5\}$ and $B = \{3, 4\}$, then $A \times B = \{(2,3), (2,4), (3,3), (3,4),(4,3), (4,4), (5,3), (5,4)\}$. In general, $A \times B = \{(a, b)|a \in A \text{ and } b \in B\}$.

Power set: The power set of set A is a set of all possible subsets of A. Let $A = \{a, b\}$, then the power set of A is $\{(\emptyset), (a), (b), (a, b)\}$. For a set of elements n, the number elements of the power set of A is 2^n.

Concatenation: If there are two sets A and B, then their concatenation is denoted by AB. Let $A = \{a, b\}$ and $B = \{c, d\}$, then $AB = \{ac, ad, bc, bd\}$. In general, $AB = \{ab|a \text{ is in } A \text{ and } b \text{ is in } B\}$.

Q. Define reflexive, symmetric, transitive and equivalence relation with examples.

Ans. Reflexive: A relation R is said to be reflexive on a non-empty set R if every element of A is related to itself by that relation R. Let $A = \{B, C, D\}$, where B, C and D are brothers. Then the relation brotherhood is a reflexive relation on the set A as $\{B, C\}$, $\{B, D\}$ and $\{C, D\}$ are all sets of brother.

Symmetric: A relation R is said to be symmetric if for two elements 'a' and 'b' in X that if a is related to b then b is related to a. Let A be a set of all students in a class. Let R be a relation called classmate. Then we can call R a symmetric relation. If a and b are two students belonging to the set, then a is a classmate of b and b is a classmate of a.

Transitive: Let R be a relation defined on a set A, then the relation R is said to be transitive if for $a, b, c \in A$ and if aRb, bRc holds good then aRc also holds good.

Let $A = \{8, 6, 4\}$, where R is a relation called greater than. If $8 > 6$ and $6 > 4$ holds good, then $8 > 4$ also holds good. Therefore, 'greater than' is a transitive relation.

Equivalence relation: A relation R is called an equivalence relation on 'A' if R is reflexive, symmetric and transitive.

2.2 GRAMMAR AND LANGUAGE

Q. Define language and grammar. Why are language and grammar needed in computer science?

Ans: To express ourselves to someone, i.e. to communicate with someone, we need some medium. That medium is language. Hindi, English and Bengali all are used to communicate among persons. Therefore, these are languages.

For constructing a language, there are some rules. Without rules, a language cannot exist. These rules are called the grammar for that language. Without grammar, a language cannot exist.

In computer science, to communicate with computer hardware, the user needs some languages for programming purposes. Like C, C++, Java. These are called Programming Language. These languages are used to communicate with the computer and the user. Therefore, they can be called language. For constructing languages, there are some rules to be followed. These rules are called the grammar for that programming language.

Q. Define grammar in the sense of automata. Justify the definition for the English language.

Ans: Grammar consists of four touples.

$$G = \{V_N, \Sigma, P, S\},$$

V_N is the set of non-terminals
Σ the set of terminals
P the set of production rule and
S the start symbol.

(Non-terminal symbols are those symbols that can be replaced multiple times. Terminal symbols are those symbols that cannot be replaced further.)

Example, let us take a sentence in English:

Bikash goes to college.

This sentence can be represented in grammatical form like this:

<Sentence> → <Subject><Predicate>
<Subject> → <Noun>/<Pronoun>
<Predicate> → <Verb Phase>
<Verb Phase> → <Verb>.<Preposition>.<Noun>
<Verb> → goes/eats/runs
<Preposition> → to/at
<Noun> → Ram/ Hari/ Bikash/College/School
<Pronoun> → I/ We/ He/ She/ They

Here,

V_N: {<Sentence>, <Subject>, <Predicate> … .}
Σ: {Ram, Hari, Bikash, He, She … etc.}
P: The production rules given above.
S: <Sentence>

2.3 CHOMSKY HIERARCHY

Q. What is the Chomsky classification of grammar? Mention the languages produced from each type of grammar. Mention the machine format for each of the languages.

Ans: Chomsky, a linguistic, classified the grammar into four types depending on the productions. These are as follows:

Type 0: Type 0 grammar is a phase structure grammar without any restriction. All grammars are Type 0 grammar.

For Type 0 grammar, the production rules are in the format of

$$\{(L_c)(NT)(R_c)\} \rightarrow \{\text{String of terminals or non-terminals or both}\}$$

L_c: Left context; R_c: Right context; NT: Non-terminal.

Type 1: Type 1 grammar is called context-sensitive grammar.

For Type 1 grammar, all production rules are in the format of context sensitive if all rules in P are of the form

$$\alpha A \beta \rightarrow \alpha \gamma \beta,$$

where $A \in NT$ (i.e. A is a single non-terminal), $\alpha, \beta \in (NT \cup \Sigma)^*$ (i.e. α and β are strings of non-terminals and terminals) and $\gamma \in (NT \cup \Sigma)^+$ (i.e. γ is a non-empty string of non-terminals and terminals).

Type 2: Type 2 grammar is called context-free grammar. In the left-hand side of the production, there will no left or right context.

For Type 2 grammar, all the production rules are in the format of

$$(NT) \rightarrow \alpha,$$

where $|NT| = 1$ and $\alpha \in (NT \cup T)^*$, NT is non-terminal and T is terminal.

Type 3: Type 3 grammar is called regular grammar. Here all the productions will be in the following forms:

$$A \rightarrow \alpha \quad \text{or} \quad A \rightarrow \alpha B,$$

where $A, B \in NT$ and $\alpha \in T$.

The Chomsky classification is called the Chomsky Hierarchy. This can be represented diagrammatically

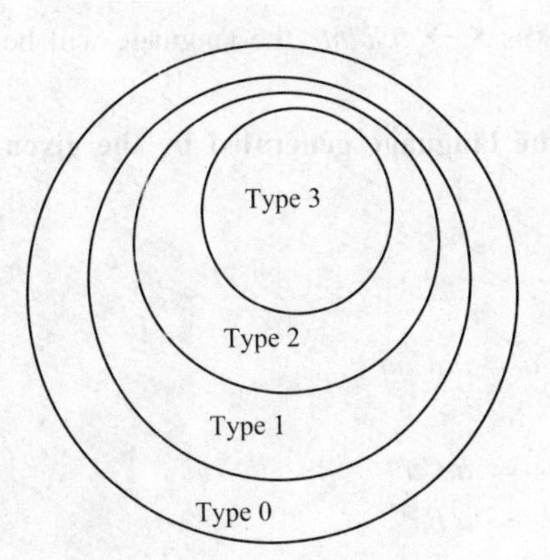

From this diagrammatical representation, we can say that all regular grammars are context-free grammar. All context-free grammar are context-sensitive grammar. All context-sensitive grammar are unrestricted grammar.

Q. Give the languages and machine format for different grammars.

Ans:

Grammar	Language	Machine Format
Type 0	Unrestricted Language	Turing Machine
Type 1	Context-sensitive Language	Linear-bounded Automata
Type 2	Context-free Language	Push Down Automata
Type 3	Regular Expression	Finite Automata

(The null alphabet is represented by ε. The null string is represented by Λ. The null set is represented by Φ.)

2.4 EXAMPLES

Q. Construct the language generated from the given grammar.

$S \rightarrow aSb/\varepsilon$

Ans: (Grammar can be represented in the form of only Production Rules. In the production rule all are given. Considering the previous grammar as example.

V_N : {S}

Σ : {a,b}

P : The above given production rules.

S : {S}

)

$S \rightarrow aSb$ and $S \rightarrow \varepsilon$ are combined into a single production. S is the start symbol. S is also a non-terminal symbol. Therefore, S can be replaced. S can be replaced by two types of strings, aSb and ε. In aSb, there is a non-terminal symbol S. Therefore, aSb is not in the language set produced from the grammar. ε will be in the language set.

In aSb there is a non-terminal S. Therefore, S can be replaced by either ε or aSb. If S is replaced by ε it will be ab, which consists of only terminals. Therefore, ab belongs to the language set.

Therefore the language will be $a^n b^n$, where the value of n will be 0, 1, 2, … n.
[n = 0 means $a0b0$ means there is no a and no b in the string means null string (Λ).]

Therefore, the language generated from the grammar will be

$$L(G) = a^n b^n, \qquad n \geq 0$$

This is denoted by the following diagram. (If the grammar was $S \rightarrow aSb/ab$, the language will be $L(G) = a^n b^n, n > 0$.)

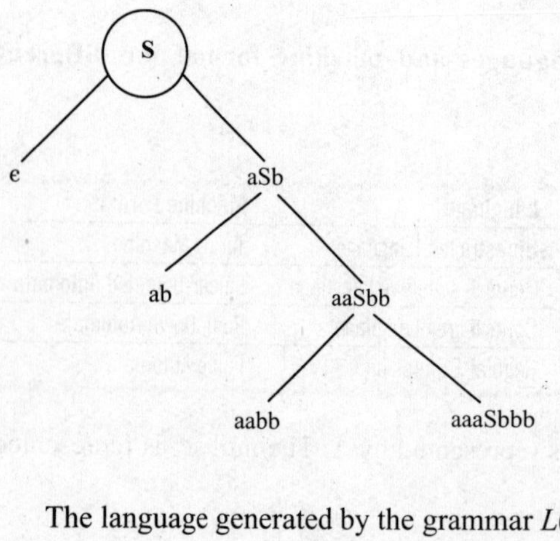

Q. Construct the language generated by the given grammar:

$S \rightarrow aCa$

$C \rightarrow aCa/b$

Ans: $S \Rightarrow aCa \Rightarrow aaCaa$

$\vdots$

$\Rightarrow a^n C a^n$

$\Rightarrow a^n b a^n$

In the language generated by the grammar, there will be at least one a. Null does not belong to the language set.

The language generated by the grammar $L(G) = a^n b a^n, n > 0$.

Q. Construct the language generated by the grammar

$S \rightarrow AbB$

$A \rightarrow aA/a$

$B \rightarrow aB/a$

Ans: $S \Rightarrow AbB \Rightarrow aAbB \Rightarrow aaAbB$

$$\vdots$$

$$\Rightarrow a^n bB \Rightarrow a^n baB \Rightarrow a^n baaB$$

$$\vdots$$

$$\Rightarrow a^n ba^m$$

In the language set generated by the grammar, there will be at least one a in both the sides of *b*. However, it may or may not be possible that in both the sides of *b*, *A* and *B* are replaced in the same number because they are different non-terminals. So, there are most chance to get different number of 'a' in both sides. Therefore, the language generated by the grammar is

$L(G) = a^n ba^m$, m, n > 0

Q. Construct the language generated from the given grammar:

$S \rightarrow aS\ /bS/\varepsilon$

Ans: In this production rule, there are three productions $S \rightarrow aS$, $S \rightarrow bS$ and $S \rightarrow \varepsilon$. In ε there is no non-terminal, so in the language set there is a null string (Λ). *S* can be replaced by *aS*, *bS* or ε. If *S* is replaced by *aS* in *aS*, it will be *aaS*. If *S* is replaced by *bS*, it will be *abS*. If *S* is replaced by *aS* in *bS*, it will be *baS*. If *S* is replaced by *bS* in *bS*, it will be *bbS*. If *S* is replaced by ε in *aS* and *bS*, it will be *a* and *b*, respectively, which will belong to the language set. By this process, we will get *aa*, *bb*, *ab*, *ba*, …, *aba*, *bab* … *abaaba*, … etc.

In a single statement, we can represent the language set as "Any combination of *a*, *b* including null."

In mathematics, it is represented as $L(G) = \{a, b\}^*$

(Any combination of *a*, *b* excluding null will be represented by $\{a, b\}^+$.)

Q. Construct the language generated from the given grammar.

$S \rightarrow aSa/bSb/C$ (*C* is also a terminal symbol.)

Ans: From the start symbol, *C* is generated, which is a terminal symbol. Therefore, *C* belongs to the language set. From *S*, two other production rules are generated *aSa* and *bSb*. In *aSa*, there is a non-terminal *S*. Therefore, *S* can be replaced by *aSa* or *bSb* or *C*. If *S* is replaced by these production rules, the strings will be *aaSaa*, *abSba* and *aCa*, respectively. Similarly, for *bSb* the strings will be *baSab*, *bbSbb* and *bCb*. Among these, *aCa* and *bCb* will be in the language set generated from the grammar.

By this process, we will get *aaCaa*, *abCba*, *baCab*, *bbCbb* … *abaCaba*, …, *ababbCbbaba* like this.

If we look into the string, we will see that before *C* there is any combination of *a* and *b* including ϵ [for the string *C*, there is no *a* and no *b*] and after *C* the string is the reverse of the previous string. If we take the string before *C* as *W*, the string after *C* will be W^R.

The language generated from the grammar will be

$L(G) = WCW^R$,

where $W \in (a, b)^*$

Q. Construct the grammar for the language a^n, $n > 0$.

Ans: The language consists of any number of *a*. As $n > 0$, in the language set there is at least one *a*. The grammar for the language is

$S \rightarrow aS/a.$

Q. Construct the grammar for the language $(ab)^n$, $n > 0$.

Ans: The language consists of any number of *ab*. [Here we can think of *ab* as a single character.] The grammar for the language is

$S \rightarrow abS/ab.$

Q. Construct the grammar for the language a^nb^n, $n > 0$.

Ans: From the string, we can say that

(i) The language consists of *a* and *b*.
(ii) In the language, *a* will appear before *b*.
(iii) Number of *a* and the number of *b* are same in any string belonging to the language set.
(iv) In the language, there is no null string.

The value of *n* is greater than 0. The lowest value of *n* is 1 here. If $n = 1$, the lowest length string that is produced from the language is *ab*. So from the start symbol *S*, *ab* is produced in the grammar there will be a production $S \rightarrow ab$.

In the language set, there are strings like *aabb*, *aaabbb* …, a^nb^n. Each time, one *a* and one *b* are added in the string. For $n = 1, 2, 3$ ….

It can be thought of as follows: in the middle, there is a non-terminal, which is replaced by adding one *a* at the left and one *b* at the right and lastly replacing that non-terminal by *ab*, which produces *aabb*, *aaabbb* ….

Therefore, the other production is

$S \rightarrow aSb.$

The grammar becomes

$S \rightarrow aSb/ab,$

where V_N: $\{S\}$, Σ: $\{a, b\}$, P: $S \rightarrow aSb/ab$, S: $\{S\}$

Q. Construct the grammar for the language $a^nc^ib^n$, $n, i \geq 0$.

Ans: From the string, we can say that

i) The language consists of *a*, *b* and *c*.
ii) In the language set, *a* comes before *c*, *c* comes before *b*.
iii) In the language set, the number of *a* and the number of *b* are the same while the number of *c* may be different.
iv) In the language set, a null string may exist.

In the language set, the number of *a* and the number of *b* are the same; that means, each time *a* and *b* come simultaneously. For a^nb^n, we have seen that there is a production rule $S \rightarrow aSb$. In the string, *c* will come in between a and b by using the production rule $S \rightarrow Sc/\varepsilon$. But if c comes directly from S, then c may come after b, if done like

$S \rightarrow Sc \rightarrow aSbc \rightarrow abc$

Therefore, abc is produced from the production rule, which does not belong to the language set. c Will not come directly from S. We have to introduce another non-terminal A.

The production rules will be like this

$S \rightarrow aSb/A$

$A \rightarrow Ac/\varepsilon$

Q. Construct the grammar for the language $a^nc^ib^n$, $n > 0$, $i \geq 0$.

Ans: In the language set c may be null as $i \geq 0$. However, there will be at least one a and one b. The grammar is

$S \rightarrow aSb/aAb$

$A \rightarrow Ac/\varepsilon$

Q. Construct the grammar for the language $a^nc^ib^n$, $n \geq 0$, $i > 0$.

Ans: In the language set a and b may be null but there will be at least one c. The grammar is

$S \rightarrow aSb/A$

$A \rightarrow Ac/c$

Q. Construct the grammar for the language $a^nb^nc^i$, $n > 0$, $i \geq 0$.

Ans: In the language set there exist a, b and c. a appears before b and b appears before c. The number of a and the number of b are the same; the number of c may be different. There will be at least one a and one b in the language set. If we look into the string, it will be clear that the string consists of two individual strings a^nb^n and c^i. Let a^nb^n is generated from the non-terminal symbol A and c^i is generated from the non terminal B. The production rule will be $S \rightarrow AB$.

a^nb^n with the condition $n > 0$ is generated from the production rule $A \rightarrow aAb/ab$, where A is the start symbol. And c^i with the condition $i \geq 0$ is generated from the production rule $B \rightarrow cB/\in$, where B is the start symbol.

The complete grammar will be

$S \rightarrow AB$

$A \rightarrow aAb/ab$

$B \rightarrow cB/\in$

Q. Construct a grammar for the language a^nb^{n+1}, $n > 0$.

Ans. Here the number of b is one more than the number of a. As $n > 0$, in the language set there is at least one a and at least two b's (as the number of b is one more than the number of a). By the production $S \rightarrow aAbb$, one a and two b's will be added to the generated language set. Now the non-terminal A can be replaced multiple times by the production rule $A \rightarrow aAb$ to produce $a^nA\,b^{n+1}$. At last A is replaced by ϵ by the production rule $A \rightarrow \epsilon$ to produce a^nb^{n+1}

Therefore the grammar for the language is

$S \rightarrow aAbb$

$A \rightarrow aAb/\epsilon$

The grammar can be generated in another way.

By two production rules $S \rightarrow aAb$ and $A \rightarrow aAb$, n number of a and n number of b are produced, where $n > 0$. At last if A is replaced by b using the production rule $A \rightarrow b$, the language set $a^n b^{n+1}$ will be produced.

Therefore the grammar for the language will be

$S \rightarrow aAb$

$A \rightarrow aAb/b$

Q. Construct a grammar for the language $a^n b^{n+1}$, $n \geq 0$.

Ans: Here the number of b is one more than the number of a. As $n \geq 0$, number of a may be zero but there will be atleast one b in the language set. So, b is in the language set. The single b is produced by the production rule $S \rightarrow b$. Using the production $S \rightarrow aSb$, n number of a and n number of b are produced. At last step S is replaced by b, using the production rule $S \rightarrow b$ to produce $a^n b^{n+1}$

Therefore the grammar for the language is

$S \rightarrow aSb/b$

Taking the previous example in consideration we can write the grammar as follows

$S \rightarrow aAbb/b$

$A \rightarrow aAb/\epsilon$

Q. Construct a grammar generating the language $a^n b^n c^i$, where $n \geq 1$, $i \geq 0$.

Ans: The language consists of two parts $a^n b^n$ where $n \geq 1$ and c^i where $i \geq 0$. Therefore, from the start symbol S, we need to take two non-terminals A and B, where A generates $a^n b^n$ with $n \geq 1$ and B generates c^i with $i \geq 0$. The grammar for the language is

$S \rightarrow AB$

$A \rightarrow aAb/ab$

$B \rightarrow Bc/\varepsilon$

Q. Construct a grammar generating the language $a^i b^n c^n$, where $n \geq 1$, $i \geq 0$.

Ans: The language consists of two parts $b^n c^n$ where $n \geq 1$ and a^i where $i \geq 0$. Therefore, from the start symbol S, we need to take two non-terminals A and B, where A generates a^i with $i \geq 0$ and B generates $b^n c^n$ with $n \geq 1$. The grammar for the language is

$S \rightarrow AB$

$A \rightarrow Aa/\varepsilon$

$B \rightarrow bBc/bc$

Q. Construct a grammar generating the language $a^n c^i b^n$, where $n \geq 1$, $i \geq 0$.

Ans: In the language, the numbers of a and b are the same, but the number of c is different. First we need to generate a production rule, which generates $a^n b^n$ with $n \geq 1$. In the middle of a^n and b^n there is a non-terminal, which generates c^i with $i \geq 0$. The grammar for the language is

$S \rightarrow aSb/aAb$

$A \rightarrow Ac/\varepsilon$

Q. Construct the grammar for palindrome of binary numbers.

Ans: A string that is read from left to right and right to left and gives the same result is called a palindrome. A palindrome can be of two types: odd palindrome and even palindrome. Odd palindromes are those types of palindromes where the number of characters is odd. Even palindromes are those types of palindromes where the number of characters is even.

A null string is also a palindrome. The palindrome will consist of '0' and '1'. A string will be a palindrome if its first and last characters are the same. The character in the *n*th position from the beginning will be the same character from the *n*th position from the last. The palindrome can start with 0 and can start with 1. 0 can come after 0 and 0 can come after 1. 1 can come after 1 and 1 can come after 0.

From the previous discussion, the grammar for the even palindrome is

$S \rightarrow 0S0/1S1/\varepsilon$ (null string is also a palindrome)

The grammar for the odd palindrome is

$S \rightarrow 0S0/1S1/0/1$

By combining the two grammars for even and odd palindromes, the final grammar will be

$S \rightarrow 0S0/1S1/0/1/\varepsilon$

Q. Find the grammar for the language a^nb^m, where $n \geq 2$, $m \geq 3$.

Ans: In the language set there will be at least two *a*'s and three *b*'s. It is not always true that the number of *b* is one more than number of *a*, as *m* and *n* are different numbers. In the language set all the *a*'s will appear before *b* so we need to introduce two different non-terminals *A* and *B* to generate a string of *a* and a string of *b*, respectively. The grammar for the language is

$S \rightarrow aaABbbb$

$A \rightarrow aA/\varepsilon$

$B \rightarrow bB/\varepsilon$

Q. Find the grammar for the language 0^m1^n, where $m \neq n$

Ans: According to the condition $m \neq n$, two cases are possible.

a) Number of 0 is more than number of 1
b) Number of 1 is more than number of 0.

Consider two start symbols S_1 and S_2, where S_1 generates the language for case a and S_2 generates the language for case b.

Case a: The language is in the form 0^m1^n. It means all 0 will come before 1. The more 0s will also come before 1. Here we can generate a grammar for producing equal number of 0 and 1. Then by considering a non-terminal A the extra 0s are added by production rule $A \rightarrow 0A/0$.

Therefore the grammar for case a is

$S_1 \rightarrow AS_1$

$S_1 \rightarrow 0S_11/\epsilon$

$A \rightarrow 0A/0$

Case b: In this case number of 1 is more than number of 0. So, the extra 1s are added at last. The grammar for case *b* is

$S_2 \rightarrow S_2B$
$S_2 \rightarrow 0S_21/\epsilon$
$B \rightarrow 1B/1$

Case a and Case b can be added by using a common start symbol S and a production rule $S \rightarrow S_1/S_2$. The complete grammar is

$S \rightarrow S_1/S2$
$S_1 \rightarrow AS_1$
$S_1 \rightarrow 0S_11/\epsilon$
$A \rightarrow 0A/0$
$S_2 \rightarrow S_2B$
$S_2 \rightarrow 0S_21/\epsilon$
$B \rightarrow 1B/1$

Q. Construct the grammar for the language $a^lb^mc^n$, where one of l, m, $n = 1$ and the remaining two are equal.

Ans: In the language set at least one of a, b or c will exist singly. The terminal elements are a and c. If in the language set there is a single a, the production rules are $S \rightarrow aS_1$ and $S_1 \rightarrow bS_1c/\varepsilon$. If in the language set there is a single c, the production rules are $S \rightarrow S_2c$ and $S_2 \rightarrow aS_2b/\varepsilon$. b is the middle element. For single b in the middle, the production rules are $S \rightarrow aS_3c$ and $S_3 \rightarrow aS_3c/b$. The grammar for the language is

$S \rightarrow aS_1/S_2c/aS_3c$
$S_1 \rightarrow bS_1c/\varepsilon$
$S_2 \rightarrow aS_2b/\varepsilon$
$S_3 \rightarrow aS_3c/b$

Q. Construct the grammar for the language 0^m1^n, where $m \geq 1$ and $n \geq 1$ and $m < n$.

Ans: According to the condition there must be alteast one 0 and one 1 in the language set. But number of 0 must be less than number of 1. The extra 1s are added at the last, because the language is in the form 0^m1^n. Here we can generate a grammar for producing equal number of 0 and 1. Then by considering a non- terminal B the extra 0s are added by production rule $B \rightarrow B1/1$

The complete grammar is

$S \rightarrow 0S1/0B1$
$B \rightarrow B1/1$

Q. Construct the grammar for the language $a^lb^mc^n$, where $l + m = n$.

Ans: The total number of a and b are equal to the total number of c. Either the number of a or the number of b may be 1. In that case, the number of c is 1. If the number of a and the number of b is zero, then the number of c is also zero. Therefore, there is production $S \rightarrow ac/bc/\varepsilon$. If in the language there is no a, then the number of b is equal to the number of c. This is the same for a language without b. The production rule is $S \rightarrow aSc/bSc$. However, in this case there is a chance of a occurring after b. The modified production is $S \rightarrow aSc/bS_1c$. The total number of a and b is equal to the total number of c; this can be solved if in each occurrence of a or b, one c is added to the language. The production rule for this case is $S_1 \rightarrow bS_1c/bc/\varepsilon$. The grammar for the language is

$S \rightarrow aSc/bS_1c/ac/bc/\varepsilon$

$S_1 \rightarrow bS_1c/bc/\varepsilon$

Q. Construct the grammar for the language L = {Set of all strings over 0, 1 containing twice as many 0 than 1}.

Ans: The language consists of 0 and 1. In the language set, the number of 0 is twice that of the number of 1. 0 and 1 can occur in any pattern. The grammar for the language is

$S \rightarrow S1S0S0S/S0S0S1S/S0S1S0S$

Q. Construct a grammar consisting of an equal number of 0 and 1.

Ans: The grammar for the language is

$S \rightarrow S0S1S/S1S0S/\varepsilon$

Q. Construct a grammar that generates all even integers up to 998.

Ans: In even numbers, the right-most number is one of 0, 2, 4, 6, 8. The middle and left-most number is one of 0, 1, 2, 3, 4, 5, 6, 7, 8, 9. We have to generate even numbers up to 998, i.e. 3 digits. Therefore, we have to consider all even numbers of one and two digits also.

$S \rightarrow A_1S_1/A_1A_2S_1$ /0 /2 /4 /6 /8

$A_1 \rightarrow$ 0/1/2/3/ 4/5/6/7/8/9

$A_2 \rightarrow$ 0/1/2/3/ 4/5/6/7/8/9

$S_1 \rightarrow$ 0/2/4/6/8

Here the production rule $S \rightarrow A_1S_1$ generates the two digits numbers. The production rule $S \rightarrow A_1A_2S_1$ generates 3 digits numbers.

Q. Construct the grammar for WW^R, where $W \in (a, b)^*$.

Ans: The string W consists of a and b. W can be a null string also. W^R is the reverse string of W. The number of characters in the string WW^R will always be even, except the null string. Therefore, the string is nothing but an even palindrome of a and b including the null string. The grammar will be

$S \rightarrow aSa/bSb/\varepsilon$

Q. Construct the grammar for the language $L = a^nb^nc^md^m$, $m, n > 0$.

Ans: The total string can be divided into two parts: (a) A string of a and b, where the number of a and the number of b are the same. (b) A string of c and d, where the numbers of c and d are the same.

From the start symbol, there will be two non-terminals A and B, where A will generate a^nb^n and B will generate c^md^m. In the language set there will be no null string. Therefore, the grammar will be

$S \rightarrow AB$

$A \rightarrow aAb/ab$

$B \rightarrow cBd/cd$

Q. Construct the grammar for the language $L = a^nc^md^mb^n$, $m, n > 0$.

Ans: In between a and b there is an equal number of c and d. The number of a and the number of b are the same.

Therefore, we have to construct a^nb^n with a non-terminal in between a^n and b^n. From that non-terminal c^md^m will be produced. Therefore, the grammar will be

$S \rightarrow aSb/aAb$

$A \rightarrow cAd/cd$

2.5 CONTEXT-SENSITIVE GRAMMAR

Q. Construct a grammar for the language $a^nb^nc^n$, where $n \geq 1$.

Ans: It is difficult to construct $a^nb^nc^n$. We construct it by the following process:

(a) First we construct $a^n\alpha^n$.

(b) Then from α^n we construct b^nc^n.

From α, generating b^nc^n is difficult, From α^n, $(bc)^n$ can be constructed. However, $(bc)^n$ is not equal to b^nc^n. Introduce a new non-terminal B:

$S \rightarrow Abc/ABSc$

$BA \rightarrow AB$

$Bb \rightarrow bb$

$A \rightarrow a$

Q. Construct a grammar for the language xx, where $x \in (a, b)^*$.

Ans:

$S \rightarrow aAS/bBS$

$S \rightarrow aAZ/bBZ$

$Aa \rightarrow aA$

$Bb \rightarrow bB$

$AZ \rightarrow Za$

$BZ \rightarrow Zb$

$Z \rightarrow \lambda$

Q. Construct a grammar for the language $\{a^nb^nc^nd^n, n \geq 1\}$.

Ans:

$S \rightarrow abcd$

$S \rightarrow aXbcd$

$Xb \rightarrow bX$

$Xc \rightarrow bYc$

$Yc \rightarrow cY$

$Yd \rightarrow Rcdd$

$cR \rightarrow Rc$

$bR \rightarrow Rb$

$aR \rightarrow aaX \mid aa$

WHAT WE HAVE LEARNED SO FAR

1. A set of rules for constructing a language is called the grammar for that language.
2. For every programming language like C, C++ and Java there is a grammar.
3. Grammar consists of four touples. $G = \{V_N, \Sigma, P, S\}$, where V_N is the set of non-terminals, Σ the set of terminals, P the set of production rule and S the start symbol.
4. Chomsky, a linguistic, classified grammar in to four types depending on the productions. The types are Type 0, i.e. unrestricted grammar, Type 1, i.e. context-sensitive grammar, Type 2, i.e. context-free grammar and Type 3, i.e. regular grammar.
5. For each of the grammar, there is a specific language, namely unrestricted language, context-sensitive language, context-free language and regular expression.
6. Unrestricted language is accepted by Turing Machine, Context-sensitive language is accepted by Linear-bounded automata, Context-free language is accepted by Push down automata and Regular language is accepted by Finite Automata.
7. For Type 0 grammar, the production rules are in the format of $\{(L_c)(NT)(R_c)\} \rightarrow$ {String of Terminals or Non-terminals or both}, where L_c id the left context, R_c the right context and NT the non-terminal.
8. For Type 1 grammar all production rules are in the format of context sensitive if all rules in P are of the form $\alpha A\beta \rightarrow \alpha\gamma\beta$, where $A \in NT$ (i.e. A is a single non-terminal), $\alpha, \beta \in (NT \cup \Sigma)^*$ (i.e. α and β are strings of non-terminals and terminals) and $\gamma \in (NT \cup \Sigma)+$ (i.e. γ is a non-empty string of non-terminals and terminals).
9. Type 2 Grammar is called context-free grammar. In the left-hand side of the production there will no left or right context. For Type 2 grammar, all the production rules are in the format of $(NT) \rightarrow \alpha$, where $|NT| = 1$ and $\alpha \in (NT \cup T)^*$, NT is the non-terminal and T the terminal.
10. Type 3 grammar is called regular grammar. Here all the productions will be in the following forms. $A \rightarrow \alpha$ or $A \rightarrow \alpha B$, where $A, B \in NT$ and $\alpha \in T$.

SOLVED PROBLEMS

1. Find the languages generated by the following grammars:

(a) $S \rightarrow aSb/aAb,\ A \rightarrow bAa/ba$ (b) $S \rightarrow 0S1/0A1,\ A \rightarrow 1A/1$

(c) $S \rightarrow 0A/0/1B,\ A \rightarrow 1A/1,\ B \rightarrow 0B/1S$

Ans:

(a) $S \rightarrow aSb \rightarrow aaSbb \stackrel{*}{\Rightarrow} a^{n-1}Sb^{b-1} \rightarrow a^nAb^n \rightarrow a^nbAab^n \stackrel{*}{\Rightarrow} a^nb^{m-1}a^{m-1}b^n \rightarrow a^nb^ma^mb^n$

The language generated by the grammar is $L(G) = a^nb^ma^mb^n$, where $m, n > 0$.

(b) $S \rightarrow 0S1 \rightarrow 00S11 \stackrel{*}{\Rightarrow} 0^{m-1}A1^{m-1} \rightarrow 0^mA1^m \rightarrow 0^m1A1^m \stackrel{*}{\Rightarrow} 0^m1^{n-1}A1^m \rightarrow 0^m1^n1^m \rightarrow 0^m1^{m+n}$

The language generated by the grammar is $L(G) = 0^m1^{m+n}$, where $m, n > 0$.

(c) First let us try to find the expressions generated by $B \rightarrow 0B/1S$ and $A \rightarrow 1A/1$. Then replace the expressions generated by A and B into $S \rightarrow 0A/1B$.

$B \rightarrow 0B \rightarrow 00B$ -----$\rightarrow 0^*B \rightarrow 0^*1S$

$A \rightarrow 1A \rightarrow 11A$ -----$\rightarrow 1^*A \rightarrow 1^*1$

$S \rightarrow 0A/0/1B$

$\rightarrow 01^*1/0/10^*1S \rightarrow (01^*1/0)(10^*1)^*$

2. Generate a CFG for the language L = Alternating sequence of a and b.

Ans: The language may start with a or with b. If the string starts with a, then the language is $(ab)^n$. If the string starts with b, then the language is $(ba)^n$. If the string starts with a, then the production rule is $S \rightarrow aA$. If the string starts with b, then the production rule is $S \rightarrow bB$. For alternating sequences of a and b, the production rules are $A \rightarrow bB$, $B \rightarrow aA$, $A \rightarrow b$, $B \rightarrow a$. The production rules are $S \rightarrow aA$, $S \rightarrow bB$, $A \rightarrow bB$, $B \rightarrow aA$, $A \rightarrow b$, $B \rightarrow a$.

3.Construct a grammar that generates all odd integers up to 999.

Ans: Odd numbers from 0 to 9 are 1, 3, 5, 7, 9. The grammar for generating 1, 3, 5, 7, 9 is $S \rightarrow 1/3/5/7/9$.

For an odd number of length 2, the grammar is $S \rightarrow AS_1$, where $A \rightarrow 0/1\ldots7/8/9$, $S_1 \rightarrow 1/3/5/7/9$.

For an odd number of length 3, the grammar is $S \rightarrow BAS_1$, where $A \rightarrow 0/1\ldots7/8/9$, $B \rightarrow 0/1\ldots7/8/9$ and $S_1 \rightarrow 1/3/5/7/9$.

4. Construct a grammar that generates $\{(01)^n \cup (10)^n\}$, where $n > 0$.

Ans: It consists of two languages, $(01)^n$ and $(10)^n$. Both are connected by union. Take A and B, two non-terminals, which generate $(01)^n$ and $(10)^n$, respectively. From the start symbol S it goes to A and B. The grammar is

$S \rightarrow A/B$

$A \rightarrow 01A/01$

$B \rightarrow 10B/10$

MULTIPLE CHOICE QUESTIONS

1. Which is correct?

   (a) $a^+ = a^*\ a^*$ (b) $a^* = a^+\ a^+$ (c) $a^+ = a^*\ a$ (d) $a^* = a^+\ a^*$

2. $(a, b)^*$ means______________.

   (a) Any combination of a, b including null (b) Any combination of a, b excluding null
   (c) Any combination of a, b but a will come first (d) None of these

3. $(a, b)^+$ means______________.

   (a) Any combination of a, b including null (b) Any combination of a, b excluding null
   (c) Any combination of a, b but a will come first (d) None of these

4. What is the language generated by the grammar $S \rightarrow aSb$, $S \rightarrow A$, $A \rightarrow aA$?

   (a) $a^m b^m$ (b) $\varnothing$ (c) $a^n b^m$ (d) $a^m b^m$

5. Which type of grammar is the following in particular $S \rightarrow aSb$, $S \rightarrow ab$?

   (a) Unrestricted (b) Context-sensitive grammar
   (c) Context-free grammar (d) Regular grammar

6. The language generated by the grammar $S \to 0S0, S \to 1S1, S \to 0, S \to 1$ is ______.
   (a) Even palindrome of 0 and 1
   (b) Odd palindrome of 0 and 1
   (c) Any combination of 0 and 1
   (d) None of these
7. The language $\{a^m b^n c^{m+n} \mid m, n \geq 1\}$ is ______.
   (a) Regular
   (b) Context free but not regular
   (c) Context sensitive but not context free
   (d) Type 0 but not context sensitive
8. Which type of grammar is the following in particular?

   $A \to aB, B \to ac, C \to bC/aD, D \to bA/b$

   (a) Context-sensitive grammar
   (b) Context-free grammar
   (c) Context free but regular in particular
   (d) Not Type 0 but context free
9. The machine format of context-sensitive grammar is ______.
   (a) Finite automata
   (b) Push down automata
   (c) Linear-bounded automata
   (d) All of the above

Ans: 1. c 2. a 3. b 4. b [Because no string of terminal is produced] 5. c 6. b 7. b 8. c 9. c

EXERCISES

1. Find the languages generated by the following grammars:
   (a) $S \to aSb/A, A \to Ac/c$
   (b) $S \to aSb/aAb, A \to Ac/\varepsilon$
   (c) $S \to aSb/aAb, A \to bA/b$
   (d) $S \to S_1/S_2, S_1 \to 0S_11/0A, A \to 0A/\varepsilon, S_2 \to 0S_21/B1, B \to B1/\varepsilon$
2. Construct grammars for the following languages:
   (a) $L = (a, b)^*$, where all a's appear before b
   (b) $L = (a, b)^*$, where there are equal numbers of a and b
   (c) $L = (a, b)^*$, where the number of b is one more than the number of a
   (d) $L = (a, b)^*$, where there is at least one a
3. Construct grammars for the following languages:
   (a) $L = a^m b^n$, where $m \neq n$.
   (b) $L = a^x b^y c^z$, where $y = x + z$
   (c) $L = a^x b^y c^z$, where $z = x + y$
   (d) $L = a^x b^y c^z$, where $x = y + z$
4. Construct grammars for the following languages:
   (a) $\{a^n b^n \mid n > 0\} \cup \{c^m d^m \mid m \geq 0\}$
   (b) $\{a^n b^n \mid n > 0\} \cup \{a^m b^m \mid m \geq 0\}$
   (c) $\{a^x b^y c^z$, where $x = y + z\} \cup \{L = a^x b^y c^z$, where $z = x + y\}$
5. Construct grammars for the following languages:
   (a) $L = (0 + 1)^*\ 11\ (11)^*$
   (b) $L =$ (Set of all strings of a, b beginning and ending with a)
   (c) $L = a^{2n+1}$, where $n > 0$

FILL IN THE BLANKS

1. For a string, any prefix of the string other than the string itself is called as the ___________ of the string.
2. For a string, any suffix of the string other than the string itself is called as the ___________ of the string.
3. If there are two sets A and B, then their intersection is denoted by ___________
4. For a set of elements n the number elements of power set of A is ___________.
5. If 2^n is the number of elements of the power set of a set then the number of element in the set is ___________.
6. A relation R is said to be ___________ if for two elements 'a' and 'b' in X that if a is related to b then b is related to a.
7. A relation R is said to be ___________ if for a,b,c e A and if aRb , bRc holds good then aRc also holds good.
8. A relation R is called as an ___________ on 'A if R is reflexive, symmetric and transitive.
9. Grammar consists of four touples- Set of Non- Terminals, ___________, Set of Production Rule, ___________
10. According to Chomsky Hierarchy there are ___________ types of grammars.
11. Type 1 Grammar is called ___________
12. Type 2 Grammar is called ___________
13. According to Chomsky Hierarchy Regular Grammar is Type ___________ grammar.
14. All languages are accepted by ___________
15. The machine format of Context Free Language is ___________
16. Linear Bounded automata is the machine format of ___________
17. The machine format of Type 3 language is ___________
18. Grammar where production rules are in the format CAB → ay6 is ___________ grammar
19. In a Context Free Grammar at the left hand side there is ___________ non terminal.
20. Type 3 language is called ___________.
21. $a^nb^nc^n$ is an example of ___________ language in particular.
22. The grammar S → aSb/A, A →Ac/c is an example of ___________ grammar in particular.
23. The grammar S → Abc/ ABSc, BA → AB, Bb → bb, A ^ a is an example of ___________ grammar in particular.
24. The grammar A → aA/ bB/a/b, B → bB/b is an example of ___________ grammar in particular
25. The language a*(a+b)b* is an example of ___________ language in particular.

26. L = Alternating sequence of 'a' and 'b' is an example of ____________ language in particular.

27. Regular Expression is accepted by type ____________ grammar.

ANSWERS

1. proper prefix	2. proper suffix	3. AnB
4. 2^n	5. n	6. symmetric
7. transitive	8. equivalence relation	9. Set of Terminals, Start Symbol
10. Four	11. Context Sensitive Grammar	12. Context Free Grammar
13. Three	14. Turing Machine	15. Push Down Automata
16. Context Sensitive Grammar	17. Finite Automata	18. Context Sensitive
19. Single	20. Regular Expression	21. Context Sensitive
22. Context Free	23. Context Sensitive	24. Regular Grammar
25. Type 4	26. Context Free	27. Three

3

Finite Automata

3.1 BASICS ABOUT FINITE AUTOMATA

Q. Define and describe the characteristics of an Automaton.

Ans. An automaton is a system where materials, energy or information are transformed and transmitted for performing some operation without direct human participation.
Any automated machine can be given as example of automaton.

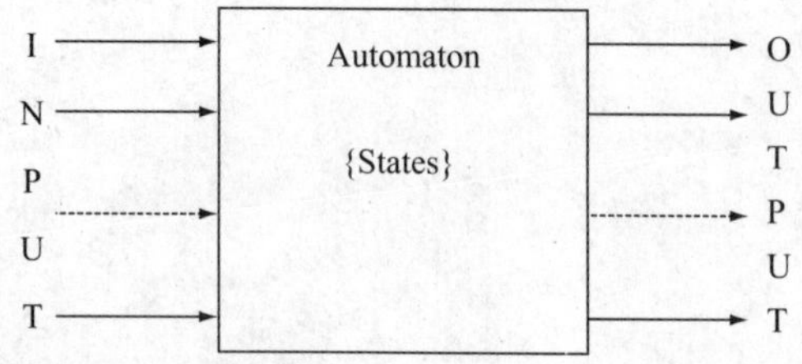

Characteristics of an automaton:

Input (I/P): Input is taken in each clock pulse. For each single instance of time $t_1, t_2, t_3, \ldots, t_n$ the input are taken as $I_1, I_2, I_3, \ldots, I_n$. As there are n number of input lines, n number of inputs will be taken in each single time instant. Input for each input line is finite and taken from a set called set of input alphabet Σ.

Output (O/P): Output is generated in each clock pulse. For each single instance of time $t_1, t_2, t_3, \ldots, t_m$, the outputs are generated as $O_1, O_2, O_3, \ldots, O_m$. Output generated from each output line is finite and belongs to a set called Output alphabet set.

State: At any discrete instant of time the automaton can be in one of the states $q_1, q_2, q_3, \ldots, q_n$. State belongs to a set called 'State' Q.

State transition: At any instant of time the automaton must be in one of the states that belong to the set Q. By getting input in a clock pulse the automaton must reside in a state. The state, in which the automaton will reside by getting that particular input, is determined by state transition. The state transition is a function of present state and present input, which produces the next state. The function is represented as δ.

Output relation: Like state transition for state there is a relation for output. Output depends either on present state and present input or present state only depending on type of machine.

Q. Define finite automata. Why it is called finite?

Ans. Finite automata (Singular: automaton) are the machine format of regular expression, which is the language format of type 3 grammar. A finite automata is defined as $M = \{Q, \Sigma, \delta, q_0, F\}$.
Where Q: Finite non-empty set of states.

Σ : Finite non-empty set of input symbols.
δ : Transitional function.
q_0: Beginning state.
F : Finite non-empty set of final states.

Finite automata are a type of finite state machines. It has finite number of states. Finite automata can be thought of a finite state machine without output.

Q. Describe the graphical and tabular representation of finite automata.

Ans. Finite automata can be represented in two ways. (a) Graphical and (b) Tabular.

In graphical representation, a state is represented as (q)

A beginning state is represented as → (q)

A final state is represented as ((q))

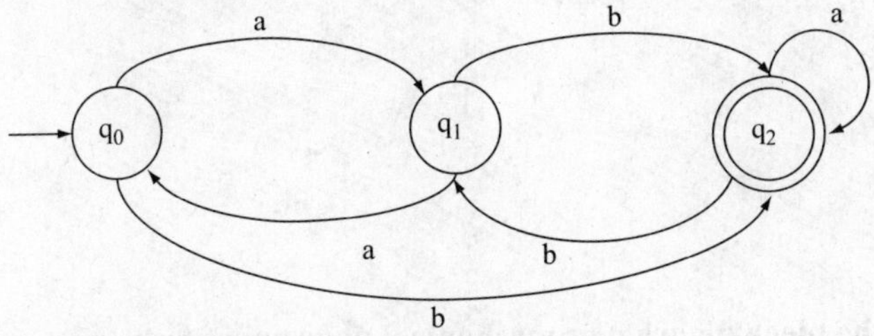

Here a finite automata is represented in graphical format.

Here,

$Q : \{q_0, q_1, q_2\}$
$\Sigma : \{a, b\}$
$\delta : \delta(q_0, a) \rightarrow q_1$

$\delta(q_0, b) \rightarrow q_2$
$\delta(q_1, a) \rightarrow q_0$
$\delta(q_1, b) \rightarrow q_2$
$\delta(q_2, a) \rightarrow q_2$
$\delta(q_2, b) \rightarrow q_1$

$q_0 : \{q_0\}$
$F : \{q_2\}$.

In tabular format a state is represented by the name of the state.
Beginning state is represented as: $\rightarrow q_n$

Final state is represented as: $\textcircled{q_n}$

For the previous finite automata, the tabular format will be

Present State	Next State	
	$a=0$	$a=1$
$\rightarrow q_0$	q_1	q_2
q_1	q_2	q_0
$\textcircled{q_2}$	q_2	q_1

Here

Q: $\{q_0, q_1, q_2\}$

Σ: $\{a, b\}$

δ: $\delta(q_0, a) \rightarrow q_1$

$\delta(q_0, b) \rightarrow q_2$

$\delta(q_1, a) \rightarrow q_0$

$\delta(q_1, b) \rightarrow q_2$

$\delta(q_2, a) \rightarrow q_2$

$\delta(q_2, b) \rightarrow q_1$

q_0: $\{q_0\}$

F: $\{q_2\}$

Q. Describe the block diagram or mechanical diagram of finite automaton. Describe each of the components.

Ans.

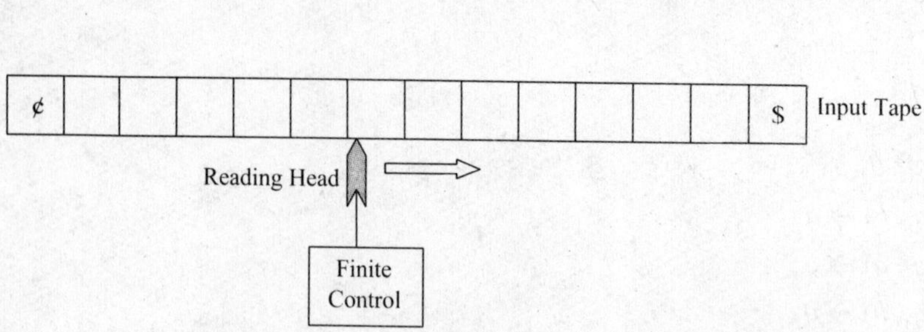

Input tape: Input tape contains the input symbol. It is divided into several squares, which contain single character of the input alphabet. Both left and right end of the input tape contain end markers. Between two end markers the input string is placed. This string is needed to be processed from left to right.

Reading Head: The head scans each square in the input tape and reads the input from the tape. The head can move from left to right or right to Left. But most of the cases the head moves from left to right. For two way finite automata and Turing machine the head can move in both directions.

Finite Control: Finite control can be considered as a control unit of a finite automaton. An automaton always resides in a state. The reading head scans the input from the input tape and sends it to finite control. In this finite control, it is decided that 'the machine is in this state and it is getting this input, so it will go to this state'. The state transition relations are written in this finite control.

3.2 TRANSITIONAL SYSTEM

Q. Define transitional system. Mention the properties of transitional functions.

Ans. A transitional system (sometimes called transitional graph) is a finite directed graph in which each node (or vertex) represents a state and the directed arc indicates the transition of the state. The label of the arc indicates input or output or both. A transitional function has two properties.

Property I: $\delta(q, \Lambda) \rightarrow q$.

It means if input is given null for a state, the machine remains in the same state.

Property II: For all string X and input symbol $a \in \Sigma$,

$$\delta(q, Xa) \rightarrow \delta[\delta(q, X), a],$$
$$\delta(q, aX) \rightarrow \delta[\delta(q, a), X].$$

Q. What are the conditions for declaring a string accepted by a finite automaton?

Ans. There are two conditions for declaring a String accepted by a finite automaton. The conditions are:

Condition I: The string must be totally traversed.
Conditions II: The machine must come to a final state.

In short it can be said that if $\delta(q_0, W) = q_n$, where W is the string given as input to the FA, q_0 is the beginning state and q_n belongs to the set of Final states, then the string W can be said accepted by the FA.

If these two conditions are fulfilled then we can declare a string accepted by a finite automaton.

If any of the conditions is failed to be fulfilled then we can declare a string is not accepted by a finite automaton.

Q. Check whether the string 011001 is accepted or not by the FA given below.

State	Input	
	0	1
$\rightarrow q_0$	q_0	q_1
q_1	q_2	q_3
q_2	q_0	q_3
(q_3)	q_1	q

Ans. For the given FA $Q = \{q_0, q_1, q_2, q_3\}$, $\Sigma = \{0, 1\}$, Beginning State is q_0 and final state is q_3 The transitional functions are given in the table.

For checking whether a string is accepted by a FA or not we assume that the input string is given input in the beginning state q_0. However, single input is given in each of the clock pulses. Therefore, at first the left most character is given input to the beginning state. From the transitional function given in the table the next state is determined. The next character of the input string is treated as input to the state just achieved. And it will process similarly till the string is finished or such a condition is arrived so that there is no transitional function mentioned in the table.

If the string is finished and the state achieved is final state then the string will be declared accepted by the machine. If it does not happen then the string will be declared not accepted.

$\delta(q_0, 011001) \rightarrow \delta(q_0, 11001)$
$\rightarrow \delta(q_1, 1001)$
$\rightarrow \delta(q_3, 001)$
$\rightarrow \delta(q_1, 01)$
$\rightarrow \delta(q_2, 1)$
$\rightarrow q_3$

q_3 is the final state of the FA. Therefore the two conditions for acceptability of a string by a FA are fulfilled. Hence the string 011001 is accepted by the given finite automata.

Q. Test whether the strings 010010, 01010 are accepted by the finite automata given below or not.

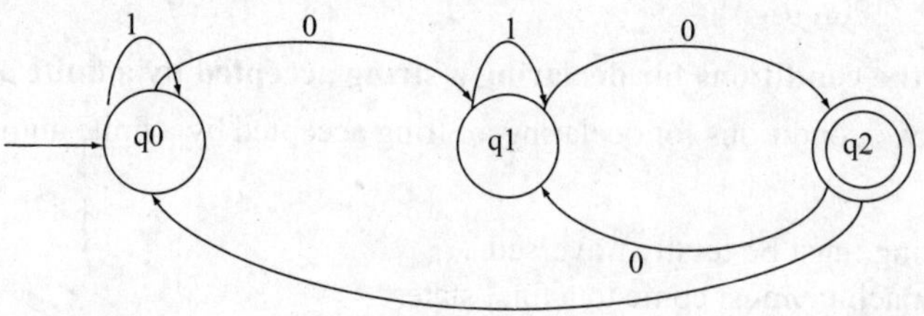

Ans.

$\delta(q_0, 010010) \rightarrow \delta(q_1, 10010)$
$\rightarrow \delta(q_1, 0010)$
$\rightarrow \delta(q_2, 010)$
$\rightarrow \delta(q_1, 10)$
$\rightarrow \delta(q_1, 0)$
$\rightarrow q_2$

q_2 is the final state of the FA. Hence the string 010010 is accepted by the FA.

$\delta(q_0, 01010) \rightarrow (q_1, 1010)$
$\rightarrow (q_1, 010)$
$\rightarrow (q_2, 10)$
$\rightarrow (q_0, 0)$
$\rightarrow q_1$

The q_1 is not final state of the FA. The String is finished. But the machine has not come to the final state. Hence the string is not accepted by the FA.

3.3 DETERMINISTIC FINITE AUTOMATA AND NON-DETERMINISTIC FINITE AUTOMATA

Q. Define deterministic finite automata (DFA) and non-deterministic finite automata (NDFA). Why are they called deterministic and non-deterministic, respectively?

Ans. Deterministic finite automata (DFA) is a finite automata where for all cases for a single input given to a single state the machine goes to a single state, i.e. all the moves of the machine can be uniquely determined by the present state and present input symbol.

A DFA can be represented as

$$M_{\text{DFA}} = \{Q, \Sigma, \delta, q_0, F\}.$$

Where δ is a transitional function mapping $Q \times \Sigma \rightarrow Q$, where $|Q| = 1$.

Non-deterministic finite automata or NDFA (NFA) is a finite automata where for some cases for a single input given to a single state the machine goes to more than one states, i.e. some the moves of the machine cannot be uniquely determined by the present state and present input symbol.

$$M_{\text{NFA}} = \{Q, \Sigma, \delta, q_0, F\}.$$

Where δ is a transitional function mapping $Q \times \Sigma \rightarrow 2^Q$ 2^Q is the power set of Q.
(Power set means set of all subsets of the set. For a set with n number of elements number of subsets or power set is 2^n. For the set {1,2,3}, the subsets are {}, {1}, {2}, {3}, {1,2}, {2.3}, {1,3}, {1,2,3}. Eight in total i.e. 2^3.)

Example:

PS	NS	
	0	1
$\rightarrow q_0$	q_0, q_1	q_2
q_1	q_2	q_1
(q_2)	q_1	q_2

Here for the state q_0 for input 0 it can to q_0 or q_1. Hence it is an example of NFA.

Q. Test whether the string '00101' is accepted by the following finite automata or not.

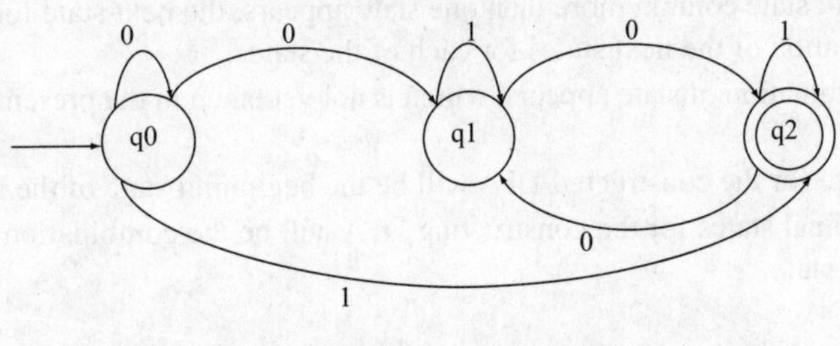

Ans. In the previous given FA, we are seeing that from q_0 for input 0 it can go to q_0 and q_1. That is for q_0 for input 0 there are two paths. Let draw a transaction diagram to clarify:

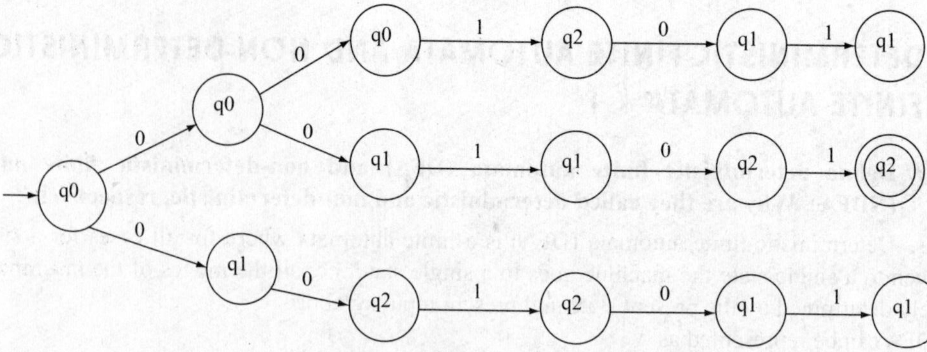

In the transaction diagram from q_0 for input string 00101 we are getting three paths. For the string 00101 the last state we are getting as q_1, q_2, q_1. Among them q_2 is the final state. That is for the string 00101 from q_0 we can reach to final state. Hence the string 00101 is accepted by the FA.

However, if someone follow path 1 and path 3, it will not be possible to reach to the final state. Then it can be declared that the string not accepted by the FA. That means it depends on the path which is being followed by the FA.

A String $w \in \Sigma^*$ is accepted by a NFA if $\delta(q_0, w)$ contains some final state.

Therefore, the string 00101 is accepted by the FA.

Q. Why do we need to convert a NFA to a DFA?

Ans. For a DFA, δ is a transitional function mapping $Q \times \Sigma \rightarrow Q$, where $|Q| = 1$.

For a NFA δ is a transitional function mapping $Q \times \Sigma \rightarrow 2^Q$, 2^Q is the power set of Q.

For a NFA for a single input given to a single state the machine can go to more than one state. Hence for a NFA it will be hard to decide for a string to be accepted by the NFA or not.

If a NFA can be converted to a DFA then this type of problem will not arise.

Implies that we have to convert $Q \times \Sigma \rightarrow 2^Q$ to $Q' \times \Sigma \rightarrow Q'$, where Q is the finite set of states for a NFA and Q' is the set of states for the converted DFA.

Q. What is the process of converting a NFA to a DFA?

Ans.

(i) Start from the beginning state of the NFA. Consider the state within [ ].

(ii) Place the next states for the beginning state for the given inputs. Put them also in [ ].

(iii) If any new combination of state appears, which is not yet taken in present state column; take that combination of state in the present state column.

(iv) If in the present state column more than one state appears, the next state for that combination will be the combination of the next states for each of the states.

(v) If no new combination of state appears, which is not yet taken in the present state column, stop the process.

(vi) Beginning state for the constructed DFA will be the beginning state of the NFA.

(vii) Final state or final states for the constructing DFA will be the combination of states containing at least one final state.

Q. Construct DFA from the given NFA.

PS	NS	
	0	1
$\rightarrow q_0$	q_0, q_1	q_2
q_1	q_2	q_1
(q_2)	q_1	q_2

Solve:

PS	NS	
	0	1
$[q_0]$	$[q_0, q_1]$	$[q_2]$
$[q_0, q_1]$	$[q_0, q_1, q_2]$	$[q_1, q_2]$
$[q_1, q_2]$	$[q_1, q_2]$	$[q_1, q_2]$
$[q_0, q_1, q_2]$	$[q_0, q_1, q_2]$	$[q_1, q_2]$
$[q_2]$	$[q_1]$	$[q_2]$
$[q_1]$	$[q_2]$	$[q_1]$

Lets replace $[q_0]$ as A, $[q_0, q_1]$ as B, $[q_1, q_2]$ as C, $[q_0, q_1, q_2]$ as D, $[q_2]$ as E and, $[q_1]$ as F

Then the constructed finite automata will be

PS	NS	
	0	1
A	B	E
B	D	C
C	C	C
D	D	C
E	F	E
F	E	F

In the finite automata, we see that in a single state, for a single input, the machine can go to only one state. Therefore, it is a DFA.

The beginning state is $[q_0]$ i.e. A. The final states are $[q_1, q_2]$ i.e. C, $[q_0, q_1, q_2]$ i.e. D, and $[q_2]$ i.e. E.

The transaction diagram for the DFA will be as follows:

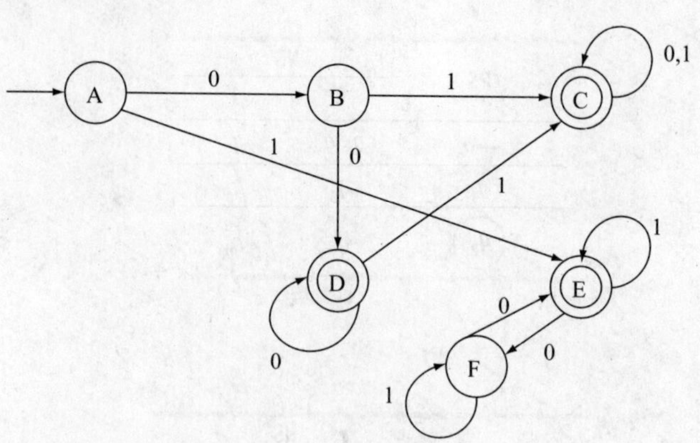

Q. Construct DFA from the given NFA.

Present Stage	Next Stage	
	0	1
$\rightarrow q_0$	q_0, q_1	q_0
q_1	q_2	q_1
q_2	q_3	q_3
(q_3)	–	q_2

Solve:

PS	NS	
	0	1
$[q_0]$	$[q_0, q_1]$	$[q_0]$
$[q_0, q_1]$	$[q_0, q_1, q_2]$	$[q_0, q_1]$
$[q_0, q_1, q_2]$	$[q_0, q_1, q_2, q_3]$	$[q_0, q_1, q_3]$
$[q_0, q_1, q_3]$	$[q_0, q_1, q_2]$	$[q_0, q_1, q_2]$
$[q_0, q_1, q_2, q_3]$	$[q_0, q_1, q_2, q_3]$	$[q_0, q_1, q_2, q_3]$

Let replace $[q_0]$ as A, $[q_0, q_1]$ as B, $[q_0, q_1, q_2]$ as C, $[q_0, q_1, q_3]$ as D, $[q_0, q_1, q_2, q_3]$ as E.

PS	NS 0	NS 1
→A	B	A
B	C	B
C	E	D
(D)	C	C
(E)	E	E

In the finite automata, we see that in a single state, for a single input, the machine can go to only one state. Hence it is a DFA.

Beginning state is A. Final state is D and E.

The transaction diagram for the DFA will be as follows.

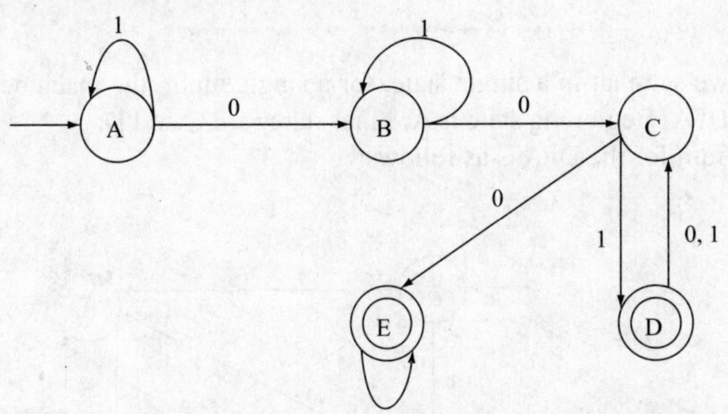

Q. Construct equivalent DFA for the given NFA.

Present Stage	Next Stage a	Next Stage b
$\rightarrow q_0$	q_0, q_1	q_2
q_1	q_0	q_1
(q_2)	–	q_0, q_1

Ans.

PS	NS a	NS b
$[q_0]$	$[q_0, q_1]$	$[q_2]$
$[q_0, q_1]$	$[q_0, q_1]$	$[q_1, q_2]$
$[q_1, q_2]$	$[q_0]$	$[q_0, q_1]$
$[q_2]$	[–]	$[q_0, q_1]$
[–]	[–]	[–]

Here for the state q_2 for input 'a' in the given NFA no state was mentioned. Therefore, we have taken it a new state [–], when converting from NFA to DFA. For the new state [–] as no next state was mentioned we have taken the same state [–] for both the inputs a and b.

(Soon we shall learn that these types of states are called dead state)

Let replace $[q_0]$ by A, $[q_0, q_1]$ by B, $[q_1, q_2]$ by C, $[q_2]$ by D, and [–] by E. The tabular representation will become:

PS	NS	
	a	*B*
A	B	D
B	B	C
C	A	B
D	E	B
E	E	E

In the finite automata, we see that in a single state, for a single input, the machine can go to only one state. Therefore, it is a DFA. Beginning state is A; Final states are C and D.

The transaction diagram for the DFA is as follows:

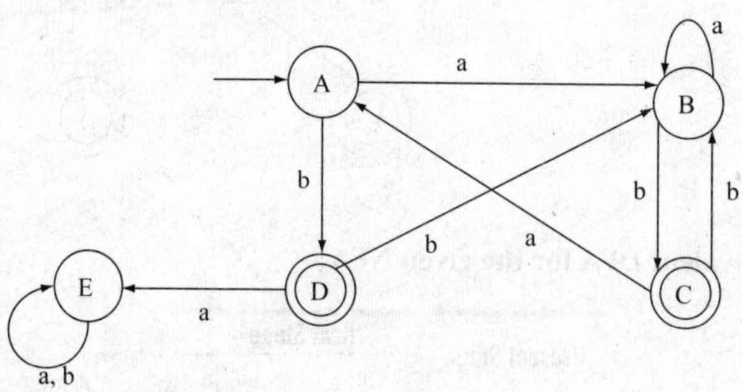

3.4 NFA WITH NULL MOVE

Q. What do you mean by NFA with ε moves? Give an example. Why is it called NFA?

Ans. If any finite automata contains any ε (null) move or transaction then that finite automata is called NFA with ε moves. As an example

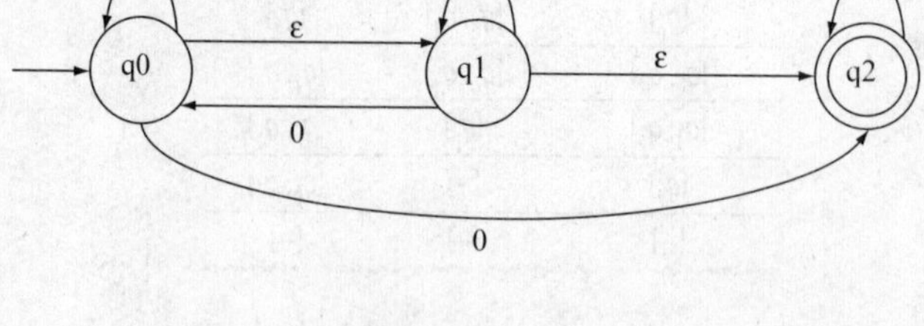

The previous finite automata contain two null moves. Hence the previous FA is NFA with null move. From the definition of NFA we know for a NFA from a single state, for a single input the machine can go to more than one state, i.e. $Q \times \Sigma \rightarrow 2^Q$, where 2^Q is the power set of **Q**.

From a state by getting ε input the machine is confined into that state. A finite automata with null move must contain at least one ε move. For this type of finite automata for input ε the machine can go to more than one states. (One is that same state and another state is the ε-transaction next state). Hence a finite automata with ε move can be called as a NFA.

For the previous finite automata

$$\delta(q_0, \varepsilon) \rightarrow q_0 \text{ and } \delta(q_0, \varepsilon) \rightarrow q_1$$
$$\delta(q_1, \varepsilon) \rightarrow q_1 \text{ and } \delta(q_1, \varepsilon) \rightarrow q_2$$

A NFA with ε move can be defined as

$$M_{\text{NFA null}} = \{Q, \Sigma, \delta, q_0, F\}.$$

Where Σ : Set of input alphabets including ε and
δ is a transitional function mapping $Q \times \Sigma \rightarrow 2^Q$ $\quad 2^Q$ is the power set of Q.

Q. What is the usefulness of NFA with ϵ move? Explain with an example.

Ans. If we want to construct finite automata that accepts a language, sometimes it becomes very difficult or seems to be impossible to construct direct NFA or DFA. But if we use NFA with ϵ moves, then the transitional diagram can be constructed and described easily.

Example: Lets assume, we are to construct a DFA that accepts any combinations of string of *a*, *b*, *c*, i.e. the string can start with *a* or *b* or *c*. After any symbol any of the symbols can come in any combination. The DFA for this:

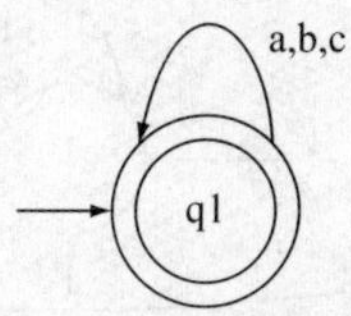

However, it is not clearly understandable how any combination of *a*, *b*, *c* can appear. However, if we represent a transitional diagram as follow:

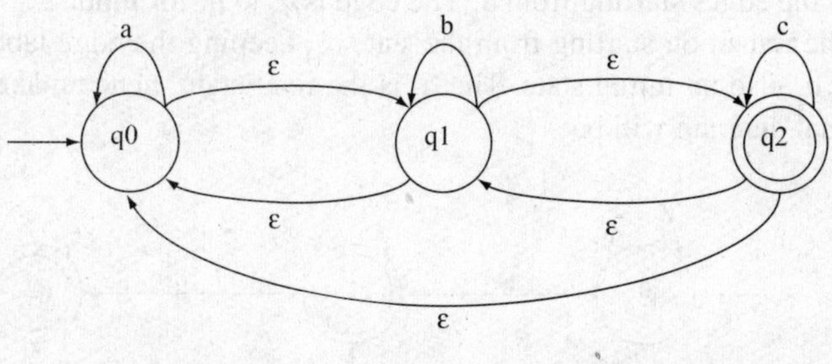

Then it is clearly understandable that the string can start with *a* or *b* or *c*, and for the null transitions from any state we can move to any other state with no input. Therefore, if *c* comes after '*a*', we can go from q_0 to q_2 easily with no input. Same thing can occur for all the other states.]

Q. How to convert a NFA with ε moves to an equivalent DFA?

Ans. Let in the NFA we want to remove the ϵ move, exists between states S_1 and S_2. This can be removed in the following way

(i) Find all the edges [transitions] those start from the state S_2.
(ii) Duplicate all these transitions starting from the state S_1, keeping the edge label same.
(iii) If S_1 is the initial state, also make S_2 as initial state.
(iv) If S_2 is the final state, also make S_1 as the final state.

Q. Convert the following NFA with null move to an equivalent DFA.

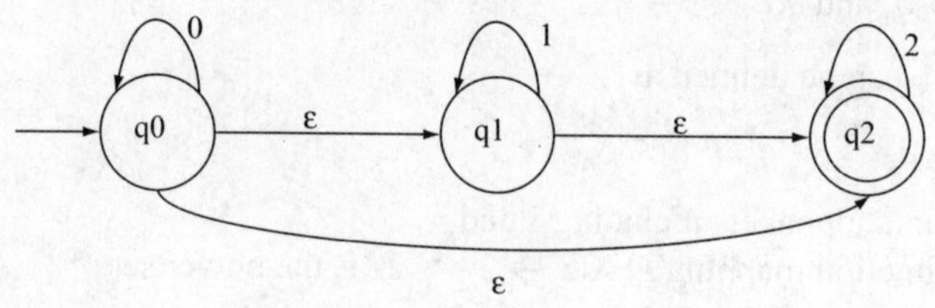

Ans. There are three null moves existing in the previous transitional diagram. The transitions are (i) From q_0 to q_1 (ii) From q_1 to q_2 (iii) From q_0 to q_2. We have to remove these null transitions step by step.

Step I: (a) Between state q_0 and q_1, there is a null move. If we want to remove that null transition, we have to find all the edges starting from q_1.The edges are q_1 to q_1 for input 1, and q_1 to q_2 for input **ϵ**.

(b) Duplicate all these transitions starting from the state q_0, keeping the edge label same. The q_0 is initial state, hence make q_1 also an initial state. The modified transitional diagram will be

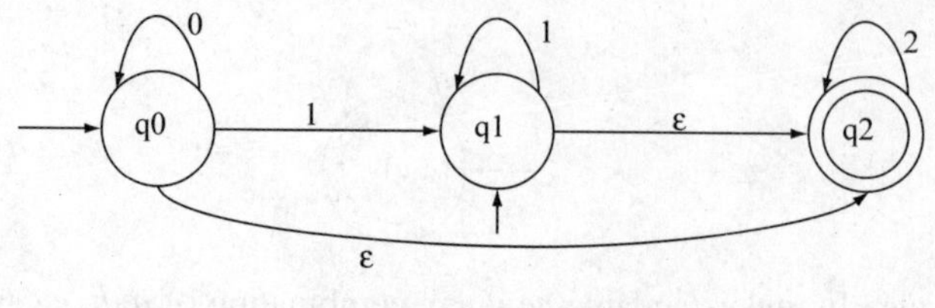

Step II: (a) Between q_1 and q_2 there is a null transaction. If we want to remove that null transition, we have to find all the edges starting from q_2.The edge is q_2 to q_2 for input 2.

(b) Duplicate the transition starting from the state q_1, keeping the edge label same. The q_1 is initial state, hence make q_2 also an initial state. The q_2 is the final state, hence make q_1 also final state. The modified transitional diagram will be

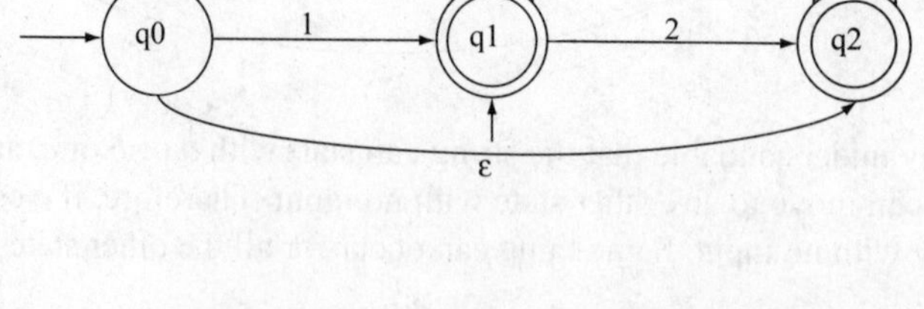

Step III: (a) Between q_0 and q_2 there is a null transaction. If we want to remove that null transition, we have to find all the edges starting from q_2. The edge is q_2 to q_2 for input 2.

(b) Duplicate the transition starting from the state q_0, keeping the edge label same. The q_0 is initial state, hence make q_2 also an initial state. The q_2 is the final state, hence make q_0 also final state. The nodified transitional diagram:

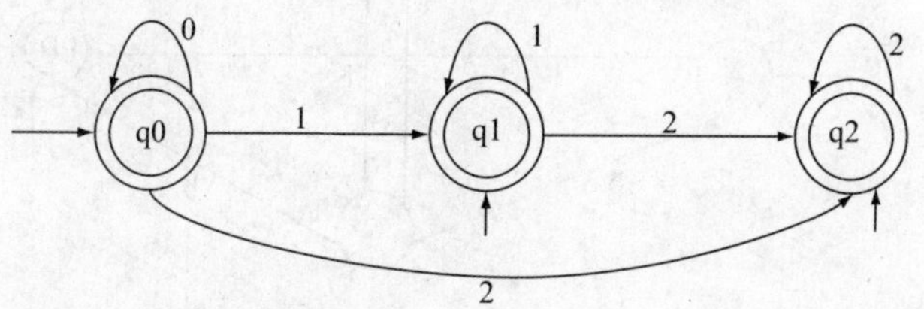

his the equivalent DFA obtained from the NFA with null transaction.

Q. Convert the following NFA with null move to an equivalent DFA.

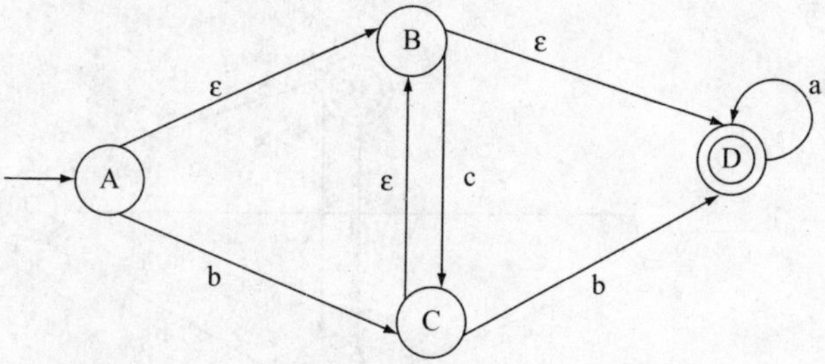

Ans. In the given NFA with ϵ move, there are three ϵ transitions: from A to B, from B to D, and from to C. We will remove the three ϵ transitions step by step.

Step I: There is a ϵ transition from A to B. If we want to remove that ϵ transition, we have to find all e edges starting from B. The edges are B to C for input c and B to D for input ϵ.

Duplicate the transition starting from the state A, keeping the edge label same. A is initial state, so ake B also an initial state. The modified transaction diagram:

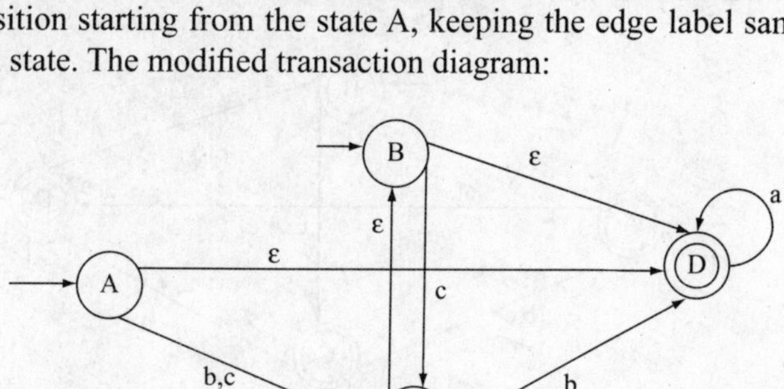

Step II: Again there are three ϵ transactions in the NFA. These are from A to D, from B to D and om C to B. Lets remove the ϵ transaction from B to D. The edge starting from D is D to D for input a. uplicate the transition starting from the state B, keeping the edge label same. As B is the initial state

D will be also initial state. As D is the final state so B will be also final state. The modified transac diagram will be

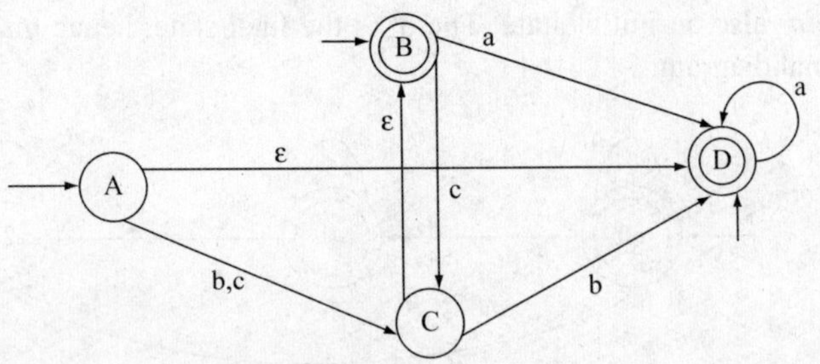

Step III: Now we are going to remove the ϵ transaction from A to D. The edge starting from D to D for input *a*. Duplicate the transition starting from the state A, keeping the edge label same. As the initial state D will be also initial state. As D is the final state so A will be also final state. The m fied transaction diagram will be

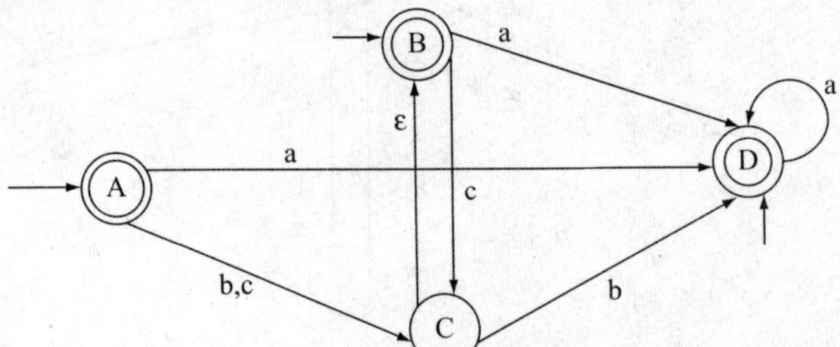

Step IV: There is only one *ϵ* transaction from C to B. To remove this, find the edges starting fro There are two, From B to D for input a and from B to C for input c. Start these edges from C. B is state so make C as final state. The modified transitional diagram will be.

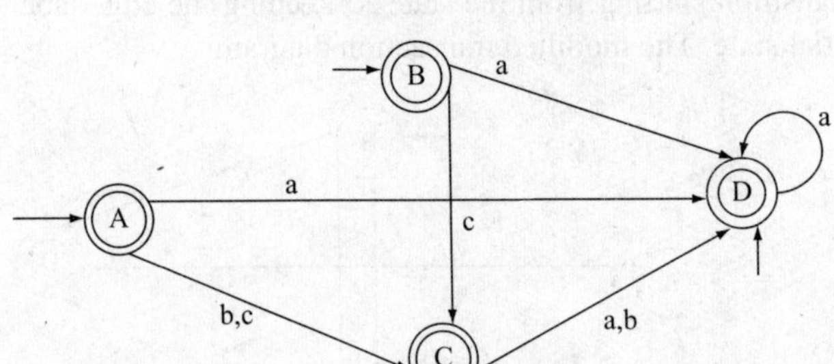

This the equivalent DFA obtained from the NFA with null transaction.

5 DEAD STATE

Q. Define dead state. What is the usefulness of Dead state? Explain with an example.

Ans. Dead state is a state where the control can enter and confined till the input ended, but no way ome out from that state.

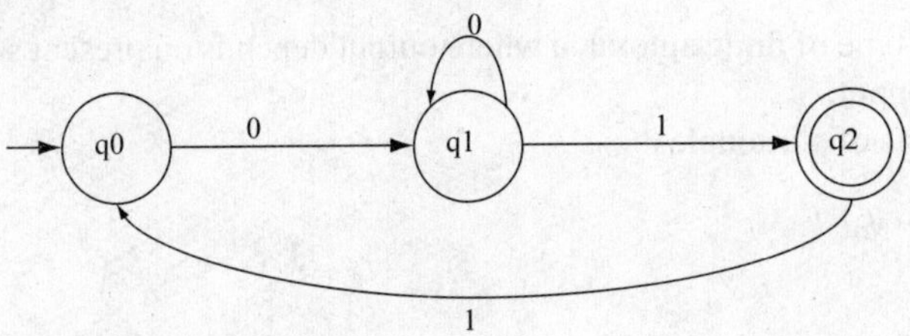

For example, for the previous finite automata from q_0 for input 0 there is a path to go to q_1. But there o path mentioned from q_0 for input 1. Same thing happens for q_2 also for input 0. Now let a string is given to test the acceptability of the string by the finite automata.

According to the condition of the acceptability, the first condition i.e. the string will be totally trased is not fulfilled. Obviously the second condition is not fulfilled.

We have to decide that the string is not accepted by the finite automata without traversing the string totally! For making the string totally traversed we have to include an extra state, let q_f, where the control will from the states for which there is only one path for one input. In the state q_f for the inputs there will self loop. Here q_f is the dead state.

By including dead state the finite automata will become

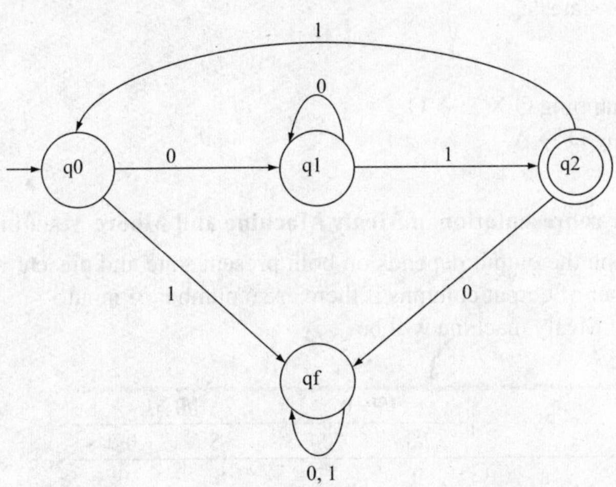

Now if we test for the acceptability of 101, the transitions are as follows

$$\delta(q_0, 101) \rightarrow \delta(\delta(q_0, 1), 01) \rightarrow \delta(\delta(q_f, 0), 1) \rightarrow \delta(q_f, 1) \rightarrow q_f.$$

String is totally traversed and reached to q_f. q_f is not the final state, so the string is not accepted by the FA. In the case we have seen that the string is finished [dead] by confined into q_f. For this reason qf is ed dead state.

3.6 FINITE AUTOMATA WITH OUTPUT

Q. Define Mealy Machine and Moore Machine.

Ans. Mealy Machine and Moore Machine are example of finite automata with outputs.

Mealy machine is one type of finite automata where output depends on present state and present input.

Moore machine is one type of finite automata where output depends on present state only but output is independent of present input.

Mealy Machine consists of six-touples:

$$M = (Q, \Sigma, \Delta, \delta, \lambda, q_0)$$

where

Q : Finite non-empty set of states;
Σ : Set of input alphabets.
Δ : Set of output alphabets.
δ : Transitional function mapping $Q \times \Sigma \rightarrow Q$
λ : Output function mapping $Q \times \Sigma \rightarrow \Delta$
q_0: Beginning state.

Moore Machine consists of six-touples

$$M = (Q, \Sigma, \Delta, \delta, \lambda, q_0)$$

where

Q : Finite non-empty set of states;
Σ : Set of input alphabets.
Δ : Set of output alphabets.
δ : Transitional function mapping $Q \times \Sigma \rightarrow Q$
λ : Output function mapping $Q \rightarrow \Delta$
q_0: Beginning state.

Q. Describe tabular representation of Mealy Machine and Moore Machine.

Ans. For Mealy machine the output depends on both present state and present input. So for mealy machine there will *n* number of output columns if there are n number of input.

So the tabular format of Mealy machine will be

PS	I/P=0		I/P=1	
	NS	O/P	NS	O/P
A	D	0	B	0
B	A	1	D	0
C	B	1	A	1
D	D	1	C	0

For Moore machine the output depends on present state only. As in a machine for present state there is only one Present state column, so there will be only one output column.

The tabular format of Moore machine will be.

PS	NS		O/P
	I/P=0	I/P=1	
A	A	B	0
B	A	C	0
C	A	C	1

Q. Describe the transitional diagram representation of Mealy machine and Moore Machine.

Ans. Mealy machine is one type of finite automata with output. Hence the transitional diagram will be like finite automata but output will be mentioned. For a Mealy Machine the output depends on present state and present input. Hence, for a Mealy machine the transitional arc will be labeled with both input and output.

Example:

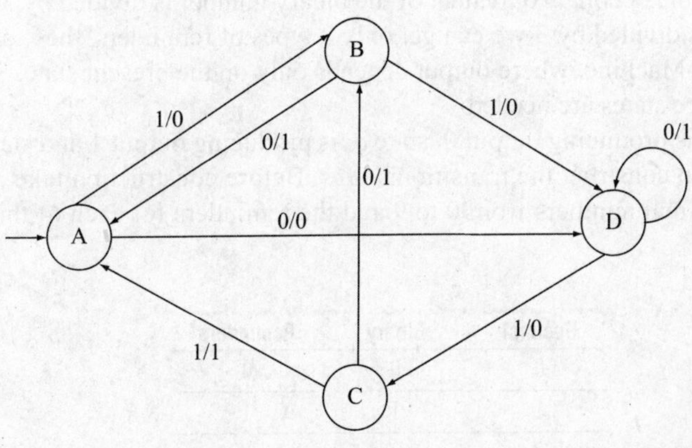

Output of Moore machine depends only on the present state. For Moore machine the states will be labeled with state name and output.

Example:

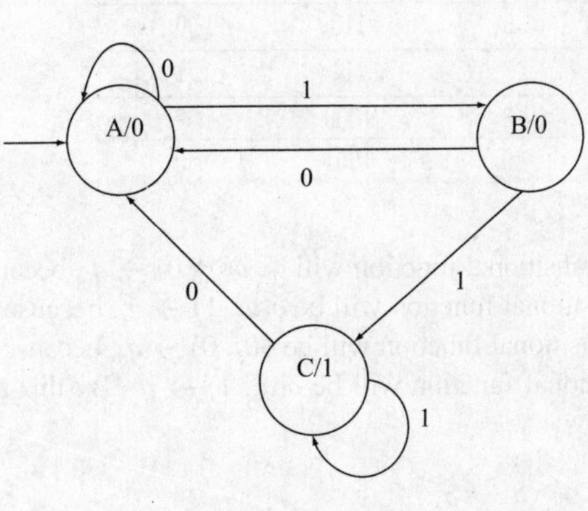

Q. Design a Mealy Machine to get complement of binary number.

Ans. For input 0 the machine will give output 1 and for input 1 the machine will give output 0. The Mealy machine:

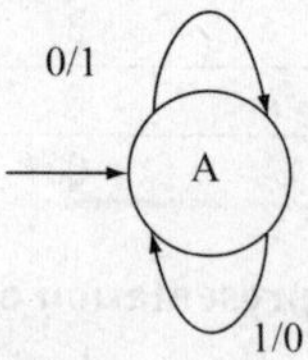

Q. Design a Moore Machine which will determine the residue mod-3 for each binary string treated as binary integer.

Ans. Binary string consists of two types of alphabet 0 and 1. Binary integer means the decimal equivalent of a binary string as integer numbers are taken as decimal. Residue mod-3 means the reminder that we get when the decimal equivalent of the binary number is divided by 3.

If a decimal number is divided by 3 we can get only 3 types of reminders, these are 0 or 1 or 2. We are constructing a Moore Machine, where output depends only on the present state. So, for three types of reminders (output) three states are needed.

Lets consider state q_0 is producing output 0, state q_1 is producing output 1 and state q_2 is producing output 2. Now we need to construct the transitional arcs. Before construction take a table containing binary equivalent of decimal numbers from 0 to 9 and the reminders for each of them, when divided by 3.

Decimal	Binary	Reminders
0	0	0
1	1	1
2	10	2
3	11	0
4	100	1
5	101	2
6	110	0
7	111	1
8	1000	2
9	1001	0

Input 0, output is 0. Therefore, transitional function will be $\delta(q_0, 0) \rightarrow q_0$, because q_0 state produce output 0. Input 1, output 1, Hence, transitional function will be $\delta(q_0, 1) \rightarrow q_1$, because q_1 state produce output 1. Input 10, output is 2. Hence, transitional function will be $\delta(q_1,0) \rightarrow q_2$, because q_2 state produce output 2. Input 11, output is 0. So, transitional function will be $\delta(q_1, 1) \rightarrow q_0$. By this process all the transitional functions can be produced.

Therefore, the Moore machine:

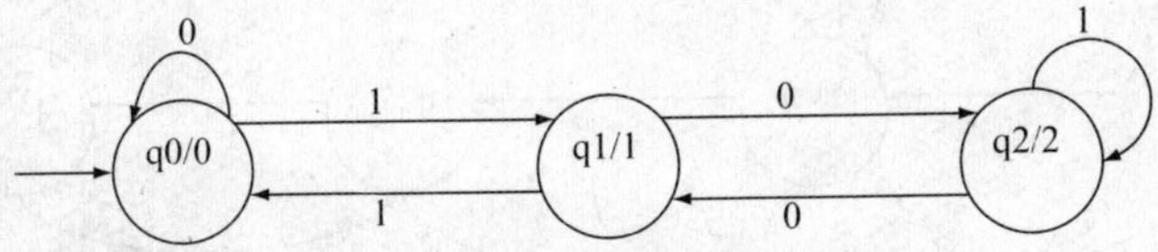

Q. Design a Mealy Machine which will determine the residue mod-3 for each binary string treated as binary integer.

Ans. The machine is a Mealy machine, so outputs depend on present state and present input.

For input 0, output is 0. Transitional function will be $\delta(q_0, 0) \rightarrow q_0$ and output function λ is $q_0 X\, 0 \rightarrow 0$. For input 1, output 1. Transitional function will be $\delta(q_0, 1) \rightarrow q_1$ and output function λ is $q_0 X\, 1 \rightarrow 1$. For input 10, output is 2. So, transitional function will be $\delta(q_1,0) \rightarrow q_2$, and output function λ is $q_1 X\, 0 \rightarrow 2$. For input 11, output is 0. Hence, transitional function will be $\delta(q_1, 1) \rightarrow q_0$, and output function λ will be $q_1 X\, 0 \rightarrow 0$. By this process all the transitional functions will be constructed. The Mealy machine for this is

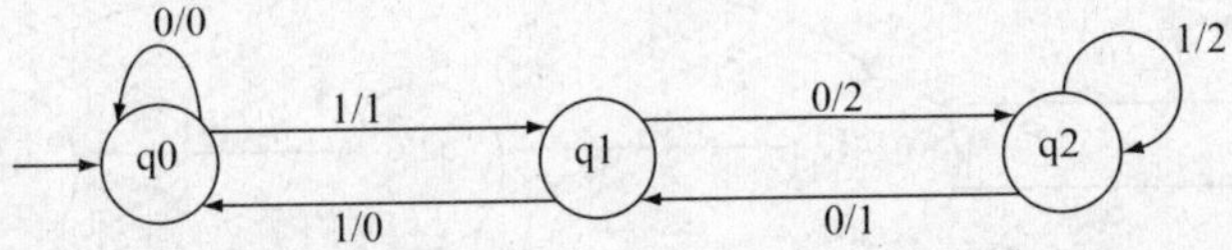

Q. Design a Moore machine which counts the occurrence of substring *aba* in a given input string.

Ans. It is one type of sequence detector. When the string *aba* will occur as a substring then output 1 will produced. For all the other cases output 0 will be produced (Overlapping sequences are also accepted).

We have to design a Moore machine, i.e. output depends only on the present state. For a string length of 3 we need four states if from a state with single input the machine goes to another new state. Let name the states as q_0, q_1, q_2, q_3. Except q_3 all the states produce output 0. In state q_0, we can get two types of input *a* or *b*. If we get '*a*' then there is a chance to get '*aba*'. So it will move forward to q_1. If we get '*b*' then there is no chance to get '*aba*' so it will confine to the same state. In q_1, again two types of input can occur, '*a*' and '*b*'. If we get '*a*', then by considering this '*a*' there is a chance to get '*aba*'. So it will confine to the same state. If we get *b* then we are two step forward to get '*aba*'. Hence the machine will move forward to state q_2. In q_2 if we get '*b*' then there is no chance to get '*aba*' except starting from the beginning. Hence it will go to q_0. If we get '*a*', we have got the string *aba*. Machine will go to state q_3. In q_3 if we get '*a*', then again there is a chance to get '*aba*'. From q_0, by getting '*a*' the machine has moved forward to q_1. So from q_2 by getting '*a*' the machine will go to q_1. If we get '*b*' then by considering the previous '*a*' again there is a chance to get '*aba*', so the machine will move to state 'q_2'.

From the above discussions the transitional functions can easily be derived. As it is Moore machine the outputs are included with the state (Output depends only on the present state not on the present input) so there is no need to derive the output functions. The Moore machine for the above problem:

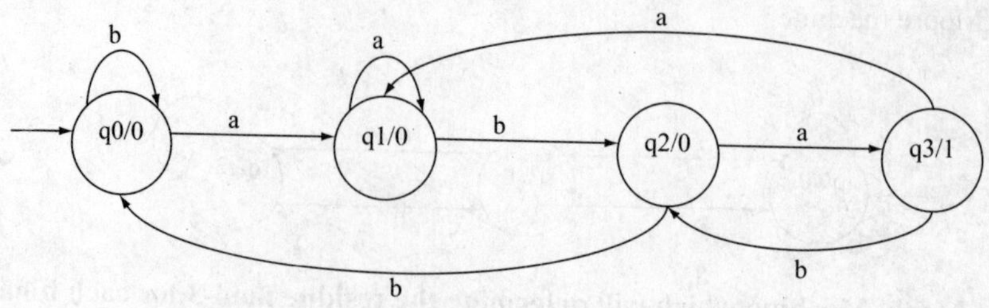

Q. Design a Mealy machine which counts the occurrence of substring *aab* in a given input string.

The machine will be Mealy machine, i.e. output depends on the present state and present input. (Discussions will be like previous)

The machine:

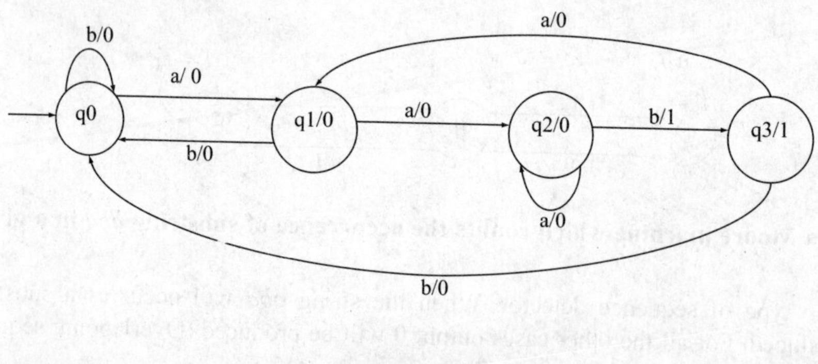

3.7 CONVERSION OF MOORE TO MEALY MACHINE BY TABULAR FORMAT

Q. What is the procedure for converting a Moore Machine to a Mealy machine?

Ans.

(i) Draw the tabular format of Mealy machine.

(ii) Put the present states of the Moore Machine in the present state column of Constructing Mealy Machine.

(iii) Put the next states of Moore machine for corresponding present states and input combination, in the next state columns of the constructing Mealy Machine for the same present states and input combination.

(iv) For the output, look into the present state column and output column of the Moore Machine. The output for Q_{Next} (Next state for present state Q_{Present} and input I/P of the constructing Mealy Machine) will be the output for that state (Q_{Next}) as a present state in the given Moore Machine.

Q. Construct Mealy Machine equivalent to the given Moore Machine.

PS	NS I/P=0	NS I/P=1	O/P
$\rightarrow q_0$	q_3	q_1	0
q_1	q_1	q_2	1
q_2	q_2	q_3	0
q_3	q_3	q_3	0

Solve:

PS	I/P=0 NS	I/P=0 O/P	I/P=1 NS	I/P=1 O/P
$\rightarrow q_0$	q_3	0	q_1	1
q_1	q_1	1	q_2	0
q_2	q_2	0	q_3	0
q_3	q_3	0	q_3	0

In the Moore Machine, for q_1 as a present state the output is 1. So in the constructing Mealy Machine for q_1 as a next state the output will be 1.

In the Moore Machine, for q_2 as a present state the output is 0. Hence in the constructing Mealy Machine for q_2 as a next state the output will be 0.

Q. Construct Mealy Machine equivalent to the given Moore Machine.

PS	NS I/P=0	NS I/P=1	O/P
$\rightarrow q_0$	q_1	q_2	1
q_1	q_3	q_2	0
q_2	q_2	q_1	1
q_3	q_0	q_3	1

Solve:

PS	I/P=0 NS	I/P=0 O/P	I/P=1 NS	I/P=1 O/P
$\rightarrow q_0$	q_1	0	q_2	1
q_1	q_3	1	q_2	1
q_2	q_2	1	q_1	0
q_3	q_0	1	q_3	1

Q. Construct Mealy Machine equivalent to the given Moore Machine.

PS	NS		O/P
	I/P=0	I/P=1	
→q_0	q_1	q_0	0
q_1	q_1	q_2	0
q_2	q_3	q_0	0
q_3	q_1	q_2	1

Solve:

PS	I/P=0		I/P=1	
	NS	O/P	NS	O/P
q_0	q_1	0	q_0	0
q_1	q_1	0	q_2	0
q_2	q_3	1	q_0	0
q_3	q_1	0	q_2	0

3.8 CONVERSION OF MEALY TO MOORE MACHINE BY TABULAR FORMAT

Q. What is the procedure for converting a Mealy Machine to a Moore machine?

Ans.

(i) Draw the tabular format of Mealy Machine first.

(ii) Look into the Next State and Output columns of the given Mealy Machine.

(iii) If for same Next state in the Next state column, the output differs in the output column, break the state q_i into different number of states. The number is equal to the number of different outputs associated with q_i.

(iv) Put the states of the present state column in the new table. The states which are broken into number of different states, put the broken states in the place of those states.

(v) Change the next states in the next state columns according to the new set of states.

(vi) Put the output from the output column of the original Mealy Machine in the new machine also.

(vii) Draw the tabular format of Moore Machine.

(viii) Put the Present states and Next States from the constructed new Mealy machine to the constructed Moore machine.

(ix) For output look into the Next State and output column of the newly constructed Mealy Machine. For the state let q_i, as a next state in the new constructed Mealy Machine if output is 0 then for q_i as a present state in the constructing Moore Machine; the output will be 0.

(x) For Moore Machine the output depends only on the present state. This means from the beginning state for Λ input we can get an output. If the output is 1, the newly constructed Moore Machine can accept zero length string, which was not accepted by given Mealy machine. To make the Moore machine does not accept Λ string, we have to add an extra state q_b (new beginning state), whose state transactions will be identical with those of the existing beginning state but output is 0.

(For a Mealy machine with m number of states and n number of output, the Moore machine will be of n number of outputs but not more than $mn + 1$ number of states.)

Q. Convert the given Mealy Machine to an equivalent Moore Machine.

PS	I/P=0		I/P=1	
	NS	O/P	NS	O/P
$\rightarrow q_0$	q_0	1	q_1	0
q_1	q_3	1	q_3	1
q_2	q_1	1	q_2	1
q_3	q_2	0	q_0	1

Solve:

Look into the next state and output columns of the given Mealy Machine. For I/P 0 for q_1 as a next state output is 1. For I/P 1 for q_1 as a next state output is 0. Same thing happens for q_2 as a next state for input 0 and input 1. So the state q_1 will be broken as q_{10} and q_{11} and the state q_2 will be broken as q_{20} and q_{21} After breaking the modified Mealy Machine will be

PS	I/P=0		I/P=1	
	NS	O/P	NS	O/P
$\rightarrow q_0$	q_0	1	q_{10}	0
q_{10}	q_3	1	q_3	1
q_{11}	q_3	1	q_3	1
q_{20}	q_{11}	1	q_{21}	1
q_{21}	q_{11}	1	q_{21}	1
q_3	q_{20}	0	q_0	1

For present state q_0 for input 1 the next state will be q_{10}, because there is no q_1 in the modified Mealy Machine. It has been broken into q_{10} and q_{11} depending on the output 0 and 1, respectively. For present state q_0 for input 1 the output is 0. Hence the next state will be q_{10}. Same cases occur for the others also. For the broken states the next states and outputs will be same as the original, from where the broken states have come.

From this the Moore Machine will be

PS	NS		O/P
	IP=0	IP=1	
$\rightarrow q_0$	q_0	q_{10}	1
q_{10}	q_3	q_3	0
q_{11}	q_3	q_3	1
q_{20}	q_{11}	q_{21}	0
q_{21}	q_{11}	q_{21}	1
q_3	q_{20}	q_0	1

For Moore machine beginning state q_0 and the output is 1. That means with null length input (no input) we are getting an output 1. Therefore, the Moore machine accepts 0 length sequence (Because here output depends only on the present state] which is not acceptable for mealy machine. To overcome this situation we must add a new beginning state q_b with same transactions as q_0 but output 0. By including the new state the Moore Machine will be.

PS	NS		O/P
	IP=0	IP=1	
$\rightarrow q_b$	q_0	q_{10}	0
q_0	q_0	q_{10}	1
q_{10}	q_3	q_3	0
q_{11}	q_3	q_3	1
q_{20}	q_{11}	q_{21}	0
q_{21}	q_{11}	q_{21}	1
q_3	q_{20}	q_0	1

Q. Convert the given Mealy Machine to an equivalent Moore Machine.

PS	I/P=0		I/P=1	
	NS	O/P	NS	O/P
$\rightarrow q_0$	q_2	z_0	q_1	z_1
q_1	q_0	z_0	q_2	z_0
q_2	q_0	z_1	q_2	z_1

Solve:

For q_0 for input 0 the outputs differs. For q_2 for input 0 and 1 the output differs. Therefore the states will be broken as q_{00}, $q_{01,}$ and q_{20}, $q_{21.}$ According to the new states the modified mealy machine:

PS	I/P=0		I/P=1	
	NS	O/P	NS	O/P
$\rightarrow q_{00}$	q_{20}	z_0	q_1	z_1
q_{01}	q_{20}	z_0	q_1	z_1
q_1	q_{00}	z_0	q_{20}	z_0
q_{20}	q_{01}	z_1	q_{21}	z_1
q_{21}	q_{01}	z_1	q_{21}	z_1

From this modified mealy machine, the Moore machine will be

PS	I/P=0		O/P
	I/P=0	I/P=1	
→q_{00}	q_{20}	q_1	Z_0
q_{01}	q_{20}	q_1	Z_1
q_1	q_{00}	q_{20}	Z_1
q_{20}	q_{01}	q_{21}	Z_0
q_{21}	q_{01}	q_{21}	Z_1

Q. Convert the given Mealy Machine to an equivalent Moore Machine.

PS	I/P=0		I/P=1	
	NS	O/P	NS	O/P
→q_0	q_2	0	q_1	0
q_1	q_0	1	q_3	0
q_2	q_1	1	q_0	1
q_3	q_3	1	q_2	0

Ans. In the next state column of the given Mealy machine the output differs for q_1 and q_3 as next state. Hence the states will be divided as q_{10}, q_{11}, and q_{30}, q_{31}, respectively. After dividing the states the modified Mealy machine will be

PS	I/P=0		I/P=1	
	NS	O/P	NS	O/P
→q_0	q_2	0	q_{10}	0
q_{10}	q_0	1	q_{30}	0
q_{11}	q_0	1	q_{30}	0
q_2	q_{11}	1	q_0	1
q_{30}	q_{31}	1	q_2	0
q_{31}	q_{31}	1	q_2	0

In the next state column of the modified mealy machine q_0 as a next state output was 0. So for the constructing Moore Machine for present state q_0 output will be 0. Same for present state q_2 the output will be 0. For the divided states like $q_{10,}$ q_{11} there is no need to mention the output as they were divided according to the distinguished output. So the constructing Moore machine will be

PS	NS		O/P
	I/P=0	I/P=1	
$\rightarrow q_0$	q_2	q_{10}	1
q_{10}	q_0	q_{30}	0
q_{11}	q_0	q_{30}	1
q_2	q_{11}	q_0	0
q_{30}	q_{31}	q_2	0
q_{31}	q_{31}	q_2	1

To get rid of the problem of occurrence of null string, we need to include another state let q_a with same transactions as of q_0 but with output 0.

The modified final Moore machine equivalent to the given Mealy machine will be

PS	NS		O/P
	I/P=0	I/P=1	
$\rightarrow q_a$	q_2	q_{10}	0
q_0	q_2	q_{10}	1
q_{10}	q_0	q_{30}	0
q_{11}	q_0	q_{30}	1
q_2	q_{11}	q_0	0
q_{30}	q_{31}	q_2	0
q_{31}	q_{31}	q_2	1

3.9 CONVERSION OF MOORE TO MEALY MACHINE BY TRANSITIONAL FORMAT

From the transitional diagram of a Moore or Mealy machine conversion can be done easily. That process is described here.

Q. Describe the process of conversion of Mealy machine from a given Moore machine.

Ans. Let a Moore machine M_o is to be converted to an equivalent Mealy machine M_C. There are certain steps for this conversion.

Step I: For a Moore machine each state is labeled with output, as for Moore machine output depends only on the present state. For the conversion, let take a state *S*; which is labeled with output *O*. Look into the incoming edges to the state *S*. These incoming edges are labeled by the input alphabets of the Moore machine. These incoming edges will be relabeled by the input alphabet as well as the output of the state *S*. The output for the state will be removed.

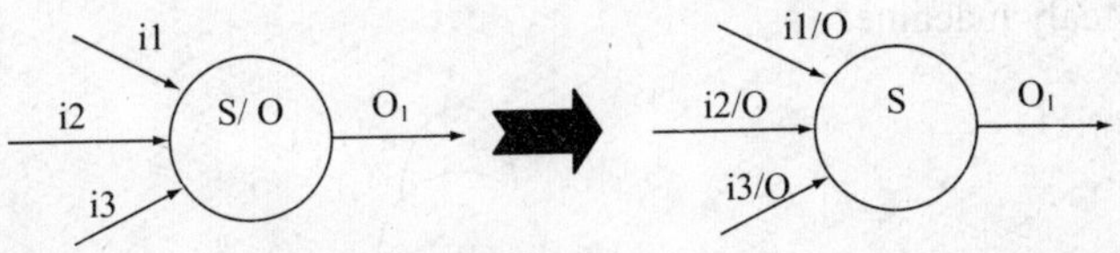

Process of conversion of Moore Machine to a Mealy Machine

Step II : Keep the outgoing edges from the state *S* as it was. (The outgoing edge of a state must be incoming edge of some other state.)

Step III: Repeat these steps for each of the states. By this we will get the Mealy machine equivalent Moore machine.

Q. Convert the following Moore machine into equivalent Mealy Machine.

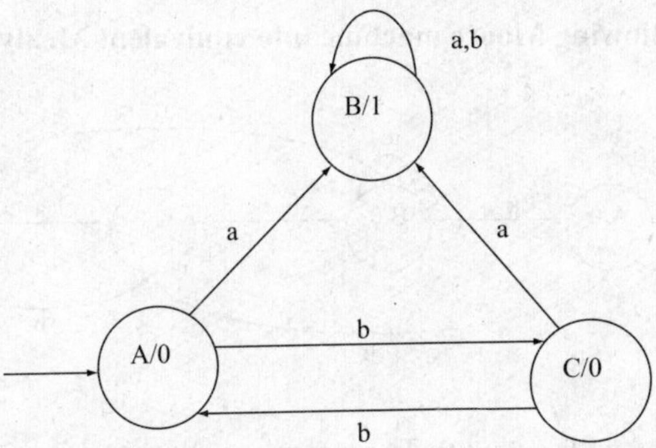

Ans.

(a) In this machine A is the beginning state. Hence start from A. For A there are two incoming arc, from C to A with input *b* and one in the form of start state indication with no input. State A is labeled with output 0. As the start state indication contains no input, it is useless, keep it as it is.

Modify the label of the incoming edge from C to B including the output of state A. Hence the label of the incoming state will be C to A with label *b*/0.

(b) State B is labeled with output 1. The incoming edges to the state B are from A to B with input *a*, B to B with input *a* and *b*, and C to B with input *a*.

Modify the labels of the incoming edges including the output of state B. Hence the labels of the incoming states will be A to B with label *a*/1, B to B with label *a*/1 and *b*/1, and C to B with label *a*/1.

(c) State C is labeled with output 0. There is only one incoming edge to this state, from A to C with input *b*.

The modified label will be *b*/0.

The converted Mealy machine:

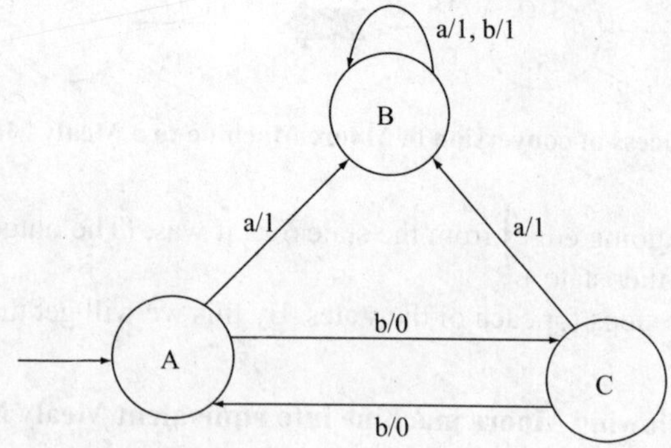

Q. Convert the following Moore machine into equivalent Mealy Machine.

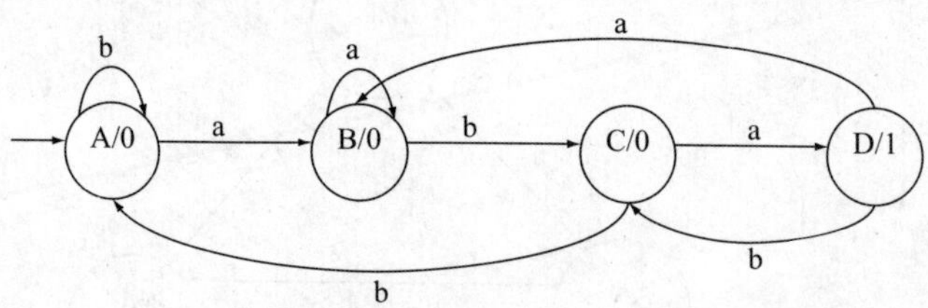

Ans. State A is labeled with output 0. The incoming edged to this state are C to A for input *b*, A to A for input *b*, and one as start state indication with no input. Ignore the edge with start state indication.

Modify the labels of the incoming edges by including the output of state A. So the modified labels will be, from A to A with label *b*/0, and from C to A with label b/0.

State B is labeled with output 0. The incoming edges to this state are, A to B for input *a*, B to B for input *a*, D to B for input *a*. The modified labels will be, A to B with label *a*/0, B to B with label *a*/0, D to B with label *a*/0.

State C is labeled with output 0. The incoming edges to this state are B to C for input *b*, and D to C for input *b*. The modified labels will be B to C with label *b*/0, D to C with label *b*/0.

State D is labeled with output 1. The incoming edge to this state is C to D for input *a*. The modified labels will be from C to D with label *a*/1.

The Mealy machine equivalent to the given Moore machine:

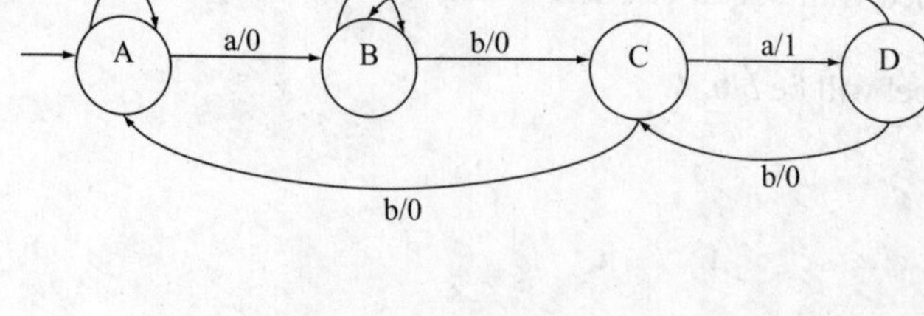

3.10 CONVERSION OF MEALY TO MOORE MACHINE BY TRANSITIONAL FORMAT

Q. Describe the process of conversion of Moore machine from a given Mealy machine.

Ans. For a given Mealy machine M_C there is an equivalent Moore Machine M_o. These can be constructed in several steps.

Step I: In mealy machine output depends on present state and present input. Hence, in the transactional diagram of a mealy machine transactional edges are labeled with input as well as output. For a state two types of edges are there, incoming edges and outgoing edges. For incoming edges it may happen that the output differs for two incoming edges like the following:

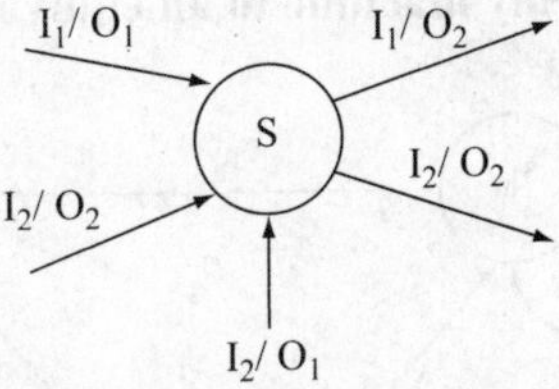

In the transitional diagram for state S, incoming edges are labeled as I_1/O_1, I_2/O_2, and I_2/O_1 and the outgoing edges are labeled as I_1/O_2 and I_2/O_2. For state S for incoming edges we are getting two types of output O_1 and O_2. These types of cases the state S will be divided into n number of parts, where n = number of different outputs for the incoming edges to the state. The output edges will be repeated for all the divided states. The transitional diagrams for the above case will be

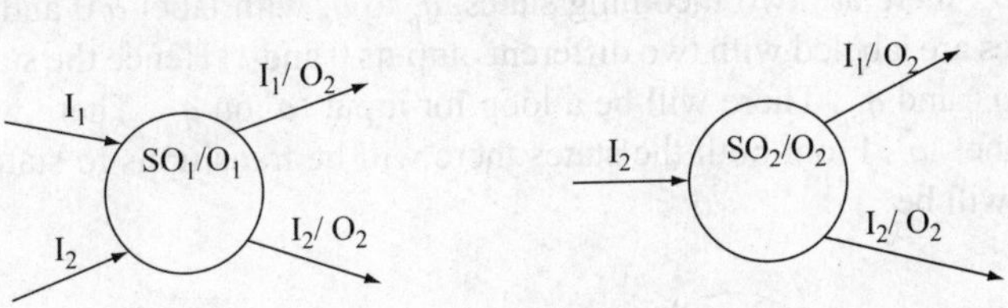

Step II: If a state has a loop and that state also need to be divided like follows:

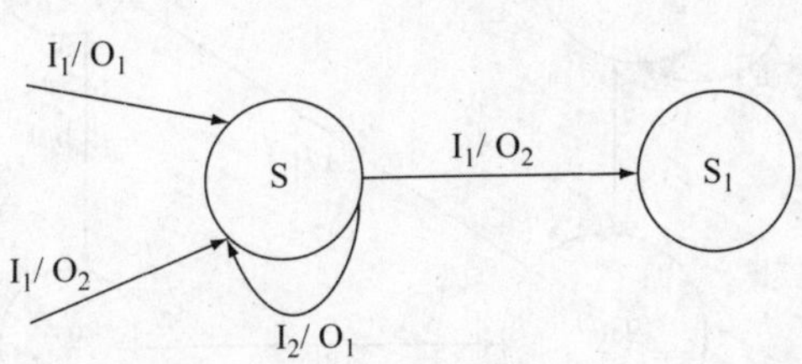

(Here for input I_1, output is O_1 as well as O_2. Hence the state S needs to be divided. The S has a loop with input I_2 and output O_1.) The state S will be divided into two states S_{O1} and S_{O2}. As the loop for input I_2 is labeled with output O_1, Hence there will be a loop on state S_{O1}. However, this loop is not possible on S_{O2}, because it produces output O_2. Hence, there will be a transition from S_{O2} to S_{O1} with input label I_2.

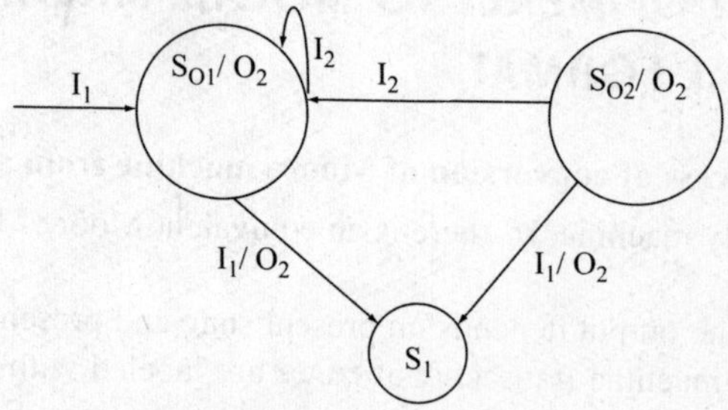

Step III: Repeat the steps I and II. By this we will get the Moore machine equivalent Mealy machine.

Q. Convert the following Mealy machine to an equivalent Moore machine.

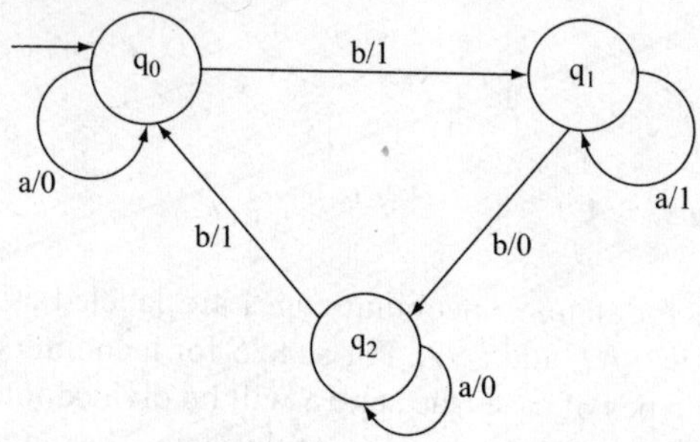

Ans. For state q_0, there are two incoming states, q_0 to q_0 with label $a/0$ and q_2 to q_0 with label $b/1$. Two incoming edges are labeled with two different outputs 0 and 1. Hence the state q_0 need to be divided into two states let q_{00} and q_{01}. There will be a loop for input 'a' on q_{00}. There will a transition from q_{01} to q_{00} with input label 'a'. From both the states there will be transitions to state q_1 with label $b/1$. The modified machine will be

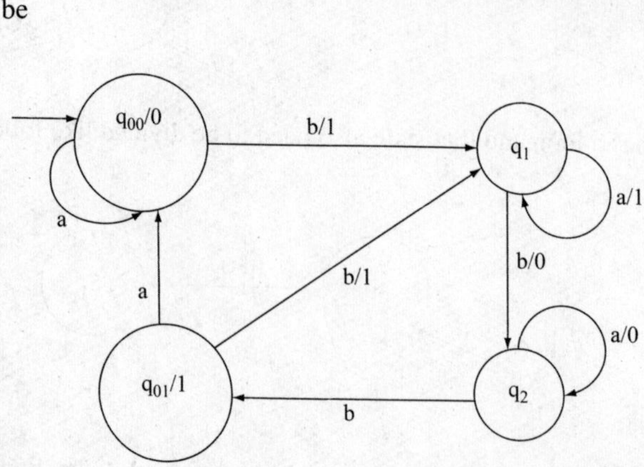

For all the other states q_1 and q_2 the outputs for all the incoming edges are 1 and 0, respectively. Hence there is no need to divide the states, the final Moore machine:

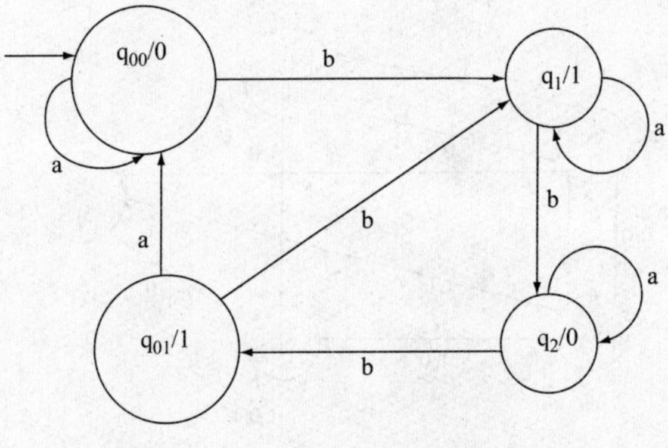

Q. Convert the following Mealy machine to an equivalent Moore machine.

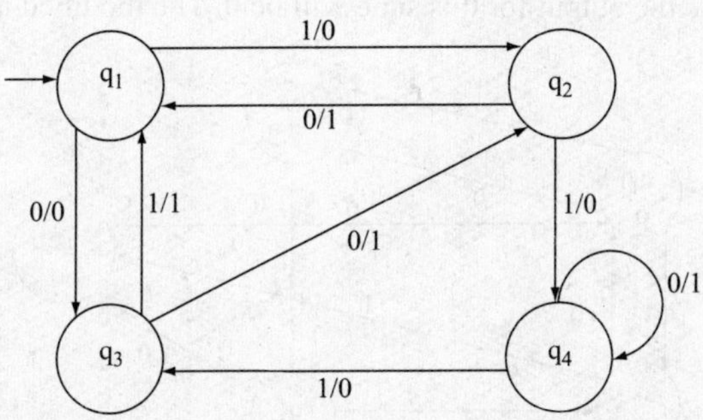

Ans. The machine contains four states. Lets start from the state q_1. The incoming edges to this state are from q_2 to q_1 with label 0/1 and from q_3 to q_1 with label 1/1. There is no difference of the outputs of the incoming edges to this state therefore in the constructing Moore machine the output for this state will be 1. The modified machine:

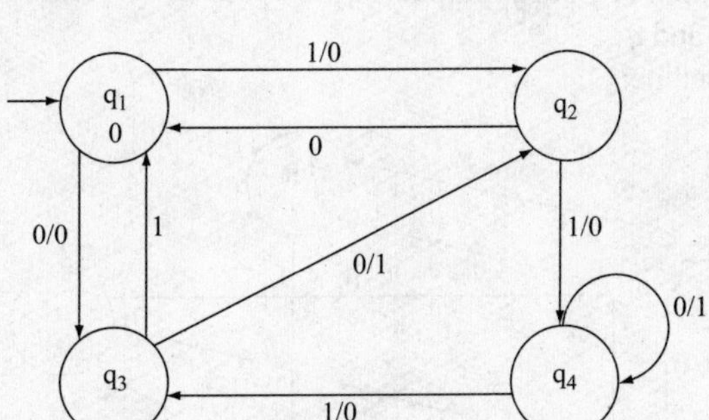

Consider the state q_2. This state contains two incoming edges, from q_1 to q_2, with label 1/0 and q_3 to q_2, with label 0/1. There are two different outputs we are getting for two incoming edges (q_1 to q_2 output 0, q_3 to q_2 output 1). Therefore the state q_2 will be divided into two, let name them q_{20} and q_{21}. The outgoing edges are duplicated for both the states generated from q_2.

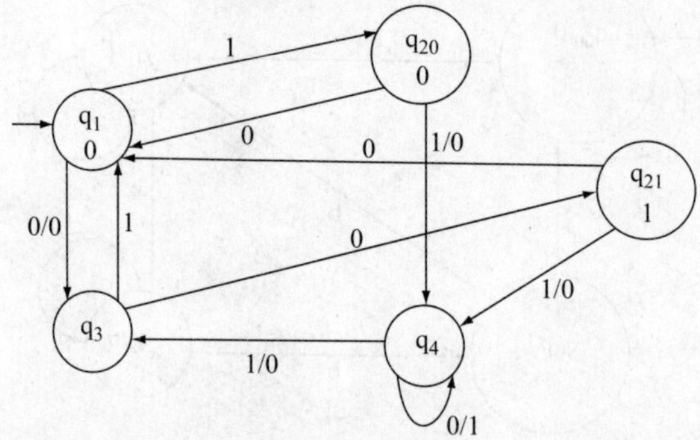

Consider state q_3. The incoming edges to this state are, from q_1 to q_3 with label 0/0 and from q_4 to q_3 with label 1/0. There is no difference of the outputs of the incoming edges to this state, therefore in the constructing Moore machine the output for this state will be 0. The modified machine:

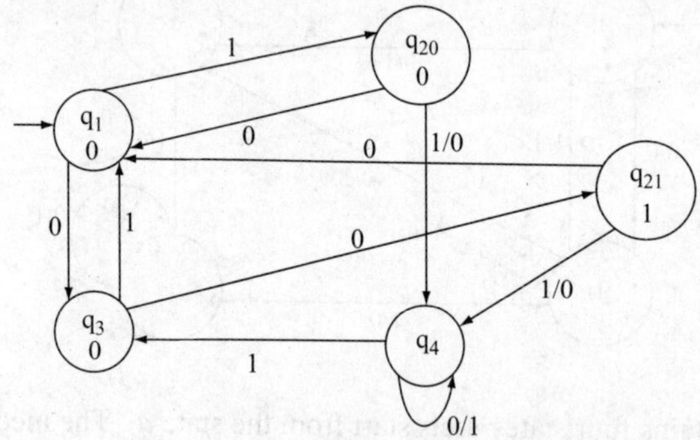

Consider the state q_4. This state contains three incoming edges, from q_{20} to q_4, with label 1/0, from q_{21} to q_4, with label 1/0 and q_4 to q_4 with label 0/1. There are two different outputs we are getting for two incoming edges (q_{20} to q_4 output 0, q_{21} to q_4 output 0, q_4 to q_4 output 1). Hence the state q_4 will be divided into two, let name them q_{40} and q_{41}.

The modified Moore machine:

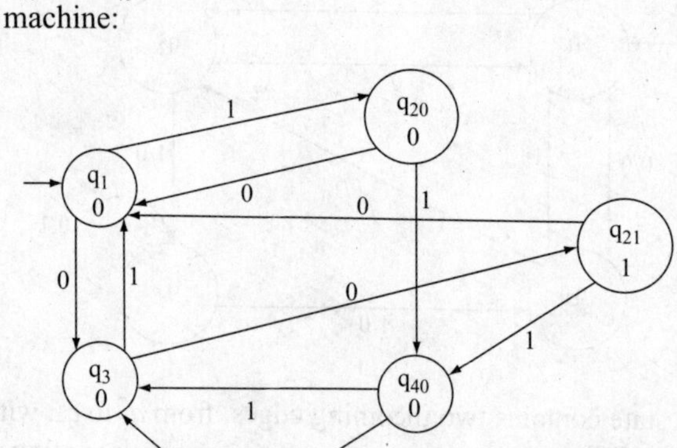

3.11 MINIMIZATION OF FINITE AUTOMATA

Q. What is the need of minimization of finite automata?

Ans. The language (regular expression) produced by a DFA is always unique. However, the reverse, i.e. a language produces a unique DFA is not true. Hence for a given language there may be different DFA s. By minimizing we can get a minimized DFA with minimum number of states and transitions which produces that particular language. DFA determines how computers manipulate regular languages (expressions). DFA size determines space/time efficiency. Hence from a DFA will minimized states need less time to manipulate a regular expression.

Q. Define dead state, inaccessible state, equivalent state, distinguishable state and k-equivalence in case of finite automata.

Ans. Dead State: A state q_i is called dead state if q_i is not a final state and for all the inputs to this state the transitions confined to that state. In mathematical notation, we can denote $q_i \notin F$ and $\delta(q_i, \Sigma) \rightarrow q_i$.

Inaccessible state: The states which can never be reached from the initial state are called in accessible state.

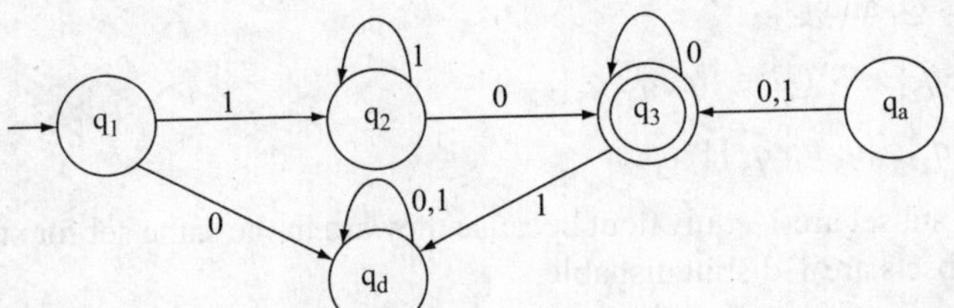

Here q_d is dead state and q_a is inaccessible state.

Equivalent State: Two states q_i and q_j of a finite automata M are called equivalent if $\delta(q_i, x)$ and $\delta(q_j, x)$ both produces final states or both of them produces non-final states for all $x \in \Sigma^*$. It is denoted by $q_i \equiv q_j$.

Distinguishable State: Two states q_i and q_j of a finite automata M are called distinguishable if for a minimum length string x, for $\delta(q_i, x)$ and $\delta(q_j, x)$ one produces final state and another produces non-final state or vice versa for all $x \in \Sigma^*$.

K-equivalent: Two states q_i and q_j of a finite automata M are called k-equivalent ($k \geq 0$) if $\delta(q_i, x)$ and $\delta(q_j, x)$ both produces final states or both of them produces non-final states for all $x \in \Sigma^*$ of length k or less.

Q. Construct a minimum state automaton from the transitional table given below.

PS	NS I/P=0	NS I/P=1
$\rightarrow q_0$	q_1	q_2
q_1	q_2	q_3
q_2	q_2	q_4
(q_3)	q_3	q_3
(q_4)	q_4	q_4
(q_5)	q_5	q_4

Solve:

In the finite automata, the states are $\{q_0, q_1, q_2, q_3, q_4, q_5,\}$. Name this set as S_0

$S0$: $\{q_0, q_1, q_2, q_3, q_4, q_5\}$. All of the states are 0 equivalent.

In the finite automata, there are two types of states final state and non-final states. Hence divide the set of states into two parts Q_1 and Q_2.

$Q1 = \{q_0, q_1, q_2\}$, $Q2 = \{q_3, q_4, q_5\}$,

$S1$: $\{\{q_0, q_1, q_2\}, \{q_3, q_4, q_5\}\}$.

States belong to same subset are 1-equivalent because they are in the same set for string length 1. States belong to different subsets are 1-distinguishable.

For input 0 and 1, q_0 is going to q_1 and q_2, respectively. Both of the states belong to same subset. For q_1 and q_2 for input 0 and 1 the next states are q_2, q_3, and q_2, q_4, respectively. For both of the states for input 0 the next state belong to one subset and for input 1 the next state belong to another subset. Therefore, q_0 can be distinguished from q_1 and q_2.

The next states for input 0 and 1 for states q_3, q_4, q_5 belong to same subset. Hence they cannot be divided.

S_2: $\{\{q_0\}, \{q_1, q_2\}, \{q_3, q_4, q_5\}\}$,

q_0 is the single state in the subset. Hence it cannot be divided.

For states q_1, q_2 for input 0 and 1 for both of the cases one state belong to one subset and another state belong to another subset. Hence they cannot be divided.

The next states for input 0 and 1 for states q_3, q_4, and q_5 belong to same subset. Hence they cannot be divided.

Therefore in the next step

S_3: $\{\{q_0\}, \{q_1, q_2\}, \{q_3, q_4, q_5\}\}$

S_2 and S_3 equivalent.

As step (n-1) and step n are same so we will stop here.
In the minimized automata number of states are 3.

The minimized finite automata in tabular format is

PS	NS	
	I/P=0	I/P=1
$\{q_0\}$	$\{q_1\}$	$\{q_2\}$
$\{q_1, q_2\}$	$\{q_2\}$	$\{q_3, q_4\}$
$\{q_3, q_4, q_5\}$	$\{q_3, q_4, q_5\}$	$\{q_3, q_4, q_4\}$

However, $\{q_1\}$, $\{q_2\}$, $\{q_3, q_4\}$ do not exist under the column of state. They are not states of the minimized finite automata, but they are subset of the states. In the next state columns by replacing the subsets by proper state the modified table will be.

PS	NS	
	I/P=0	I/P=1
$\{q_0\}$	$\{q_1, q_2\}$	$\{q_1, q_2\}$
$\{q_1, q_2\}$	$\{q_1, q_2\}$	$\{q_3, q_4, q_5\}$
$\{q_3, q_4, q_5\}$	$\{q_3, q_4, q_5\}$	$\{q_3, q_4, q_5\}$

As q_0 is the beginning state of the original finite automata $\{q_0\}$ will be the beginning state of minimized finite automata. As q_3, q_4, and q_5 are the final states of the original finite automata so the set of the states containing any of the states as element will be final state. Here all the states are contained in a single set $\{q_3, q_4, q_5\}$, hence it is the final state. By replacing $\{q_0\}$ as A, $\{q_1, q_2\}$ as B and $\{q_3, q_4, q_5\}$ as C, the modified minimized finite automata will be.

PS	Next State	
	I/P=0	I/P=1
→A	B	B
B	B	C
(C)	C	C

The transitional diagram of the minimized finite automata will be.

Q. Construct a minimum state automaton from the transitional table given below.

PS	NS	
	I/P=0	I/P=1
A	F	B
B	C	G
C	C	A
D	G	C
E	F	H
F	G	C
G	E	G
H	C	G

A is initial state and C is final state

Ans. In the finite automata the states are **{A,B,C,D,E,F,G,H }**. Name this set as S_0

S_0: {A,B,C,D,E,F,G,H }. All of the states are 0 equivalent.

In the finite automata there are two types of states final state and non-final states. Hence divide the set of states into two parts Q_1 and Q_2.

Q_1 = {C}, Q_2 = {A,B,D,E,F,G,H},

S_1: {{C} {A,B,D,E,F,G, H}}.

States belong to same subset are 1-equivalent because they are in the same set for string length 1. States belong to different subsets are 1- distinguishable.

The C is single state, hence it cannot be divided. Among the states {A,B,D,E,F,G,H} for {B,D,F,H} for input either 0 or 1, the next state belong to {C} which is different subset (From B with input 0 goes to C, from D with input 1 goes to C, from F with input 1 goes to C, H with input 0 goes to C).

For the other states {A,E,G} for input either 0 or 1 the next state belongs to Q_2.

So Q_2 can be divided into two parts {A,E,G} and {B,D,F,H}. Let name them Q_3 and Q_4.

The divided sets will be

S_2: {{C}, {A,E,G}, {B,D,F,H}}.

Consider the subset of states {A,E,G}. A and E with input 0 and 1 both go to F,B and F,H, respectively, i.e. to the subset {B,D,F,H}. The G with input 0 and 1 go to E,G, i.e. the same subset. Hence {A,E,G} will be divided into two subsets {A,E} and {G}.

The subset {B,D,F,H} can be divided depending on the input and next state combination. B and H produce next state C and G for input 0 and 1, respectively.

The D and F produce next state G and C for input 0 and 1, respectively. Hence the set **{B,D,F,G}** will be divided into two subsets {B,H} and {D,F}.

The divided sets will be

S_3: {{C}, {A,E}, {G}, {B,H}, {D,F}}.

The subsets cannot be divided further. Hence these are the states of minimized DFA. Lets rename the subsets as q_0, q_1, q_2, q_3 and q_4. Initial state was A, hence here initial state is {A,E}, i.e. q_1. Final state was C, hence here final state is {C}, i.e. q_0. The tabular representation of minimized DFA is

PS	NS	
	I/P=0	I/P=1
(q_0)	q_0	q_1
→q_1	q_4	q_3
q_2	q_1	q_2
q_3	q_0	q_2
q_4	q_2	q_0

3.12 MYHILL-NERODE THEOREM

Q. Define Equivalence Relation and Right Invariant.

Ans.

(a) A relation R in set S is Reflexive if xRx for every x in S.

(b) A relation R in set S is symmetric if for x,y in S, yRx, whenever xRy.

(c) A relation R in set S is transitive if for x,y and z in S, xRz whenever xRy and yRz.

A relation R in set S is called equivalence relation if it is reflexive, symmetric and transitive.

Right Invariant: An equivalence relation R on strings of symbols from some alphabet Σ is said to be right invariant if for all $x, y \in \Sigma^*$ with $x\,R\,y$ and all $w \in \Sigma^*$ we have that $xw\,R\,yw$. This definition states that an equivalence relation has the right invariant property if two equivalent strings (x and y) that are in the language still are equivalent if a third string (w) is appended to the right of both of them.

Q. State Myhill Nerode Theorem.

Ans. Myhill Nerode Theorem states that the following three statements are equivalent.

(a) The set L, a subset of Σ^*, is accepted by a DFA, i.e. L is a regular language.

(b) There is a right-invariant equivalence relation R of finite index such that L is the union of some of the equivalence classes of R.

(c) Let equivalence relation R_L be defined as xR_Ly, if and only if for all z in Σ^*, xz is in L exactly when yz is in L then R_L is of finite index.

Q. How Myhill Nerode Theorem can be applied in minimizing a DFA?

Ans.

Step I: Build a two-dimensional Matrix labeled by the states of the given DFA at the left and bottom side. The major diagonal and the upper triangular part will be put dash.

Step II: One of the three symbols, X, x or 0 will be put in the locations where there is no dash.

(a) Mark X at *p*, *q* in lower triangular part such that *p* is final state and *Q* is non-final state.
(b) Make distinguished pair combination of the non-final states. If there are *n* number of non-final states there will be nC_2 number of distinguished pairs.

Take a pair (*p*, *q*) and find (*r*, *s*), such that $r = \delta(p, a)$ and $s = \delta(q, a)$. If in the place of (*r*, *s*) there is *X* or *x*, in the place of (*p*, *q*) there will be *x*.

(c) If (*r,s*) is neither *X* nor *x*, then (*p,q*) will be 0.
(d) Repeat *b* and *c* for final states also.

Step III: The combination of states where there is 0, they will be the states of the minimized machine.

Q. Minimize the following DFA using Myhill Nerode theorem.

PS	NS	
	I/P=a	I/P=b
→A	B	E
B	C	D
C	H	I
D	I	H
E	F	G
F	H	I
G	H	I
H	H	H
I	I	I

Here C,D,F,G are final states.

Ans.

Step I: Divide the states of the DFA into two subsets final (*F*) and non-final (*Q-F*).

F = {C,D,F,G}, *Q-F* = {A,B,E,H,I}.

Make a two-dimensional matrix labeled at left and button by the states of the DFA.

A	—	—	—	—	—	—	—	—	—
B		—	—	—	—	—	—	—	—
C			—	—	—	—	—	—	—
D				—	—	—	—	—	—
E					—	—	—	—	—
F						—	—	—	—
G							—	—	—
H								—	—
I									—
	A	B	C	D	E	F	G	H	I

Step II: (a) The following combinations are the combination of beginning and final state.

(A,C), (A,D), (A,F), (A,G), (B,C), (B,D), (B,F), (B,G), (E,C), (E,D), (E,F), (E,G), (H,C), (H,D), (H,F), (H,G), (I,C), (I,D), (I,F), (I,G).

Put X in these combinations of states.

The modified matrix:

A	—	—	—	—	—	—	—	—	—
B		—	—	—	—	—	—	—	—
C	X	X	—	—	—	—	—	—	—
D	X	X		—	—	—	—	—	—
E			X	X	—	—	—	—	—
F	X	X			X	—	—	—	—
G	X	X			X		—	—	—
H			X	X		X	X	—	—
I			X	X		X	X		—
	A	B	C	D	E	F	G	H	I

(b) The pair combination of non-final states are **(A,B), (A,E), (A,H), (A,I), (B,E), (B,H), (B,I), (E,H), (E,I), (H,I).**

$r = \delta(\text{A},a) \rightarrow$ B $s = \delta(\text{B},a) \rightarrow$ C, in the place of (B,C) there is *X*. Hence in the place of (A, B) there will be *x*.

Same like $(r,s) = \delta((\text{A, E}), (a) \rightarrow$ (B, F) (there is X). In the place of (A,E) there will be *x*.

$(r,s) = \delta((\text{A,H}), (\text{a}) \rightarrow$ (B,H) (neither X nor *x*). In the place of (A,H) there will be 0.

$(r,s) = \delta((\text{A,I}), (\text{a}) \rightarrow$ (B,I) (neither X nor *x*). In the place of (A,I) there will be 0.

$(r,s) = \delta((\text{B,E}), (\text{a}) \rightarrow$ (C,F) (neither X nor x). In the place of (B,E) there will be 0.

$(r,s) = \delta((\text{B,H}), \text{a}) \rightarrow$ (C,H) (there is X). In the place of (B,H) there will be *x*.

$(r,s) = \delta((\text{B,I}), (\text{a}) \rightarrow$ (C,I) (there is X). In the place of (B,I) there will be *x*.

$(r,s) = \delta((\text{E,H}), (\text{a}) \rightarrow$ (F,H) (there is X). In the place of (E,H) there will be *x*.

$(r,s) = \delta((\text{E,I}), (\text{a}) \rightarrow$ (F,I) (there is X). In the place of (E,I) there will be *x*.

$(r,s) = \delta((\text{H,I}), (\text{a}) \rightarrow$ (H,I) (neither X nor x). In the place of (H,I) there will be 0.

(c) The pair combination of final states are **(C,D), (C,F), (C,G), (D,F), (D,G), (F,G).**

$(r,s) = \delta((\text{C,D}), (\text{a}) \rightarrow$ (H,I) (neither X nor x). In the place of **(C,D)** there will be 0.

$(r,s) = \delta((\text{C,F}), (\text{a}) \rightarrow$ (H,H) (There is dash, neither X nor *x*). In the place of **(C,F)** there will be 0.

$(r,s) = \delta((\text{C,G}), (\text{a}) \rightarrow$ (H,H) (neither X nor x). In the place of **(C,G)** there will be 0.

$(r,s) = \delta((\text{D,F}), (\text{a}) \rightarrow$ (I,H) (neither X nor x). In the place of **(D,F)** there will be 0.

$(r,s) = \delta((\text{D,G}), (\text{a}) \rightarrow$ (I,H) (neither X nor x). In the place of **(D,G)** there will be 0.

$(r,s) = \delta((\text{F,G}), (\text{a}) \rightarrow$ (H,H) (neither X nor x). In the place of **(F,G)** there will be 0.

The modified matrix will be

B	x							
C	X	X						
D	X	X	0					
E	x	0	X	X				
F	X	X	0	0	X			
G	X	X	0	0	X	0		
H	x	x	X	X	x	X	X	
I	x	x	X	X	x	X	X	0
	A	B	C	D	E	F	G	H

The combination of entries 0 are the states of the modified machine. The states of the minimized machine are [A], [B,E], [C,D], [C,F], [C,G], [D,F], [D,G], [F,G], [H,I].

For the minimized machine M'

$Q' = (\{A\}, \{B,E\}, \{C,D,F,G\}, \{H,I\})$.

[C,D], [C,F], [C,G], [D,F], [D,G] and [F,G] are grouped into single state [C,D,F,G] because all the previous combination of states are produced from these 4 states taking 2 states in a group.

$\Sigma = \{a,b\}$.

δ' :

PS	NS	
	a	*b*
{A}	{B,E}	{B,E}
{B,E}	{C,D,F,G}	{C,D,F,G}
{C,D,F,G}	{H,I}	{H,I}
{H,I}	{H,I}	{H,I}

q'_0 : {A}.

F' : {C,D,F,G}.

Q. Minimize the following finite automata by Myhill Nerode Theorem.

PS	NS	
	I/P=a	I/P=b
→A	B	F
B	A	F
C	G	A
D	H	B
E	A	G
F	H	C
G	A	D
H	A	C

Here F,G,H are final states.

Ans.

Step I: Divide the states of the DFA into two subsets Final **(F)** and non-final **(Q–F)**.

F={E,F,G}, Q–F = {A,B,C,D}

Make a two-dimensional matrix labeled at left and button by the states of the DFA.

A	—	—	—	—	—	—	—	—
B		—	—	—	—	—	—	—
C			—	—	—	—	—	—
D				—	—	—	—	—
E					—	—	—	—
F						—	—	—
G							—	—
H								—
	A	B	C	D	E	F	G	H

Step II: (a) The following combinations are the combination of beginning and final state.

(A,E), (A,F),(A,G),(B,E), (B,F),(B,G),(C,E),(C,F),(C,G),(D,E),(D,F),(D,G)

Put X in these combinations of states.

The modified matrix will be

B							
C							
D							
E							
F	X	X	X	X	X		
G	X	X	X	X	X		
H	X	X	X	X	X		
	A	B	C	D	E	F	G

(b) The pair combination of non-final states are (A,B), (A,C), (A,D), (A,E), (B,C), (B,D), (B,E), (C,D), (C,E), (D,E).

$r = \delta(A,a) \rightarrow B \quad s = \delta(B,a) \rightarrow A$, in the place of (A,B) there is neither X nor x. Hence in the place of (A,B) there will be 0.

Same like $(r,s) = \delta((A,C), a) \rightarrow$ (B,G) (there is X). In the place of **(A,C)** there will be x.

$(r,s) = \delta((A,D), (a) \rightarrow$ (B,H) (there is X). In the place of **(A,D)** there will be x.

$(r,s) = \delta((A,E), (a) \rightarrow$ (B,A) (there is neither X nor x). In the place of (A,E) there will be 0

$(r,s) = \delta((B,C), (a) \rightarrow$ (A,G) (there is X). In the place of (B,C) there will be x.

$(r,s) = \delta((B,D), (a) \rightarrow$ (A,H) (there is X). In the place of (B,D) there will be x.

$(r,s) = \delta((B,E), (a) \rightarrow$ (A,A) (there is neither X nor x, only dash). In the place of (B,E) there will be 0.

$(r,s) = \delta((C,D), (a) \rightarrow$ (G,H) (there is neither X nor x). In the place of (C,D) there will be 0.

$(r,s) = \delta((C,E), (a) \rightarrow$ (G,A)) (there is X). In the place of (C,E) there will be x.

$(r,s) = \delta((D,E), (a) \rightarrow$ (H,A) (there is X). In the place of (D,E) there will be x.

6. For a NFA for some cases for a single input given to a single state the machine goes to more than one states, i.e. $Q \times \Sigma \rightarrow 2^Q$.
7. NFA can be constructed to an equivalent DFA.
8. A finite automata is called a NFA with null move if there exists a null transaction, i.e. $Q \times \varepsilon \rightarrow Q$.
9. Dead state is a state where the control can enter and confined till the input ended, but no way to come out from that state,
10. In Mealy Machine output depends on present state and present input.
11. In Moore Machine output depends on only present state.
12. Myhill Nerode Theorem is used to minimize a finite automata.
13. Two way finite automata are machines which can traverse (read) an input string in both directions (Left and right).
14. Finite automata is used in designing Lexical analyzer.

SOLVED PROBLEMS

1. Test whether the following string is accepted by the following finite automata or not.

(a) 0001101 (b) 01010

PS	NS 0	NS 1
$\rightarrow q_0$	q_2	q_3
q_1	q_0	q_2
q_2	q_1	q_3
q_3	q_3	q_1

Ans.

(a) $\delta(q_0, 0001101) \rightarrow \delta(q_2, 001101)$
$\rightarrow \delta(q_1, 01101)$
$\rightarrow \delta(q_0, 1101)$
$\rightarrow \delta(q_3, 101)$
$\rightarrow \delta(q_1, 01)$
$\rightarrow \delta(q_0, 1)$
$\rightarrow q_3$.

As q_3 is the final state so the string is accepted by the given finite automata.

(b) $\delta(q_0, 01010) \rightarrow \delta(q_2, 1010)$
$\delta(q_3, 010) \rightarrow \delta(q_3, 10)$
$\rightarrow \delta(q_1, 0)$
$\rightarrow q_0$

The q_0 is a non-final state. Hence the string is not accepted by the given finite automata.

2. Test whether the following string is accepted by the following finite automata or not.

(a) 0111100 (b) 11010

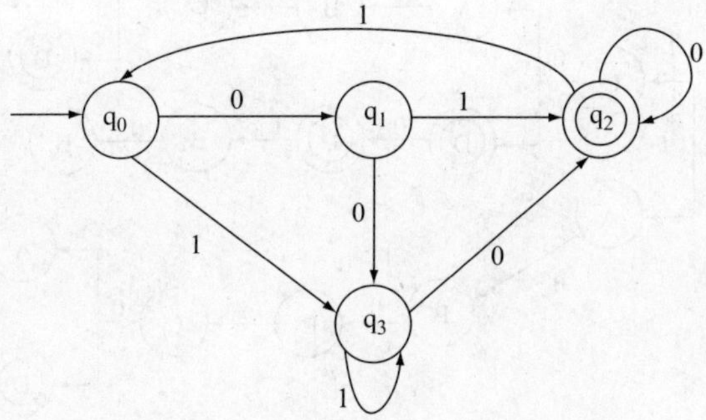

Ans.

(a) $\delta(q_0, 0111100) \rightarrow \delta(q_1, 111100)$
$\rightarrow \delta(q_2, 11100)$
$\rightarrow \delta(q_0, 1100)$
$\rightarrow \delta(q_3, 100)$
$\rightarrow \delta(q_3, 00)$
$\rightarrow \delta(q_2, 0)$
$\rightarrow q_2.$

The q_2 is the final state. Therefore, the string is accepted by the given finite automata.

(b) $\delta(q_0, 11010) \rightarrow \delta(q_3, 1010)$
$\rightarrow \delta(q_3, 010)$
$\rightarrow \delta(q_2, 10)$
$\rightarrow \delta(q_0, 0)$
$\rightarrow q_1$

q_1 is a non-final state. Therefore, the string is not accepted by the given finite automata.

3. Test whether the string 10010 is accepted by the following NFA or not.

PS	NS	
	$a=0$	$a=1$
→A	B	A, C
B	B	C
C	A, D	B
D	D	B

Ans.

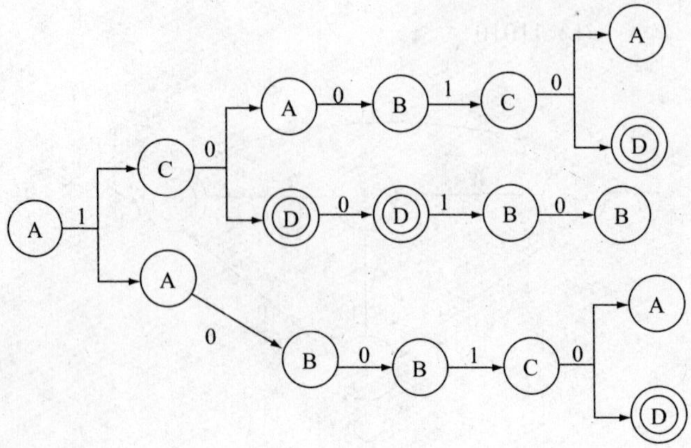

For the string 10010 we are getting terminal state as D which is a final state for two cases. Therefore, the string is accepted by the NFA.

4. Convert the following NFA into an equivalent DFA.

PS	NS	
	$a=0$	$a=1$
$\rightarrow q_0$	q_0, q_1	q_0
q_1	q_2, q_3	q_1
q_2	q_3	q_3
(q_3)	–	q_2

Ans. This is an NFA because here for present state q_0 with input 0 the control moves to q_0, q_1.

PS	NS	
	$a=0$	$a=1$
$[q_0]$	$[q_0, q_1]$	$[q_0]$
$[q_0, q_1]$	$[q_0, q_1, q_2, q_3]$	$[q_0, q_1]$
$[q_0, q_1, q_2, q_3]$	$[q_0, q_1, q_2, q_3]$	$[q_0, q_1, q_2, q_3]$

For simplification let replace $[q_0]$ by A, $[q_0, q_1]$ by B, $[q_0, q_1, q_2, q_3]$ by C. Here A is the initial state and C is the final state as it contains the state q_3.

The simplified DFA is

PS	NS	
	$a=0$	$a=1$
$\rightarrow$A	B	A
B	C	B
(C)	C	C

4. Convert the following NFA into an equivalent DFA.

PS	NS	
	$a=0$	$a=1$
$\rightarrow q_0$	q_0, q_1	q_0, q_2
q_1	q_3	–
q_2	–	q_3
(q_3)	q_3	q_3

Ans.

PS	NS	
	$a=0$	$a=1$
$[q_0]$	$[q_0, q_1]$	$[q_0, q_2]$
$[q_0, q_1]$	$[q_0, q_1, q_3]$	$[q_0, q_2]$
$[q_0, q_2]$	$[q_0, q_1]$	$[q_0, q_2, q_3]$
$[q_0, q_1, q_3]$	$[q_0, q_1, q_3]$	$[q_0, q_2, q_3]$
$[q_0, q_2, q_3]$	$[q_0, q_1, q_3]$	$[q_0, q_2, q_3]$

For simplification let replace $[q_0]$ by A, $[q_0, q_1]$ by B, $[q_0, q_2]$ by C, $[q_0, q_1, q_3]$ by D and $[q_0, q_2, q_3]$ by E. Here A is the initial state and D and E are the final state as they contains the state q_3.

The simplified DFA is

PS	NS	
	$a=0$	$a=1$
→A	B	C
B	D	C
C	B	E
(D)	D	E
(E)	D	E

5. Convert the following NFA with ∈ move to an equivalent DFA.

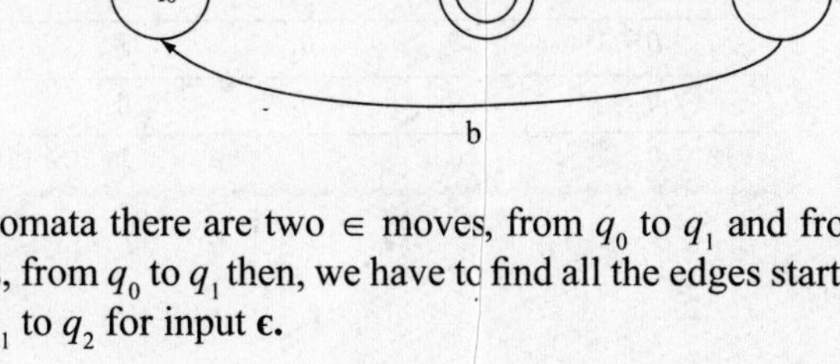

Ans. In the given automata there are two ∈ moves, from q_0 to q_1 and from q_1 to q_2. If we want to remove the first ∈ moves, from q_0 to q_1 then, we have to find all the edges starting from q_1. The edges are q_1 to q_1 for input a, and q_1 to q_2 for input **є**.

Duplicate all these transitions starting from the state q_0, keeping the edge label same. The q_0 is initial state, so make q_1 also an initial state. The q_1 is the final state, therefore make q_0 as final state. The modified transitional diagram:

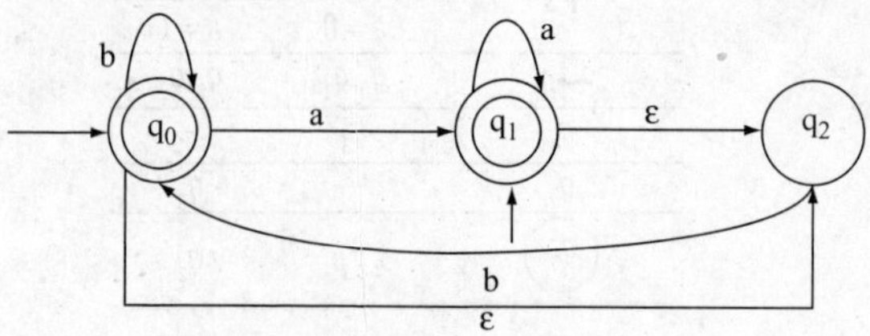

Again there are two ∈ moves, from q_0 to q_2 and from q_1 to q_2. If we want to remove the null transition from q_0 to q_2, we have to find all the edges starting from q_2. The edges are q_2 to q_0 for input *b*. Duplicate this transition starting from the state q_0, keeping the edge label same. The modified transitional diagram: (As in q_0 there is a loop with label *b*, we need not to make another loop with the same label.)

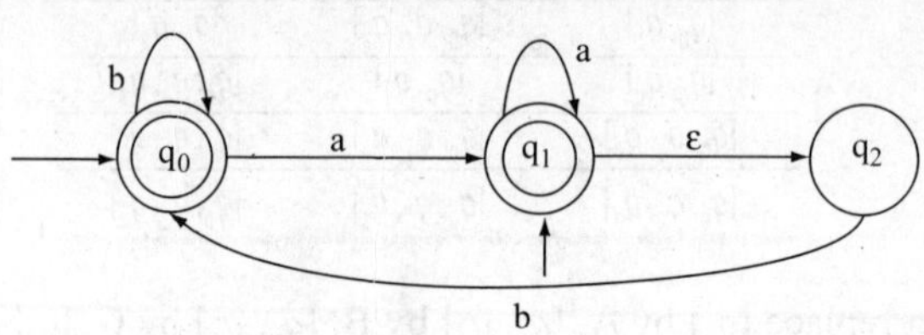

If we want to remove the null transition from q_1 to q_2, we have to find all the edges starting from q_2. The edges are q_2 to q_0 for input *b*. Duplicate this transition starting from the state q_1, keeping the edge label same. Here q_1 is initial state, hence make q_2 also an initial state. The modified transitional diagram:

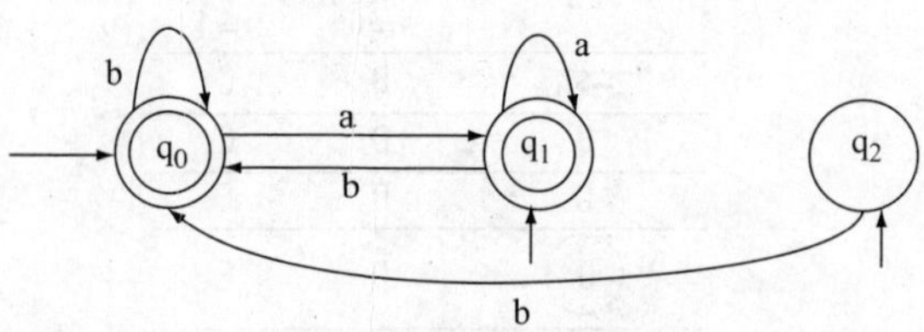

6. Convert the following Moore machine to equivalent Mealy machine by tabular format.

PS	NS		O/P
	I/P=0	I/P=1	
$\rightarrow q_0$	q_2	q_1	0
q_1	q_0	q_3	1
q_2	q_3	q_4	1
q_3	q_4	q_1	0
q_4	q_4	q_2	1

Ans. The equivalent Mealy machine is

PS	I/P=0		I/P=1	
	NS	O/P	NS	O/P
$\rightarrow q_0$	q_2	1	q_1	1
q_1	q_0	0	q_3	0
q_2	q_3	0	q_4	1
q_3	q_4	1	q_1	1
q_4	q_4	1	q_2	1

7. Convert the following Moore machine to equivalent Mealy machine by tabular format.

PS	NS		O/P
	I/P=0	I/P=1	
$\rightarrow q_0$	q_1	q_3	1
q_1	q_0	q_2	0
q_2	q_4	q_1	0
q_3	q_4	q_3	1
q_4	q_3	q_1	0

Ans.

The equivalent Mealy machine is

PS	I/P=0		I/P=1	
	NS	O/P	NS	O/P
$\rightarrow q_0$	q_1	0	q_3	1
q_1	q_0	1	q_2	0
q_2	q_4	0	q_1	0
q_3	q_4	0	q_3	1
q_4	q_3	1	q_1	0

8. Convert the following Mealy machine to equivalent Moore machine by tabular format.

PS	I/P=0		I/P=1	
	NS	O/P	NS	O/P
$\rightarrow q_0$	q_1	1	q_2	1
q_1	q_3	0	q_0	1
q_2	q_4	0	q_3	1
q_3	q_1	0	q_4	0
q_4	q_2	1	q_4	0

Ans. In the next state column of the given Mealy machine the output differs for q_1 and q_3 as next state. Therefore, the states will be divided as $q_{10,}$ q_{11} and q_{30}, q_{31}, respectively. After dividing the states the modified Mealy machine:

PS	I/P=0		I/P=1	
	NS	O/P	NS	O/P
→q_0	q_{11}	1	q_2	1
q_{10}	q_{30}	0	q_0	1
q_{11}	q_{30}	0	q_0	1
q_2	q_4	0	q_{31}	1
q_{30}	q_{10}	0	q_4	0
q_{31}	q_{10}	0	q_4	0
q_4	q_2	1	q_4	0

The converted Moore machine is

PS	NS		O/P
	I/P=0	I/P=1	
→q_0	q_{11}	q_2	1
q_{10}	q_{30}	q_0	0
q_{11}	q_{30}	q_0	1
q_2	q_4	q_{31}	1
q_{30}	q_{10}	q_4	0
q_{31}	q_{10}	q_4	1
q_4	q_2	q_4	0

To get rid of the problem of occurrence of null string, we need to include another state let q_a with same transactions as of q_0 but with output 0.

The modified final Moore machine equivalent to the given Mealy machine is

PS	NS		O/P
	I/P=0	I/P=1	
q_a	q_{11}	q_2	0
q_0	q_{11}	q_2	1
q_{10}	q_{30}	q_0	0
q_{11}	q_{30}	q_0	1
q_2	q_4	q_{31}	1
q_{30}	q_{10}	q_4	0
q_{31}	q_{10}	q_4	1
q_4	q_2	q_4	0

9. Convert the following Mealy machine to equivalent Moore machine by tabular format.

PS	I/P=0		I/P=1	
	NS	O/P	NS	O/P
$\rightarrow q_0$	q_0	1	q_1	0
q_1	q_3	1	q_3	1
q_2	q_1	1	q_2	1
q_3	q_2	0	q_0	1

Ans. In the next state column of the given Mealy machine the output differs for q_2 and q_3 as next state. Therefore the states will be divided as $q_{10,}$ q_{11} and q_{20}, q_{21}, respectively. After dividing the states the modified Mealy machine will be

PS	I/P=0		I/P=1	
	NS	O/P	NS	O/P
$\rightarrow q_0$	q_0	1	q_{10}	0
q_{10}	q_3	1	q_3	1
q_{11}	q_3	1	q_3	1
q_{20}	q_{11}	1	q_{21}	1
q_{21}	q_{11}	1	q_{21}	1
q_3	q_{20}	0	q_0	1

The converted Moore machine:

PS	I/P=0		O/P
	I/P=0	I/P=1	
$\rightarrow q_0$	q_0	q_{10}	1
q_{10}	q_3	q_3	0
q_{11}	q_3	q_3	1
q_{20}	q_{11}	q_{21}	0
q_{21}	q_{11}	q_{21}	1
q_3	q_{20}	q_0	1

To get rid of the problem of occurrence of null string, we need to include another state let q_a with same transactions as of q_0 but with output 0.

The modified final Moore machine equivalent to the given Mealy machine:

PS	I/P=0		O/P
	I/P=0	I/P=1	
$\rightarrow q_a$	q_0	q_{10}	0
q_0	q_0	q_{10}	1
q_{10}	q_3	q_3	0
q_{11}	q_3	q_3	1
q_{20}	q_{11}	q_{21}	0
q_{21}	q_{11}	q_{21}	1
q_3	q_{20}	q_0	1

10. Convert the following Moore machine into equivalent Mealy Machine by transitional format.

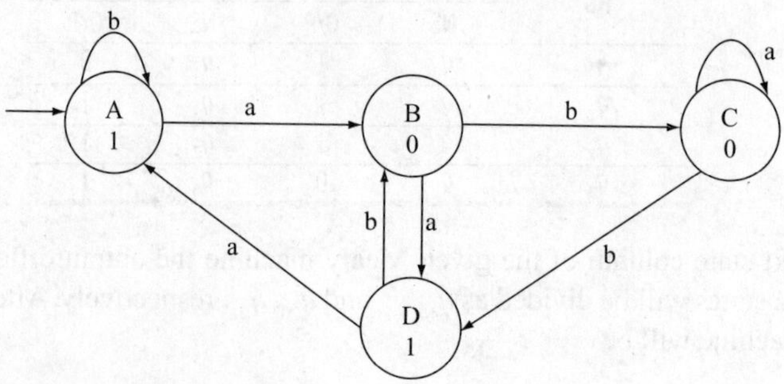

Ans.

(a) In this machine A is the beginning state. Therefore start from A. For A there are three incoming arc, from A to A with input *b* and one in the form of start state indication with no input and the last is from D to A with input *a*. State A is labeled with output 1. As the start state indication contains no input, it is useless, keep it as it is.

Modify the label of the incoming edge from D to A and from A to A including the output of state A. Hence the label of the incoming state will be D to A with label a/1 and A to A with label b/1.

(b) State B is labeled with output 0. The incoming edges to the state B are from A to B with input a, D to B with input *b*. Modify the labels of the incoming edges including the output of state B. So the labels of the incoming states will be A to B with label a/0, D to B with label b/0.

(c) State C is labeled with output 0. There are two incoming edges to this state, from B to C with input *b* and from C to C with input *a*. The modified label will be B to C with label b/ 0, and C to C with label a/ 0.

(d) State D is labeled with output 1. There are two incoming edges to this state, from B to D with input *a*, and from C to D with input *b*. The modified label will be B to D with label *a*/1, and C to D with label *b*/1. The converted Mealy machine:

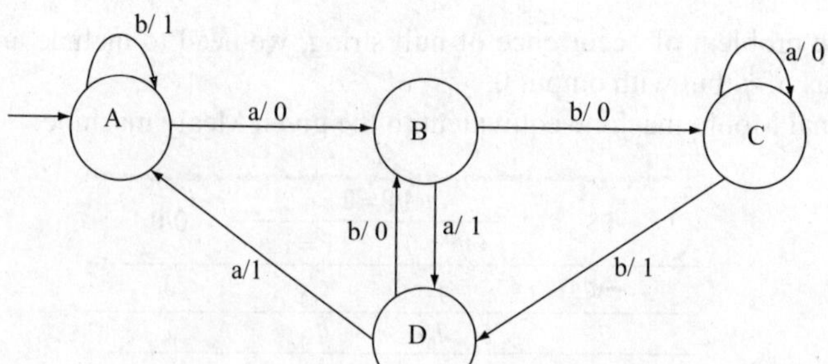

11. Convert the following Mealy machine into equivalent Moore Machine by transitional format.

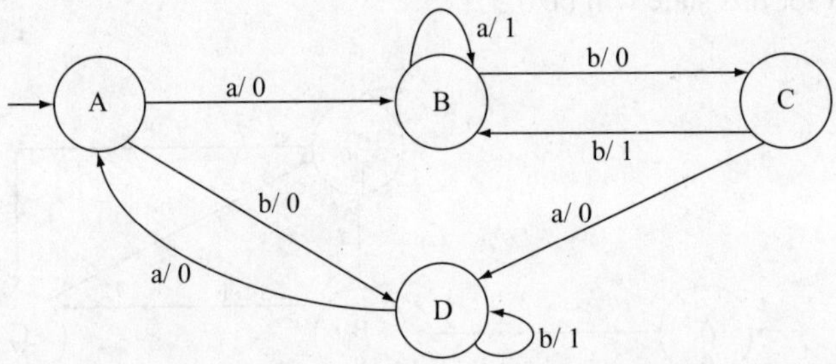

Ans. The machine contains four states. Lets start from the state A. The incoming edges to this state are from D to A with label *a*/0. There is no difference of the outputs of the incoming edges to this state so in the constructing Moore machine the output for this state will be 0.

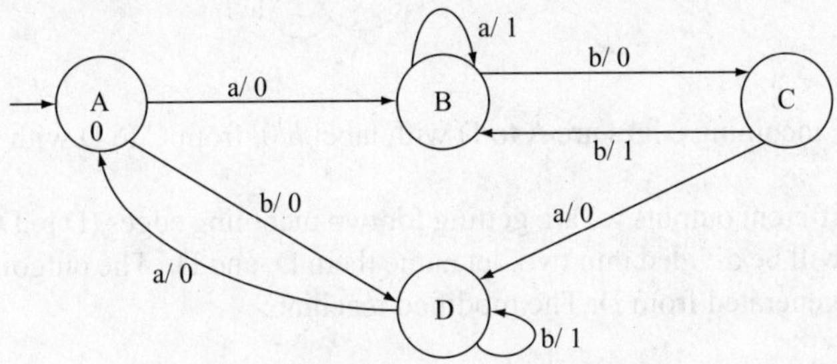

For the state B, the incoming edges are B to B with label *a*/1, from A to B with label *a*/0 and from C to B with label *b*/1.

There are two different outputs we are getting for two incoming edges (B to B output 1, A to B output 0). So, the state B will be divided into two, lets name them B_0 and B_1. The outgoing edges are duplicated for both the states generated from B. The modified machine:

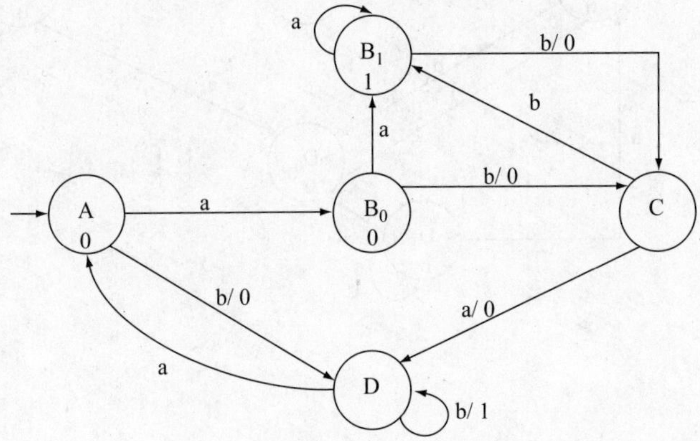

For the state A, the incoming edges to this state are from B_0 to C with label *b*/0 and B_1 to C with label *b*/0. There is no difference of the outputs of the incoming edges to this state so in the constructing Moore machine the output for this state will be 0.

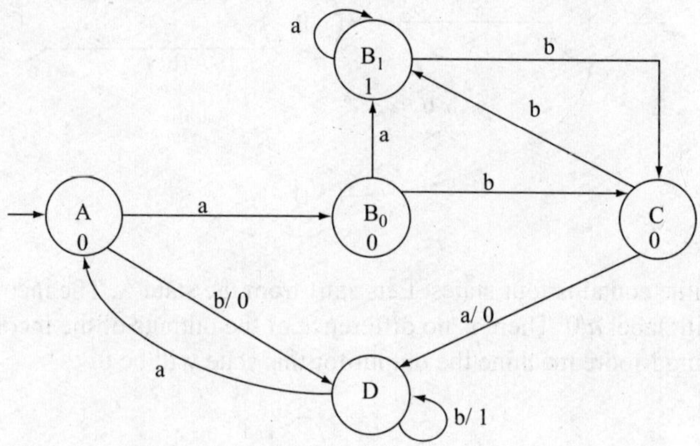

For the state D, the incoming edges are A to D with label *b*/0, from C to D with label *a*/0 and from D to D with label *b*/1.

There are two different outputs we are getting for two incoming edges (D to D output 1, C to D output 0). So, the state D will be divided into two, let name them D_0 and D_1. The outgoing edges are duplicated for both the states generated from D. The modified machine:

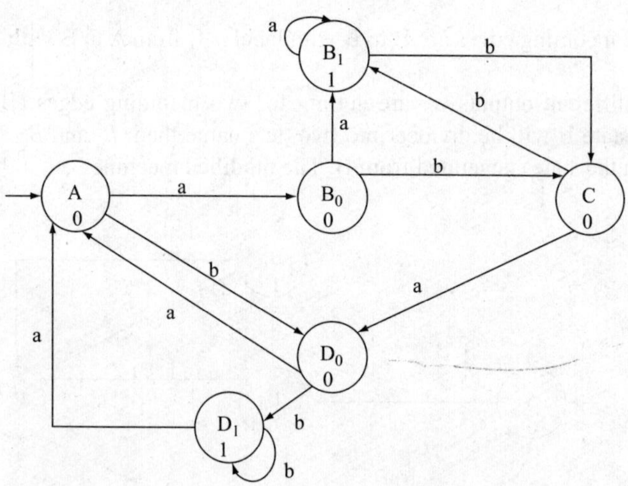

12. Minimize the following finite automata.

PS	NS	
	I/P=a	I/P=b
→A	B	F
B	A	F
C	G	A
D	H	B
E	A	G
F	H	C
G	A	D
H	A	C

Here F,G,H are final states.

Ans. In the Finite automata the states are {A,B,C,D,E,F,G,H }. Name this set as $S_{0.}$

S_0: {A,B,C,D,E,F,G,H } All of the states are 0 equivalent.

In the finite automata, there are two types of states Final State and Non-Final States. So divide the set of states into two parts Q_1 and Q_2.

$Q1$ = {F, G, H}, $Q2$ = {A, B, C, D, E}.

S_1: {{F, G, H} {A, B, C, D, E}}.

States belong to same subset are 1-equivalent because they are in the same set for string length 1. States belong to different subsets are 1- distinguishable.

The next states of F are H and C. The next states of G and H are A, D and A, C, respectively.

A, D and A, C belong to the same subset but H and C are belong to different subset. Hence, F, G, H are divided into {F}, {G, H}.

For input 0 the next states of A, B, C, D and E are B, A, G, H and A, respectively. For input 1 the next states of A, B, C, D and E are F, F, A, B and G, respectively. Hence, the set {A, B, C, D, E } is divided into {A, B, E} and {C, D}.

S_2: {{F} {G, H} {A, B, E} {C, D}}

By the same process {A, B, E} is divided into {A, B}, {E}.

S_3: {{F} {G, H} {A, B} {E} {C, D}} = {{A, B}, {C, D}, {E}, {F}, {G, H}}

The set further is not dividable. So these are the states of minimized DFA. Let rename the subsets as q_0, q_1, q_2, q_3 and q_4. Initial state was A, Hence here initial state is {A,B}, i.e. q_0. Final state were F, G and H, hence here final states are {F}, i.e. q_3 and {G,H}, i.e. q_4. The tabular representation of minimized DFA is

PS	NS I/P=0	NS I/P=1
$\rightarrow q_0$	q_0	q_3
q_1	q_4	q_0
q_2	q_0	q_4
(q_3)	q_4	q_1
(q_4)	q_0	q_1

13. Design a Mealy and Moore Machine for detecting a sequence 1010 where overlapping sequences are also accepted. The Moore Machine that you have got, convert it to Mealy Machine. Are any differences coming? How will you prove that the two Mealy machines are equivalent?

Ans.

The Mealy Machine is

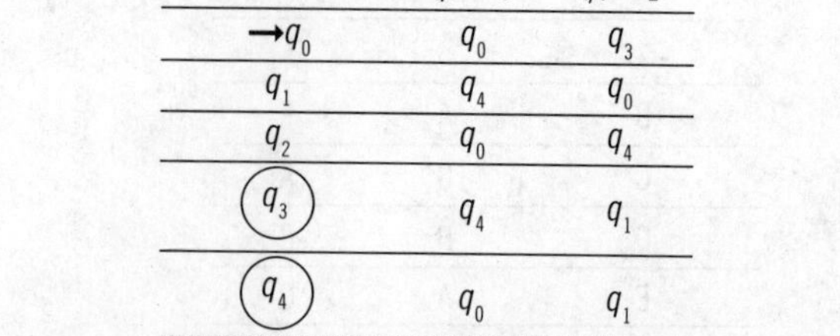

The Moore Machine:

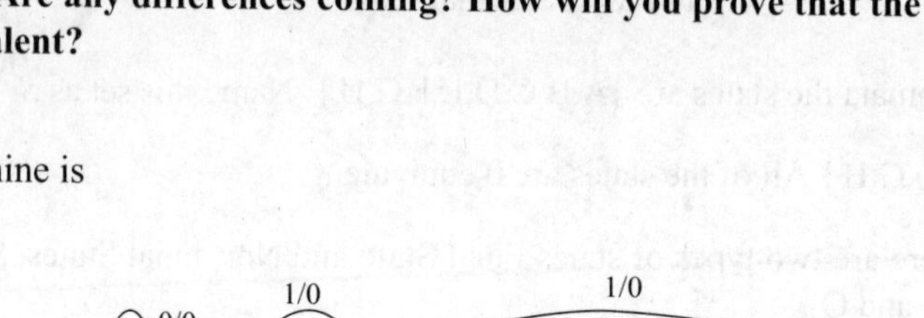

The converted Mealy machine from the given Moore Machine is (By using transactional format)

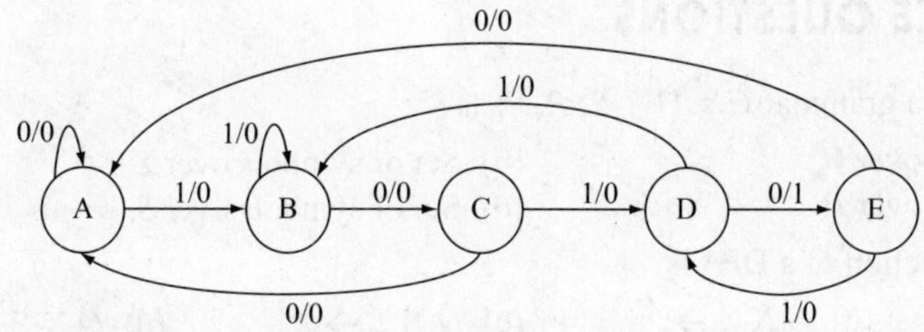

This is surely different from the previously constructed Mealy Machine in number of states and in transactions.

But these two Mealy machines are equivalent. This can be proved by finding the equivalent partitions of the second machine.

The tabular format of the previous machine is

PS	NS, z	
	x=0	x=1
A	A, 0	B, 0
B	C, 0	B, 0
C	A, 0	D, 0
D	E, 1	B, 0
E	A, 0	D, 0

$P_0 = \{A,B,C,D,E\}$,
$P_1 = \{A,B,C,E\}\{D\}$,
$P_2 = \{A,B\}\{C,E\}\{D\}$,
$P_3 = \{A\}\{B\}\{C,E\}\{D\}$,
$P_4 = \{A\}\{B\}\{C,E\}\{D\}$.

Rename the states as S_1, S_2, S_3, S_4

PS	NS, z	
	x=0	x=1
S_1 (A)	S_1, 0	S_2, 0
S_2 (B)	S_3, 0	S_2, 0
S_3 (C, E)	S_1, 0	S_4, 0
S_4 (D)	S_3, 1	S_2, 0

The machine is same as the first mealy machine.

MULTIPLE CHOICE QUESTIONS

1. A language L from a grammar $G = \{V_N, \Sigma, P, S\}$ is
   (a) Set of symbols over V_N
   (b) Set of symbols over Σ,
   (c) Set of symbols over P
   (d) Set of symbols over S.
2. The transitional function of a DFA is
   (a) $Q \times \Sigma \rightarrow Q$ (b) $Q \times \Sigma \rightarrow 2^Q$ (c) $Q \times \Sigma \rightarrow 2^n$ (d) $Q \times \Sigma \rightarrow Q^n$
3. The transitional function of a NFA is
   (a) $Q \times \Sigma \rightarrow Q$ (b) $Q \times \Sigma \rightarrow 2^Q$ (c) $Q \times \Sigma \rightarrow 2^n$ (d) $Q \times \Sigma \rightarrow Q^n$
4. Maximum number of states of a DFA converted from a NFA with n states is
   (a) n (b) n^2 (c) 2^n (d) None of these.
5. Basic limitations of finite state machine is
   (a) It cannot remember arbitrarily large amount of information,
   (b) In cannot remember state transitions,
   (c) In cannot remember grammar for a language,
   (d) It cannot remember language generated from a grammar.
6. The string WW^R is not recognized by any FSM because
   (a) A FSM cannot remember arbitrarily large amount of information,
   (b) A FSM cannot fix the mid point,
   (c) A FSM cannot match W with W^R,
   (d) A FSM cannot remember first and last inputs.
7. A finite automata recognizes
   (a) Any Language
   (b) Context Sensitive Language
   (c) Context Free Language
   (d) Regular Language.
8. Which is true for Dead State?
   (a) It cannot be reached anytime,
   (b) There is no necessity of the state,
   (c) If control enters no way to come out from the state,
   (d) If control enters FA deads.
9. Which is true for Moore Machine?
   (a) Output depends on present state,
   (b) Output depends on present input,
   (c) Output depends on present state and present input,
   (d) Output depends on present state and past input.
10. Which is true for Mealy Machine?
    (a) Output depends on present state
    (b) Output depends on present input
    (c) Output depends on present state and present input
    (d) Output depends on present state and past input

11. Which is true for in accessible state?
    (a) It cannot be reached anytime,
    (b) There is no necessity of the state,
    (c) If control enters no way to come out from the state,
    (d) If control enters FA deads.
12. In Mealy Machine O/P is associated with
    (a) Present state (b) Next state (c) Input (d) None of these
13. In Moore Machine O/P is associated with
    (a) Present state (b) Next state (c) Input (d) None of these
14. Which type string is accepted by the following finite automata?
    (a) All string (b) Null string (c) No string (d) All of the above

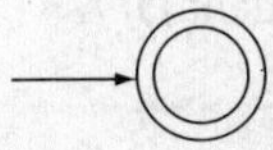

Ans: 1. b 2. a 3. b 4. c 5. a 6. b 7. d 8. c 9. a 10. c 11. a 12. b 13. a 14. b

EXERCISES

1. Test whether the following strings are accepted by the given finite automata or not.
   (a) 01010 (b) 1010100 (c) 0100101

PS	NS	
	a=0	a=1
$\rightarrow q_0$	q_1	q_2
q_1	q_3	q_2
q_2	q_2	q_3
(q_3)	q_3	q_0

2. Test whether the following strings are accepted by the given finite automata or not.
   (a) 100010 (b) 0001101 (c) 1000

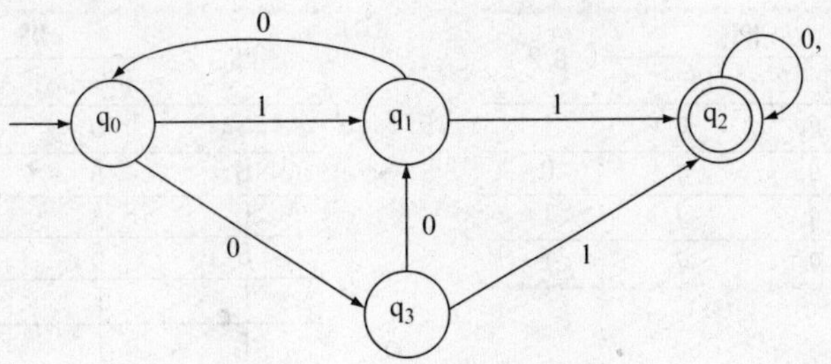

3. Test whether the following string 101001 is accepted by the given finite automata or not taking all possible combination of transitional path.

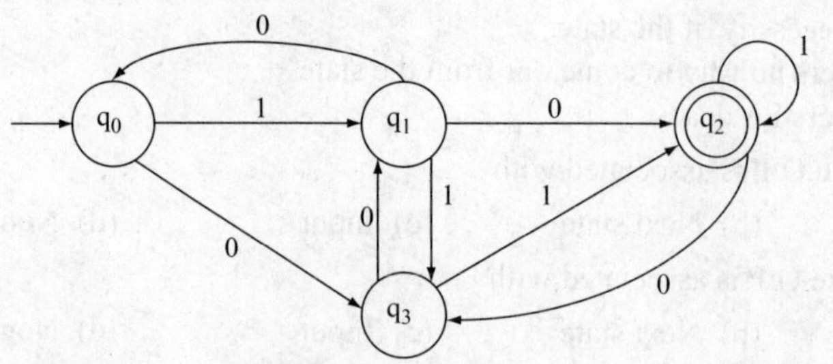

Why are you getting different result? Explain.

4. Convert the following NFA s into equivalent DFA s.

(a)

PS	NS	
	a=0	a=1
→A	B	A, C
B	B	C
C	A, D	B
(D)	D	B

(b)

PS	NS	
	a=0	a=1
→q_0	q_0	q_0, q_1
(q_1)	–	q_2
q_2	q_2	q_2

(c)

PS	NS	
	a=0	a=1
→A	A	A, B
B	C	–
C	–	D
(D)	D	D

5. Convert the following NFA s with null move to equivalent DFA s.

a)

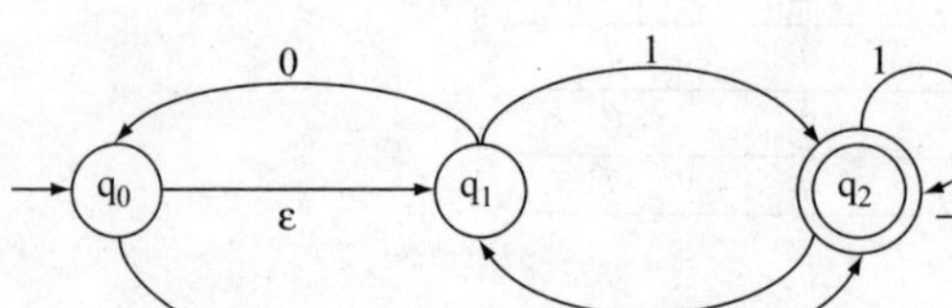

b)

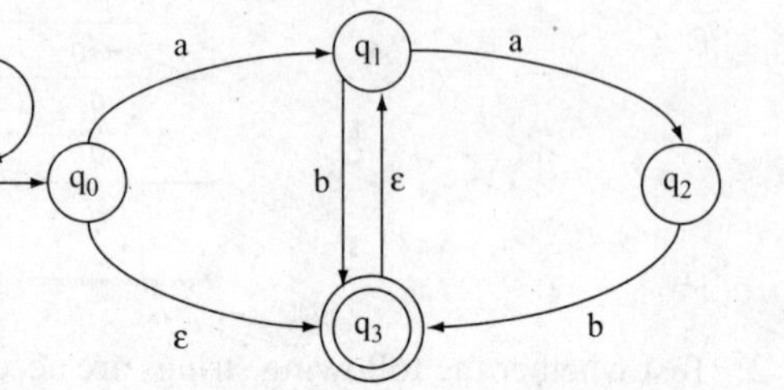

6. Convert the following Moore Machines into equivalent Mealy Machines.

(a)

PS	NS		O/P
	I/P=0	I/P=1	
→q_0	q_3	q_1	1
q_1	q_1	q_2	0
q_2	q_2	q_3	1
q_2	q_3	q_3	1

(b)

PS	NS		O/P
	I/P=0	I/P=1	
→A	D	B	1
B	A	E	0
C	A	E	1
D	C	A	0
E	F	D	0
F	F	D	1

7. Convert the following Mealy Machines into equivalent Moore Machines.

(a)

PS	I/P=0		I/P=1	
	NS	O/P	NS	O/P
A	E	0	C	0
B	F	0	C	1
C	E	0	A	0
D	F	0	A	1
E	A	0	D	0
F	D	0	E	1

(b)

PS	I/P=0		I/P=1	
	NS	O/P	NS	O/P
A	B	0	C	0
B	D	0	E	1
C	A	0	A	1
D	E	1	E	1
E	E	1	C	0

8. Convert the following Moore Machine into equivalent Mealy machine by transitional format.

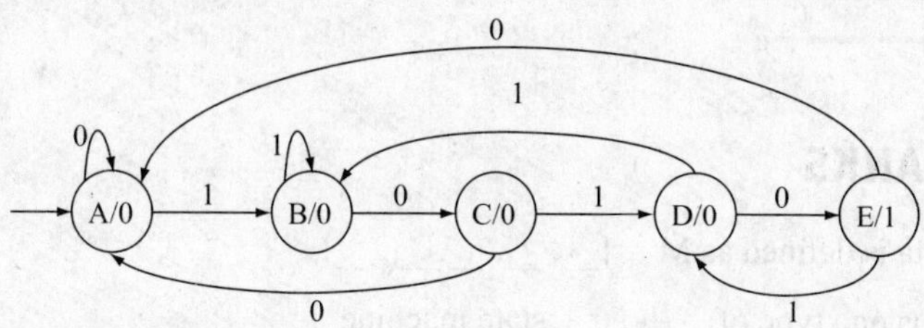

9. Convert the following Mealy Machine into equivalent Moore machine by transitional format.

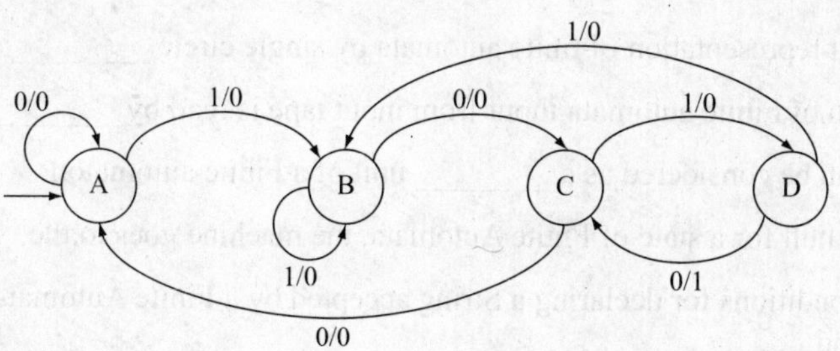

10. Minimize the following finite automata by finding equivalent state method..

(a)

PS	NS	
	I/P=0	I/P=1
→A	E	C
B	C	A
C	B	G
D	G	A
E	F	B
F	E	D
G	D	G

(b)

PS	NS	
	I/P=0	I/P=1
→A	B	H
B	F	D
C	D	E
D	C	F
E	D	C
F	C	C
G	C	D
H	C	A

11. Minimize the following finite automata by MyHill Nerode Theorem.

PS	NS	
	I/P=0	I/P=1
→A	B	F
B	G	C
(C)	A	C
D	C	G
E	H	F
F	C	G
G	G	E
H	G	C

FILL IN THE BLANKS

1. A Finite Automata is defined as M = {__, __, __, __, __}.
2. Finite Automata is one type of ________ state machine
3. In graphical format representation of finite automata by double circle ________ state is represented.
4. In tabular format representation of finite automata by single circle ________ state is represented.
5. In block diagram of Finite automata input from input tape is read by ________.
6. Finite control can be considered as a ________ unit of a Finite automaton.
7. If input is given null for a state of Finite Automata, the machine goes to the ________.
8. There are two conditions for declaring a String accepted by a Finite Automaton. The conditions are ________ and ________.
9. For DFA the transitional function δ is represented by Q X Σ → ________.
10. DFA is a Finite Automata where for all cases for a single input given to a single state the machine goes to a ________ state.
11. In NFA δ is a transitional function mapping Q X Σ → ________.
12. If any Finite Automata contains any ϵ (null) move or transaction then that Finite Automata is called ________ with ϵ moves.
13. A state where the control can enter and confined till the input ended, but no way to come out from that state is called ________.
14. Mealy Machine and Moore Machine are example of Finite Automata with ________.
15. For Mealy machine the output depends on ________ and ________.
16. For Moore machine the output depends on ________.

17. The states which can never be reached from the initial state are called ________ state.

18. A relation R in set S is called equivalence relation if it is ________, ________ and ________.

19. A relation R in set S is ________ if for x,y in S, yRx whenever xRy.

20. A relation R in set S is ________ if for x,y and z in S, xRz whenever xRy and yRz.

21. R is ________ then for all x,y and z , xRy => xzRyz.

22. Myhill-Nerode Theorem is used for ________.

23. A two way finite automata is like Finite Automata but can traverse in ________.

24. Lexical analyzer is designed by ________.

25. Maximum number of states of a DFA converted from a NFA with n states is ________.

26. A Finite Automata recognizes ________ language.

ANSWERS

1. Q, S, 8, q0, F
2. finite
3. final
4. final
5. Reading head
6. Control
7. same state
8. string must be totally traversed, The machine must come to a Final state
9. Q
10. Single
11. 2^Q
12. NFA
13. Dead State
14. outputs
15. present state, present input
16. Present State
17. in accessible
18. reflexive, symmetric, transitive
19. symmetric
20. transitive
21. right invariant
22. Minimization of FA
23. Both direction
24. Finite Automata
25. 2^n

4

Regular Expression

4.1 BASICS OF REGULAR EXPRESSION

Q. What is Regular Expression?

Ans. A regular expression can be defined as a language or string accepted by a finite automata.

We know that a finite automata consists of five touples $\{Q, \Sigma, \delta, q_0, F\}$. Among them a Regular Expression is a string on Σ, i.e. it will consist only with input alphabets.

In short a Regular Expression is written as RE.

Q. Give some formal recursive definition of Regular Expression

Ans.

(i) Any terminals, i.e. the symbols belong to **Σ** are Regular Expression. Null string(**Λ**) and Null set(Ø) are also Regular Expression.

(ii) If P and Q are two Regular Expressions then the union of the two Regular Expressions denoted by $P + Q$ is also a Regular Expression.

(iii) If $\boldsymbol{P}$ and $\boldsymbol{Q}$ are two Regular Expressions then their concatenation denoted by $\boldsymbol{PQ}$ is also a Regular Expression.

(iv) If $\boldsymbol{P}$ is a Regular Expression then the iteration (repetition or closure) denoted by $\boldsymbol{P}^*$ is also a Regular Expression.

(v) If $\boldsymbol{P}$ is a Regular Expression then **(*P*)** is a Regular Expression.

(vi) The expressions got by repeated application of the rules from (i) to (v) over Σ are also Regular Expression.

Q. Describe three basic operations on Regular Expression.

Ans. Three basic operations are Union, Concatenation and closure.

Operation of union on Regular Expression: If R_1 and R_2 are two Regular Expression s over Σ then $L(R_1 \text{ U } R_2)$ is denoted by $L(R_1 + R_2)$.

$L(R_1 \text{ U } R_2)$ is a string from R_1 or a string from R_2.

$L(R_1 + R_2) = L(R_1) \text{ U } L(R_2)$.

Operation of Concatenation on Regular Expression: If R_1 and R_2 are two Regular Expression s over Σ then $L(R_1 \cap R_2)$ is denoted by $L(R_1R_2)$.

$L(R_1 \cap R_2)$ is a string from R_1 followed by a string from R_2.

$L(R_1R_2) = L(R_1)L(R_2)$.

Operation of Closure on Regular Expression: If R_1 and R_2 are two Regular Expressions over Σ then $L(R^*)$ is a string obtained by concatenating n elements for $n \geq 0$.

Q. Define Kleene's Closure with example. What is the difference with Closure?

Ans.

Kleene's Closure: It is defined as a set of all strings including null (Λ) obtained from the alphabets of the set Σ. It is denoted as Σ^*.

If $\Sigma = \{0\}$, then $\Sigma^* = \{\Lambda, 0, 00, 000, \ldots\ldots\}$,

If $\Sigma = \{0, 1\}$, then $\Sigma^* = \{\Lambda, 0, 1, 01, 00, 11, 010, 011, 100, \ldots\ldots\}$.

Difference

(i) Closure is nothing but iteration of 0 to ∞ times, but Kleene's Closure is set including Λ.

(ii) Closure is applied on Regular Expression, but Kleene's Closure is applied on Σ

(iii) If $R = 01$, then Closure on R denoted by R^* are Λ, 01, 0101, 010101,…, etc., i.e. iteration of the same string 01.

If $\Sigma = \{0, 1\}$ then Kleene's Closure denoted by $\Sigma^* = \{\Lambda, 0, 1, 01, 00, 11, 010, 011, 100, \ldots\}$, i.e. set of any combinations of 0 and 1 including Λ.

Q. Describe the following REs in English language.

(i) 10^*1 (ii) a^*b^* (iii) $(ab)^*$ (iv) $(a^* + b^*)\, c^*$ (v) $(00)^*(11)^*1$.

Ans.

(i) The strings that we get from the Regular Expression $\mathbf{10^*1}$ are {11, 101, 1001, 10001, …}. From the set we can conclude that the strings that are generated from the Regular Expression s are beginning with 1 and ending with 1. In between 1 and 1 there are any numbers of 0.

So we can describe in English like this:

Set of all strings, beginning and ending with 1 *with any number of* 0 *in between two* 1.

(ii) The strings that we get from the Regular Expression a^*b^* are $a^*.b^*$, i.e.

$\{\Lambda, a, aa, aaa, \ldots\}.\{\Lambda, b, bb, bbb, \ldots\} = \{\Lambda, a, b, aa, bb, ab, abb, aab, \ldots\}$

from the set we can conclude that the strings that are generated from the Regular Expression, contain any number of 'a' followed by any number of 'b',

so we can describe in English like this:

Set of all strings of 'a' *and* 'b' *containing any number of* 'a' *followed by any number of* 'b'.

(iii) The strings that we get from the Regular Expression $(ab)^*$ are $\{\Lambda, ab, abab, ababab, \ldots\}$.

In English it can be said as:

Set of all string of a *and* b *with equal number of* a *and* b *containing* 'ab' *as repetition.*

(iv) $(a^* + b^*)$ means any combination of a or any combination of b. The c^* means any combination of c, which is concatenated with $(a^* + b^*)$.

In English it can be described as

Any combination of 'a' *or any combination of* 'b' *followed by any combination of* 'c'.

(v) The strings that we get, from the Regular Expression $\mathbf{(00)^*(11)^*1}$, are $\{1, 001, 111, 00111, \ldots\}$. In the string there are always odd number of 1 and even number of 0.

In English it can be described as:

Set of all strings of '0' and '1' with even number 0 followed by odd number of 1.

Q. Construct Regular Expression from the description given below.

(i) A Regular Expression consists of any combination of a and b; beginning with a, and ending with b.

(ii) A language of any combination of a and b containing abb as a substring.

(iii) Regular Expression of a and b containing at least 2 'a's.

(iv) Write Regular Expression for the language $L = \{a^n b^m \mid \text{where } m + n \text{ is even}\}$.

(v) A Regular Expression of a and b, having exactly one 'a'.

Ans.

(i) The Regular Expression consists of any combination of a and b, i.e. $(a + b)^*$. But the Regular Expression starts with a and ends with b. In between a and b any combination of a and b occurs. So the Regular Expression is

$L = a(a + b)^*b$.

(ii) In the Regular Expression abb occurs as a substring. The R.E. consists of any combination of a and b. The substring abb may occur at the beginning, at the middle, or at the last. If abb occurs at the beginning then after abb there is any combination of a and b. If abb occurs at the middle then before and after abb there are any combination of a and b. If abb occurs at the last then before abb there is any combination of a and b.

So the Regular Expression is $L = (a + b)^*abb(a + b)^*$.

(iii) The expression consists of a and b and it contains atleast two a. There may be more than two a. So any combination of 'a' and 'b' can occur before the first 'a', before the second 'a', i.e. after the first 'a' and after the second 'a'.

So the Regular Expression will be $L = (a + b)^*a(a + b)^*\, a(a + b)^*$

(iv) The Regular Expression consists of n number of 'a' followed by m number of 'b'. However, $m + n$ is always even. This is possible if

(a) m and n both are even or (b) m and n both are odd.

If m and n are both even then the expression will be $(aa)^*(bb)^*$.

If m and n are both odd then the expression will be $(aa)^*a(bb)^*b$

By combining these two the Regular Expression will be

$L = (aa)^*(bb)^* + (aa)^*a(bb)^*b$.

(v) In the Regular Expression there is exactly one 'a'. Before and after a there is any combination of b.

Hence the Regular Expression will be $L = b^*ab^*$.

Q. Mention the identities of Regular Expression.

Ans. We all know that by using two points one and only one straight line can be drawn. This statement is taken as a true and based on that the Geometry stands. This cannot be proved. This is taken as a universal truth. This type of statements is called Identities.

For Regular Expression there are also some identities.

(i) $\emptyset + R = R + \emptyset = R$

(ii) $\emptyset R = R\emptyset = \emptyset$

(iii) $\Lambda R = R\Lambda = R$

(iv) $\Lambda^* = \Lambda$ and $\emptyset^* = \Lambda$

(v) $R + R = R$

(vi) $R^*R^* = R^*$

(vii) $R^*R = RR^*$

(viii) $(R^*)^* = R^*$

(ix) $\Lambda + RR^* = \Lambda + R^*R = R^*$

(x) $(PQ)^*P = P(QP)^*$

(xi) $(P + Q)^* = (P^*Q^*)^* = (P^* + Q^*)^*$

(xii) $(P + Q)R = PR + QR$.

Q. From the Identities of Regular Expression prove that

$\mathbf{(1 + 100^*) + (1 + 100^*)(0 + 10^*)(0 + 10^*)^* = 10^*(0 + 10^*)^*}$.

Ans. LHS

$(1 + 100^*) + (1 + 100^*)(0 + 10^*)(0 + 10^*)^*$

$= (1 + 100^*)\ [\wedge + (0 + 10^*)(0 + 10^*)^*]$

$= (1 + 100^*)(0 + 10^*)^*$ [According to $\mathbf{\Lambda + RR^* = R^*}$]

$= 1(\Lambda + 00^*)(0 + 10^*)^*$

$= 10^*(0 + 10^*)^* =$ RHS.

Q. From the Identities of Regular Expression prove that

$\mathbf{\wedge + 1^*(011)^*[1^*(011)^*]^* = (1 + 011)^*}$

Ans. Take $\mathbf{1^*(011)^*}$ as P then the LHS becomes

$\wedge + PP^*$
$= P^*$
$= [1^*(011)^*]^* = (1 + 011)^* =$ RHS [As $(P + Q)^* = (P^*Q^*)^*$].

Q. From the Identities of Regular Expression prove that

$$\mathbf{10 + (1010)^*[\wedge + \wedge(1010)^*] = 10 + (1010)^*}$$

Ans. LHS $= 10 + (1010)^*[\wedge + \wedge(1010)^*]$

$\Rightarrow 10 + (1010)^*[\wedge + (1010)^*]$ *As* $\wedge R = R$

$\Rightarrow 10 + \wedge(1010)^* + (1010)^* (1010)^*$

$\Rightarrow 10 + (1010)^* + (1010)^*$ As $\wedge R = R$ and $RR = R$

$\Rightarrow 10 + (1010)^* =$ RHS As $R + R = R$

4.2 ARDEN THEOREM

Q. State and prove Arden's theorem.

Ans.

Arden's Theorem:

Statement: Let $\boldsymbol{P}$ and $\boldsymbol{Q}$ be two Regular Expression s over Σ. If $\boldsymbol{P}$ does not contain Λ, then for the equation

$\boldsymbol{R = Q + RP}$ has a unique (one and only one) solution $\boldsymbol{R = QP^*}$.

Proof:

Now point out the statements in Arden's Theorem in General form.

(i) $\boldsymbol{P}$ and $\boldsymbol{Q}$ are two Regular Expressions.

(ii) $\boldsymbol{P}$ does not contain $\boldsymbol{\Lambda}$ symbol.

(iii) $\boldsymbol{R = Q + RP}$ has a solution, i.e. $\boldsymbol{R = QP^*}$

(iv) This solution is the one and only one solution of the equation.

If $\boldsymbol{R = QP^*}$ is a solution of the equation $\boldsymbol{R = Q + RP}$ then by putting the value of $\boldsymbol{R}$ in the equation we shall get the value '0'.

$$\boldsymbol{R = Q + RP}$$
$$\boldsymbol{R - Q - RP = 0}$$

LHS $\qquad \boldsymbol{R - Q - RP}$

(Putting the value of R in the LHS we get)

$$\boldsymbol{QP^* - Q - QP^* P}$$
$$\boldsymbol{= QP^* - Q(\wedge + P^* P)}$$
$$\boldsymbol{= QP^* - QP^*} \quad \textbf{[As } (\wedge + R^*R) = R^* \textbf{]}$$
$$\boldsymbol{= 0}$$

So from here it is proved that $\boldsymbol{R = QP^*}$ is a solution of the equation $\boldsymbol{R = Q + RP}$.

Now we have to prove that $\boldsymbol{R = QP^*}$ is the one and only one solution of the equation $\boldsymbol{R = Q + RP}$.

As $\boldsymbol{R = Q + RP}$, so put the value of $\boldsymbol{R}$ again and again in the RHS of the equation.

$$\begin{aligned} R &= Q + RP \\ &= Q + (Q + RP)P \\ &= Q + QP + RPP \\ &= Q(\Lambda + P) + RPP \\ &= Q(\Lambda + P) + (Q + RP)PP \\ &= Q(\Lambda + P) + QPP + RPPP \\ &= Q(\Lambda + P + PP) + RPPP \end{aligned}$$

After several steps we shall get

$$R = Q(\Lambda + P + P^2 + P^3 + \ldots + P^n) + RP^{n+1}.$$

Now let a string w belongs to $\boldsymbol{R}$. If w is a Λ string then in which part the Λ will belong?

This string will belong to either in $Q(\Lambda + P + P^2 + P^3 + \text{----} P^n)$ part or in $\boldsymbol{RP^{n+1}}$ part. However, according to point number (ii) $\boldsymbol{P}$ does not contain $\boldsymbol{\Lambda}$, so the string w does not belong to $\boldsymbol{RP^{n+1}}$. So it will obviously belong to $\boldsymbol{Q(\Lambda + P + P^2 + P^3 + \text{----} P^n)}$ which is nothing but $\boldsymbol{QP^*}$. $\boldsymbol{[(\Lambda + P + P^2 + P^3 + \text{----} P^n)}$ is any combination of $\boldsymbol{P}$ including $\boldsymbol{\Lambda}$].

As this string belongs only in one part so $\boldsymbol{R}$ and $\boldsymbol{QP^*}$ represents the same set. That means $\boldsymbol{R = QP^*}$ is the unique solution of the equation $\boldsymbol{R = Q + RP}$.

Q. How Regular Expression can be constructed from Finite Automata by Algebraic Method using Arden's Theorem.

Ans.

There are some assumptions:

(i) In the transitional graph there will be no Λ-move.

(ii) In the Finite Automata there will be only one initial state.

For the Finite Automata given above there is no Λ-move. And it has only one initial state.

Now we have to construct equations for all the three states. There will be n number of equations if there are n-states.

For any Finite Automata these equations will be constructed in the following way.

<State Name> = Σ[<State Name from which inputs are coming>.<input>]

For the beginning state there is an arrow at the beginning coming from no state. Therefore, a Λ will be added with the equation of beginning state.

Then these equations have to be solved by the Identities of Regular Expression. The expression consists of only the input symbols of Σ, for the final state is the Regular Expression for the Finite Automata.

Q. Construct a Regular Expression from the given Finite Automata by Algebraic Method using Arden's Theorem

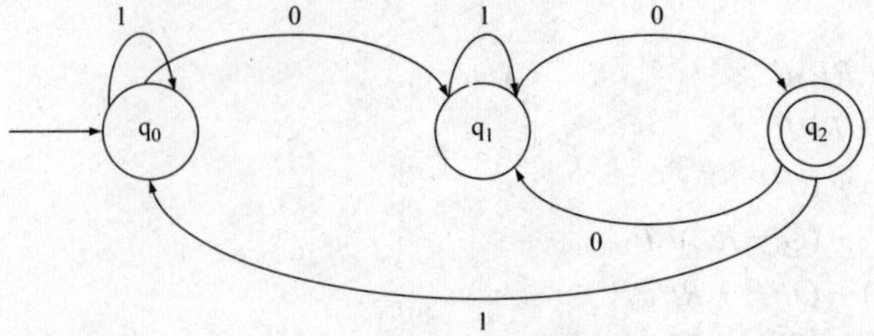

Ans.

For the above given Finite Automata the equations will be

$q_0 = q_0.1 + q_2.1 + \Lambda$ (i)

$q_1 = q_0.0 + q_1.1 + q_2.0$ (ii)

$q_2 = q_1.0$ (iii)

Put the value of q_2 in equation no. (ii)

$$q_1 = q_0.0 + q_1.1 + q_1.0.0$$
$$= q_0.0 + q_1(1 + 0.0)$$

This equation is in the form $\boldsymbol{R = Q + RP}$ where $\boldsymbol{R = q_1, Q = q_0.0}$ **and** $\boldsymbol{P = (1 + 0.0)}$

So the solution of the equation will be $\boldsymbol{R = QP^*}$, **i.e.** $\boldsymbol{q_1 = q_0.0. (1 + 0.0)^*}$

Put the value $q_2 = q_1.0$ in equation no. (i).

We will get

$$q_0 = q_0.1 + q_1.0.1 + \Lambda$$

Again put the value of q_1 in the above equation, we will get

$$q_0 = q_0.1 + q_0.0. (1 + 0.0)^*.0.1 + \Lambda$$
$$q_0 = q_0(1 + 0.(1 + 0.0)^*.0.1) + \Lambda$$

This equation is in the form $\boldsymbol{R = Q + RP}$, where $\boldsymbol{R = q_0, Q = \Lambda}$ and $\boldsymbol{P = (1 + 0.(1 + 0.0)^*.0.1)}$. So the solution of the equation:

$$q_0 = \Lambda.[1 + 0.(1 + 0.0)^*.0.1]^*$$
$$= [1 + 0.(1 + 0.0)^*.0.1]^*$$

Therefore $q_1 = [1 + 0.(1 + 0.0)^*.0.1]^*.0. (1 + 0.0)^*$

and $q_2 = [1 + 0.(1 + 0.0)^*.0.1]^*.0. (1 + 0.0)^*.0.$

As q_2 is the final state of the Finite automata so all strings will halt on this state. So the Regular Expression will be $[1 + 0.(1 + 0.0)^*.0.1]^*.0. (1 + 0.0)^*.0$ accepting the Finite Automata.

Q. Construct a Regular Expression from the given Finite Automata by Algebraic Method using Arden's Theorem

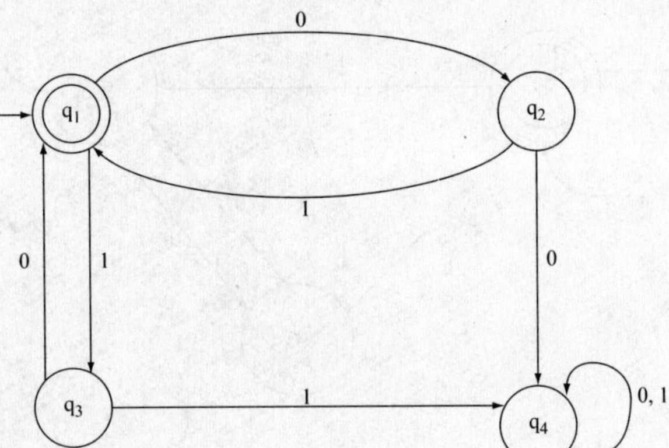

Ans.

For the above given Finite Automata the equations will be

$q_1 = q_2 1 + q_3 0 + \Lambda$ (i)

$q_2 = q_1 0$ (ii)

$q_3 = q_1 1$ (iii)

$q_4 = q_2 0 + q_3 1 + q_4 0 + q_4 1$ (iv)

Solution:

Substituting the value of q_2 and q_3 in q_1 we get.

$q_1 = q_1 01 + q_1 10 + \Lambda,$

$q_1 = q_1(01 + 10) + \Lambda.$

If q_1 is treated as R, Λ as Q and $(01 + 10)$ as P then the equation will become $R = Q + RP$

The solution for the equation will be $R = QP^*$.

Therefore $q_1 = \Lambda(01 + 10)^*$, i.e. $q_1 = (01 + 10)^*$ [As $\Lambda.R = R$]

As q_1 is the only final state so the string accepted by the Finite Automata is $(01 + 10)^*$

[We are seeing that we do not need the equation (iv), i.e. the equation for q_4 in the solution process. Here equation (iv) is redundant.]

Q. Construct a Regular Expression from the given Finite Automata by Algebraic Method using Arden's Theorem.

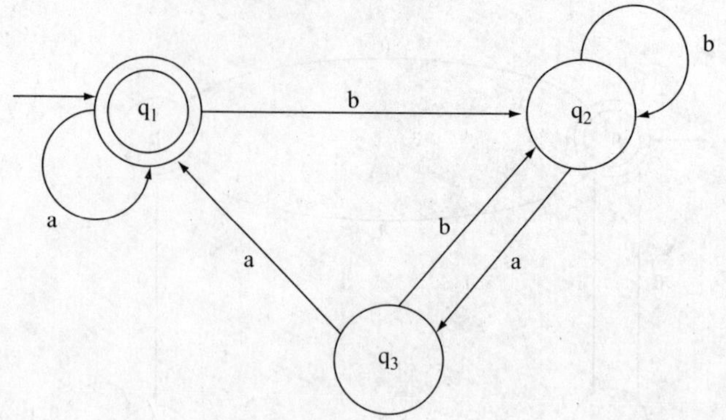

Ans. For the given Finite Automata the equations:

$q_1 = q_1.a + q_3.a + \wedge,$ (i)

$q_2 = q_2.b + q_3.b + q_1.b,$ (ii)

$q_3 = q_2.a.$ (iii)

Solution:

$q_3 = q_2.a$, replace this in equation (ii). The equation will become

$q_2 = q_2.b + q_2.a.b + q_1.b,$

$= q_2(b + a.b) + q_1.b.$

The equation is in the format of $R = Q + RP$, $q_2[R] = q_2[R](b + a.b)[P] + q_1.b\ [Q]$.

The solution will be $R = QP^*$ i.e. $q_2 = q_1 b.(b + ab)^*$.

Replace the value of q_2 in equation (iii).

$q_3 = q_1 b.(b + ab)^*.a.$

Replace the value of q_3 in equation (i),

$q_1 = q_1.a + q_1 b.(b + ab)^*.a.a + \wedge,$

$= q_1.[a + b.(b + ab)^*.a.a] + \wedge.$

The equation is in the format of $R = Q + RP$, $q_1[R] = q_1[R].[a + b.(b + ab)^*.a.a][P] + \wedge[Q]$. The solution of the equation will be $R = QP^*$, i.e. $q_1 - \wedge.[a + b.(b + ab)^*.a.a]^*$,

i.e. $q_1 = [a + b.(b + ab)^*.a.a]^*$ [According to $\mathbf{\Lambda R = R\Lambda = R}$]

q_1 is the final state, so the Regular Expression accepting the Finite Automata is

$[a + b.(b + ab)^*.a.a]^*.$

4.3 CONSTRUCTION OF FINITE AUTOMATA EQUIVALENT TO A REGULAR EXPRESSION

Q. What is the process of construction of Finite Automata equivalent to a Regular Expression?

Ans. The Regular Expression is the language format of finite automata. There are two steps for making a finite automata from an Regular Expression.

Step I: From the given Regular Expression an equivalent transitional system (Finite Automata) with Λ move has to be constructed.

Step II: From the transitional system with Λ moves a DFA need to be constructed.

For constructing **Step I** again there are several steps.

(i) Take two states one is Beginning state and another is Final state. Make a transition from Beginning state to Final state and place the Regular Expression in between the beginning and final state.

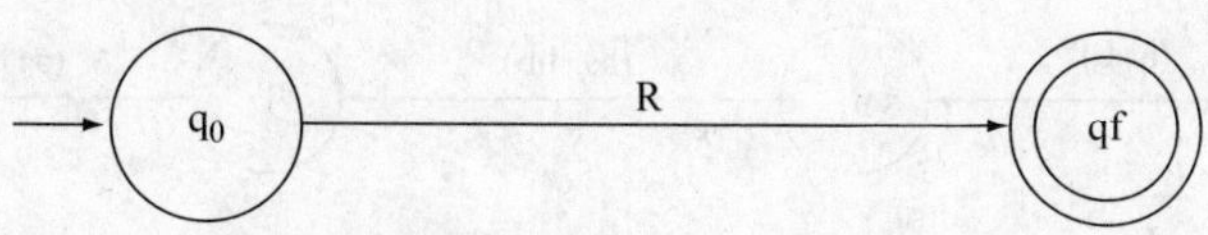

(ii) If in the Regular Expression there is a ' + ' (union) sign, then there are parallel paths between the two states.

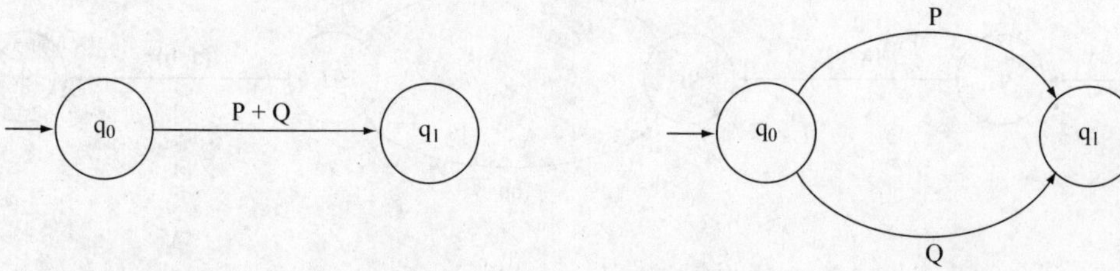

(iii) If in the Regular Expression there is a '.' (dot) sign, then one extra state will be added between the two states.

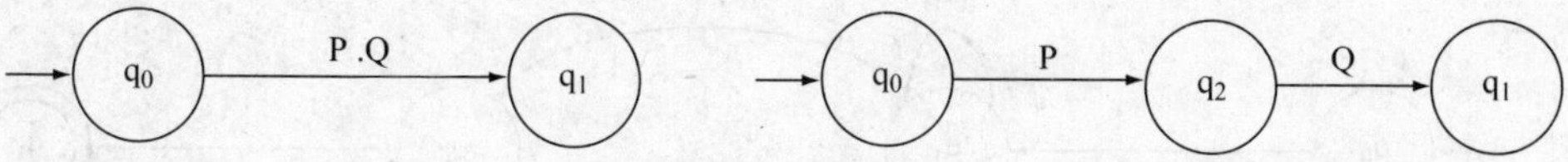

(iv) If in the Regular Expression there is a '*' (closure) sign, then a loop will be added to the next state putting label Λ between the two states.

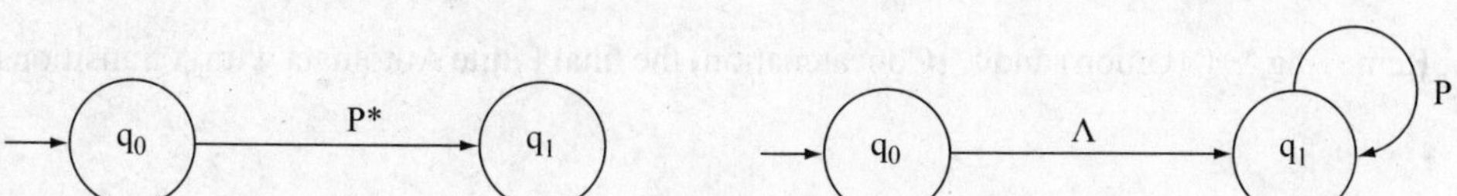

Q. Construct Finite Automata equivalent the Regular Expression.

$L = (a + b)^*(aa + bb)(a + b)^*$.

Ans.

I. Two states are taken. One is beginning state and another is final state. The Regular Expression is placed between the two states with a transition from beginning state to final state.

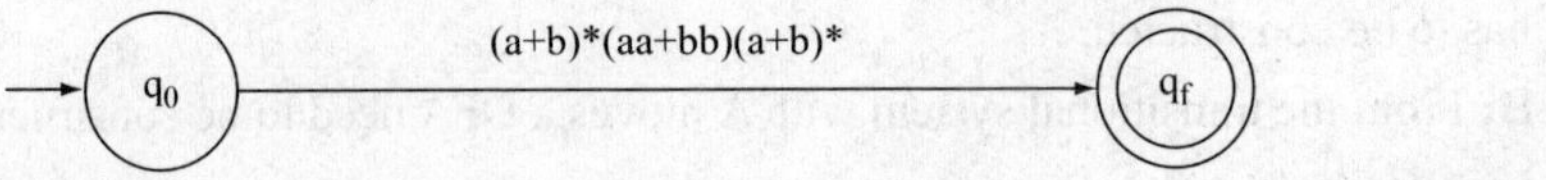

II. In the Regular Expression there are two '.' (Concatenation), between $(a + b)^*$ and $(aa + bb)$, and $(aa + bb)$ and $(a + b)^*$, two extra states will be added between q_0 and q_f.

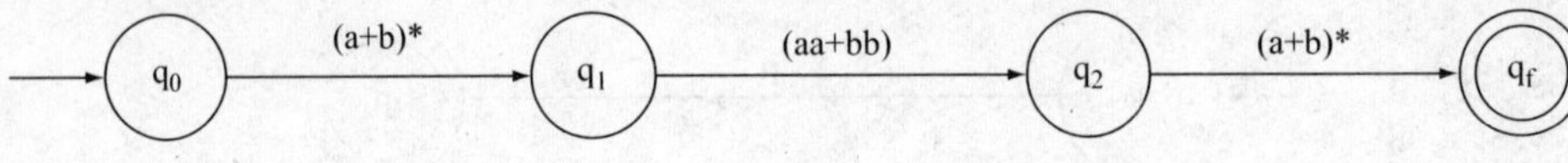

III. In *aa* and *bb* there is a ' + ' (Union) sign. Therefore between q_1 and q_2 there will be parallel paths.

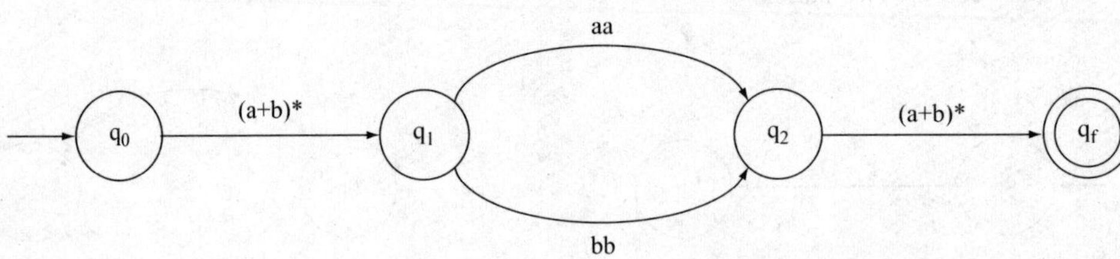

IV. There are two '*' (Closure) signs between q_0 and q_1, and q_2 and q_f. So, loop with label $a + b$ will be added to q_1 and q_f, making transitions between q_0, q_1 and q_2, q_f with label Λ.

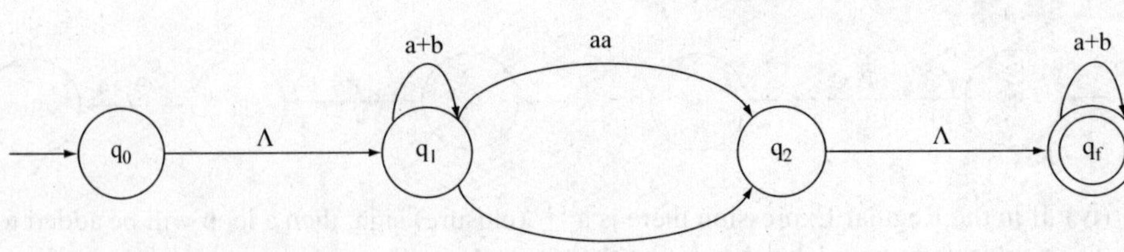

V. Removing ' + ' (Union) and '.'(Concatenation) the final Finite Automata with Λ transitions will be.

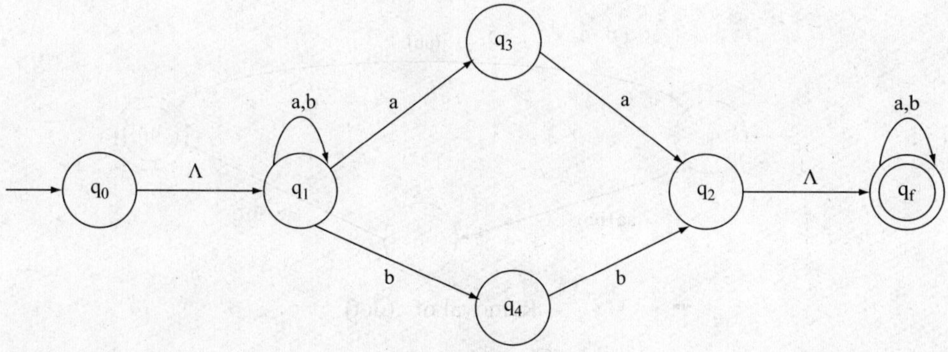

VI. Between q_0, q_1 and q_2, q_f there is a label Λ. It means from q_0 by getting no input it can reach to q_1, same thing is for q_2 and q_f. So q_0 and q_1 may be treated as same state, same for q_2 and q_f. The transitions from q_1 and q_f will be added with q_0 and q_2, respectively with same label.

By removing the Λ transactions the Finite Automata will be

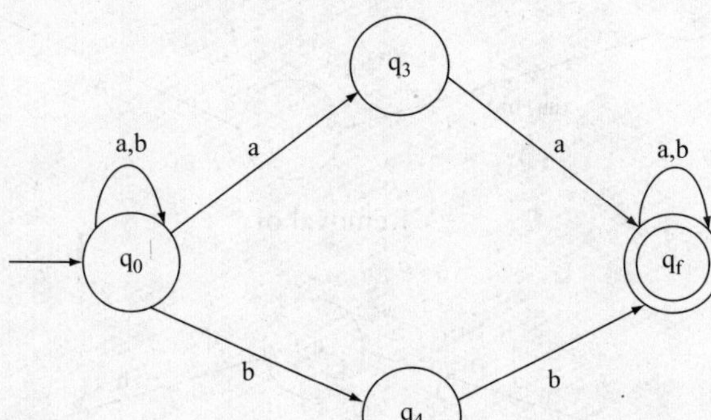

Q. Construct Finite Automata equivalent to the Regular Expression.

$L = ab + (aa + bb)(a + b)^*$

Ans.

I.

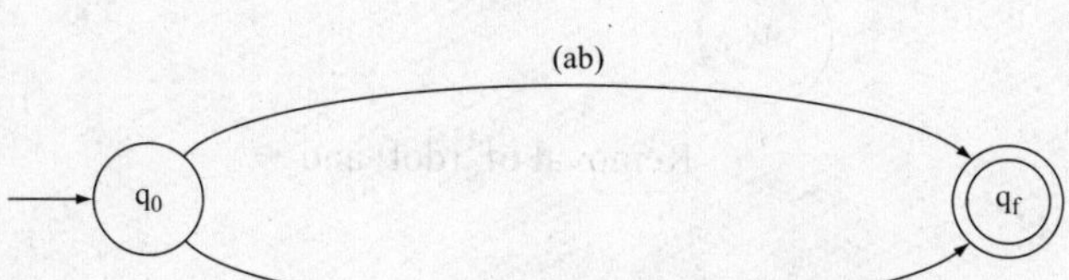

Removal of +

II.

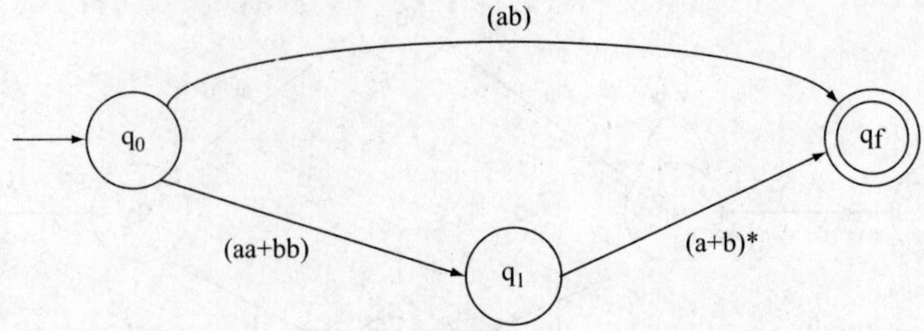

Removal of .(dot)

III.

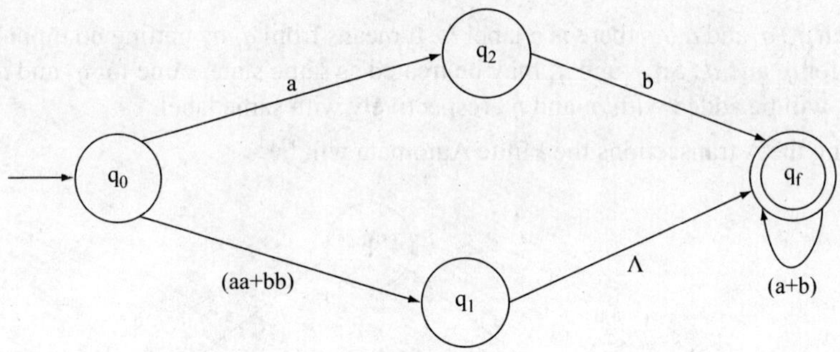

Removal of *

IV.

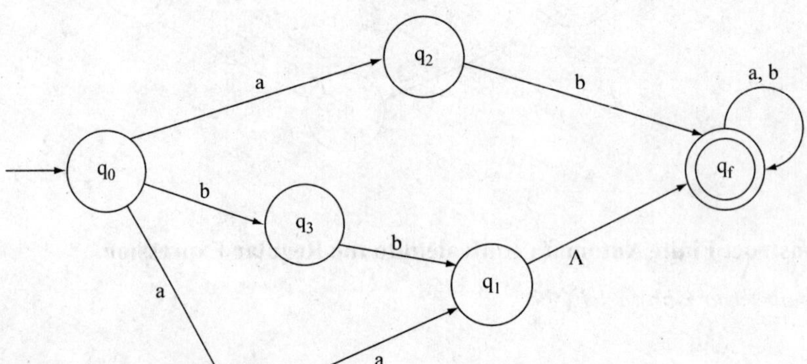

Removal of .(dot) and +

V.

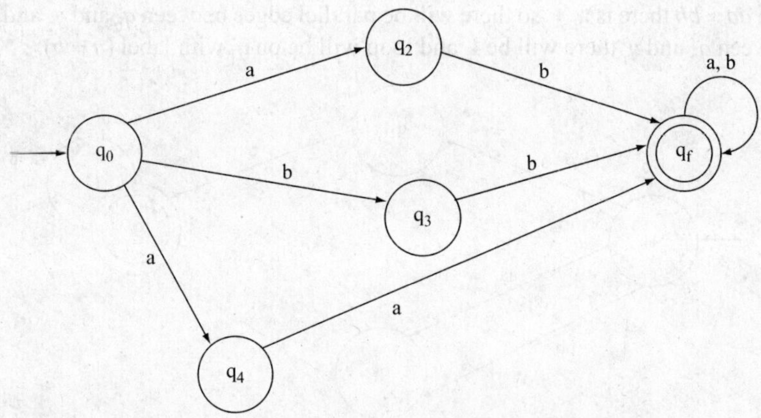

Q. Construct Finite Automata equivalent the Regular Expression.

$L = ab + (aa + bb)(a + b)^*$

Ans. Step I: Take a beginning state q_0 and a final state q_f .Between the beginning and final state place the Regular Expression.

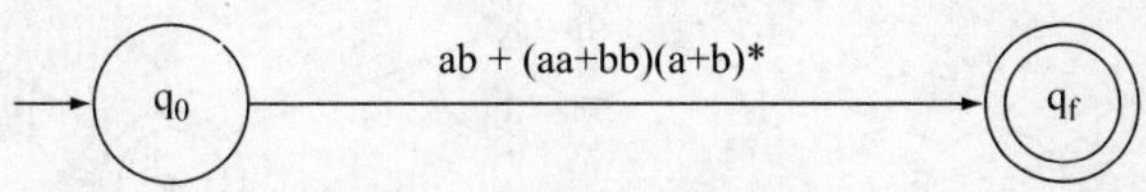

Step II: Between *ab* and $(aa + bb)(a + b)^*$ there is a + sign, so there will be parallel edges between q_0 and q_f.

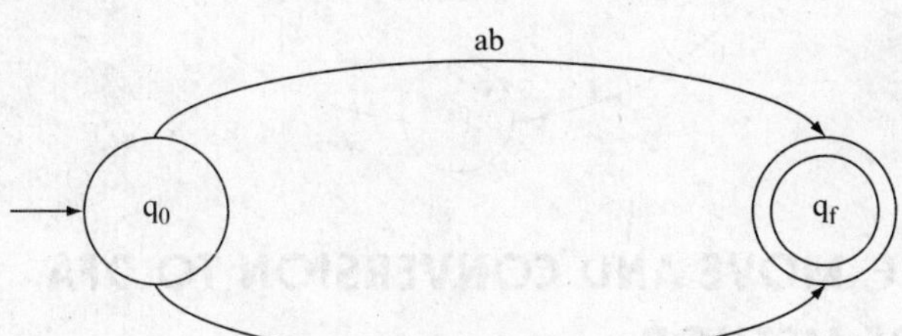

Step III: Between '*a*' and '*b*' there is a '.' (dot), so extra state will be added. Between $(aa + bb)$ and $(a + b)^*$ another extra state will also be added.

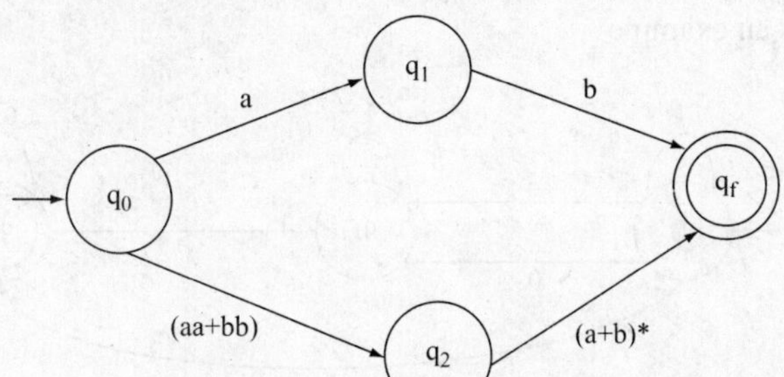

Step IV: In $aa + bb$ there is a +, so there will be parallel edges between q_0 and q_2 and in $(a + b)^*$ there is a *. So between q_2 and q_f there will be L and loop will be on q_f with label $(a + b)$.

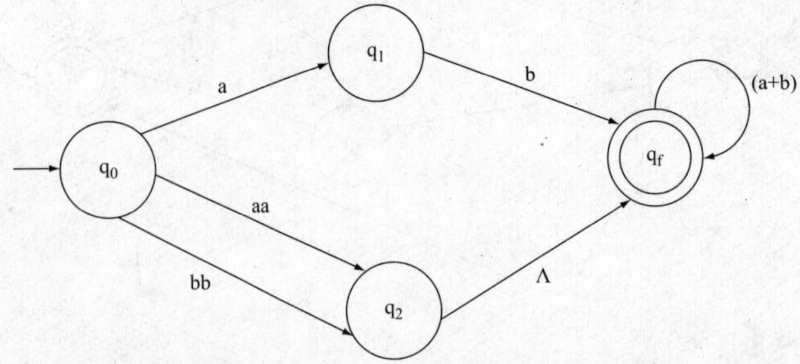

Step V: *aa* and *bb* there is .(dot). So, two extra states will be added between q_0 and q_2 [one for *aa* and another *bb*]. $(a + b)$ on q_f will be made loop with label *a,b*. Between q_2 and q_f there is a L, that is with no input, control can go to q_2 to q_f. So, q_2 and q_f are equivalent state. The final finite automata for the given Regular Expression will be.

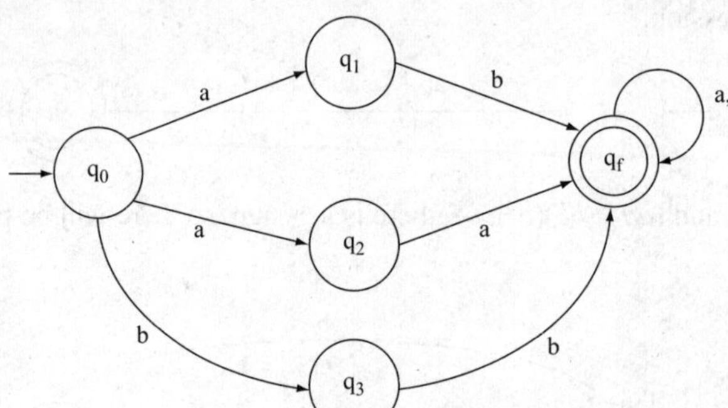

4.4 NFA WITH ∈ MOVE AND CONVERSION TO DFA BY ∈ – CLOSURE METHOD

Q. What do you mean by NFA with ∈ moves? Give an example. Why is it called NFA?

Ans.

If any Finite Automata contains any ∈ (null) move or transaction then that Finite Automata is called NFA with ∈ moves. As an example

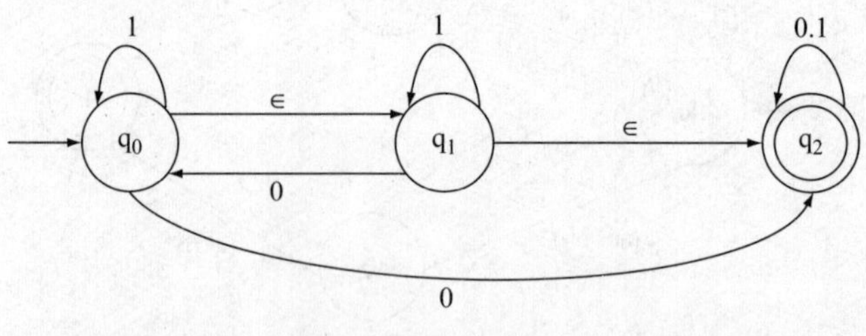

The previous Finite Automata contain two null moves. So the previous FA is NFA with null move.

From the definition of NFA we know for a NFA from a single state for a single input the machine can go to more than one state, i.e. $Q \times \Sigma \rightarrow 2^Q$, Where 2^Q is the power set of Q.

From a state by getting $\in$ input the machine is confined into that state. A Finite Automata with null move must contain at least one $\in$ move. For this type of Finite Automata for input $\in$ the machine can go to more than one state. (One is that same state and another state is the ε- transaction next state). So a Finite Automata with $\in$ move can be called as a NFA.

For the previous Finite Automata

$$\delta(q_0, \in) \rightarrow q_0 \text{ and } \delta(q_0, \in) \rightarrow q_1$$

$$\delta(q_1, \in) \rightarrow q_1 \text{ and } \delta(q_1, \in) \rightarrow q_2$$

A NFA with $\in$ move can be defined as

$$M_{\text{NFA null}} = \{Q, \Sigma, \delta, q_0, F\}.$$

Where Σ: Set of input alphabets including $\in$. and

δ is a transitional function mapping $Q \times \Sigma \rightarrow 2^Q$ 2^Q is the power set of Q.

Q. Define $\in$ closure. Clarify it by a suitable example.

Ans. $\in$ – closure of a state is defined as the set of all states S, such that it can reach from that state to all the states in S with input $\in$ (i.e. with no input).

Example: Consider the following NFA with $\in$ moves.

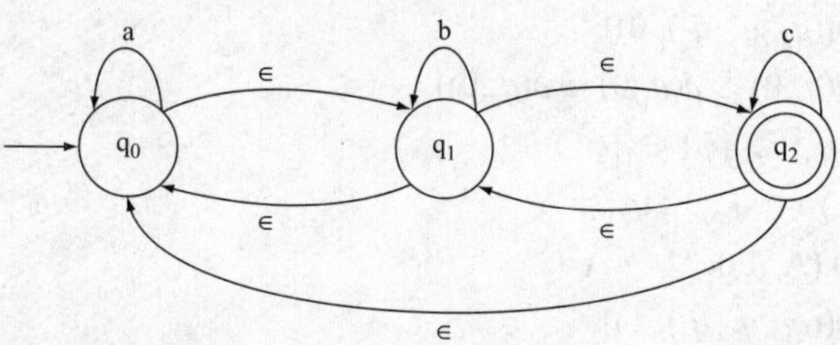

From state q_0 by input $\in$ (i.e. with no input) we can reach to state q_1 and q_2. With no input we can reach to the same state, i.e. q_0. Therefore, we can write

$\in$–closure $(q_0) = \{q_0, q_1, q_2\}$

Same like $\in$–closure$(q_1) = \{q_0, q_1, q_2\}$

$\in$–closure $(q_2) = \{q_0, q_1, q_2\}$ (From q_1 with no input we can reach to q_0, from q_2 with no input we can reach to q_1, so from q_2 with no input we can reach to q_0)

Q. How to convert a NFA with $\in$ move to a DFA?

Ans. Step I: Find $\in$–closure of all the states.

Step II: Construct transitional function δ' for the beginning state for all inputs. The function δ' will be calculated like the following

$$\delta'(Q, \text{i/p}) = \in\text{–closure}(\delta(Q, \text{i/p})).$$

Let $\in$–closure(A) $= \{q_1, q_2, q_3\} = Q$, Therefore the previous equation will become

$$\delta'(Q, i/p) = \in\text{–}closure(\delta(\{q_1, q_2, q_3\}, i/p))$$

$$= \in\text{–closure}[\delta(q_1, \text{i/p}) \cup \delta(q_2, \text{i/p}) \cup \delta(q_3, \text{i/p})].$$

Step III: First find ∈ –closure of the initial state. Rename the set of states as a new state. Then find function δ' of that state for all inputs. If δ' of that state for all inputs is constructed then it is called that the state is marked (Fuily Traversed for all the inputs). If any new combinations of state, other than the marked state appear in the process of marking then rename that as a new state.

Step IV: Repeat step III for all new unmarked states. If no the new state appears, then stop construction.

Step V: In this process the states which contain final state as entry are final state of the constructed new DFA.

Q. Convert the following NFA with ∈ –move to an equivalent DFA.

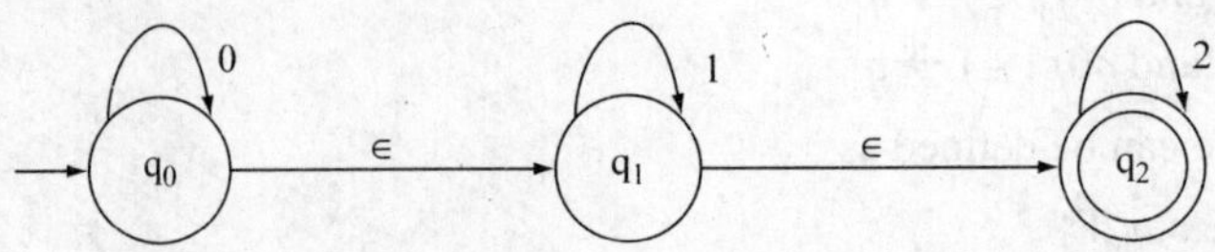

Ans. $\in\text{-closure}(q_0) = \{q_0, q_1, q_2\}$
$\in\text{-closure}(q_1) = \{q_1, q_2\}$
$\in\text{-closure}(q_2) = \{q_2\}$

$\in\text{-closure}(q_0) = \{q_0, q_1, q_2\}$. Let rename this state as A. Then construct δ' function for the new unmarked state A for input 0, 1 and 2.

$\delta'(A, 0) = \in\text{-closure}(\delta (A, 0))$
$= \in\text{-closure } (\delta((q_0, q_1, q_2), 0))$
$= \in\text{-closure } (\delta(q_0,0) \cup \delta(q_1,0) \cup \delta(q_2,0))$
$= \in\text{-closure } (\{q_0\} \cup \{\phi\} \cup \{\phi\})$
$= \in\text{-closure}(q_0) = \{ q_0, q_1, q_2\} = A$

$\delta'(A, 1) = \in\text{-closure } (\delta (A, 1))$
$= \in\text{-closure } (\delta((q_0, q_1, q_2), 1))$
$= \in\text{-closure } (\delta(q_0,1) \cup \delta(q_1,1) \cup \delta(q_2,1))$
$= \in\text{-closure } (\{\varphi\} \cup \{ q_1\} \cup \{\varphi\})$
$= \in\text{-closure } (q_1) = \{ q_1, q_2\}$.

As it is new combination of state other than A so rename it as B.

$\delta'(A, 2) = \in\text{-closure } (\delta (A, 2))$
$= \in\text{-closure } (\delta(q_0, q_1, q_2), 2)$
$= \in\text{-closure } (\delta(q_0,2) \cup \delta(q_1,2) \cup \delta(q_2,2))$
$= \in\text{-closure } (\{\varphi\} \cup \{ f\} \cup \{ q_2\})$
$= \in\text{-closure } (q_2) = \{q_2\}$.

As it is new combination of state other than A and B so rename it as C.

As δ' is constructed for all inputs on A so A is marked.

B is till unmarked.

Then construct δ' function for the new unmarked state B for input 0, 1 and 2.

$\delta'(B, 0) = \in\text{-closure } [\delta (B, 0)]$
$= \in\text{-closure } [\delta(q_1, q_2), 0]$
$= \in\text{-closure } [\delta(q_1,0) \cup \delta(q_2,0)]$
$= \in\text{-closure } (\{\varphi\} \cup \{\varphi\})$
$= \in\text{-closure } (\varphi) = \varphi$

$\delta'(B, 1) = \in\text{-closure } [\delta (B, 1)]$
$= \in\text{-closure } [\delta(q_1, q_2), 1]$
$= \in\text{-closure } [\delta(q_1,1) \cup \delta(q_2,1)]$
$= \in\text{-closure } (\{\varphi\})$
$= \in\text{-closure } (q_1) = \{q_1, q_2\} = B.$

$\delta'(B, 2) = \in\text{-closure } [\delta (B, 2)]$
$= \in\text{-closure } [\delta(q_1, q_2), 2]$
$= \in\text{-closure } [\delta(q_1,2) \cup \delta(q_2,2)]$
$= \in\text{-closure } (\{\varphi\} \cup \{ q_2\})$
$= \in\text{-closure } (q_2) = \{q_2\} = C.$

As δ' is constructed for all inputs on B so B is marked.

C is till unmarked.

Then construct δ' function for the new unmarked state C for input 0, 1 and 2.

$\delta'(C, 0) = \in\text{-closure } [\delta (C, 0)]$
$= \in\text{-closure } [\delta(q_2), 0]$
$= \in\text{-closure } [\delta(q_2,0)]$
$= \in\text{-closure } (\{\varphi\})$
$= \in\text{-closure}(\varphi) = \varphi$

$\delta'(C, 1) = \in\text{-closure } [\delta (C, 1)]$
$= \in\text{-closure } [\delta(q_2), 1]$
$= \in\text{-closure } [\delta(q_2,1)]$
$= \in\text{-closure } (\{\varphi\})$
$= \varphi$

$\delta'(C, 2) = \in\text{-closure } [\delta (C, 2)]$
$= \in\text{-closure } [\delta(q_2), 2]$
$= \in\text{-closure } [\delta(q_2,2)]$
$= \in\text{-closure } (\{q_2\}) = \{q_2\} = C.$

As A, B and C all contain q_2, which is final state, so A, B, C all are final states.

The equivalent DFA

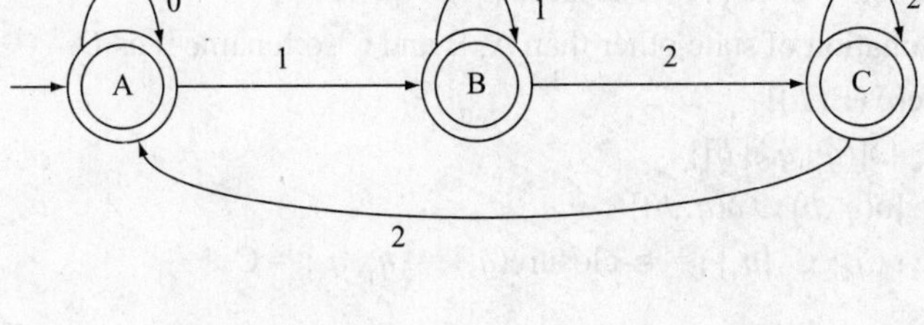

Q. Convert the following NFA with ∈- move to an equivalent DFA.

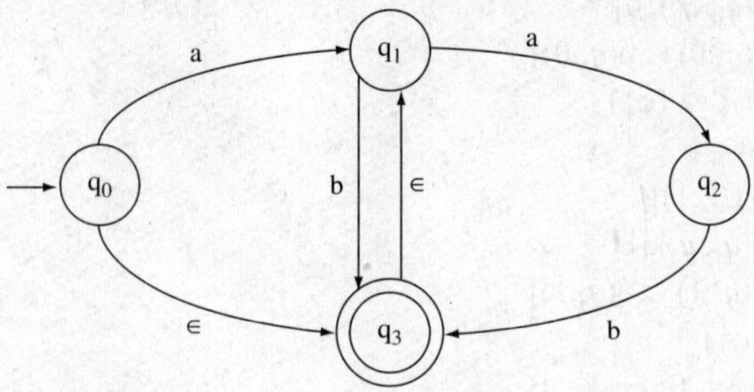

Ans. ∈-Closure $(q_0) = \{q_0, q_3, q_1\}$
∈-Closure $(q_1) = \{q_1\}$
∈-Closure $(q_2) = \{q_2\}$
∈-Closure $(q_3) = \{q_3, q_1\}$

∈-closure$(q_0) = \{q_0, q_1, q_3\}$. Lets rename this state as A. Then construct δ' function for the new unmarked state A for input 'a' and 'b'.

Then construct δ' function for the new unmarked state A for input 'a' and 'b'.

$\delta'(A, a)$ = ∈-closure$(\delta(A, a))$
= ∈-closure $\{\delta[(q_0, q_1, q_3), a]\}$
= ∈-closure $[\delta(q_0,a) \cup \delta(q_1,a) \cup \delta(q_3,a)]$
= ∈-closure $(\{q_1\} \cup \{q_2\} \cup \{\varphi\})$
= ∈-closure $(q_1, q_2) = \{q_1, q_2\}$.

As it is new combination of state other than A so rename it as B.

$\delta'(A, b)$ = ∈-closure $[\delta(A, b)]$
= ∈-closure $\{\delta[(q_0, q_1, q_3), b]\}$
= ∈-closure $[\delta(q_0,b) \cup \delta(q_1,b) \cup \delta(q_3,b)]$
= ∈-closure $(\{\varphi\} \cup \{q_3\} \cup \{\varphi\})$ = ∈-closure$(q_1) = \{q_3, q_1\}$

As it is new combination of state other than A and B so rename it as C.

As δ' is constructed for all inputs on A so A is marked.

B is till unmarked.

Then construct δ' function for the new unmarked state B for input 'a' and 'b'.

$\delta'(B, a)$ = ∈-closure$[\delta(B, a)]$
= ∈-closure $\{\delta[(q_1, q_2), a]\}$
= ∈-closure $[\delta(q_1,a) \cup \delta(q_2,a)]$
= ∈-closure $(\{q_2\} \cup \{\varphi\})$ = ∈-closure $(q_2) = \{q_2\}$.

As it is a new combination of state other than A, B and C so rename it as D.

$\delta'(B, b)$ = ∈-closure$[\delta(B, b)]$
= ∈-closure $\{\delta[(q_1, q_2), b]\}$
= ∈-closure $[\delta(q_1,b) \cup \delta(q_2,b)]$
= ∈-closure $(\{q_3\} \cup \{q_3\})$ = ∈-closure$(q_3) = \{q_1, q_3\}$ = C.

As δ' is constructed for all inputs on B so B is marked.

C is till unmarked.

Then construct δ' function for the new unmarked state C for input 'a' and 'b'.

$\delta'(C, a) = \in\text{-closure } [\delta(C, a)]$
$= \in\text{-closure } \{\delta[(q_1, q_3), a]\}$
$= \in\text{-closure } [\delta(q_1,a) \cup \delta(q_3,a)]$
$= \in\text{-closure } (\{q_2\} \cup \{\varphi\})$
$= \in\text{-closure } (q_2) = \{q_2\} = D.$

$\delta'(C, b) = \in\text{-closure } [\delta\ (C, b)]$
$= \in\text{-closure } \{\delta[(q_1, q_3), b]\}$
$= \in\text{-closure } [\delta(q_1,b) \cup \delta(q_3,b)]$
$= \in\text{-closure } (\{q_3\} \cup \{\varphi\})$
$= \in\text{-closure } (q_3) = \{q_1, q_3\} = C.$

As δ' is constructed for all inputs on C so C is marked.

The D is still unmarked.

Then construct δ' function for the new unmarked state D for input 'a' and 'b'.

$\delta'(D, a) = \in\text{-closure } [\delta\ (D, a)]$
$= \in\text{-closure } \{\delta[(q_2), a)]\}$
$= \in\text{-closure } [\delta(q_2,a)]$
$= \in\text{-closure } (\{\varphi\})$
$= \varphi$

$\delta'(D, b) = \in\text{-closure } [\delta\ (D, b)]$
$= \in\text{-closure } \{\delta[(q_2), b]\}$
$= \in\text{-closure } [\delta(q_2,b)]$
$= \in\text{-closure } (\{q_3\})$
$= \{q_1, q_3\} = C.$

As the state C contains q_3 so it is final state.

The equivalent DFA is

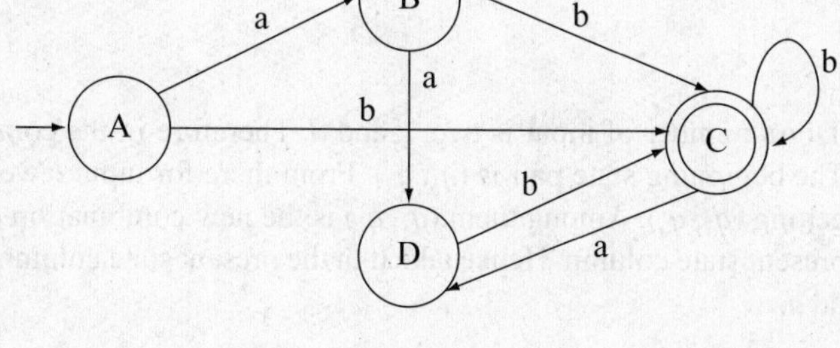

4.5 EQUIVALENCE OF TWO FINITE AUTOMATA AND TWO REGULAR EXPRESSIONS

Q. What are the steps to declare two Finite Automata equivalents?

Ans. Let there are two Finite Automata M and M′ where number of input symbols are the same.

(i) Make a comparison table with $n + 1$ columns, where n is the number of input symbols.

(ii) In the first column there will be pair of vertices (q, q') where $q \in$ M and $q' \in$ M′. The first pair of vertices will be the initial states of the two machines M and M′. Second column consists of (q_a, q'_a). Where q_a is reachable from the initial state of the machine M for the first input, and q'_a is reachable from the initial state of the machine M′ for the first input. The other n–2 columns consist of pair of vertices from M and M′ for n–1 inputs, where $n = 2, 3, \ldots, n-1$.

(iii) If any new pair of States appears in any of the n—1 next state columns, which were not taken in the First column; take that pair in the present state column and construct subsequent column elements like the first row.

(iv) If a pair of states (q, q') appear in any of the n columns for a pair of states in the present state column, where q is the final state of M and q' is the non-final state of M′ or vice versa, terminate the construction and conclude that M and M′ are not equivalent.

(v) If no new pair of states appears, which were not taken in the First Column and step (iv) does not hold stop construction and declare M and M′ are equivalent.

Q. Find whether the two DFAs are equivalent or not.

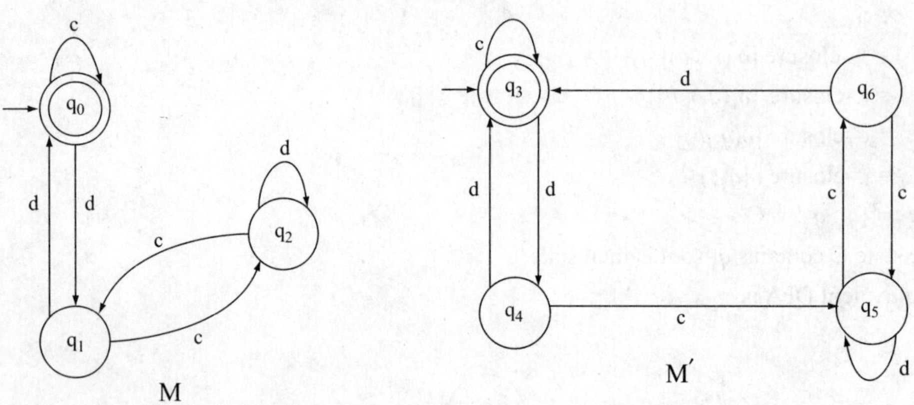

Ans.

In the previous two DFAs number of input is two, c and d. Therefore in the comparison table there will be three columns. The beginning state pair is (q_0, q_3). From there for input c we are getting (q_0, q_3) and for input d we are getting (q_1, q_4). Among them (q_1, q_4) is the new combination of states which has not appeared yet in the present state column. Hence take it in the present state column and construct next state pairs for input c and d.

	NS	
	For I/P C $(q_{c,} q'_c)$	For I/P d $(q_{d,} q'_d)$
(q_0, q_3)	(q_0, q_3)	(q_1, q_4)
(q_1, q_4)	(q_2, q_5)	(q_0, q_3)
(q_2, q_5)	(q_1, q_6)	(q_2, q_5)
(q_1, q_6)	(q_2, q_5)	(q_0, q_3)

After the fourth step no new state combinations have appeared. Hence further construction is stopped. In the whole table no such type of combination of states appears where one state is Final state of one machine and other is the non-final state of another machine.

Therefore, two DFAs are equivalent.

Q. Find whether the two DFAs are equivalent or not.

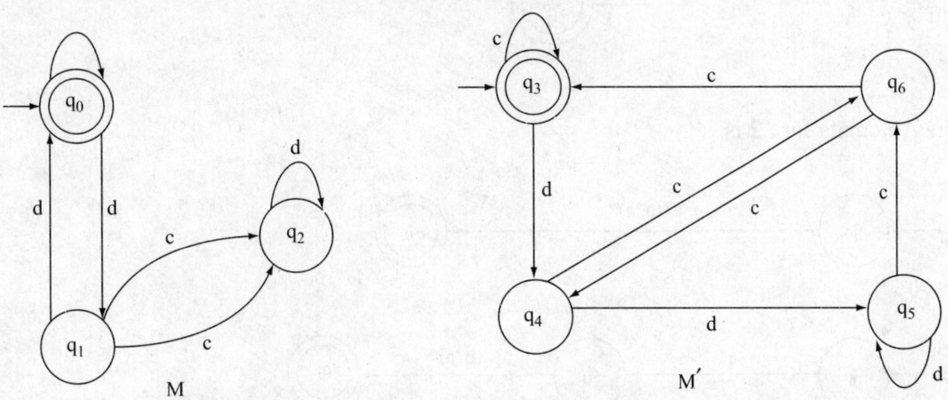

In the previous two DFAs number of input is two *c* and *d*. Hence in the comparison table there will be three columns. The beginning state pair is (q_0, q_3).

Present State (q, q′)	Next State	
	For I/P *c* $(q_{c,} q'_c)$	For I/P *d* $(q_{d,} q'_d)$
(q_0, q_3)	(q_0, q_3)	(q_1, q_4)
(q_1, q_4)	(q_2, q_6)	(q_0, q_5)

(q_0, q_5) is a combination of states where q_0 is the Final state of the machine M and q_5 is the Non-Final state of the machine M′. Hence we shall stop construction declaring two machines are not equivalent.

Q. How will you prove that two Regular Expressions are equivalent?

Ans. For every Regular Expression there is an accepting Finite Automata. If the finite automata constructed from both of the Regular Expressions are same, then we can say that two Regular Expressions are equivalent.

Q. Prove that the following Regular Expressions are Equivalent.

$L1 = (a + b)^*$ $L2 = a^*(b^*a)^*$

Ans. The Finite Automata for $L1$ is

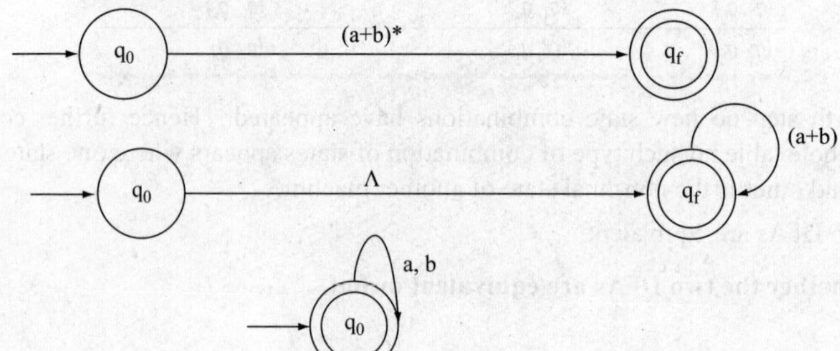

Finite Automata for $L2$ is

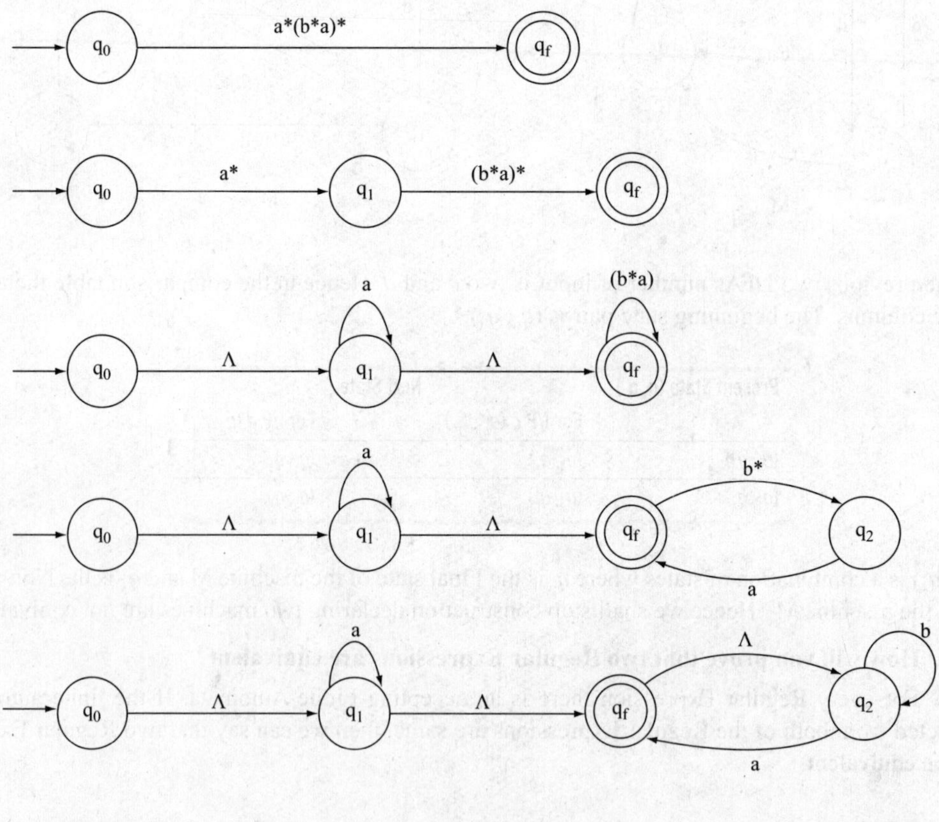

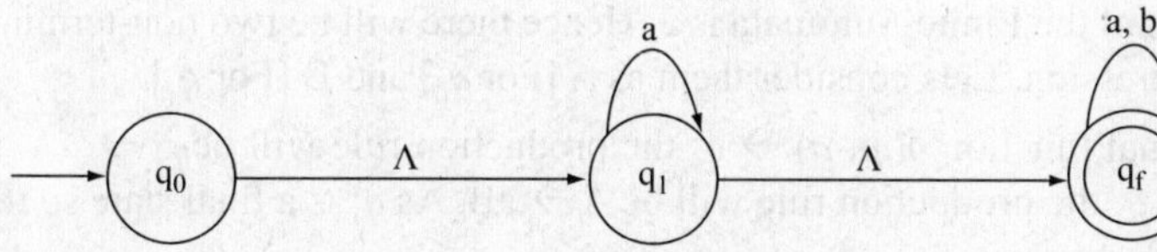

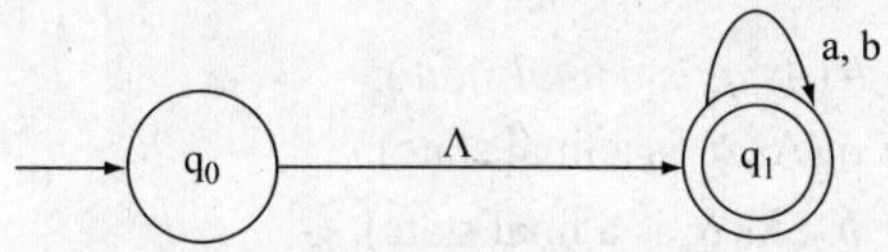

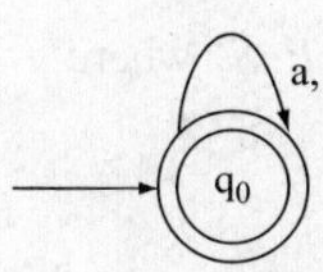

We are seeing the Finite Automata Generated by two Regular Expressions, $L1$ and $L2$ are same. Hence we can decide that the two Finite Automata are Equivalent.

4.6 CONSTRUCTION OF REGULAR GRAMMAR FROM A REGULAR EXPRESSION

Q. What is the process of generating a Regular Grammar from a Regular Expression?

Ans. From a Regular Expression the Regular grammar for the Regular Expression can be made.

Step I: Construct the equivalent FA for the given Regular Expression (Eliminate all null moves).

Step II: Number of Non-terminals of the grammar will be equal to the number of states of the FA.

Step III: For all transitional functions in the form $\delta(Q_1, a) \rightarrow Q_2$, $[Q_1, Q_2 \in Q$ and $a \in \Sigma]$the production rules will be in the form A→ $a\text{A}_1$. If Q_2 is a final state then for the transitional function $\delta(Q_1, a) \rightarrow Q_2$ the production rules will be A→ $a\text{A}_1$ and A → a. The start symbol will be the symbol representing the initial state of the FA.

Q. Construct Regular Grammar for the Regular Expressions.

(i) $a^*(a+b)b^*$ **(ii)** $ab(a+b)^*$ **(iii)** $10 + (0 + 11)0^*1$

Ans.

(i) The Deterministic Finite Automata for the string $a^*(a+b)b^*$ is

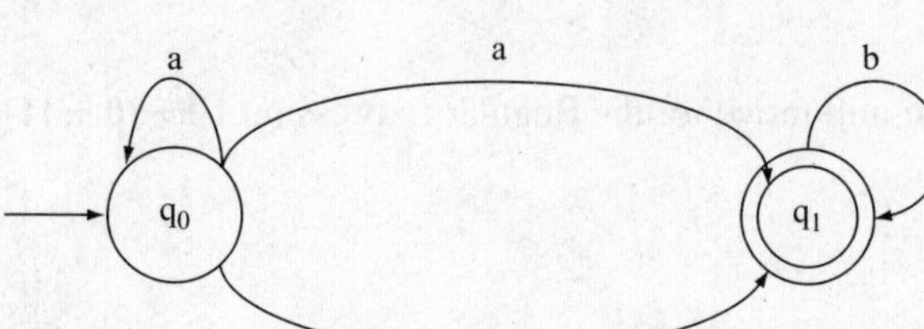

Number of states of the Finite Automata is 2. Hence there will be two non-terminals in the Grammar for the Regular Expression. Lets consider them as A [For q_0] and B [For q_1].

For the transitional function $\delta(q_0, a) \rightarrow q_0$ the production rule will be A → *a*A. For the transitional function $\delta(q_0, \text{a}) \rightarrow q_1$ the production rule will be A → aB. As q_1 is a final state so there will be another production rule A → *a*

$\delta(q_0, b) \rightarrow q_1$: *A → bB and A → b* (*As* q_1 *is a final state*),
$\delta(q_1, a) \rightarrow q_1$: B → *a*B and B → *a* (As q_1 is a final state),
$\delta(q_1, b) \rightarrow q_1$: B → *b*B and B → *b* (As q_1 is a final state).

Start symbol will be A as q_0 is the beginning state.

The grammar G for the Regular Expression $a^*(a + b)b^*$ is $\{V_N, \Sigma, P, S\}$ where

$V_N = \{A,B\}$,
$\Sigma = \{a,b\}$,

P: {A → *a*A/ *b*B/*a*/*b*, B → *a*B/*b*B/*a*/*b*},

S: {A},

(ii) The DFA for the string $ab(a + b)^*$ is

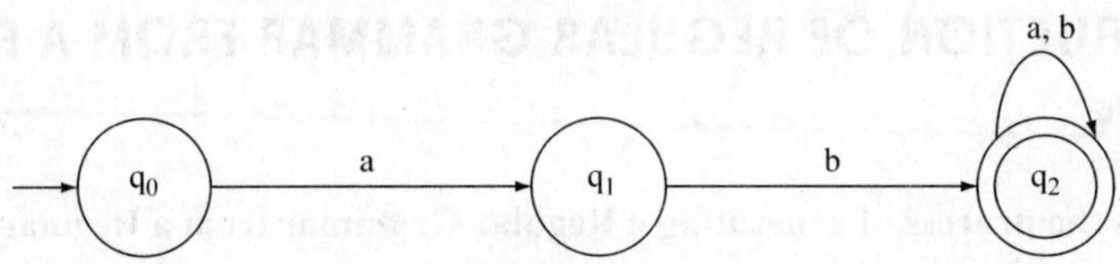

There are three states in the DFA. Number of Non-terminals for the Grammar of the Regular Expression will be 3. Let take them as A (For q_0), B(For q_1) and C (For q_2).

For the transitional function $\delta(q_0, a) \rightarrow q_1$ the production rule will be A → *a*B

$\delta(q_1, b) \rightarrow q_2$:*B → bC and B → b*[*As* q_2 *is final state*],
$\delta(q_2, a) \rightarrow q_2$: C → *a*C and C → *a* [As q_2 is final state],
$\delta(q_2, b) \rightarrow q_2$: C → *b*C and C → *b* [As q_2 is final state].

Start symbol will be A as q_0 is the beginning state.

The grammar G for the Regular Expression $ab(a + b)^*$ is $\{V_N, \Sigma, P, S\}$, where

$V_N = \{A, B, C\}$,
$\Sigma = \{a, b\}$,

P: {A → *a*B, B → *b*C/*b*, C → *a*C/ *b*C/ *a*/ *b*},

S: {A}.

(iii) The NFA without null move for the Regular Expression $\mathbf{10 + (0 + 11)0^*1}$ is

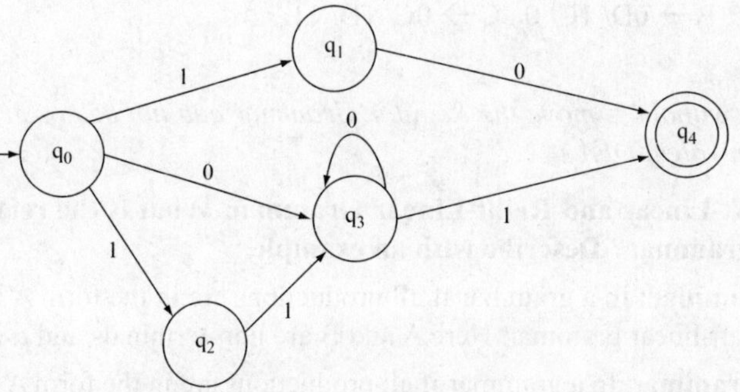

The equivalent DFA for the above NFA will is

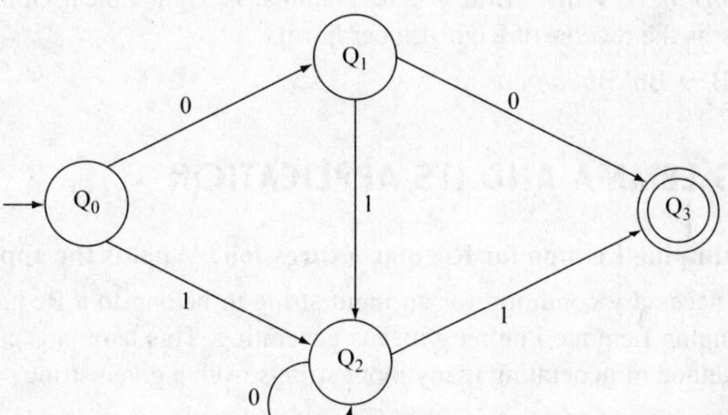

There are four states of the DFA for the Regular Expression **10 + (0 + 11)0*1.** Hence for the Grammar of the Regular Expression there will be four non-terminals. Lets consider them as A [For Q_0], B [For Q_1], C [For Q_2] and D [For Q_3].

Now we have to construct the Production rules of the Grammar.

For the transitional function $\delta(Q_0, 0) \rightarrow Q_1$, the production rule will be A → 0B

Same like.

$\delta(Q_0, 1) \rightarrow Q_2$, *the production rule will be A → 1C,*

$\delta(Q_1, 0) \rightarrow Q_3$ the production rule will be B → 0D and B → 0 (As Q_3 is final state),

$\delta(Q_1, 1) \rightarrow Q_2$, the production rule will be B → 1C,

$\delta(Q_2, 0) \rightarrow Q_2$, the production rule will be C → 0C,

$\delta(Q_2, 1) \rightarrow Q_3$, the production rule will be C → 1D and C → 1 (As Q_3 is final state).

Start symbol will be A as Q_0 is the beginning state.

The grammar G for the Regular Expression **10 + (0 + 11)0*1** is $\{V_N, \Sigma, P, S\}$, where

$V_N = \{A,B,C,D\}$,

$\Sigma = \{0,1\}$,

P: {A → 0B/ 1C, B → 0D/ 1C/ 0 , C → 0C/ 1D/ 1},

S: {A}.

(*N.B. From NFA without ∈ move the Regular Grammar can not be constructed. We can do this by constructing the equivalent DFA.*)

Q. Define Left-Linear and Right-Linear Grammar. What is the relation between these two forms of grammar? Describe with an example.

Left-Linear Grammar: In a grammar if all productions are in the form A → Bα or A → α then that grammar is called left-linear grammar. Here A and B are non-terminals and α is a string of terminals.

Right-Linear Grammar: In a grammar if all productions are in the form A → αB or A → α then that grammar is called right-linear grammar. Here A and B are non-terminals and α is a string of terminals.

Left-Linear grammar is the reverse of Right-Linear grammar and vice versa. Let there is a regular grammar A → *a*A/ *b*B/ *b*, B → *a*B/ *b*B/ *a*/ *b*. The grammar is Right-Linear Grammar. The Left-Linear form of the grammar is the reverse of Right-Linear Form.

A → A*a*/ B*b*/ *b*, B → B*a*/ B*b*/ *a*/*b*.

4.7 PUMPING LEMMA AND ITS APPLICATION

Q. What is Pumping Lemma for Regular Expression? What is the application of it?

Ans. There is a necessary condition for an input string to belong to a Regular set. This necessary condition is the Pumping Lemma. Pumping means generating. This lemma is called Pumping Lemma because it gives a method of generating many input strings from a given string.

As Pumping lemma is a necessary condition for a string belongs to a Regular set, it is used to prove that certain sets are not regular. If any set fulfills all the conditions of Pumping Lemma it cannot be said confirm that the set is regular.

But the reverse is true, i.e. if any set breaks the conditions of Pumping Lemma it can be said confirm that the set is not regular. So Pumping Lemma is used to prove that certain sets are not regular.

Q. State and prove Pumping Lemma for Regular Expression.

Ans. Pumping Lemma: Let M = $\{Q, \Sigma, \delta, q_0, F\}$ is a Finite Automata with *n* number of states. Let *L* is a Regular Set accepted by M. Let *w* is a string belongs to the set *L* and w|≥ *m*. If $m \geq n$, i.e. length of the string is greater than or equal to the number of states, then there exists *x*, *y*, *z* such that $w = xyz$, where$|xy| \leq n, |y| > 0$ and $xy^iz \in L$ for each $i \geq 0$.

[It needs some clarification, after we shall go to the proof section of it.

Lets consider the following Finite Automata. Here from q_0 by getting *a* it goes to q_1 and from q_1 by getting *b* it goes to q_2, which is the Final state. The Finite Automata consists of three states, q_0, q_1, q_2. The string that is accepted by the Finite Automata is *ba*. Length of the string is 2 which is less than the number of states of the Finite Automata.

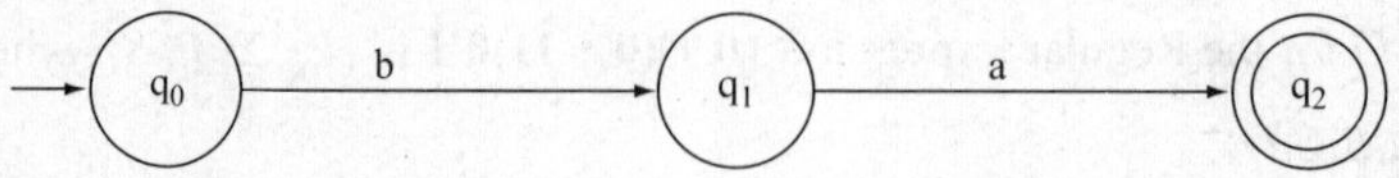

Here from a state by getting a single input it goes to a single distinct state. But if the length of the string is equal or greater than the number of states of the Finite Automata, then from a state by getting single input it is not possible to get all single distinct states. There must be repetition of at least a single state. This can be described by the following diagrams.

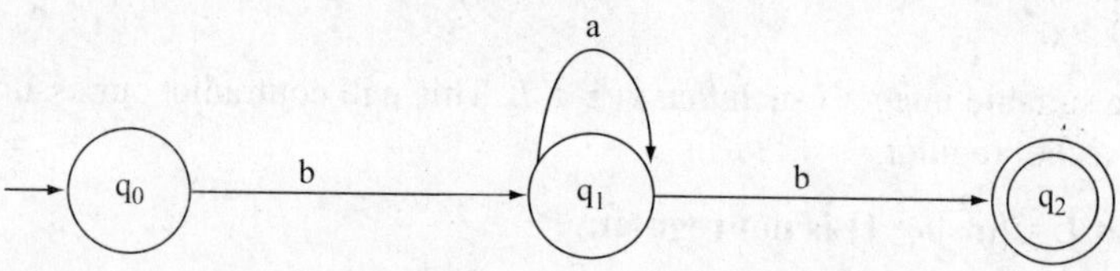

The Regular Expression accepted by the Automata is ba^*b. The expression can be divided into three parts x, y, z where y is the looping portion, x is the portion before looping and z is the portion after the looping portion.]

Proof:

Let w be a string of length m, where m is greater that n, the number of state of the finite automata accepting the string w.

$w = a_1a_2a_3\ldots a_m \qquad |w| = m \geq n$

Starting from the beginning state q_0, by getting the string w as input the machine will go to the final state.

In general

$$\delta\,(q_0, a_1a_2a_3\ldots a_i) = q_i \quad \text{for i} = 1,2,3, \ldots m.$$

The set of the states followed by the string w in the transitional path from beginning state to final state are $Q_n = \{q_0, q_1, q_2, \ldots, q_m\}$. Number of states in the set is m.

But number of states of the Finite Automata accepting the string w is n. As $m \geq n$ so at least two states in the set Q_n must coincide.

Take two integers j and k, where $0 \leq j < k \leq n$. Among the various pairs of repeated states, take a pair q_j, q_k. The string w can be decomposed into three substrings $a_1a_2 \ldots a_j$, $a_{j+1} \ldots a_k$ and $a_{k+1} \ldots a_m$. Lets denote them as x, y, and z, respectively. As $k \leq n$ so length of the string $a_1 \ldots a_k$ is $\leq n$, i.e. $|xy| \leq n$ and $w = xyz$.

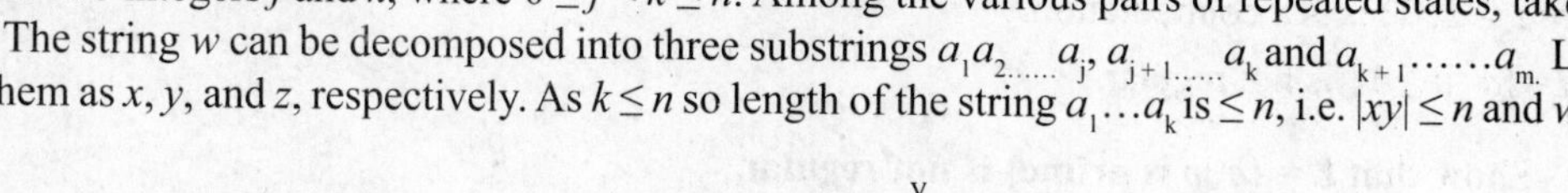

The automaton starts from the initial state q_0. On applying the string x it reaches to the state q_j. On applying the string y it comes back to q_j as $q_j = q_k$. So on applying the string y, i number of times (where $i \geq 0$) on q_j, it will be in the same state q_j. On applying z on q_j the automaton will reach to the final state. Hence the string xy^iz with $i \geq 0$ belongs to the language set L, i.e. $xy^iz \in L$.

Q. How Pumping Lemma can be applied to prove that certain sets are not regular?

Ans. Pumping lemma is used to prove that certain sets are not regular. This needs certain steps.

Step I: Assume the set L is regular. Let n be the number of states of the finite automata accepting L.

Step II: Choose a string w ($w \in L$) such that $|w| \geq n$. By using pumping lemma we can write $w = xyz$, with $|xy| \leq n$ and $|y| > 0$.

Step III: Find a suitable integer i such that $xy^iz \notin L$. This will contradict our assumption. From here L will be declared as not regular.

Q. Show that $L = \{a^{i^2} \mid i \geq 1\}$ is not regular.

Ans.

Step I: Assume the set L is regular. Let n be the number of states of the finite automata accepting the set L.

Step II: Let $w = a^{n^2}$. $|w| = n^2$ which is greater than n, the number of states of the finite automata accepting L. By using pumping lemma, we can write $w = xyz$ with $|xy| \leq n$ and $|y| > 0$.

Step III: Take $i = 2$. Hence the string will become xy^2z.

$$|xy^2z| = |x| + 2|y| + |z| > |x| + |y| + |z| \text{ as } |y| > 0.$$

From step II we know $|w| = |xyz| = |x| + |y| + |z| = n^2$.

So $|xy^2z| > n^2$

Again $|xy^2z| = |x| + 2|y| + |z| = |x| + |y| + |z| + |y| = n^2 + |y|$

As $|xy| \leq n$ so, $|y| \leq n$

Therefore $|xy^2z| \leq n^2 + n$

From the previous derivations we can write

$$n^2 < |xy^2z| \leq n^2 + n < n^2 + n + n + 1$$

$$n^2 < |xy^2z| < (n + 1)^2.$$

Hence $|xy^2z|$ lies between n^2 and $(n + 1)^2$. They are square of two consecutive positive integers. In between square of two consecutive positive integers no square of positive integer belongs. But a^{i^2} where $i \geq 1$ is a perfect square of an integer. Hence the string derived from it, i.e. $|xy^2z|$ is also a square of an integer, which lies between square of two consecutive positive integers. This is not possible.

So $xy^2z \notin L$. This is a contradiction.

So, $L=\{a^{i^2} \mid i \geq 1\}$ is not regular.

Q. Show that $L = \{a^p \mid p$ is prime$\}$ is not regular.

Ans.

Step I: Assume the set L is regular. Let n be the number of states in the finite automaton accepting L.

Step II: Let p is a prime number which is greater than n. Let the string $w = a^p$, $w \in L$. By using Pumping lemma we can write $w = xyz$ with $|xy| \leq n$ and $|y| > 0$. As the string w consists of only 'a' so x, y, and z are also string of 'a's. Let $y = a^m$ for some m with $1 \leq m \leq n$.

Step III: Let take $i = p + 1$. $|xy^iz|$ will be $|xyz| + |y^{i-1}|$

$$|xy^iz| = |xyz| + |y^{i-1}|$$

$$= p + (i - 1)\,|y| \qquad [xyz = a^p]$$

$= p + (i - 1)m \qquad [y = a^m]$

$= p + pm \qquad [i = p + 1]$

$= p(1 + m).$

$p(1 + m)$ is not a prime number as it has factors p and $(1 + m)$ including 1 and $p(1 + m)$. Hence, $xy^iz \notin L$. This is a contradiction.

Therefore $L = \{a^p \mid p \text{ is prime}\}$ is not regular.

Q. Show that $L=\{a^{i^3} \mid i \geq 1\}$ is not regular.

Ans.

Step I: Assume the set L is regular. Let n be the number of states of the finite automata accepting the set L.

Step II: Let $L = a^{n^3}$. The $|w| = n^3$ which is greater than n, the number of states of the finite automata accepting L. By using pumping lemma, we can write $w = xyz$ with $|xy| \leq n$ and $|y| > 0$.

Step III: Consider $i = 3$. Therefore the string will become xy^3z.

$$|xy^3z| = |x| + 3|y| + |z| = |x| + |y| + |z| + 2|y| = n^3 + 2|y|$$

As $|xy| \leq n$ so, $|y| \leq n$

Therefore $|xy^3z| = n^3 + 2|y| \leq n^3 + n < n^3 + 3n^2 + 3n + 1 < (n + 1)^3$.

As $|y| > 0$ so, $|xy^3z| = |xyz| + 2|y| > n^3$.

We can write

$$n^3 < |xy^3z| < (n + 1)^3$$

xy^3z is a perfect cube which lies between n^3 and $(n + 1)^3$, i.e. two consecutive perfect cube numbers. In between cube of two consecutive positive integers no cube of positive integer belongs. But a^{i^3} where $i \geq 1$ is a perfect cube of an integer. Hence the string derived from it, i.e. $|xy^3z|$ is also a cube of an integer, which lies between cube of two consecutive positive integers. This is not possible. Therefore $xy^3z \notin L$. This is a contradiction. So, $L=\{a^{i^3} \mid i \geq 1\}$ is not regular.

Q. Show that $L=\{a^nb^n$ where $n \geq 1\}$ is not regular.

Ans.

Step I: Suppose the set L is regular. Let n be the number of states of the finite automata accepting L.

Step II: Let $w = a^nb^n$, $|w| = 2n > n$. By pumping lemma we can write w = xyz with $|xy| \leq n$ and $|y| > 0$.

Step III: We want to find a suitable i so that $xy^iz \notin L$.

The string y can be of any of the following:

(i) y is a string of only 'a', i.e. $y = a^k$ for some $k \geq 1$

(ii) y is a string of only 'b', i.e. $y = b^k$ for some $k \geq 1$

(iii) y is a string of both 'a', and 'b', i.e. $y = a^kb^l$ for some k, $1 \geq 1$

For Case (i) take $i = 0$. As $xyz = a^nb^n$, $xy^0z = xz$ will be $a^{n-k}b^n$.

As $k \geq 1$, $(n-k) \neq n$, So $xy^0z \notin L$.

For Case (ii) take $i = 0$. As $xyz = a^nb^n$, xy^0z = xz will be a^nb^{n-k}.

As $k \geq 1$, $(n-k) \neq n$, So $xy^0z \notin L$.

For Case (iii) take $i = 2$. As $xyz = a^n b^n$, $xy^2z = xyyz$.

We know $xyz = a^n b^n = a^{n-k} a^k\, b^l\, b^{n-l}$, Therefore $xyyz$ will be

$a^{n-k} a^k\, b^l\, a^k\, b^l\, b^{n-l} = a^n b^l a^k b^n$, which is not in the form $a^n b^n$. So $xy^2z \notin L$

For all the three cases we are getting contradiction. Therefore L is not regular.

Q. Show that L = palindrome over $\{a,b\}$ is not regular.

Ans.

Step I: Suppose the set L is regular. Let n be the number of states of the finite automata accepting L.

Step II: Let $w = a^n b a^n$, $|w| = (2n + 1) > n$. By pumping lemma we can write $w = xyz$ with $|xy| \leq n$ and $|y| > 0$.

Step III: We want to find a suitable i so that $xy^iz \notin L$. The string y may consists of only 'a' let a^j where $j > 0$.

Let take $i = 0$. $xyz = a^n b a^n = a^{n-j} a^j\, b a^n$. Therefore $xy^0z = a^{n-j} b a^n$.

As $j > 0$, $n - j \neq n$. So $a^{n-j} b a^n$ is not a palindrome.

So $xy^0z \notin L$. Hence it is proved that L is not Regular.

Q. Show that $L = \{ww$, where $w \in (a,b)^*\}$ is not regular

Ans.

Step I: Let consider the set L is regular. Let n be the number of states of the finite automata accepting L.

Step II: Let $ww = a^n b a^n b \in L$, so $|ww| = 2(n + 1) > n$. By applying pumping lemma we can write $w = xyz$ with $|xy| \leq n$ and $|y| > 0$.

Step III: We want to find a suitable i so that $xy^iz \notin L$. The string consist of 'a' and 'b'. Therefore y can be of any of these

(i) y has no 'b', i.e. $y = a^k$.

(ii) y has only one 'b' (because the string is $a^n b a^n b$).

Let take $i = 0$ in case I. If $i = 0$, then $xy^0z = xz$ and it is in the form $a^{n-k} b a^n b$ or $a^n b a^{n-k} b$.

This is not in the form ww, i.e. $xz \notin L$. Hence L is not regular.

In case II, if we take $i = 0$ then $xy^0z = xz$ which contain only one 'b'. Which is not in the form ww, i.e. $xz \notin L$. Hence L is not regular.

Q. Show that $L = \{a^n b a^n$, where $n \geq 1\}$ is not regular.

Ans.

Step I: Assume that L is regular. Let n be the number of states of the finite automata accepting L.

Step II: Let $w = a^n b a^n$. Hence $|w| = 2n + 1 > n$. According to pumping lemma we can write $w = xyz$, with $w = xyz$ with $|xy| \leq n$ and $|y| > 0$.

Step III: We want to find a suitable i so that $xy^iz \notin L$. The string consist of 'a' and 'b'. So y can be of any of these:

(i) y has no 'b', i.e. $y = a^k$

(ii) y has only one 'b' [because the string is $a^n b a^n$]

For Case I take $i = 2$.

The string $xyz = a^{n-k} a^k b a^n$ or $a^n b a^k a^{n-k}$

Therefore, $xy^2z=a^{n-k}a^{2k}ba^n=a^{n+k}ba^n$ or $a^nba^{2k}a^{n-k}=a^nba^{n+k}$.

As $k \neq 0$, $(n + k) \neq n$. Therefore $xy^2z \notin L$.

This is a contradiction so L is not regular.

For Case II let take $i = k$. So $xy^kz = a^nb^ka^n$. This is not in the form a^nba^n. Therefore $xy^kz \notin L$.

This is a contradiction so L is not regular.

Q. Show that $L = \{a^nb^nab^{n+1}\}$ is not regular.

Ans.

Step I: Assume that L is regular. Let n be the number of states of the finite automata accepting L.

Step II: Let $w = a^nb^nab^{n+1}$, so $|w| = (3n + 2) > n$. By using pumping lemma we can write $w = xyz$, with $w = xyz$ with $|xy| \leq n$ and $|y| > 0$.

Step III: We want to find a suitable i so that $xy^iz \notin L$. The string consist of 'a' and 'b'. Hence y can be of any of these

(a) y contain only 'a', let $y = a^k$.

(b) y contain only 'b', let $y = b^l$

(c) y contain 'a' and 'b' both, let $y = b^ka$.

For case I, take $i = 0$.

$$w = xyz = (a^{n-k})(a^k)(b^nab^{n+1})$$

$xy^0z = a^{n-k}\,b^nab^{n+1}$ which is not in the form $a^nb^nab^{n+1}$.

For case II take $i = 0$

$$w = xyz = (a^nb^{n-l})(b^l)ab^{n+1}$$

$xy^0z = a^nb^{n-l}\,ab^{n+1}$ which is not in the form $a^nb^nab^{n+1}$.

For case III, take $i = 2$

$$w = xyz = a^nb^{n-k}(b^ka)^2\,b^{n+1}$$

$= a^nb^na\,b^kab^{n+1}$, which is not in the form $a^nb^nab^{n+1}$.

In all the three cases there are contradiction, hence the language is not regular.

Q. Show that the language containing the set of all balanced parenthesis is not regular.

Ans.

Step I: Assume that L is regular. Let n be the number of states of the finite automata accepting L.

Step II: Let w = (((….()….))) = $(^n)^n$. $|w| = 2n > n$. By using pumping lemma we can write $w = xyz$, with $w = xyz$ with $|xy| \leq n$ and $|y| > 0$.

Step III: We want to find a suitable i so that $xy^iz \notin L$. The string consists of '(' and ')'. So y can be of any of these

(a) y consists of only '(' let $y = (^k$

(b) y consists of only ')', let $y =)^k$

(c) y consists of both '(' and ')', let $y = (^k)^k$

For case I, take $i = 0$.

$w = xyz = (^{n-k} (\ ^k)^n$

$xy^0z = (^{n-k})^n$ which is not set of all balanced parenthesis.

For case II, take $i = 0$.

$w = xyz = (^n\ )\ ^k)^{n-k}$

$xy^0z = (^n)^{n-k}$ which is not set of all balanced parenthesis.

For case III, take $i = 2$.

$w = xyz = (^{n-k}(^k)^k)^{n-k}$

$xy^2z = (^n)^k(^k)^n$ which is not set of all balanced parenthesis.

In all the three cases there are contradiction, hence the language is not regular.

Q. Show that $L = \{0^n1^{2n}$, where $n \geq 1\}$ is not regular.

Ans.

Step I: Assume that L is regular. Let n be the number of states of the finite automata accepting L.

Step II: Let $w = 0^n1^{2n}$, where n^3 1. $|w| = 3n > n$. By using pumping lemma we can write $w = xyz$, with $|xy| \leq n$ and $|y| > 0$.

Step III: We want to find a suitable i so that $xy^iz \notin L$. The string consists of '0' and '1'. y can be any of the following forms

y consists of only '0', let $y = 0^k$

y consists of only '1', let $y = 1^k$

y consists of both '0' and '1'. Let $y = 0^k1^k$

For case I, take $i = 0$.

$w = xyz = 0^n1^{2n} = 0^{n-k}0^k1^{2n}$

$xy^0z = 0^{n-k}1^{2n}$, as $k \neq 0$, $(n-k) \neq n$.

For case II, take $i = 0$.

$w = xyz = 0^n1^{2n} = 0^n1^k1^{2n-k}$

$xy^0z = 0^n1^{2n-k}$, as $k \neq 0$, $(2n-k) \neq n$.

For case III, take $i=2$.

$w = xyz = 0^n1^{2n} = 0^{n-k}0^k1^k1^{2n-k}$

$xy^2z = 0^n1^k0^k1^{2n}$, which is not in the form 0^n1^{2n}.

For all the three cases we are getting contradiction, therefore L is not regular.

4.8 CLOSURE PROPERTIES OF REGULAR SET

Q. What do you mean by closure property? Give an example.

Ans. A set is closed (under an operation) if and only if the operation on two elements of the set produces another element of the set. If an element outside the set is produced, then the operation is not closed. Closure is a property which describes when we combine any two elements of the set; the result is also included in the set.

If we multiply two *real numbers*, we will get another real number. Since this process is always true, it is said that the real numbers are "closed under the operation of multiplication". There is simply no way to escape the set of real numbers when multiplying.

Let $S = \{1,2,3,4,5,6,7,8,9,10,\ldots\}$ is a set of real numbers.

$1 \times 2 = 2,$

$2 \times 3 = 6,$

$5 \times 2 = 10.$

All are included in the set of real numbers.

Therefore we can say real numbers are closed under the operation of multiplication.

Q. Prove that two Regular Expressions L_1 and L_2 over Σ are closed under union operation.

Ans. We have to prove that if L_1 and L_2 are regular over Σ, then their union, i.e. $L_1 \cup L_2$ will be also regular.

As L_1 and L_2 are regular over Σ, there must exist finite automata $M_1 = (Q_1, \Sigma, \delta_1, q_{01}, F_1)$ and $M_2 = (Q_2, \Sigma, \delta_2, q_{02}, F_2)$ such that $L_1 \in M_1$ and $L_2 \in M_2$

Assume that there is no common states between Q_1 and Q_2, i.e. $Q_1 \cap Q_2 = \wedge$.

Define another Finite Automata $M_3 = (Q, \Sigma, \delta, q_0, F)$, where

(i) $Q = Q_1 \cup Q_2 \cup \{q_0\}$, where q_0 is a new state $\notin Q_1 \cup Q_2$

(ii) $F = F_1 \cup F_2$

(iii) Transitional function δ is defined as $\delta(q_0, \epsilon) \rightarrow \{q_{01}, q_{02}\}$

and $\delta(q, \Sigma) \rightarrow \delta_1(q, \Sigma)$ if $q \in Q_1$

$\delta(q, \Sigma) \rightarrow \delta_2(q, \Sigma)$ if $q \in Q_2$

It is clear from the previous discussion that from q_0 we can reach to either initial state q_1 of M_1 or initial state q_2 of M_2.

Transitions for the new Finite Automata M are same like the transitions of M_1 and M_2.

As $F = F_1 \cup F_2$ so any string accepted by M_1 or M_2 will also be accepted by M

Therefore $L_1 \cup L_2$ is also regular.

Example:

Let $L_1 = a^*(a+b)b^*$

$L_2 = ab(a+b)^*$

The Finite Automata M_1 accepting L_1 is

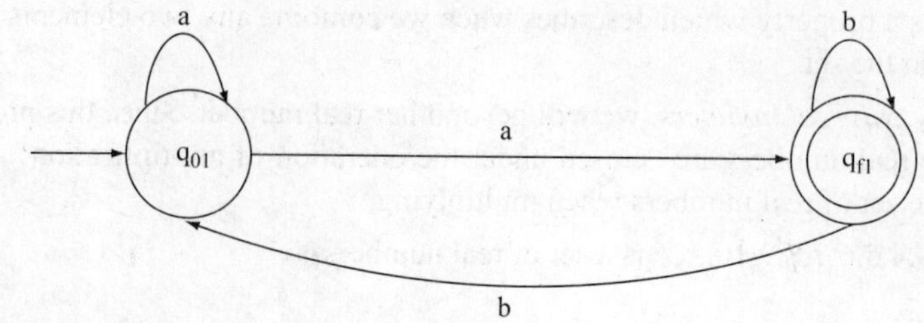

The Finite Automata M_2 accepting L_2 is

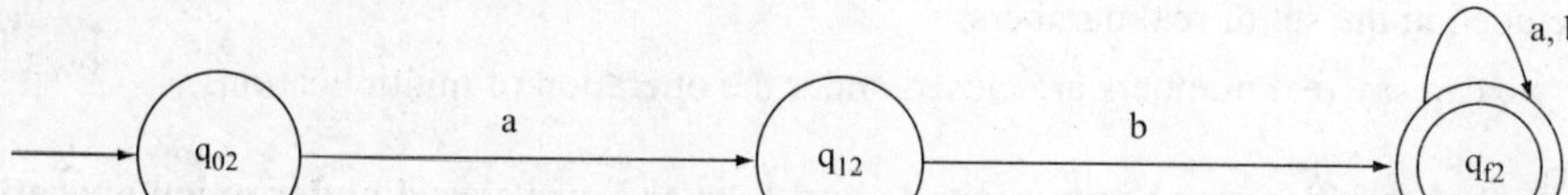

The machine M produced by combining M_1 and M_2 is

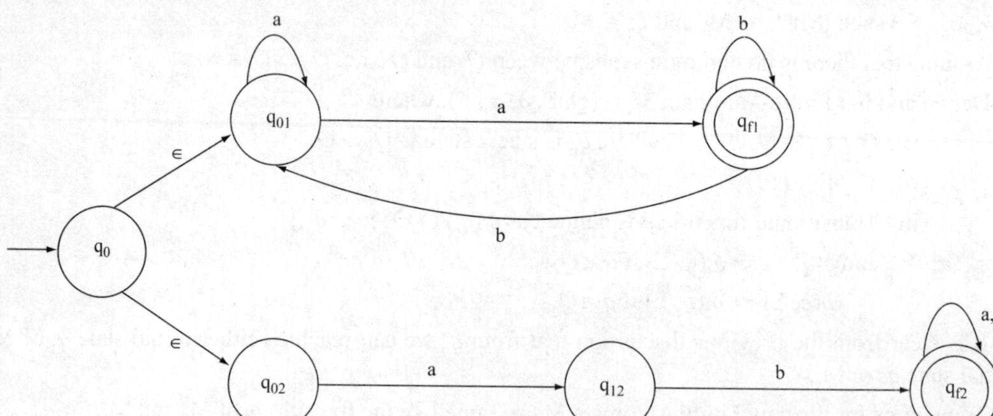

It accepts $L_1 \cup L_2$

Q. Prove that complement of a Regular Expression is also regular.

Ans. If L is regular we have to prove that L^T is also Regular.

As L is Regular there must be a Finite Automata $M = (Q, \Sigma, \delta, q_0, F)$ accepting L. M is a Finite Automata, so M has a transitional system.

Let construct another transitional system M′ with the state diagram of M but reversing the direction of the directed edges. M′ can be designed as follows

(i) Set of States of M′ is same as M

(ii) Set of input symbols of M′ is same as M

(iii) Initial state of M′ is same as Final state of M [M′ is reverse direction of M]

(iv) Final state of M′ is same as initial state of M [M′ is reverse direction of M]

Let a string w belongs to L, i.e. $w \in$ M. Therefore, there is a path from q_0 to F with path value w. By reversing the edges we get a path from F to q_0 (Beginning and Final state of M′) in M′. The path value is reverse of w, i.e. w^T. Therefore $w^T \in$ M′.

So the reverse of the string w is regular.

Let L = ab(a+b)*

The Finite Automata M accepting L is

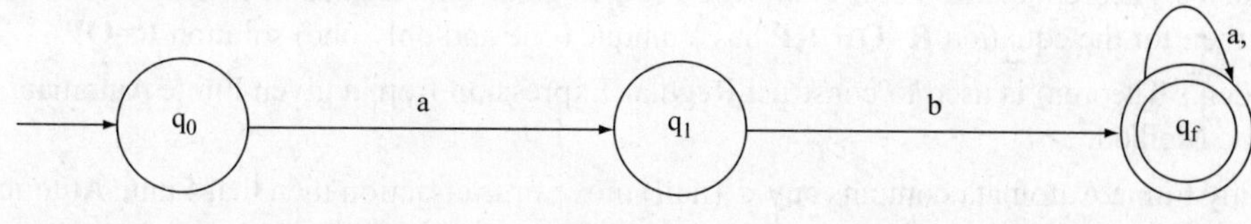

The reverse of The finite automata M′ accepting L^c is

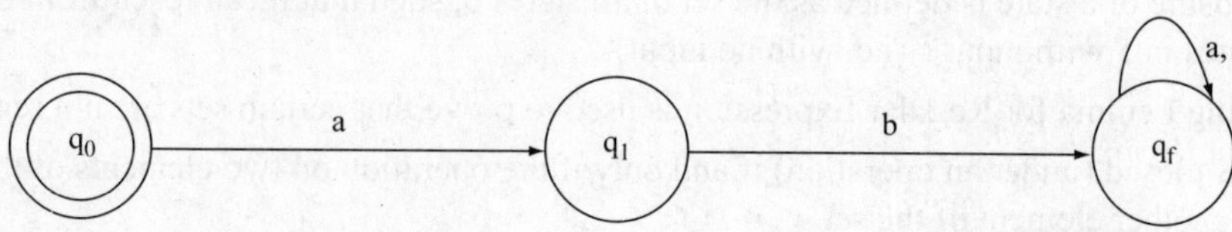

M′ accepts (a+b)*ba which is reverse of L.

Therefore $w \notin L$, i.e. $\Sigma^* - L^{\prime}L$. However, $\Sigma^* - L$ is accepted by M′ which is a Finite Automata.

Replace this by $\Sigma^* - L \neq L$

Q. If L is regular and L is a subset of Σ^*, prove that $\Sigma^* - L$ is also a regular set.

Ans. As L is Regular there must be a Finite Automata M = $(Q, \Sigma, \delta, q_0, \text{F})$ accepting L. Let construct another DFA M′ = $(Q, \Sigma, \delta, q_0, \text{F}')$, where F′ = Q–F. Therefore two DFA differ only in their final states. A final state of M is a nonfinal state of M′ and vice versa.

Let take a string w which is accepted by M′. Therefore $\delta(q_0, w) \in \text{F}'$, i.e. $\delta(q_0, w) \in (Q - \text{F})$.

The string w cannot be accepted by M, because $\delta(q_0, w) \notin$ F[As F does not belong to $(Q - \text{F})$].

Therefore $w \notin L$, i.e. $\boldsymbol{\Sigma^* - L \neq L}$. However, $\boldsymbol{\Sigma^* - L}$ is accepted by M′ which is a Finite Automata.

Therefore $\boldsymbol{\Sigma^* - L}$ is a regular set

Q. Prove that two Regular Expressions L_1 and L_2 over Σ are closed under intersection operation.

Ans. From D'Morgan's theorem we know

$$L_1 \cap L_2 = (L_1^C \cup L_2^C)^C$$

We know if L_1 and L_2 are regular then L_1^C and L_2^C are also regular.

As L_1^C and L_2^C are regular, $\boldsymbol{L_1^C \cup L_2^C}$ is also regular (Regular Expression are closed under union operation.)

As $L_1^C \cup L_2^C$ is regular so their complement $\boldsymbol{(L_1^C \cup L_2^C)^C}$ is also regular.

So $\boldsymbol{L_1 \cap L_2}$ is also regular, i.e. the regular sets are closed under intersection.

WHAT WE HAVE LEARNED SO FAR

1. A Regular Expression can be defined as a language or string accepted by a Finite Automata.
2. Any terminal symbols, null string ($\wedge$), null set (ϕ) are Regular Expression.
3. Union, Concatenation, Iteration of two Regular Expressions or any combination of them are also Regular Expression.
4. Arden's Theorem states that if **P** and **Q** be two Regular Expressions over Σ. If **P** does not contain Λ, then for the equation **R=Q + RP** has a unique (one and only one) solution **R=QP***.
5. Arden's Theorem is used to construct Regular Expression from a given Finite Automata by Algebraic Method.
6. If any Finite Automata contains any $\in$ (null) move or transaction then that Finite Automata is called NFA with $\in$ moves.
7. $\in$ – closure of a state is defined as the set of all states S, such that it can reach from that state to all the states in S with input ϵ (i.e. with no input).
8. Pumping Lemma for Regular Expression is used to prove that certain sets are not regular.
9. A set is closed (under an operation) if and only if the operation on two elements of the set produces another element of the set.
10. Closure is a property which describes when we combine any two elements of the set; the result is also included in the set.
11. Regular Expressions are closed under Union, Complementation, and Intersection operation.

SOLVED PROBLEMS

1. Describe the following Regular Expressions in English Language.

(i) $a(a + b)^*b$ (ii) $(a + b)^*aba(a + b)^*$ (iii) $(0 + 1)^*1(0 + 1)^*0(0 + 1)^*$

Ans. (i) The language starts with 'a' and ends with 'b'. In the middle of 'a' and 'b' there is any combination of 'a' and 'b'. Hence the Regular Expression described in English language

{Set of any combination of 'a' and 'b' beginning with 'a' and ending with 'b'}

(ii) The expression is divided into three parts $(a + b)^*$, aba, and $(a + b)^*$. In each element of the language set there is aba as substring. In English language, the Regular Expression is described as

{Set of any combination of 'a' and 'b' containing 'aba' as substring}

(iii) The expression is divided into five parts $(0 + 1)^*$, 1, $(0 + 1)^*$, 0 and $(0 + 1)^*$. In each element of the language set there is 1 and 0, where 1 appears first. In English language the Regular Expression is described as

{Set of any combination of '0' and '1' containing atleast one 1 and one 0}.

2. Find Regular Expression for the following:

(a) Set of Languages of any combination of 'a' and 'b' beginning with 'a'.

(b) Set of languages of any combination of '0' and '1' containing atleast one double symbol.

(c) Set of languages of any combination of '0' and '1' containing no double symbol

Ans. (a) Set of any combination of 'a' and 'b' is denoted by $(a + b)^*$. The Regular Expression is

$\boldsymbol{L = a(a + b)^*}$.

(b) The language consists of two symbols '0' and '1'. Double [same] symbol means either 00 or 11. Part of the language containing atleast one double symbol is denoted by (00 + 11). Therefore the language of any combination of '0' and '1' containing atleast one double symbol is expressed as $\boldsymbol{L = (0 + 1)^* (00 + 11) (0 + 1)^*}$.

(c) The language consists of two symbols '0' and '1'. Double [same] symbol means either 00 or 11. According to the condition, in the language 00 or 11 will not appear. The language may start with '0' or start with '1'. The language start with '0' with no double symbol is $(01)^*$. The language start with '1' with no double symbol is $(10)^*$.

The expression is $\boldsymbol{L = (01)^* + (10)^*}$

3. Construct a Regular Expression from the given Finite Automata by Algebraic Method using Arden's Theorem.

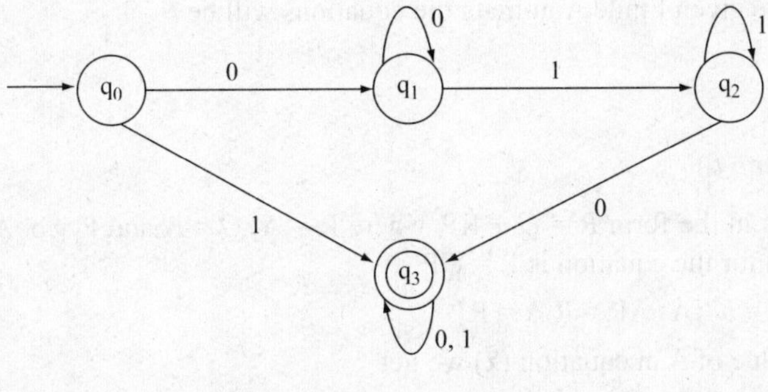

Ans. For the above given Finite Automata the equations

$$q_0 = \Lambda \quad \text{(i)}$$
$$q_1 = q_0 0 + q_1 0 \quad \text{(ii)}$$
$$q_2 = q_1 1 + q_2 1 \quad \text{(iii)}$$
$$q_3 = q_2 0 + q_0 1 + q_3 (0 + 1) \quad \text{(iv)}$$

Put the value of q_0 in equation q_1. $q_1 = 0 + q_1 0$. The equation is in the form R = Q + RP, where R = q_1, Q = 0 and P = 0. By Arden theorem the solution of the equation is R = QP* i.e.

$q_1 = 00^*$.

Substituting the value q_1 in equation (3) we get $q_2 = 00^*1 + q_2 1$.

The equation is in the form R = Q + RP, where R = q_2, Q = 00^*1 and P = 1. By Arden theorem the solution of the equation is R = QP^* i.e.

$q_2 = 00^*11^*$.

Substituting the value of q_2 and q_0 in equation (4) we get

$q_3 = (00^*11^*0 + 1) + q_3\,(0 + 1)$.

The equation is in the form R = Q + RP, where R = q_3, Q = $(00^*11^*0 + 1)$ and P = (0 + 1). By Arden theorem the solution of the equation is R = QP^* i.e.

$q_3 = (00^*11^*0 + 1)\,(0 + 1)^*$.

As q_3 is the final state so the Regular Expression generated from the given Finite Automata is $(00^*11^*0 + 1)\,(0 + 1)^*$.

4. Construct a Regular Expression from the given Finite Automata by Algebraic Method using Arden's Theorem.

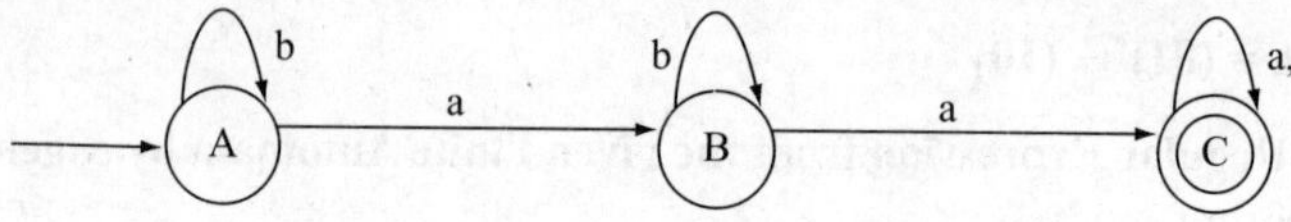

Ans. For the above given Finite Automata the equations will be

$A = \Lambda + Ab$ (*i*)

$B = Aa + Bb$ (ii)

$C = Ba + C(a + b)$ (iii)

The equation (1) is in the form R = Q + RP, where R = A, Q = Λ and P = b. According to Arden's Theorem, the solution for the equation is R = QP^*.

Therefore, $A = \Lambda b^* = b^*$ [As ΛR = R Λ = R].

Substituting the value of A in equation (2) we get

$B = b^*a + Bb$

The equation is in the format R = Q + RP, where R = B, $Q = b^*a$, and P = b. According to Arden's Theorem, the solution for the equation is R = QP^*.

Therefore, $B = b^*ab^*$.

Substituting the value of B in equation (3) we get

$C = b^*ab^*a + C(a + b)$.

The equation is in the format R = Q + RP, where R = C, $Q = b^*ab^*a$ and P = $(a + b)$. According to Arden's Theorem, the solution for the equation is R = QP^*.

So $C = b^*ab^*a(a + b)^*$.

As C is the final state so the Regular Expression accepted by the finite automata is $b^*ab^*a(a + b)^*$

5. Construct a Regular Expression from the given Finite Automata by Algebraic Method using Arden's Theorem.

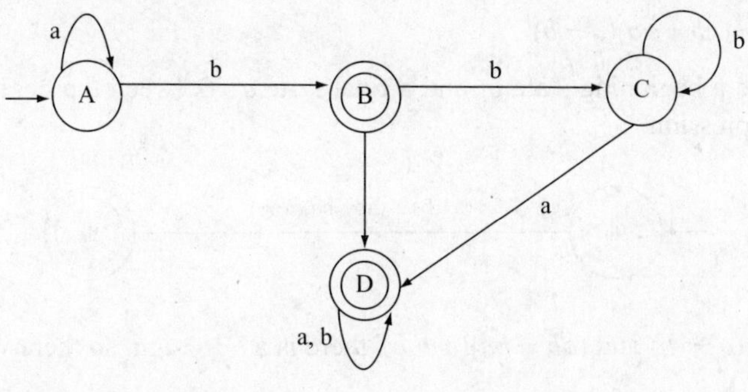

Ans. For the above given Finite Automata the equations will be

$A = \Lambda + Aa,$ (*i*)

$B = Ab,$ (*ii*)

$C = Bb + Cb,$ (iii)

$D = Ba + Ca + D(a + b).$ (iv)

The equation (1) is in the form $R = Q + RP$, where $R = A$, $Q = \Lambda$, and $P = a$. According to Arden's Theorem, the solution for the equation is $R = QP^*$.

Therefore $A = \Lambda a^* = a^*$ [As $\Lambda R = R\Lambda = R$].

Substituting the value of A in equation (2) we get

$$B = a^*b.$$

Substituting the value of B in equation (3) we get

$$C = a^*bb + Cb.$$

This is in the format $R = Q + RP$, where $R = C$, $Q = a^*bb$, and $P = b$. According to Arden's Theorem, the solution for the equation is $R = QP^*$.

$$C = a^*bbb^*.$$

Substituting the value of B and C in equation (4) we get

$$D = a^*ba + a^*bbb^*a + D(a + b).$$

This is in the format $R = Q + RP$, where $R = D$, $Q = a^*ba + a^*bbb^*a$ and $P = a + b$. According to Arden's Theorem, the solution for the equation is $R = QP^*$.

$$D = (a^*ba + a^*bbb^*a)(a + b)^*.$$

In the finite automata there are two final states B and D. Therefore, the Regular Expression accepted by the finite automata:

$L = a^*b + (a^*ba + a^*bbb^*a)(a + b)^*$

6. Construct Finite Automata equivalent to the Regular Expression.

$L = (a + b) + (ab + ba)(a + b)^*$

Ans. Step I: Take a beginning state q_0 and a final state q_f. Between the beginning and final state place the Regular Expression.

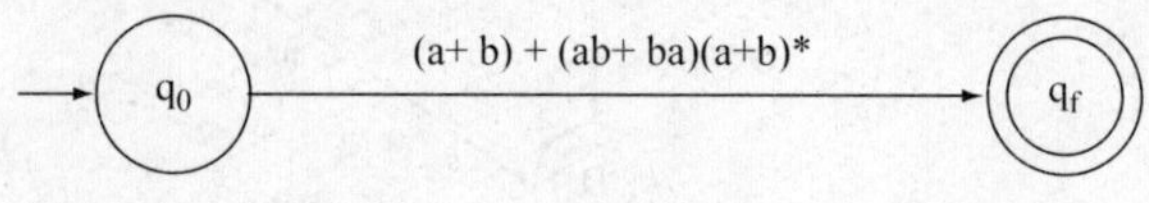

Step II: Between $(a + b)$ and $(ab + ba)(a + b)^*$ there is a ' + ' sign, so there will be parallel edges between q_0 and q_f.

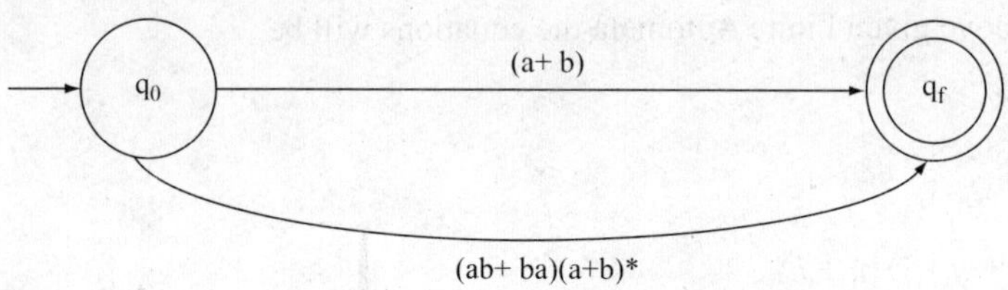

Step III: Between $(ab + ba)$ and $(a + b)^*$ there is a '.' (dot) sign, so a extra state is added between q_0 and q_f.

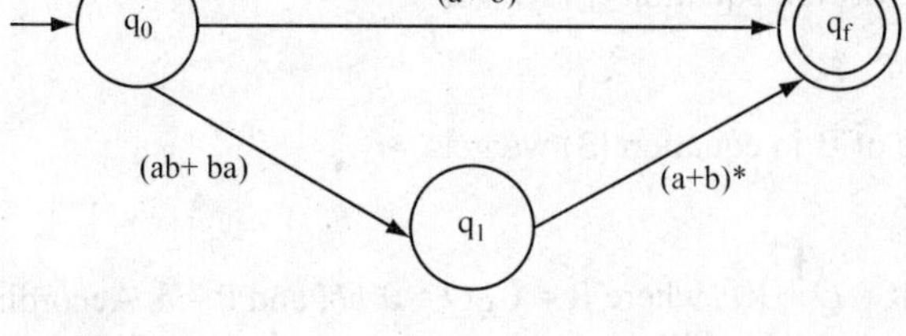

Step IV: Between ab and ba there is ' + ' sign, so there will be parallel edges between q_0 and q_1.

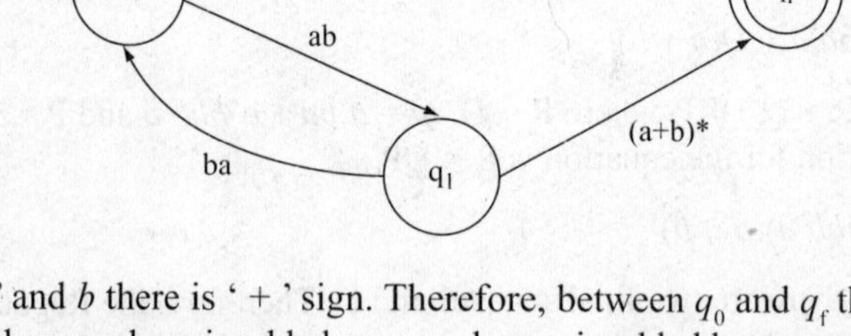

Step V: Between 'a' and b there is ' + ' sign. Therefore, between q_0 and q_f there is parallel edge. As there is a '*' in $(a + b)$, hence a loop is added on q_f and an $\in$ is added between q_1 and q_f.

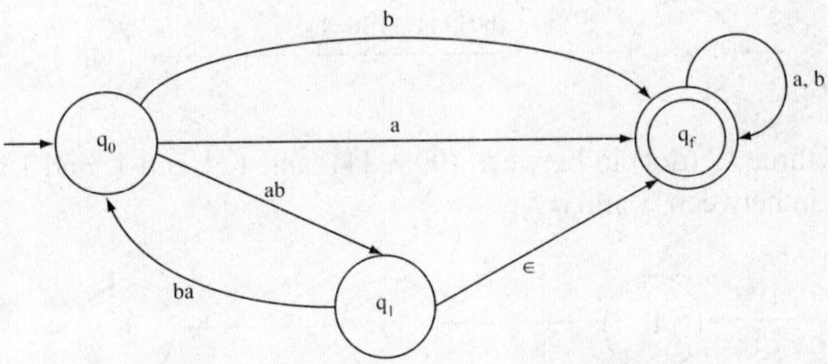

Step VI: Between 'a' and 'b' and between 'b' and 'a' there are '.'(dot). Therefore, two extra states are added between q_0 and q_1.

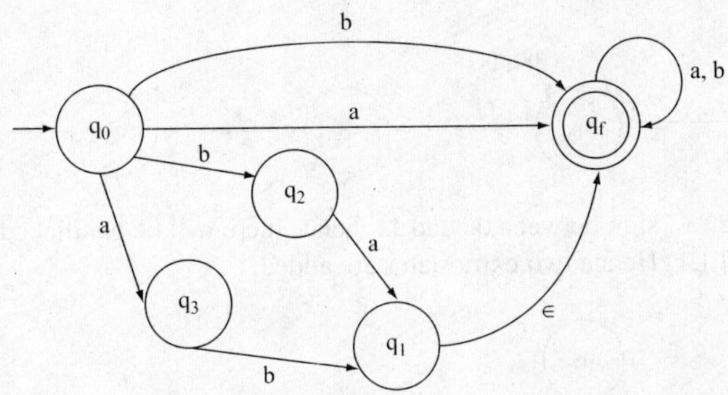

Step VII: Between q_1 and q_f there is an ∈. To remove that ∈, merge q_1 and q_f. Now two transition from q_2 and q_3 is added on q_f.

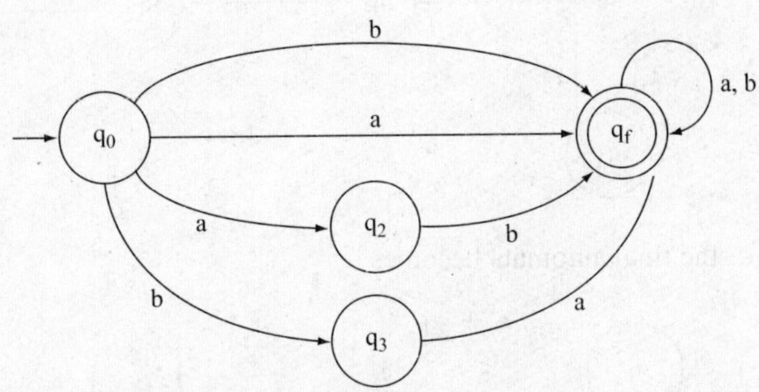

7. **Construct Finite Automata equivalent to the Regular Expression.**

$$L = (00 + 11)^* 11 (0 + 1)^*$$

Ans.

Step I: Take a beginning state q_0 and a final state q_f. Between the beginning and final state place the Regular Expression.

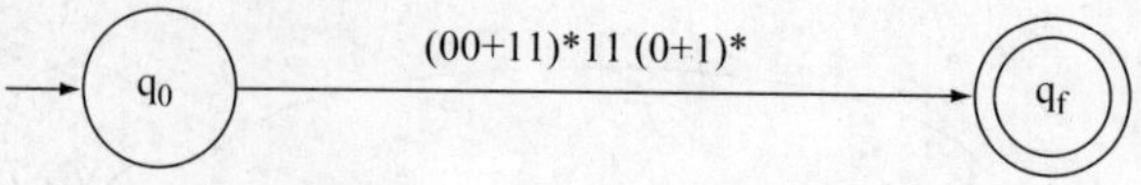

Step II: There are three '.' (dot) in between $(00 + 11)^*$ and 1, 1 and 1, and 1 and $(0 + 1)^*$. So three extra states are added in between q_0 and q_f.

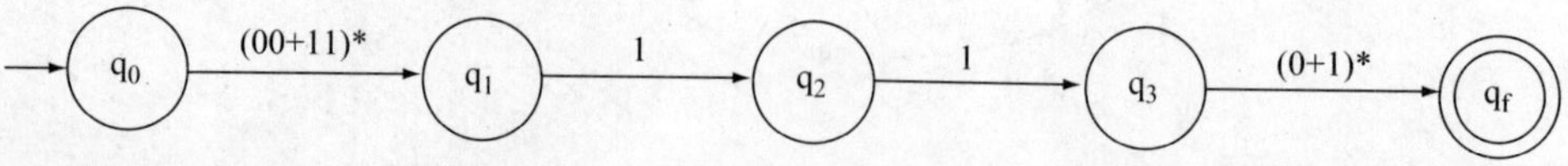

Step III: There are two * in the Regular Expression. Hence, there will be self loop on q_1 and q_f. And $\in$ transition will be in between q_0 and q_1, and q_3 and q_f.

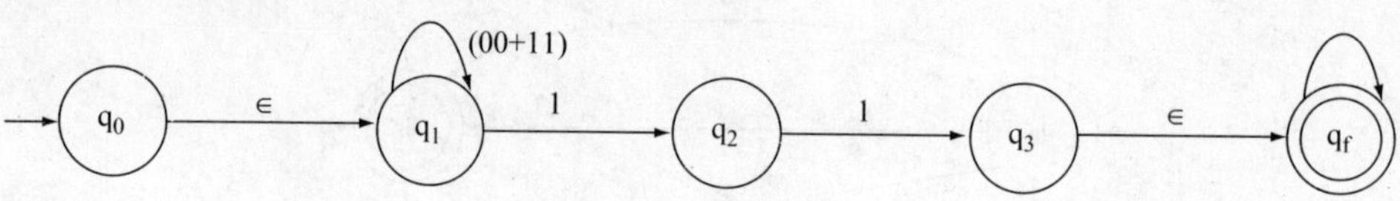

Step IV: There is a ' + ' sign between 00 and 11, hence there will be parallel edges. And two '.'(dot) sign (between 0, 0 and 1,1) Hence two extra states are added.

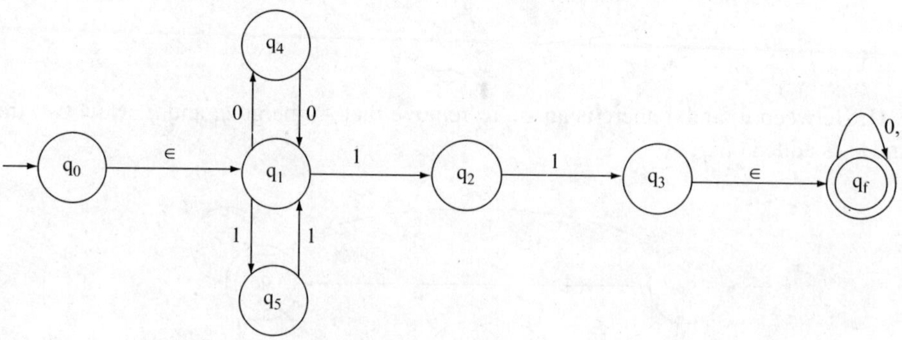

Step V: Removing $\in$, the final automata becomes

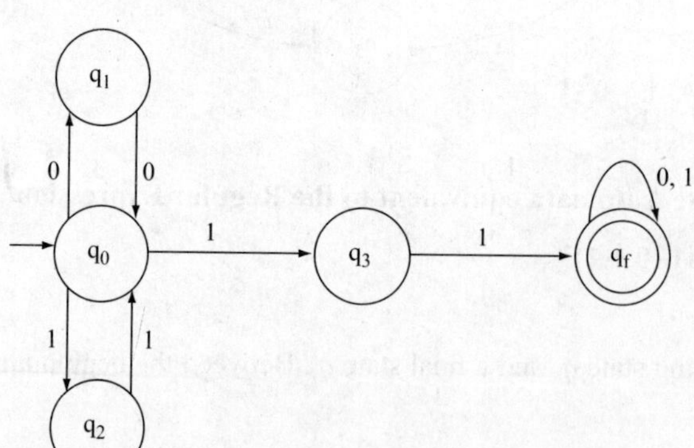

8. Convert the following NFA with ∈ –move to an equivalent DFA.

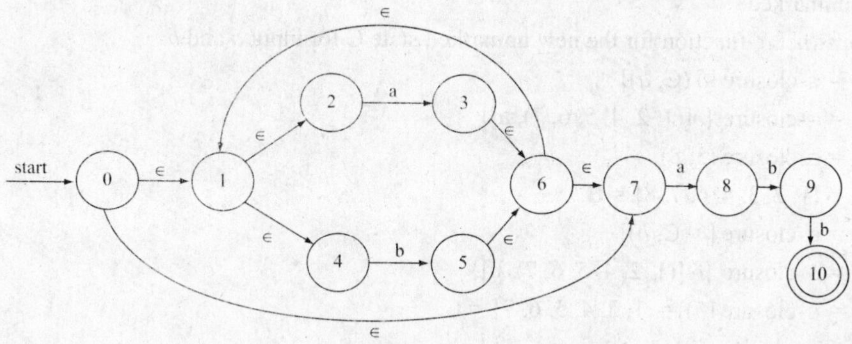

Ans.

∈-closure (0) = {0,1,2,4,7}
∈-closure (1) = {1, 2, 4}
∈-closure (2) = {2}
∈-closure (9) = {9}
∈-closure (3) = {1, 2, 3, 4, 6, 7}
∈-closure (4) = {4}
∈-closure (5) = {1, 2, 4, 5, 6, 7}
∈-closure (10) = {10}
∈-closure (6) = {1, 2, 4, 6, 7}
∈-closure (7) = {7}
∈-closure (8) = {8}

As 0 is the beginning state so start with ∈-closure(0) = {0,1,2,4,7}. Let rename it as A.

A is till unmarked.

Then construct δ′ function for the new unmarked state A for input *a* and *b*.

$\delta'(A, a)$ = ∈-closure (δ (A, *a*))
= ∈-closure (δ((0,1,2,4,7), *a*))
= ∈-closure (3, 8)
= {1, 2, 3, 4, 6, 7, 8}

New state so rename it as B.

$\delta'(A, b)$ = ∈-closure(δ (A, *b*))
= ∈-closure (δ((0,1,2,4,7), *b*))
= ∈-closure (5) = {1, 2, 4, 5, 6, 7}

New state so rename it as C.

B is till unmarked.

Then construct δ′ function for the new unmarked state B for input *a* and *b*.

$\delta'(B, a)$ = ∈-closure(δ (B, *a*))
= ∈-closure (δ((1, 2, 3, 4, 6, 7, 8), *a*))
= ∈-closure (3, 8)
= {1, 2, 3, 4, 6, 7, 8} = B

$\delta'(B, b)$ = ∈-closure (δ (B, *b*))
= ∈-closure (δ((1, 2, 3, 4, 6, 7, 8), *b*))
= ∈-closure (5, 9)
= {1, 2, 4, 5, 6, 7, 9}.

New state so rename it as D.

C is till unmarked.

Then construct δ' function for the new unmarked state C for input a and b.

$\delta'(C, a) = \in\text{-closure } [\delta (C, a)]$

$= \in\text{-closure } \{\delta[(1, 2, 4, 5, 6, 7), a]\}$

$= \in\text{-closure } (3, 8)$

$= \{1, 2, 3, 4, 6, 7, 8\} = B.$

$\delta'(C, b) = \in\text{-closure } [\delta (C, b)]$

$= \in\text{-closure } \{\delta [(1, 2, 4, 5, 6, 7), b]\}$

$= \in\text{-closure } (5) = \{1, 2, 4, 5, 6, 7\} = C.$

D is till unmarked.

Then construct δ' function for the new unmarked state D for input a and b.

$\delta'(D, a) = \in\text{-closure}(\delta (D, a))$

$= \in\text{-closure } \{\delta[(1, 2, 4, 5, 6, 7, 9), a]\}$

$= \in\text{-closure } (3, 8)$

$= \{1, 2, 3, 4, 6, 7, 8\} = B$

$\delta'(D, b) = \in\text{-closure}\{\delta (D, b)\}$

$= \in\text{-closure } \{\delta[(1, 2, 4, 5, 6, 7, 9), b]\}$

$= \in\text{-closure } (5) = \{1, 2, 4, 5, 6, 7, 10\}$

New state so rename it as E.

$\delta'(E, a) = \in\text{-closure}[\delta (E, a)]$

$= \in\text{-closure } \{\delta[(1, 2, 4, 5, 6, 7, 10), a]\}$

$= \in\text{-closure } (3, 8)$

$= \{1, 2, 3, 4, 6, 7, 8\} = B$

$\delta'(E, b) = \in\text{-closure}[\delta (E, b)]$

$= \in\text{-closure } \{\delta[(1, 2, 4, 5, 6, 7, 10), b]\}$

$= \in\text{-closure } (5) = \{1, 2, 4, 5, 6, 7\} = C$

Here final state is E.

The equivalent DFA:

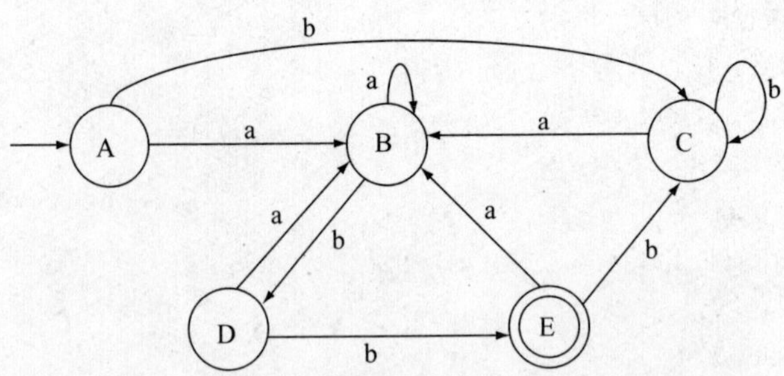

9. Construct Regular Grammar for the Regular Expression $L = (a + b)^*(aa + bb)(a + b)^*$

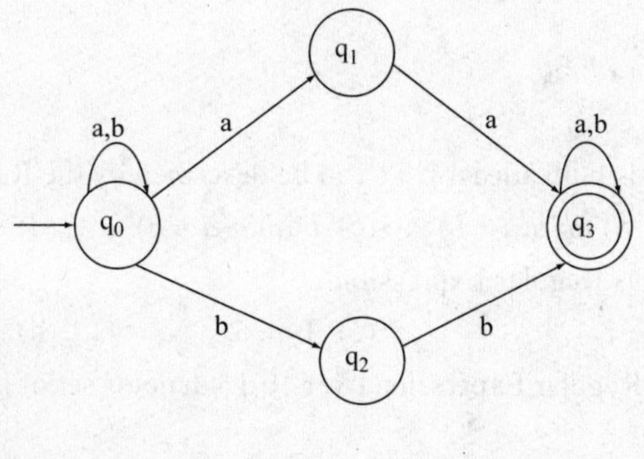

Ans. The NFA for the Regular Expression

There are four states in the finite automata. Therefore, in the regular grammar there are four non-terminals.

Lets consider them as A [For q_0], B [For q_1], C [For q_2] and D [For q_3].

Now we have to construct the Production rules of the Grammar.

For the state q_0 the production rules are

A → aA, A → bA, A → aB, A → bC.

For the state q_1 the production rules are

B → aD, B → a [As D is final state].

For the state q_3 the production rules are

C → bD, C → b [As D is final state].

For the state q_4 the production rules are

D → aD, D → bD, D → a/b

The grammar = {V_N, S, *P*, *S*}

V_N= {*A, B, C, D*} *S* ={*a, b*}

P: A → *a*A/ *b*A/ *a*B/ *b*C

B → *a*D/*a*

C → bD/*b*

D → *a*D/*b*D/*a*/*b*

MULTIPLE CHOICE QUESTIONS

1. Machine format of Regular Expression is

(a) Finite Automata (b) Push Down Automata
(c) Turing Machine (d) All of the above.

2. Regular Expression is accepted by
   (a) Finite Automata
   (b) Push Down Automata
   (c) Turing Machine
   (d) All of the above.
3. The language of all words with atleast 2 a's can be described by the Regular Expression
   (a) $(ab)^*a$ (b) $(a+b)^*ab^*a(a+b)^*$ (c) $b^*ab^*a(a+b)^*$ (d) All of the above
4. Which type of language is Regular Expression?
   (a) Type 0 (b) Type 1 (c) Type 2 (d) Type 3.
5. Which of the following Regular Expression over {0,1} denotes set of all strings not containing 100 as substring?
   (a) $(1+0)^*0^*$ (b) 0^*1010^* (c) 0^*1^*01 (d) All of the above.
6. $\wedge + RR^* = ?$
   (a) R (b) R^* (c) R^+ (d) $\wedge$.
7. What is the solution for the equation $R = Q + RP$ (If P and Q are Regular Expression and P does not contain $\wedge$)
   (a) $R = QP^*$ (b) $R = QP$ (c) $R = PQ^*$ (d) $R = P^*Q^*$.
8. Which is true for $\in$ -closure of a state.
   (a) All the states reachable from the state with input null excluding the state
   (b) The state only
   (c) All the other states
   (d) All the states reachable from the state with input null.
9. Pumping lemma for Regular Expression is used to prove that
   (a) Certain sets are Regular
   (b) Certain Sets are not Regular
   (c) Certain Regular Grammar produce Regular Expression
   (d) Certain Regular Grammar does not produce Regular Expression
10. Regular sets are closed under
   (a) Union (b) Concatenation (c) Kleene Closure (d) All of the above.

Ans. 1. a 2. d 3. b 4. d 5. c 6. b 7. a 8. d 9. b 10. d.

EXERCISES

1. Prove that $(0 + 011^*) + (0 + 011^*)(01 + 0100^*)(01 + 0100^*)^* = 01^*(010^*)^*$.
2. Find Regular Expression for the followings
   (a) Set of all strings over (a, b) containing exactly one a
   (b) Set of all strings over (a, b) containing atleast two a's
   (c) Set of all strings over (0, 1) containing exactly two a's
   (d) Set of all strings over (a, b) beginning and ending with b.

(e) Set of all strings over (0, 1) containing 010 as substring
(f) Set of all strings over (0, 1) not containing substring 00.

3. Describe the following Regular Expressions in English language

(a) b^*ab^* (b) $(a + b)^* aba(a + b)^*$ (c) $a(a + b)^*ab$

4. Find Regular Expressions corresponding to the automaton generated by the following Finite Automata.

(a)

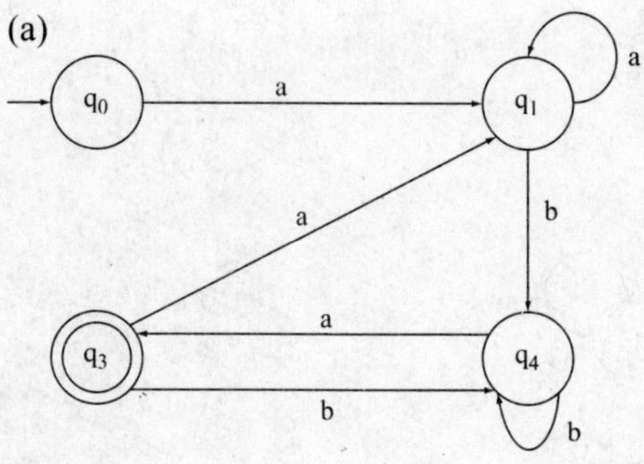

(b)

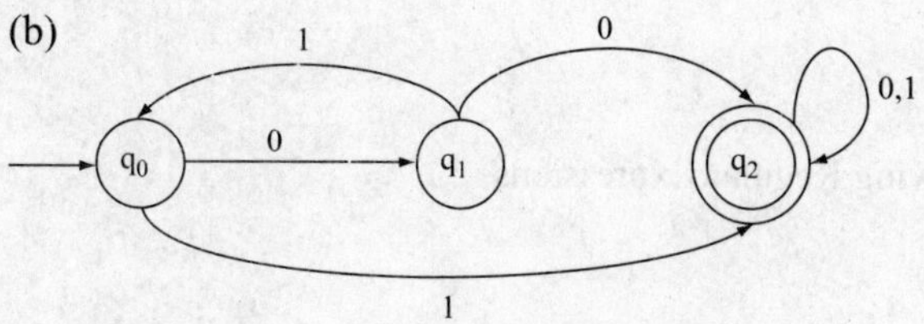

(c)

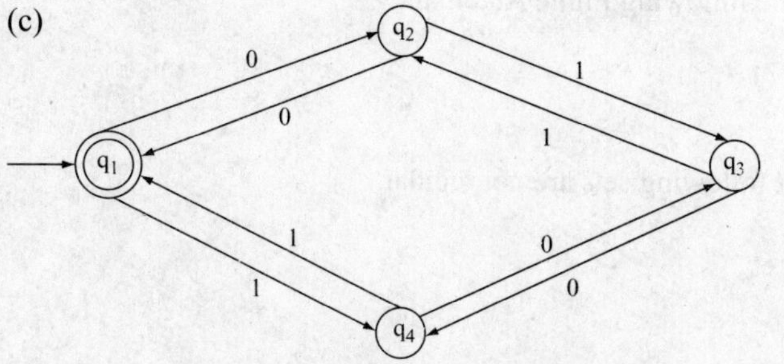

5. Convert the following NFA with null move to an equivalent DFA by $\in$ closure method.

(a)

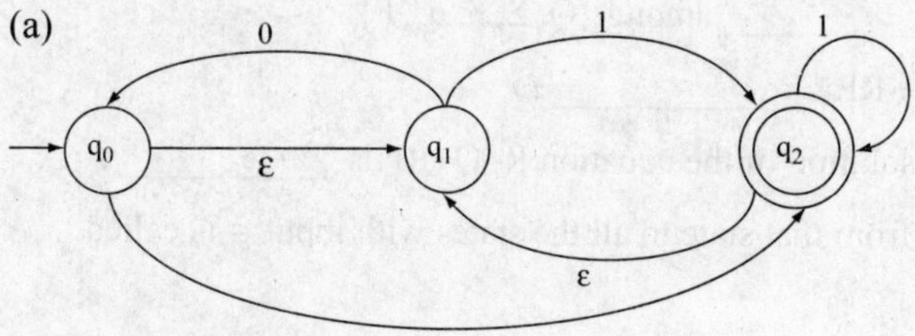

(b)

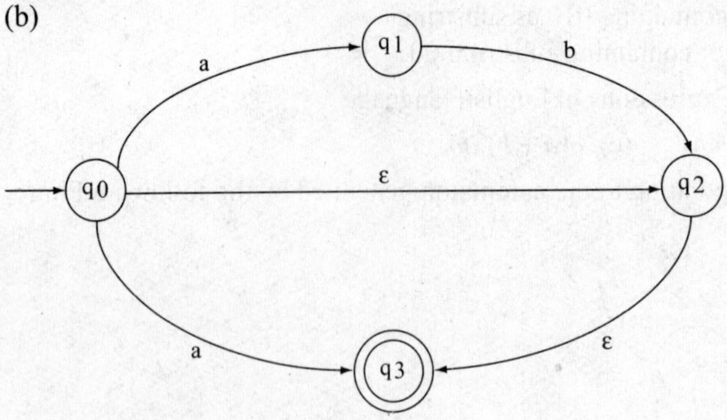

(c)

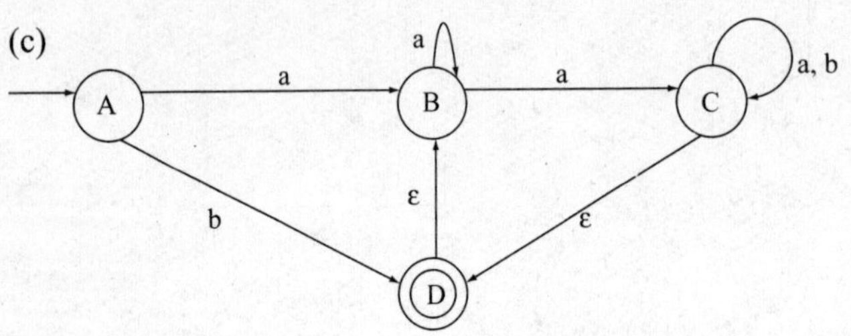

6. Develop Finite Automata for the following Regular Expressions
   (a) $(a^*ab + ba)^*a^*$
   (b) $(ab + a)^*(aa + b)$
   (c) $10 + (0 + 11)0^*1$
7. Construct Regular Grammar for the following Finite Automata.
   (a) $ab + (aa + bb)(a + b)^*$
   (b) $01(00 + 11)^*11^*$
   (c) $a^*(aa + bb)^* + b^*(ab + ba)^*$
8. Using Pumping Lemma show that following sets are not regular.
   (a) $L = \{a^n b^m, \text{ where } 0 < n < m\}$
   (b) $L = \{a^n b^{n+1}, \text{ where } n > 0\}$
   (c) $L = \{a^i b^j c^k, \text{ where } i,j,k > 0\}$

FILL IN THE BLANKS

1. Regular Expression is a string on __________ among $\{Q, \Sigma, \delta, q_0, F\}$
2. If R is a Regular Expression then $\wedge + RR^* =$ __________.
3. According to Arden's Theorem the solution of the equation R=Q+RP is __________.
4. Set of all states that can be reached from that state to all the states with input $\in$ is called __________

5. For the following NFA with ∈ move ∈ closure of q1 is ___________

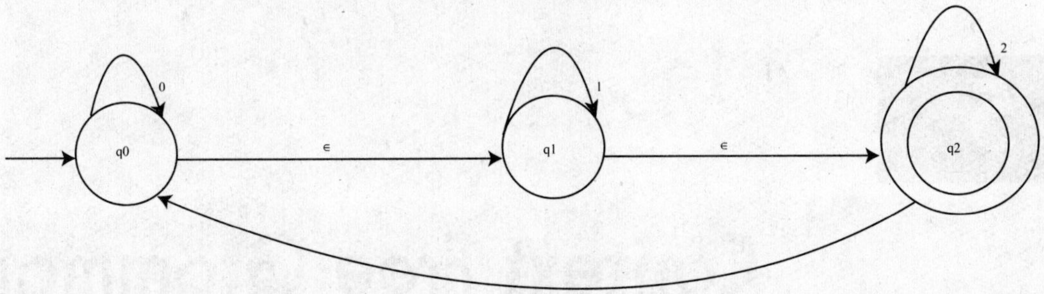

6. A grammar where all productions are in the form A → Ba or A → **a** then that grammar is called ___________

7. A grammar where all productions are in the form A → **a**B or A → **a** then that grammar is called ___________.

8. Pumping Lemma for Regular Expression is used to prove that certain sets are not ___________.

9. The property which describes when we combine any two elements of the set; the result is also included in the set is called ___________

10. If any Finite Automata contains any ∈ (null) move or transaction then that Finite Automata is called ___________.

11. Machine format of Regular Expression is ___________

ANSWERS

1. Σ	2. **R***	3. R = QP*
4. ∈ closure	5. q0, q1, q2	6. left linear grammar
7. right linear grammar	8. Regular	9. Closure property
10. NFA with ∈ moves	11. Finite Automata	

5

Context Free Grammar

5.1 CONTEXT FREE GRAMMAR: DEFINITION AND EXAMPLES

Q. Define context free grammar. Why is it called context free?

Ans. According to Chomsky Hierarchy, Context Free Grammar (CFG) is Type 2 Grammar.

In mathematical description we can describe it as

Where all the production are in the form $\alpha \rightarrow \beta$, where $\alpha \in V_N$, i.e. set of non-terminals and $|\alpha| = 1$, i.e. there will be only one non-terminal at the left-hand-side and $\beta \in V_N \cup \Sigma$, i.e. β is a combination of non-terminals and terminals.

Before describing why this type of grammar is called context free, we have to know the definition of context. Non-terminals symbols are the producing symbols because they produce some extra symbols. So the production rules are in the format of

{A string consists of at least one non-terminal} → {A string of terminals and/or non-terminals}. If any symbol is present with the producing non-terminal at the left-hand-side of the production rule then that extra symbol is called context. Context can be of two types (a) left context; (b) right context.

In context free grammar, at the left-hand-side of each production rules there is only one non-terminal. (No context is added with it). For this reason this type of grammar is called context free grammar.

Q. Construct a CFG for the language $L = \{WCW^R \mid W \in (a,b)^*\}$.

Ans. W is a string of any combination of a and b. Hence, W^R is also a string of any combination of a and b, but it is a string which is the reverse of W. The C is a terminal symbol like a, b. Hence if we take C as a mirror we will be able to see the reflection of W in the W^R part.

Like C, $abCba$, $abbaCabba$ like this. It means there is some generating symbol in the middle by replacing which it adds same terminal symbol before and after C. As $W \in (a,b)^*$ so null symbol are also accepted in the place of a,b. That means only C is accepted by this language set.

From the above discussion the production rules will be:

$S \rightarrow aSb/bSb/C$.

The Grammar will be $G = \{V_N, \Sigma, P, S\}$, where

V_N: $\{S\}$,
Σ: $\{a, b, C\}$,
P: $S \rightarrow aSb/bSb/C$,
S: $\{S\}$.

Q. Construct a CFG for the Regular Expression (0 + 1)* 0 1*.

Ans. If we describe the regular expression in English language it will be any combination of 0 and 1 followed by single 0 and ends with any number of 1.

In this regular expression a single 0 is in between $(0 + 1)^*$ and 1^*. That is, in the language set only 0 can exist. For constructing the grammar for this regular expression keep the single 0 as fixed. Then before and after of this 0 consider two non-terminals A and B, which can be replaced multiple times.

Hence, the production rule (P) of the Grammar for constructing this regular expression will be

$S \rightarrow A0B$,
$A \rightarrow 0A/\ 1A/\epsilon$,
$B \rightarrow 1B/\epsilon$,

The Grammar will be $G = \{V_N, \Sigma, P, S\}$, where

V_N: $\{S, A, B\}$,
Σ: $\{0, 1, \epsilon\}$,
S: $\{S\}$.

Q. Construct a CFG for the RE (011 + 1)* (01)*

Sol.

The regular expression consists of two parts $(011 + 1)^*$ and $(01)^*$. Hence from the start symbol we are taking two non-terminals each of them is producing one part. (011 + 1) can be written as 011/ 1. As it is any combination of (represented by *) so null string is also included in the language set.

From the above discussion the production rules (P) of the grammar will be

$S \rightarrow BC$,
$B \rightarrow AB/\epsilon$,
$A \rightarrow 011/1$,
$C \rightarrow DC/\epsilon$,
$D \rightarrow 01$.

The grammar will be $G = \{V_N, \Sigma, P, S\}$, where

V_N: $\{S, A, B, C, D\}$,
Σ: $\{0, 1, \epsilon\}$,
S: $\{S\}$.

Q. Construct a CFG for a string in which there will be equal number of binary digits.

Ans. Binary digits means 0 and 1. We have to construct a Grammar for a string where there will be equal number of 0 and 1. These numbers may come in any order, but in the string the number of 0 and 1 will be equal. Hence the string may start with 0, may start with 1. 0 can come after 0 or 1 can come after 0. 1 can come after 1 or 0 can come after 1.

The production rules (P) for this Grammar will be

$S \rightarrow 0S0/1S1/0S1/1S0/\ \in$

The Grammar will be $G = \{V_N, \Sigma, P, S\}$, where

V_N: $\{S\}$,
Σ: $\{0,1, \epsilon\}$,
S: $\{S\}$.

Q. Construct a CFG for the string $[abba(baa)^n aab(aaba)^n \mid n \geq 0]$.

Ans. In English language the description for the string will be *abba* followed by any number of (*baa*) followed by *aab* followed by any number of *aaba*, in which number of *baa* and number of *aaba* are same. Value of *n* may be 0. Hence the string *abbaaab* is also accepted by the language set. One thing to be noticed in the string that, number of (*baa*) and number of (*aaba*) are same in the string.

The production rule (*P*) for the grammar of this language set will be

$S \rightarrow abbaA$
$A \rightarrow (baa)A(aaba)$
$A \rightarrow aab$

The grammar will be $G = \{V_N, \Sigma, P, S\}$, where

V_N: $\{S, A\}$,
Σ: $\{a, b\}$,
S: $\{S\}$.

Q. Construct a CFG for $\{a^n b^n c^m d^m \mid n, m \geq 1\}$

Ans. The string can be described like this: A string of equal number of *a* and *b* followed by equal number of *c* and *d*.

In this string, number of *a* and number of *b* will be same, and number of *c* and number of *d* will be same. Break the string into two parts A and B. Both are non-terminals. A will generate the string *anbn* and B will generate the string $c^m d^m$.

Now the Production rules (P) for the Grammar of the language will be

$S \rightarrow AB$,
$A \rightarrow aAb/ab$,
$B \rightarrow cBd/cd$.

The Grammar will be $G = \{V_N, \Sigma, P, S\}$, where

V_N: $\{S, A, B\}$,
Σ: $\{a, b, c, d\}$,
S: $\{S\}$.

Q. Construct a grammar for the language $\{a^n b^m c^m d^n \mid m, n \geq 1\}$

Ans. In this string number of *a* and number of *d* are same, and number of *b* and number of *c* are same. Here *a* comes first followed by *b*, *c*, and *d*. But the problem of breaking the string into two parts is that here *b* and *c* come in the middle of *a* and *d*. In this case, if we take a non-terminal for generating $b^m c^m$ then the problem will be solved.

Now the production rules (P) for the grammar of the language will be

$S \rightarrow aSd/aAd$,
$A \rightarrow bAc/bc$.

The grammar will be $G = \{V_N, \Sigma, P, S\}$, where

V_N: $\{S, A\}$,

Σ: $\{a,b,c,d\}$,

S: $\{S\}$.

5.2 DERIVATION AND PARSE TREE

Q. Define left-most derivation and right-most derivation.

Ans. In the process of generating a language from a given production rules of a grammar, the non-terminals are replaced by the corresponding strings of the right-hand-side of the production. But if there are more than one non-terminal then it must be determined which one will be replaced. Depending on this selection derivation are divided into two parts (a) left most derivation; (b) right-most derivation.

(a) A derivation is called a left most derivation if we replace only the left most non-terminal by some production rule at each step of the generating process of the language from the grammar.

(b) A derivation is called a right most derivation if we replace only the right most non-terminal by some production rule at each step of the generating process of the language from the grammar.

Q. Construct the string 0100110 from the Grammar given below by using
(a) left most derivation
(b) right most derivation

$S \rightarrow 0S/1AA$

$A \rightarrow 0/1A/0B$

$B \rightarrow 1/0BB$

Ans.

Left most derivation

$S \rightarrow 0\underline{S} \rightarrow 01\underline{A}A \rightarrow 010\underline{B}A \rightarrow 0100\underline{B}BA \rightarrow 01001\underline{B}A \rightarrow 010011\underline{A} \rightarrow 0100110$

(The replaced non-terminals are underlined.)

Right most derivation

$S \rightarrow 0\underline{S} \rightarrow 01A\underline{A} \rightarrow 01\underline{A}0 \rightarrow 010\underline{B}0 \rightarrow 0100B\underline{B}0 \rightarrow 0100\underline{B}10 \rightarrow 0100110$

(The replaced non-terminals are underlined.)

Q. Construct the string *abbbb* from the Grammar given below by using
(a) Left most derivation
(b) Right most derivation

$S \rightarrow aAB$

$A \rightarrow bBb$

$B \rightarrow A/\epsilon$

Ans.

Left most derivation

$S \rightarrow a\underline{A}B \rightarrow ab\underline{B}bB \rightarrow ab\underline{A}bB \rightarrow abb\underline{B}bbB \rightarrow abbbb\underline{B} \rightarrow abbbb$

Right most derivation

$S \rightarrow aAB \rightarrow aA \rightarrow abBb \rightarrow abAb \rightarrow abbBbb \rightarrow abbbb$

Q. What is parsing? Define parse tree. What are the conditions for constructing a parse tree from a CFG? Why parse tree construction is only possible for CFG?

Ans.

Parsing a string is finding a derivation for that string from a given grammar.

Parse tree is the tree representation of deriving a context free language (CFL) from a given Context free Grammar. These types of trees are some times called derivation trees.

"A parse tree is an ordered tree in which left-hand-side of a production represents a parent node and children nodes are represented by the production's right-hand-side."

Conditions for constructing a parse tree from a CFG

(i) Each vertex of the tree must have a label. The label is a non-terminal or terminal or null (Λ).

(ii) The root of the tree is the start symbol, i.e. S.

(iii) The label of the internal vertices are non-terminal symbols $\in V_N$.

(iv) If there is a production $A \rightarrow X_1X_2\ldots\ldots X_K$. Then for a vertex, label A, the children of that node will be $X_1X_2\ldots\ldots X_K$.

(v) A vertex n is called a leaf of the parse tree if its label is a terminal symbol $\in \Sigma$ or null (Λ).

Parse Tree construction is only possible for CFG. This is because the properties of a tree match with the properties of CFG.

Here we are describing the similar properties of a Tree and a CFG.

(a) For a tree there must have some root. For every CFG there is a single start symbol.

(b) Each node of a tree has single label. For every CFG at the left-hand-side there is a single non-terminal.

(c) A child node is derived from a single parent. For constructing a CFL from a given CFG a non-terminal is replaced by a suitable string at the right-hand-side (If for a non-terminal there are multiple productions). Each of the characters of the string is generating a node. That is for each single node there is a single parent.

For these similarities a parse tree can only be generated for a CFG.

(*NB: Parse tree is not possible context sensitive grammar because there are production like* bB→aa *or* AA→ B *that means at the left-hand-side there may be more than one symbols.*)

Q. Find the parse tree for generating the string 0100110 from the grammar given below.

$S \rightarrow 0S/1AA$

$A \rightarrow 0/1A/0B$

$B \rightarrow 1/0BB$

Ans.

For generating the string 0100110 from the above given CFG the Left Most derivation will be

$S \rightarrow 0\underline{S} \rightarrow 01\underline{A}A \rightarrow 010\underline{B}A \rightarrow 0100\underline{B}BA \rightarrow 01001\underline{B}A \rightarrow 010011\underline{A} \rightarrow 0100110$

The parse tree for this derivation:

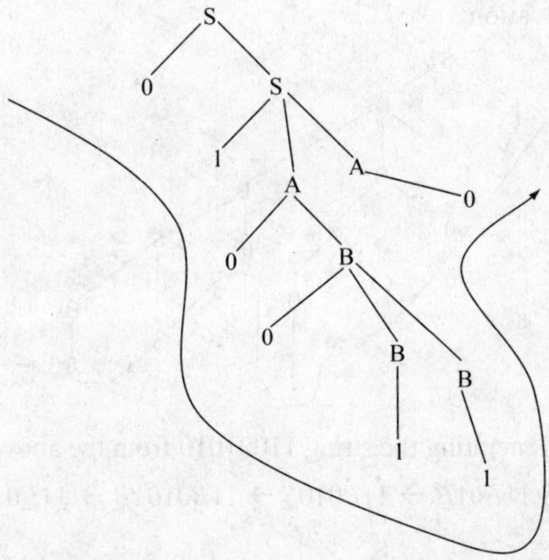

For generating the string 0100110 from the above given CFG the right most derivation will be

$S \rightarrow 0\underline{S} \rightarrow 01A\underline{A} \rightarrow 01\underline{A}0 \rightarrow 010\underline{B}0 \rightarrow 0100B\underline{B}0 \rightarrow 0100\underline{B}10 \rightarrow 0100110$

The parse tree for this derivation:

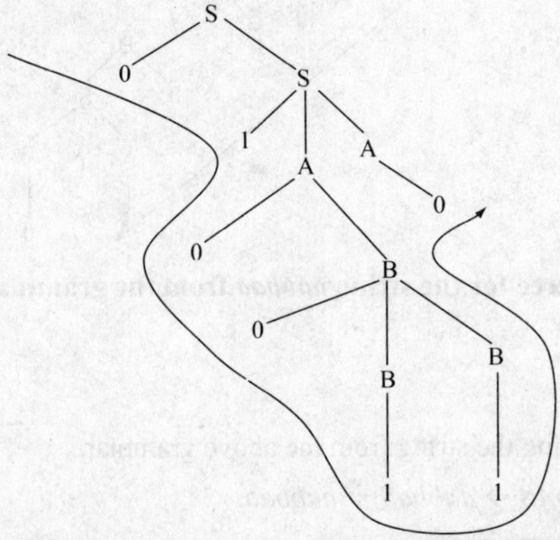

(*NB: When you will be told to generate a parse tree you can generate that by left most derivation or right most derivation.*)

Q. Find the parse tree for generating the string 11001010 from the given grammar.

$S \rightarrow 1B/0A$
$A \rightarrow 1/1S/0AA$
$B \rightarrow 0/0S/1BB$

Ans.

For Generating the string 11001010 from the above given CFG the left most derivation will be.

$S \rightarrow 1\underline{B} \rightarrow 11\underline{B}B \rightarrow 110\underline{S}B \rightarrow 1100AB \rightarrow 11001B \rightarrow 110010S \rightarrow 1100101B \rightarrow 11001010.$

The parse tree for this derivation:

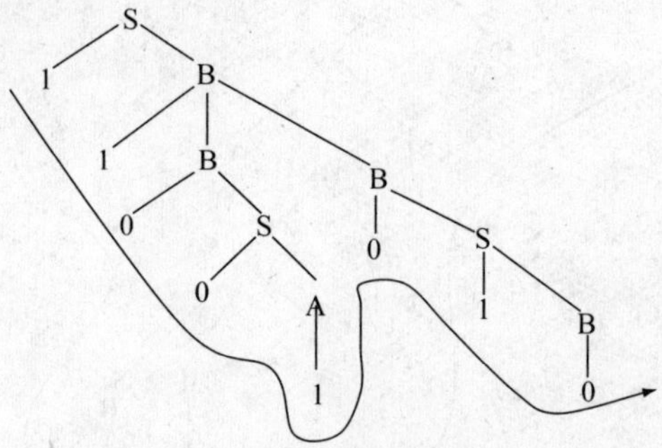

The left most derivation for Generating the string 11001010 from the above given CFG:

$S \rightarrow 1\underline{B} \rightarrow 11B\underline{B} \rightarrow 11B0\underline{S} \rightarrow 11B01\underline{B} \rightarrow 11B010\underline{S} \rightarrow 11B0101\underline{B} \rightarrow 11\underline{B}01010 \rightarrow 11001010$

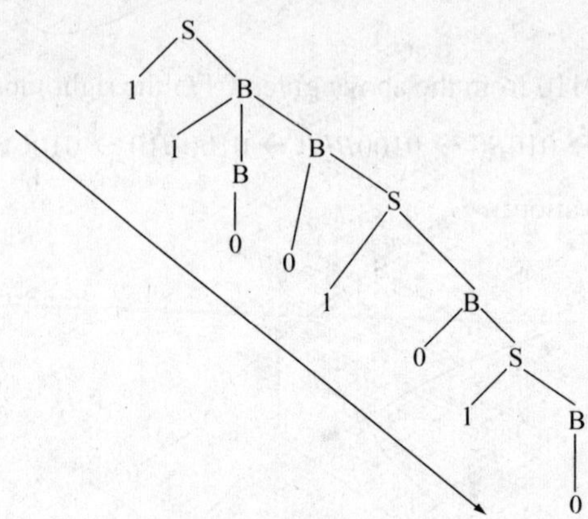

Q. Construct a parse tree for the string *aabbaa* from the grammar given below.

S* → *a*/*aAS
A* →*SS*/ *SbA*/ *ba

Ans.

The derivation for generating the string from the above grammar.

$S \rightarrow a\underline{A}S \rightarrow a\underline{S}bAS \rightarrow aab\underline{A}S \rightarrow aabba\underline{S} \rightarrow aabbaa.$

The derivation tree:

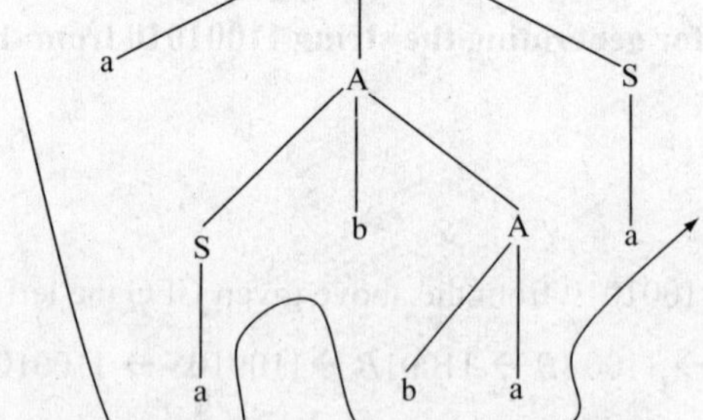

5.3 AMBIGUITY

Q. What do you mean by ambiguous language or ambiguous grammar? Explain with an example.

Ans. For generating a string from a given grammar we have to derive the string step by step from the production rules of the given grammar. For this derivation we know two types of derivations (i) left most derivation and (ii) right most derivation. Except these two there is also one approach called mixed approach. Here particularly left most or right most is not maintained in each step, whereas any of the non-terminals present in the deriving string is replaced by suitable production rule.

By this processes different types of derivation can be generated for deriving a particular string from a given grammar. For each of the derivations a parse tree is generated.

Different parse trees generated from the different derivations may be same or may be different.

A grammar of a language is called ambiguous if any of the cases for generating a particular string; more than one left most derivation or more than one right most derivation or more than one parse tree can be generated

Lets assume there is a grammar

$S \rightarrow aS/AS/A$,

$A \rightarrow AS/a$.

Generate the string *aaa* from the given grammar.

Sol. The string can be generated in many ways. Here we are giving two ways.

(i) $S \rightarrow aS \rightarrow aAS \rightarrow aaS \rightarrow aaA \rightarrow aaa$

(ii) $S \rightarrow A \rightarrow AS \rightarrow ASS \rightarrow aAS \rightarrow aaS \rightarrow aaA \rightarrow aaa$

The parse tree for derivation (i) The parse tree derivation (ii)

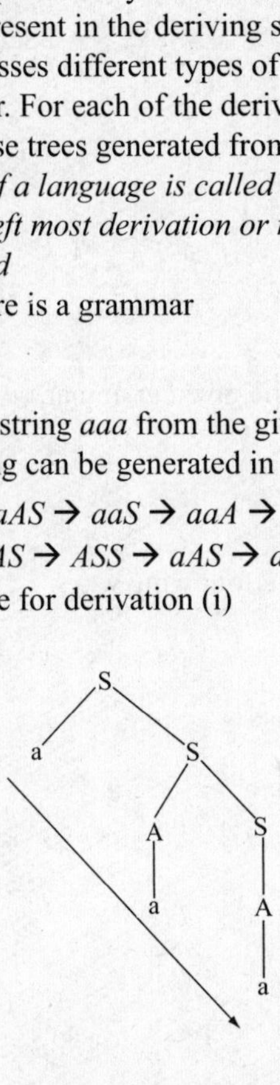

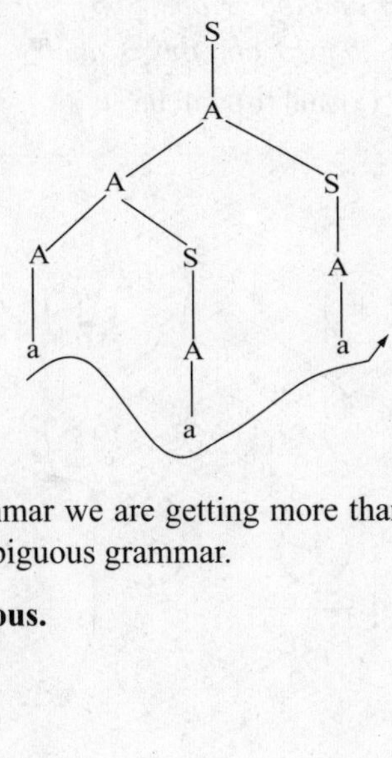

Here for the same string derived from the same grammar we are getting more than one parse tree. Hence according to the definition, the grammar is an ambiguous grammar.

Q. Prove that the following grammar is ambiguous.

V_N: {S},

Σ: {*id*, + ,*},

P: $S \rightarrow S + S/S * S$/id,

S: {S}.

Ans. Let take a string *id* + *id***id*.

The string can be generated in the following ways

(a) $S \rightarrow S + \underline{S} \rightarrow \underline{S} + S * S \rightarrow id + \underline{S} * S \rightarrow id + id * \underline{S} \rightarrow id + id * id,$

(b) $S \rightarrow S * S \rightarrow S + S * S \rightarrow id + S * S \rightarrow id + id * S \rightarrow id + id * id.$

The parse tree for (a): The parse tree for (b)

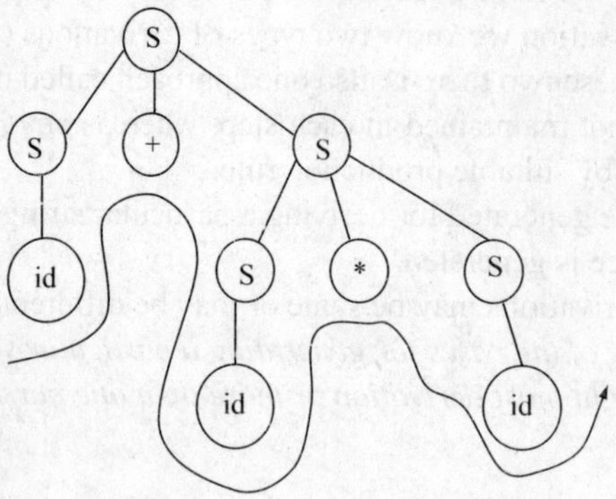

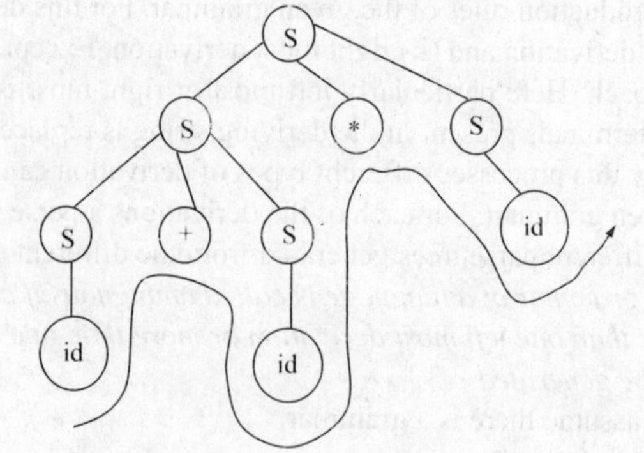

As we are getting two parse tree for generating a string from the given grammar, so the Grammar is ambiguous.

Q. Prove that the following grammar is ambiguous.

$$S \rightarrow a/abSb/aAb \quad A \rightarrow bS/aAAb$$

Ans. Take a string *abababb*. The string can be generated in the following ways

(a) $S \rightarrow ab\underline{S}b \rightarrow aba\underline{A}bb \rightarrow abab\underline{S}bb \rightarrow abababb$

(b) $S \rightarrow a\underline{A}b \rightarrow ab\underline{S}b \rightarrow aba\underline{A}bb \rightarrow abab\underline{S}bb \rightarrow abababb$

Parse trees for (a) and (b) will be

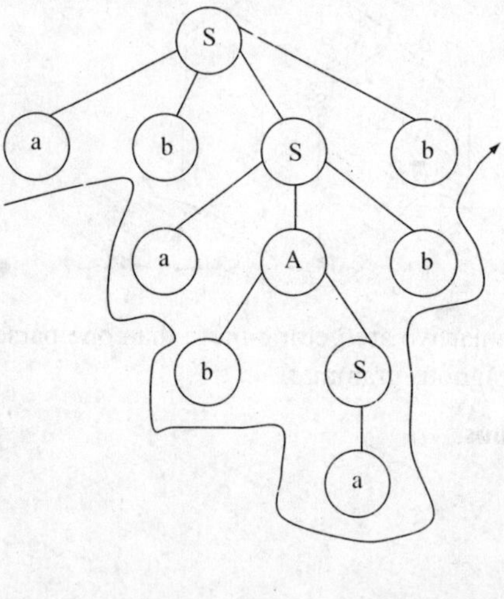

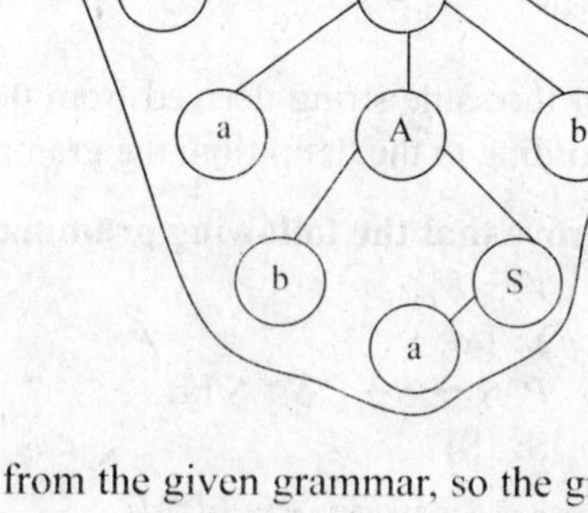

As we are getting two parse tree for generating a string from the given grammar, so the grammar is ambiguous.

Q. Prove that the following grammar is ambiguous.

$S \rightarrow 0Y / 01$

$X \rightarrow 0XY / 0$

$Y \rightarrow XY1 / 1$

Ans. Take a string **000111.** The string can be derived in the following ways.

(a) $S \rightarrow 0\underline{Y} \rightarrow 0\underline{X}Y1 \rightarrow 00\underline{X}YY1 \rightarrow 000\underline{Y}Y1 \rightarrow 0001\underline{Y}1 \rightarrow 000111$

(b) $S \rightarrow 0\underline{Y} \rightarrow 0X\underline{Y}1 \rightarrow 0\underline{X}XY11 \rightarrow 00\underline{X}Y11 \rightarrow 000\underline{Y}11 \rightarrow 000111$

Parse trees for (a) and (b) will be

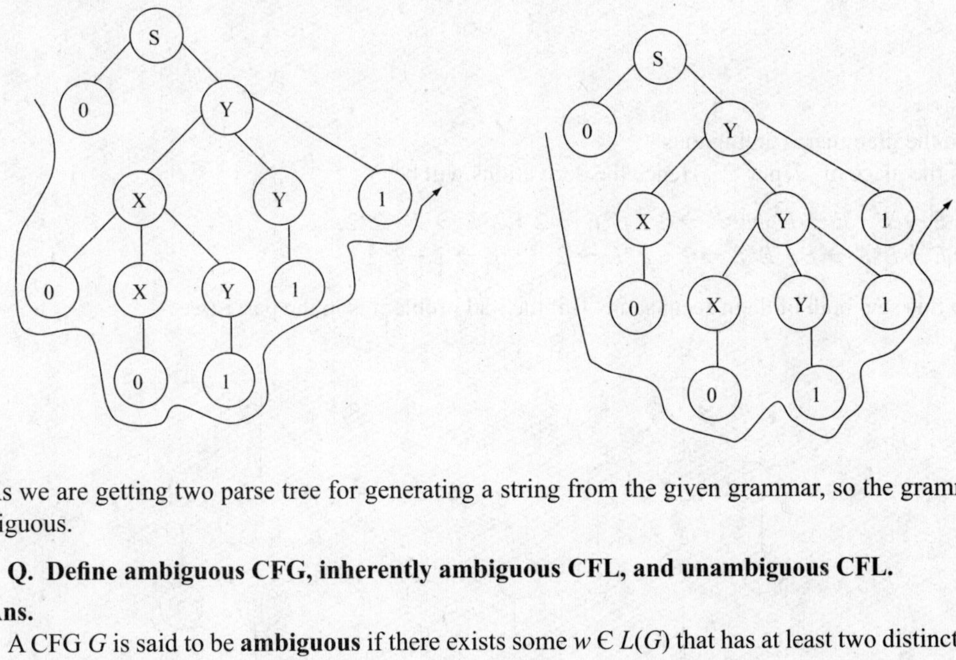

As we are getting two parse tree for generating a string from the given grammar, so the grammar is ambiguous.

Q. Define ambiguous CFG, inherently ambiguous CFL, and unambiguous CFL.

Ans.

(a) A CFG G is said to be **ambiguous** if there exists some $w \in L(G)$ that has at least two distinct parse trees.

(b) A CFL L is said to be **inherently ambiguous** if all its grammars are ambiguous.

(c) If L is a CFL for which there exists an unambiguous grammar, then L is said to be **unambiguous.** (Even one grammar for L is unambiguous, and then L is an unambiguous language.)

Q. Does ambiguous grammar create problem? Explain with a suitable example.

Ans. Yes, ambiguous grammar create problem. Lets take an example

For a grammar G, the production rule is $E \rightarrow E + E' E^*E/a$.

From here we have to construct $a + a^*a$.

The string can be generated in two different ways

(a) $E \rightarrow E + E \rightarrow E + E^*E \rightarrow a + E^*E \rightarrow a + a^*E \rightarrow a + a^*a$

(b) $E \rightarrow E^*E \rightarrow E + E^*E \rightarrow a + E^*E \rightarrow a + a^*E \rightarrow a + a^*a$

So for these two cases two parse trees are

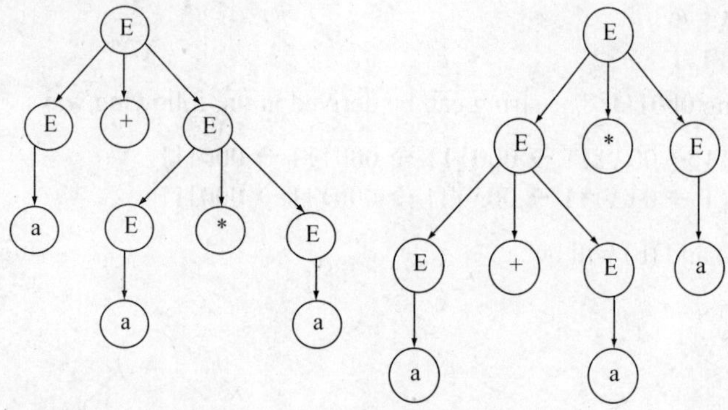

So the grammar is ambiguous.

In the place of '*a*' put '2'. Hence the derivations will be

(a) $E \rightarrow E + E \rightarrow E + E{*}E \rightarrow 2 + E{*}E \rightarrow 2 + 2{*}E \rightarrow 2 + 2{*}2$,

(b) $E \rightarrow E{*}E \rightarrow E + E{*}E \rightarrow 2 + E{*}E \rightarrow 2 + 2{*}E \rightarrow 2 + 2{*}2$.

Upto this step both of them seem same. But the real problem is in the parse tree.

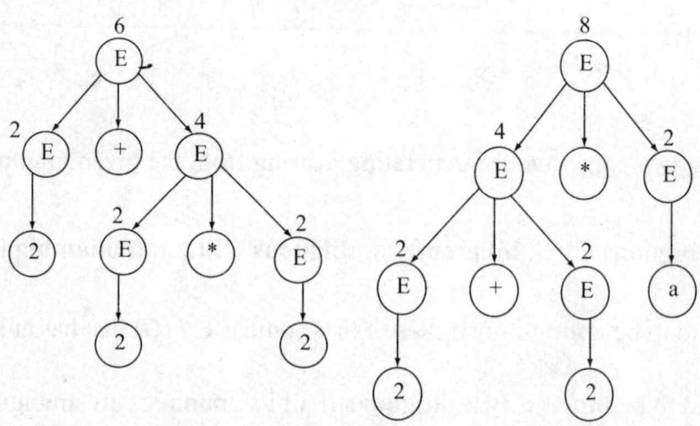

The correct result is **2 + 2*2 = 2 + 4 = 6** (according to the rules of mathematics * has higher precedence over +).

From here we can decide that ambiguity is bad for programming language.

Q. How can we remove ambiguity from a grammar?

Ans. There is no particular rule to remove ambiguity from a context free grammar. Some times ambiguity can be removed by hand. In the previous case, ambiguity can be removed by setting priority to the operators ' + ' and '*'. If '*' is set as higher priority than ' + ' then ambiguity can be removed. More bad news is that some CFL have only ambiguous Grammar. That means in no way the ambiguity can be removed. This type of ambiguity is called inherent ambiguity.

5.4 LEFT RECURSION AND LEFT FACTORING

Q. What is left recursion? Describe with an example.

Ans. A context-free grammar is called left recursive if a non-terminal 'A' as a left most symbol appears alternatively at the time of derivation either immediately (called direct left-recursive) or through some other non-terminal definitions (called indirect/hidden left-recursive).

In other words a grammar is left recursive if it has a non-terminal 'A' such that there is a derivation.

$$A \overset{+}{\Rightarrow} A\alpha \quad \text{for some string } \alpha$$

Example:

Direct Left Recursion:

Let the grammar is $A \rightarrow A\alpha/\beta$, where α and β consists of terminal and/or non-terminals but β does not start with A.

At the time of derivation if we start from A and replace A by the production $A \rightarrow A\alpha$, then for all the time A will be the left most non-terminal symbol.

Indirect Left Recursion:

Take a grammar in the form

$A \rightarrow B\alpha/\gamma$,

$B \rightarrow A\beta/\delta$,

where α, β, γ, and δ consist of terminal and/or non-terminal.

At the time of derivation if we start from A replace the A by the production $A \rightarrow B\alpha$ and after that the B is replaced by the production $B \rightarrow A\beta$, then A will appear again as a left most non-terminal symbol. This is called indirect left recursion.

In general a grammar in the form

$A_0 \rightarrow A_1\alpha_1/$ ---

$A_1 \rightarrow A_2\alpha_2/$ ---

⋮

$A_n \rightarrow A_0\alpha_{(n+1)}/$ ---

is indirect left recursive grammar.

(*NB: Left recursive grammar is to be converted into a non-left recursive grammar because top down parsing technique cannot handle left recursion. top down parsing is a part of compiler design*).

Q. How to convert a left recursive grammar into a non-left recursive grammar?

Ans. Immediate left recursion can be removed by the following process. This is called Moore's proposal. For a grammar in the form

$A \rightarrow A\,\alpha \mid \beta$, where β does not start with A.

The equivalent grammar after removing left recursion becomes

$A \rightarrow \beta A'$,

$A' \rightarrow \alpha A' \mid \varepsilon$.

In general for a grammar in the form $A \rightarrow A\alpha_1 | \ldots | A\,\alpha_m | \beta_1 | \ldots | \beta_n$, where $\beta_1 \ldots \beta_n$ do not start with A, the equivalent grammar after removing left recursion is

$A \rightarrow \beta_1 A' | \ldots | \beta_n A'$
$A' \rightarrow \alpha_1 A' | \ldots | \alpha_m A' | \varepsilon$

For indirect left recursion removal there is an algorithm

Arrange non-terminals in some order: $A_1 \ldots A_n$

- for i from 1 to n do{
  - for j from 1 to i-1 do {
    replace each production
    $A_i \rightarrow A_j\,\gamma$
    by
    $A_i \rightarrow \alpha_1\,\gamma | \ldots | \alpha_k\,\gamma$
    where $A_j \rightarrow \alpha_1 | \ldots | \alpha_k$
    }
- eliminate immediate left-recursions among A_i productions

}

Q. Remove left recursion from the following grammar.

$E \rightarrow E + T | T$
$T \rightarrow T{*}F | F$
$F \rightarrow id | (E)$

Ans. In the grammar there are two immediate left recursions $E \rightarrow E + T$ and $T \rightarrow T * F$

By using Moore's proposal the left recursion $E \rightarrow E + T$ is removed as

$E \rightarrow TE'$ and $E' \rightarrow + TE' / \in$.

The left recursion $T \rightarrow T{*}F$ is removed as

$T \rightarrow F\,T'$
$T' \rightarrow {*}F\,T' | \in$

The context free grammar after removing left recursion becomes

$E \rightarrow T\,E'$
$E' \rightarrow + T\,E' | \in$
$T \rightarrow F\,T'$
$T' \rightarrow {*}F\,T' | \in$
$F \rightarrow id | (E)$

Q. Remove left recursion from the following grammar.

$S \rightarrow Aa | b$
$A \rightarrow Sc | d.$

Ans. The grammar has indirect left recursion. Rename S as A_1 and A as A_2. The grammar is

$A_1 \rightarrow A_2 a / b,$
$A_2 \rightarrow A_1 c / d.$

For $i = 1, j = 1$, there is no production in the form $A_1 \rightarrow A_1\alpha$.

For $i = 2, j = 1$, there is a production in the form $A_2 \rightarrow A_1\alpha$. The production is $A_2 \rightarrow A_1 c$. According to the algorithm for removal of indirect left recursion the production becomes

$A_2 \rightarrow A_2 ac / bc.$

This left recursion for the production $A_2 \rightarrow A_2ac/ bc/ d$ is removed and the production rules are

$A_2 \rightarrow bcA_2' / dA_2'$
$A_2' \rightarrow acA_2' / \in$

The actual non-left recursive grammar is

$S \rightarrow Aa/ b,$
$A \rightarrow bcA' / dA',$
$A' \rightarrow acA' /\in.$

Q. Remove left recursion from the following grammar.

$S \rightarrow Aa \mid b$
$A \rightarrow Ac \mid Sd \mid f$

Ans. The grammar has indirect left recursion. Rename S as A_1 and A as A_2. The grammar is

$A_1 \rightarrow A_2a/ b,$
$A_2 \rightarrow A_2c/ A_1d/ f.$

For $i = 1, j = 1$, there is no production in the form $A_1 \rightarrow A_1\alpha$.
For $i = 2, j = 1$, there is a production in the form $A_2 \rightarrow A_1\alpha$. The production is $A_2 \rightarrow A_1d$.

According to the algorithm for removal of indirect left recursion the production becomes

$A_2 \rightarrow A_2ad/ bd.$

The A_2 production is $A_2 \rightarrow A_2c/A_2ad/bd/f$.

This left recursion for the production $A_2 \rightarrow A_2c/A_2ad/bd/f$. is removed and the production rules are

$A_2 \rightarrow bdA_2'$
$A_2 \rightarrow fA_2'$
$A_2' \rightarrow cA_2'/ adA_2'.$

The actual non-left recursive grammar is

$S \rightarrow Aa \mid b$
$A \rightarrow bdA/ / fA/$
$A' \rightarrow cA' / adA'$

Q. What is left factoring? Describe with an example.

Ans. Let in a grammar there is a production rule in the form $A \rightarrow \alpha\beta_1/ \alpha\beta_2/.../ \alpha\beta_n$. The parser generated from this kind of grammar is not efficient as it requires backtracking. To avoid this problem we need to left factor the grammar.

Let the string that we need to construct is $\alpha\beta_2$. The parser is a computer program. It will check only one symbol at a time. Therefore, first it will take 'α'. For getting 'α', there are n number of productions. But which production is to be chosen? Let it has chosen $A \rightarrow \alpha\beta_1$. After traversing '$\alpha$', it will take the next symbol 'β_2' in the string. But from the current situation it is not possible to get 'β_2'. So, the parser needs to traverse back again. This is called backtracking. Left Factor solves this problem of backtracking.

To left factor a grammar, we collect all productions that have the same left-hand-side Non-Terminal and begin with the same terminal symbols on the right-hand-side. We combine the common strings into a single production and then append a new non-terminal symbol to the end of this new production. Finally, we create a new set of productions using this new non-terminal for each of the suffixes to the common production.

After left factoring the above grammar is transformed into:

$A \rightarrow \alpha A_1$

$A1 \rightarrow \beta_1 / \beta_2 / \ldots / \beta_n.$

Q. Left Factor the following grammar.

$A \rightarrow \underline{a}bB \mid \underline{a}B \mid cdg \mid cdeB \mid cdfB$

Ans. In the previous grammar, the right-hand-side productions *abB* and *aB* both starts with '*a*'. So they can be left factored. Same way *cdg*, *cdeB* and *cdfB* all starts with '*cd*'. So they can also be left factored.

The left factored grammar is

$A \rightarrow aA'$

$A' \rightarrow bB / B$

$A \rightarrow cdA''$

$A'' \rightarrow g / eB / fB$

5.5 SIMPLIFICATION OF CFG

Q. Why do we need to simplify a CFG?

Ans. Context free grammar may contain different types of useless symbols, unit productions, and null productions. These types of symbols and productions increase number of steps in generating a language from a CFG. Reduced grammar contains less number of non-terminals and productions, so the time complexity for language generating process becomes less from reduced grammar.

Q. What are processes of simplification of a CFG?

Ans. Context free grammar can be simplified in the following three processes.

(i) Removal of useless symbols
  (a) Removal of non-generating symbols
  (b) Removal of non-reachable symbols
(ii) Removal of unit productions
(iii) Removal of null productions.

Q. Define non-generating symbol and non-reachable symbol.

Ans. Non-generating symbols are those symbols, which do not produce any terminal string.

Non-reachable symbols are those symbols, which cannot be reached at any time starting from the start symbol.

Q. How useless symbols can be removed from a given context free grammar?

Ans. Useless symbols are of two types (a) non-generating, and (b) non-reachable.

These two types of useless symbols can be removed according to the following process

(a) Find the non-generating symbols, i.e. the symbols which do not generate any terminal string. If start symbol is found non-generating leave that symbol. Because start symbol cannot be removed, as the language generating process start from that symbol.
(b) For removing non-generating symbols remove those productions whose right-side and/or left-side contain those symbols.

(c) Now find the non-reachable symbols, i.e. the symbols which cannot be reached, starting from the start symbol.

(d) Remove the non-reachable symbols like rule (b)

[*There is no hard and first rule for which symbol (non-generating or non-reachable) will be removed first, but most of the cases non-generating symbol is removed first, then non-reachable symbol is removed. However, depending upon the situation this can be changed.*]

Q. Remove Useless symbols from the given Context Free Grammar.

$S \rightarrow AC$
$S \rightarrow BA$
$C \rightarrow CB$
$C \rightarrow AC$
$A \rightarrow a$
$B \rightarrow aC/b$

Ans. There are two types of useless symbols, non-generating symbol and non-reachable symbol. First we are finding non-generating symbols.

Those symbols which do not produce any terminal string are non-generating symbol.

Here *S* and *C* are non-generating symbol as they do not produce any terminal string. But *S* is the start symbol, so it cannot be removed.

So we have to remove the symbol *C*. To remove *C*, all the productions containing *C* as a symbol (left-hand-side or right-hand-side) must be removed. By removing the productions the minimized grammar will be

$S \rightarrow BA,$
$A \rightarrow a,$
$B \rightarrow b.$

Now we have to find non-reachable symbols, the symbols which cannot be reached at any time starting from the start symbol. There is no non-reachable symbol in the grammar. So the minimized form of the grammar by removing useless symbols is

$S \rightarrow BA,$
$A \rightarrow a,$
$B \rightarrow b.$

Q. Remove useless symbols from the given CFG.

$S \rightarrow aB/\ bX$
$A \rightarrow BAd/\ bSX\ /a$
$B \rightarrow aSB/\ bBX$
$X \rightarrow SBD/\ aBx\ /ad$

Sol. First we are going to find non-generating symbols, the non-terminals which do not produce any terminal string.

Here *S* and *B* are not producing any terminal string, so they are non-generating symbol. But *S* cannot be removed as it is start symbol. To remove *B* from the production rules of the given grammar, all the productions containing *B* as a symbol will be removed. By removing *B* from the grammar the modified production rules will be

$S \rightarrow bX,$
$A \rightarrow bSX/\ a,$
$X \rightarrow ad.$ -------------------------(a)

Now we have to find non-reachable symbols, the symbols which cannot be reached starting from the start symbol.

Here in (a) the symbol A cannot be reached by any path at any time starting from the start symbol S. So A is a non-reachable symbol. To remove A, all the productions containing A as a symbol will be removed. By removing A from the production rules of the grammar the minimized grammar will be.

$S \rightarrow bX,$
$X \rightarrow ad.$

Q. Remove useless symbol from the given grammar.

$S \rightarrow aAa$
$A \rightarrow bBB$
$B \rightarrow ab$
$C \rightarrow aB$

Sol. First we are going to remove Non-generating symbols, the non-terminals which do not produce any terminal string. Here S, A and C are non-generating symbols. However, as S is the start symbol it cannot be removed. However, A and C will be removed. The production rules containing A and/or C as a symbol will be removed. By removing A and C the production becomes

$B \rightarrow ab$. However there is no meaning of the grammar containing this single production rule and no start symbol. Therefore, we have to first remove the non-reachable symbols then non-generating symbols.

Here non-reachable symbols are B and C, But B is a generating symbol, so B cannot be removed. By removing C the production rules of the grammar becomes.

$S \rightarrow aAa$
$A \rightarrow bBB$
$B \rightarrow ab.$

Here non-generating symbols are S and A. However, any one of them cannot be removed. If we remove there will be no existence of the grammar or the language generating power of the grammar will be hampered.

Q. Reduce the following CFG by removing useless symbols from the grammar.

$S \rightarrow aC/ SB$
$A \rightarrow bSCa / ad$
$B \rightarrow aSB/ bBC$
$C \rightarrow aBC/ ad$

Sol. First we are going to remove the non-generating symbols from the production rules. Here S and B are not producing any terminal string, so they are non-generating symbols. But S is the start symbol so it cannot be removed. So, only B will be removed. By removing B the grammar becomes

$S \rightarrow aC$
$A \rightarrow bSCa/ ad$
$C \rightarrow ad$

Now we have to find the non-reachable symbols, the non-terminals which cannot be reached starting from the start symbol. Here symbol A cannot be reached by any path starting from the start symbol. Therefore, A will be removed. By removing A the production becomes

$S \rightarrow aC$
$C \rightarrow ad$

This is the reduced format of the grammar by removing useless symbols.

Q. What is unit production? What the problems unit production create in CFG? What is the procedure to remove unit production from a given context free grammar?

Ans. Production in the form **non-terminal → Single non-terminal** is called unit production. Unit production increases the number of steps as well as complexity at the time of generating language from the grammar. This will be clear if we take an example.

Lets assume there is a grammar ***S → AB, A → E, B→C, C → D, D →b, E→a.*** From here when we are going to generate a language then it will be generated by the following way

S → AB → EB →aB → aC → aD → ab, Number of steps are 6.

The grammar by removing unit production and as well as minimizing will be

S →AB, A→a, B → b.

From the language will be generated by the following way ***S → AB → aB → ab***, Number of steps is 3.

Procedure to remove unit production:

There is an algorithm to remove unit production from a given CFG.

```
While (there exist a unit production NT → NT)
{
  select a unit production A →B
  for(every non-unit production B →α)
  {
   add production A → α to the grammar.
   eliminate A →B from grammar.
  }
}
```

Q. Remove unit production from the following grammar.

S → AB, A → E, B→C, C → D, D →b, E→a

Ans. In this grammar unit productions are ***A →E, B→ C* and *C →D***. if we want to remove the unit production *A → E* from the grammar first we have to find a non-unit production in the form *E →* {Some string of terminal or non-terminal or both}. There is a production *E → a*. Hence the production *A → a* will be added to the production rule. And the modified production rule will be

S → AB, A → a, B → C, C →D, D →b, E →a.

For removing another unit production *B →C* we have to find a non-unit production *C →*{Some string of terminal or non-terminal or both}. However, there is no such production found. For removing a unit production *C →D* we have found a non-unit production *D →b*. So the production C →*b* will be added to the production rule set and C→ D will be removed. The modified production rule will be

S → AB, A → a, B → C, C →b, D →b, E →a.

Now the unit production *B →C* will be removed by *B →b* as there is a non-unit production *C →b*. The modified production rule will be

S → AB, A → a, B → b, C →b, D →b, E →a.

[*This is the grammar without unit production, but it is not minimized. There are useless symbols (non-reachable symbol)* C, D, *and* E. *Therefore, if we want to minimize the grammar these symbols will be removed. By removing the useless symbols the grammar will be*

S → AB, A →a, B →b]

Q. Remove unit production from the following grammar.
$S \rightarrow AB, A \rightarrow a, B \rightarrow C, C \rightarrow D, D \rightarrow b$.

Ans. The unit productions in the grammar are $B \rightarrow C, C \rightarrow D$.
To remove unit production $B \rightarrow C$ we have to search for a non-unit production $C \rightarrow$ {Some string of terminal or non-terminal or both}. There is no such production rule found. So, we are trying to remove the unit production $C \rightarrow D$.

There is a non-unit production $D \rightarrow b$. So, the unit production $C \rightarrow D$ will be removed by including a production $C \rightarrow b$.

The modified production rules will be

$S \rightarrow AB, A \rightarrow a, B \rightarrow C, C \rightarrow b, D \rightarrow b$

There is a unit production $B \rightarrow C$ exists. This unit production can be removed by including a production $B \rightarrow b$ to the grammar.

The modified production rules will be

$S \rightarrow AB, A \rightarrow a, B \rightarrow b, C \rightarrow b, D \rightarrow b$.

In this grammar no unit production exists.

(This grammar is unit production free, but not minimized. There are useless symbols in the form of non-reachable symbols. Here non-reachable symbols are C *and* D, *which cannot be reached starting from the start symbol* S. *By removing the useless symbols the grammar will become* **S →AB, A → a, B →b.**)

Q. Remove Unit production from the following grammar.

$S \rightarrow aX/ Yb/ Y$
$X \rightarrow S$
$Y \rightarrow Yb/ b$

Ans. The unit productions in the grammar are $S \rightarrow Y$ and $X \rightarrow S$. To remove unit production $S \rightarrow Y$, we have to find a non-unit production where $Y \rightarrow$ {Some string of terminal or non-terminal or both}. There is a non-unit production $Y \rightarrow Yb/ b$. The unit production $S \rightarrow Y$ will be removed by including production $S \rightarrow Yb/ b$ in the production.

The modified production rules will be

$S \rightarrow aX/ Yb/b$
$X \rightarrow S$
$Y \rightarrow Yb/ b$

In the previous production rules there is a unit production $X \rightarrow S$. This production can be removed by including the production $X \rightarrow aX/Yb/b$ to the production rules.

The modified production rules will be.

$S \rightarrow aX/Yb/b$,
$X \rightarrow aX/Yb/b$,
$Y \rightarrow Yb/b$.

(*This is also minimized grammar.*)

Q. Remove Unit production from the following grammar.

$S \rightarrow AA$
$A \rightarrow B/BB$
$B \rightarrow abB/b/bb$

Ans. In the previous grammar there is a unit production $A \rightarrow B$. To remove the unit production we have to find a non-unit production $B \rightarrow$ {Some string of Terminal or Non-terminal or both}. There is a non-unit production $\boldsymbol{B \rightarrow abB/b/bb}$. So the unit production $A \rightarrow B$ can be removed by including the production $A \rightarrow abB/b/bb$ to the production rule.

The modified production rule will be

$\boldsymbol{S \rightarrow AA}$

$\boldsymbol{A \rightarrow BB/abB/b/bb}$

$\boldsymbol{B \rightarrow abB/b/bb.}$

(*This is also minimized grammar.*)

Q. What do you mean by null production? When null production cannot be removed? What is the procedure to remove null production?

Ans. A production in the form $NT \rightarrow \epsilon$ is called null production.

If **Λ** (null string) is in the language set generated from the grammar, then that null production cannot be removed.

That is if we get $S \stackrel{*}{\Rightarrow} \epsilon$ then that null production cannot be removed from the production rules.

Procedure to remove null production:

Step I: If $A \rightarrow \epsilon$ is a production to be eliminated then we look for all productions, whose right side contain A.

Step II: Replace each occurrence of A in each of these productions to obtain the non-ϵ production.

Step III: These non-null productions must be added to the grammar to keep the language generating power same.

Q. Remove ϵ production from the following grammar.

$\boldsymbol{S \rightarrow aA,}$

$\boldsymbol{A \rightarrow b/\epsilon.}$

Sol. In the previous production rules there is a null production $A \rightarrow \epsilon$. The grammar does not produce null string as a language so this null production can be removed.

According to step I we have to look for all productions whose right side contain A. There is one $S \rightarrow aA$.

According to second step we have to replace each occurrence of **'A'** in each of the productions. There is only one occurrence of **'A'** in $S \rightarrow aA$. So after replacing it will become $S \rightarrow a$.

According to step three, these productions will be added to the grammar.

Hence the grammar will be

$\boldsymbol{S \rightarrow aA/a,}$

$\boldsymbol{A \rightarrow b.}$

Now in the new production rules there is no null production.

Q. Remove ϵ production from the following grammar.

$\boldsymbol{S \rightarrow aX/ bX}$

$\boldsymbol{X \rightarrow a/b/\epsilon.}$

Sol. In the previous grammar there is a null production $X \rightarrow \boldsymbol{\epsilon}$. In the language set produced by the grammar there is no null string, so this null production can be removed.

For removing this null production we have to look for all the productions whose right side contains *X*. There are two such productions in the grammar *S* → *aX* and *S* → *bX*.

We have to replace each occurrence of '*X*' in each of the productions to obtain non-null production. In both the productions *X* has occurred only once. Therefore, after replacing the productions will become *S* → *a* and *S* → *b*, respectively.

These productions must be added to the grammar to keep the language generating power same. So, after adding these, productions the grammar will be

S → aX/ bX/ a/ b,
X → a/ b.

Q. Remove ϵ production from the following grammar.
S → ABaC,
A → BC,
B → b/ ϵ,
C → D/ ϵ,
D → d.

Sol. In the previous grammar there are two null productions *B* → **ϵ** and *C* → **ϵ.** The grammar does not produce any null string. So these null productions can be removed to obtain a non-null production.

To remove the null production *B* → **ϵ** we have to find the productions whose right side contain *B*. There are two productions in the grammar *S* → *ABaC* and *A* → *BC*.

We have to replace each occurrence of *B* in each of the productions by null to obtain non-null production. In the previous two cases *B* has occurred only once. After replacing *B* by null the productions will become *S* → *AaC* and *A* → *C*. These productions will be added to the grammar to keep the language generating power same.

To remove the null production *C* → **ϵ** we have to find those productions whose right side contain *C*. There are two productions *S* → *ABaC* and *A* → *BC*.

We have to replace each occurrence of *C* in each of the productions by null to obtain non-null production. In the previous two cases *C* has occurred only once. After replacing *C* by null the productions will become *S* → *ABa* and *A* → *B*. These productions will be added to the grammar to keep the language generating power same.

In the previous two productions *S* → *ABaC* and *A* → *BC*, *B* and *C* both are there. But we have replaced *B* and *C* in two steps. If simultaneously *B* and *C* are replaced by null, the productions will become *S* → *Aa* and *A* → **ϵ**, respectively. These productions will also be added to keep the language generating power same.

So, after removing the two null productions *B* → **ϵ** and *C* → **ϵ**, the modified grammar will become

S → ABaC / AaC/ ABa/ Aa,
A → BC/ C/ B/ ϵ,
B → b,
C → D,
D → d.

Again in this grammar there is a null production *A* → **ϵ.** By removing the null production according to the previous way the modified grammar will become

S → ABaC / AaC/ ABa/ Aa/ BaC / aC/ Ba/ a,
A → BC/ C/ B,

$B \rightarrow b$,
$C \rightarrow D$,
$D \rightarrow d$.

The grammar is not in minimized format because there are three unit productions $A \rightarrow C$, $A \rightarrow B$ and $C \rightarrow D$. By removing the unit productions from the grammar, the minimized grammar will become

$S \rightarrow ABaC$ / AaC/ ABa/ Aa/ BaC / aC/ Ba/ a,
$A \rightarrow BC$/ d/ b,
$B \rightarrow b$,
$C \rightarrow d$,
$D \rightarrow d$.

Again in the grammar there is a non-reachable symbol D. By removing the non-reachable symbol the minimized grammar will be

$S \rightarrow ABaC$ / AaC/ ABa/ Aa/ BaC / aC/ Ba/ a,
$A \rightarrow BC$/ d/ b,
$B \rightarrow b$,
$C \rightarrow d$.

Q. Remove ϵ production from the following grammar.
$S \rightarrow ABAC$,
$A \rightarrow aA$/ ϵ,
$B \rightarrow bB$/ ϵ,
$C \rightarrow c$.

Sol. In the grammar there are two null productions. $A \rightarrow \epsilon$ and $B \rightarrow \epsilon$. The grammar does not produce any null string. So these null productions can be removed to obtain a non-null production.

To remove the null production $A \rightarrow \epsilon$ we have to find all the productions whose right-hand-side contain A. There are two productions $S \rightarrow ABAC$ and $A \rightarrow aA$. Among them in the production $S \rightarrow ABAC$ there are two A and one B. We have to replace each occurrence of A in each of the productions by null to obtain non-null production. By replacing we get $S \rightarrow ABC$, $S \rightarrow BAC$, $S \rightarrow BC$ (First right most, then left most then both) and $A \rightarrow a$ (For $A \rightarrow aA$).

To remove null production $B \rightarrow \epsilon$ we have to find all the productions whose right side contains B. There are two productions $S \rightarrow ABAC$ and $B \rightarrow bB$, each of them have single occurrence of B. For obtaining non-null productions we have to replace each occurrence of B in each of the productions by null. By replacing we get $S \rightarrow AAC$ and $B \rightarrow b$.

In the production $S \rightarrow ABAC$, there are both A and B. But we have replaced A and B in two separate steps. If simultaneously A and B are replaced by null, the productions will become

$S \rightarrow AC$, $S \rightarrow C$.

So, after removing the two null productions $A \rightarrow \epsilon$ and $B \rightarrow \epsilon$, the modified grammar will become

$S \rightarrow ABAC$/ ABC/ AAC/ BAC/ BC/ AC/ C,
$A \rightarrow aA$/ a,
$B \rightarrow bB$/ b,
$C \rightarrow c$.

There is no null production in the grammar.

Q. Remove ϵ production from the following grammar.
$S \rightarrow aS/ A$,
$A \rightarrow aA/ \epsilon$.

Sol. In the previous grammar there is a null production $A \rightarrow \epsilon$. But in the language set generated by the grammar there is a null string, which can be generated by the following way $S \rightarrow A \rightarrow \epsilon$. As null string is in the language set so the null production cannot be removed from the grammar.

5.6 NORMAL FORM

Q. What is called normal form of a grammar? What is the utility of normal form?
For a grammar the right-hand-side (RHS) of a production can be any string of variables and terminals, i.e. $(V_N \cup \Sigma)^*$. A grammar is said to be in normal form when every production of the grammar has some specific form. That means except allowing any member of $(V_N \cup \Sigma)$ on the RHS of the productions, we permit only specific members on the RHS of the production. But these restrictions should not hamper the language generating power of the grammar.

Utility of Normal Form:
When a grammar is made in normal form, every production of the grammar is converted in some specific form. These help us to design some algorithm to answer certain questions. Similarly if a CFG is converted into CNF, one can easily answer whether the language generated by the grammar, i.e. $L(G)$ is finite or not. For a CFG converted into CNF the parse tree generated from the CNF is always a Binary tree. Same like if a CFG is converted in GNF then a PDA accepting the language generated by the grammar can easily be designed.

Q. Define Chomsky normal form. What is the process of converting a CFG into CNF?
A CFG is called in CNF if all the productions of the grammar are in the following form
non-terminal → String of exactly two non-terminals
non-terminal → Single Terminal

Process:
Step I:
(a) Eliminate all ϵ – production.
(b) Eliminate all unit production.
(c) Eliminate all useless symbols.

Step II:
If (all the productions are in the form *NT* → string of exactly two *NT*s or *NT* → Single Terminal)
Declare the CFG is in CNF. And stop

Else
follow step III and/or IV and/or V.

Step III: (Elimination of terminals on the R.H.S. of length two or more)
Consider any production of the form
$NT \rightarrow T_1T_2....T_n$, where $n \geq 2$ (*T* means Terminal and *NT* means non-terminal).

For a terminal T_i introduce a new variable (non-terminal) say NT_1 and a corresponding production $NT_i \rightarrow T_i$. Repeat this for every terminal on the RHS so that every productions of the grammar has either a single terminal or two or more variables.

Step IV: (Restriction of number of variables on the RHS to two).

Consider any production of the form

$NT \rightarrow NT_1NT_2...NT_n$, where $n \geq 3$.

The production $NT \rightarrow NT_1NT_2...NT_n$ is replaced by new productions

$NT \rightarrow NT_1A_1$

$A_1 \rightarrow NT_2A_2$

$A_2 \rightarrow NT_3A_3$

$A_{n-2} \rightarrow NT_{n-1}NT_n$

Here A_i s are new variables.

Step V: (Conversion of string containing terminals and non-terminals, to string of non-terminal on the RHS)

Consider any production of the form

$NT \rightarrow T_1T_2....T_nNT_1...NT_n$, where $n \geq 1$.

For the part $T_1T_2....T_n$, follow **Step III**

Check the resultant string by Step II. If not in CNF follow **Step IV.**

By this process the generated new grammar is in CNF.

Q. Convert the following grammar into CNF.

$S \rightarrow bA/ aB$

$A \rightarrow bAA/ aS/ a$

$B \rightarrow aBB/ bS/ a$

Sol. The productions $S \rightarrow bA$, $S \rightarrow aB$, $A \rightarrow bAA$, $A \rightarrow aS$, $B \rightarrow aBB$, $B \rightarrow bS$ are not in CNF. So we have to convert these into CNF. Let replace terminal **'*a*'** by non-terminal C_a and terminal **'*b*'** by non-terminal C_b. Hence two new productions will be added to the grammar

$C_a \rightarrow a$ and $C_b \rightarrow b$.

By replacing *a* and *b* by new non-terminals and including the two productions the modified grammar will be

$S \rightarrow C_bA/ C_aB$

$A \rightarrow C_bAA/ C_aS/a$

$B \rightarrow C_aBB/ C_bS/a$

In the modified grammar all the productions are not in CNF. The productions $A \rightarrow C_bAA$ and $B \rightarrow C_aBB$ are not in CNF, because they contain more than two non-terminals at the right-hand-side. Let replace ***AA*** by a new non-terminal ***D*** and ***BB*** by another new non-terminal ***E***. Hence two new productions will be added to the grammar $D \rightarrow AA$ and $E \rightarrow BB$. Therefore, the new modified grammar will be

$S \rightarrow C_bA/ C_aB$

$A \rightarrow C_bD/ C_aS/a$

$B \rightarrow C_aE/ C_bS/a$

$D \rightarrow AA$

$E \rightarrow BB$

$C_a \rightarrow a$

$C_b \rightarrow b$

Q. Convert the following grammar into CNF.

$S \rightarrow ABa$
$A \rightarrow aab$
$B \rightarrow AC$
$C \rightarrow a$

Ans. Except $B \rightarrow AC$, all the productions in the grammar are not in CNF. We have to convert them into CNF keeping the language generating power same.

Lets replace **'*a*'** by D_a and **'*b*'** by D_b. Hence two new productions $D_a \rightarrow a$ and $D_b \rightarrow b$ will be added to the grammar. By replacing **'*a*'** by D_a and **'*b*'** by D_b and adding two productions the modified grammar:

$S \rightarrow ABD_a$
$A \rightarrow D_aD_aD_b$
$B \rightarrow AC$
$D_a \rightarrow a$
$D_b \rightarrow b$
$C \rightarrow a$

$S \rightarrow ABD_a$ and $A \rightarrow DaD_aD_b$ are not in CNF. Take two non-terminals E and F. Replace AB by E and D_aD_a by F. Therefore, two new productions $E \rightarrow AB$ and $F \rightarrow D_aD_a$ will be added to the grammar. By replacement and adding the productions the modified grammar will be

$S \rightarrow ED_a$
$A \rightarrow FD_b$
$B \rightarrow AC$
$D_a \rightarrow a$
$D_b \rightarrow b$
$E \rightarrow AB$
$F \rightarrow D_aD_a$
$C \rightarrow a$

In the previous grammar all the productions are in the form of **non-terminal → String of exactly two non-terminals or non-terminal → Single Terminal.** Hence the grammar is in CNF.

Q. Convert the following grammar into CNF.

$E \rightarrow E + E$
$E \rightarrow E * E$
$E \rightarrow id$

Where $\Sigma = \{+, *, id\}$

Ans. Except $E \rightarrow id$ all the other productions of the grammar are not in CNF. In the grammar $E \rightarrow E + E$ and $E \rightarrow E * E$ there are two terminals + and *. Take two non-terminals C and D for replacing '+' and '*', respectively. Two new productions will be added to the grammar. By replacing '+' and '*' the modified production rules will be

$E \rightarrow ECE$
$E \rightarrow EDE$
$E \rightarrow id$
$C \rightarrow +$
$D \rightarrow *$

In the production rules $E \rightarrow ECE$ and $E \rightarrow EDE$ there are three non-terminals. Replace *EC* by another non-terminal *F* and *ED* by *G*. Therefore, two new productions $F \rightarrow EC$ and $G \rightarrow ED$ will be added to the grammar. By replacing and adding the new productions the modified grammar will be

$E \rightarrow FE$
$E \rightarrow GE$
$E \rightarrow id$
$C \rightarrow +$
$D \rightarrow *$
$F \rightarrow EC$
$G \rightarrow ED$

In the previous grammar all the productions are in the form of **non-terminal → String of exactly two non-terminals or non-terminal → Single Terminal.** Hence the grammar is in CNF.

Q. Convert the following grammar into CNF

$S \rightarrow abAB$
$A \rightarrow bAB / \epsilon$
$B \rightarrow BAa / \epsilon$

Ans. In the grammar there are two null productions $A \rightarrow \epsilon$ and $B \rightarrow \epsilon$. First these productions must be removed, after that the grammar can be converted into CNF. After removing the null production $A \rightarrow \epsilon$ the modified grammar will be

$S \rightarrow abAB / abB$
$A \rightarrow bAB / bB$
$B \rightarrow Ba$

After removing the null production $B \rightarrow \epsilon$ the modified grammar will be

$S \rightarrow abAB / abA / abB / ab$
$A \rightarrow bAB / bA / bB / b$
$B \rightarrow Ba / Aa / a$

Now this grammar can be converted into CNF. In the grammar except $A \rightarrow b$ and $B \rightarrow a$ all the productions are not in CNF. Let take two non-terminals C_a and C_b which will replace *a* and *b*, respectively. Therefore, two new productions $C_a \rightarrow a$ and $C_b \rightarrow b$ will be added to the grammar. After replacing and adding new productions the modified grammar will be

$S \rightarrow C_aC_bAB / C_aC_bA / C_aC_bB / C_aC_b$
$A \rightarrow C_bAB / C_bA / C_bB / b$
$B \rightarrow BC_a / AC_a / a$
$C_a \rightarrow a$
$C_b \rightarrow b$

In this modified grammar $S \rightarrow CaC_bAB$, $S \rightarrow C_aC_bA$ $S \rightarrow C_aC_bB$ and $A \rightarrow C_bAB$ are not in CNF. Let take two another non-terminals *D* and *E*, which will be replaced in the place of CaC_b and *AB*, respectively. Hence, two new productions $D \rightarrow CaC_b$ and $E \rightarrow AB$ will be added to the grammar. By replacing and adding two new productions the modified grammar will be

$S \rightarrow DE / DA / DB / C_aC_b$
$A \rightarrow C_bE / C_bA / C_bB / b$
$B \rightarrow BC_a / AC_a / a$
$D \rightarrow C_aC_b$
$E \rightarrow AB$

$C_a \rightarrow a$
$C_b \rightarrow b$

In the previous grammar all the productions are in the form of **non-terminal → String of exactly two non-terminals or non-terminal → Single Terminal.** Hence the grammar is in CNF.

Q. Define Greibach normal form (GNF). What is the application of GNF?

Ans. A grammar is said to be in GNF if every productions of the grammar is of the form

non-terminal → (Single Terminal)(String of non-terminals)
non-terminal → Single Terminal
In one line it can be said that all the productions will be in the form
non-terminal → (Single Terminal)(non-terminal)*
(* means any combination of *NT* s including null)

Application:
If a CFG can be converted into GNF, then from that GNF, the Pushdown Automata (Machine Format of a CFG) accepting the CFL can easily be designed.

Q. What is the process of converting a given CFG into GNF?

Ans. Before going into detail about the process of converting a CFG into GNF we have to know two lemmas which are useful for the conversion process.

Lemma I: If $G = (V_N, \Sigma, P, S)$ be a CFG. And if $A \rightarrow A\alpha$ and $A \rightarrow \beta_1/\beta_2/\ldots/\beta_n$ belongs to the Productions rules(P) of G. Then a new grammar $G' = (V_N, \Sigma, P', S)$ can be constructed by replacing $A \rightarrow \beta_1/\beta_2\ldots/\beta_n$ in $A \rightarrow A\alpha$, which will produce

$A \rightarrow \beta_1\alpha/\beta_2\alpha/\ldots/\beta_n\alpha$ This production belongs to P' in G'.
It can be proved that $L(G) = L(G')$

Lemma II: Let $G = (V_N, \Sigma, P, S)$ be a CFG and the set of A productions belongs to P be $A \rightarrow A\alpha_1/A\alpha_2/\ldots/A\alpha_m/\beta_1/\beta_2/\ldots/\beta_n$.

Introduce a new non-terminal X. Let $G' = (V'_N, \Sigma, P', S)$ where $V'_N = (V_N \cup X)$ and P' can be formed by replacing the A-productions by

1. $A \rightarrow \beta_i \quad 1 \le i \le n$
   $A \rightarrow \beta_i X,$
2. $X \rightarrow \alpha_j \quad 1 \le j \le m$
   $X \rightarrow \alpha_j X.$

It can be proved that $L(G) = L(G')$.

[The main production was $A \rightarrow A\alpha_j/\beta_i$. If we replace $A \rightarrow A\alpha_j$ in the production $A \rightarrow A\alpha_j$, the production will become $A \rightarrow A\alpha_j\alpha_j$. Then replace A by β_i. The production will become $A \rightarrow \beta_i\,\alpha_j\alpha_j$.
If we replace $A \rightarrow \beta_i$ in the production $A \rightarrow A\alpha_j$, the production will become $A \rightarrow \beta_i\alpha_j$.
Take another non-terminal X, which will be replaced in the place of the string after αj in both the productions $A \rightarrow \beta_i\,\alpha_j\alpha_j$ and $A \rightarrow \beta_i\alpha_j$. So the A productions will be $A \rightarrow \beta_i$ and $A \rightarrow \beta_i X$ and X productions will be $X \rightarrow \alpha_j$ or $X \rightarrow \alpha_j\alpha_j\ldots\alpha_j$ i.e. $X \rightarrow \alpha_j X$. Hence the lemma II is correct.]

Process for Conversion a CFG into GNF

Step I: Eliminate null productions and unit productions from the Grammar and convert the Grammar into CNF.

Step II: Rename the non-terminals of V_N as $(A_1, A_2\ldots\ldots A_n)$ with start symbol A_1

Step III: Using **Lemma I** modify the productions. Such that left-hand-side variable subscript is less than or equal to right-hand-side starting variable subscript, that is in mathematical notation it can be said all the productions will be in the form $A_i \rightarrow A_jV$ where $i \leq j$.

Step IV: By repeating applications of **Lemma I** and **Lemma II,** all the productions of the modified grammar will come into GNF.

Q. Convert the following grammar into GNF.

$S \rightarrow AA/a$

$A \rightarrow SS/b$

Ans.

Step I: There is no unit productions and no null production in the grammar. The given grammar is in CNF.

Step II: In the grammar there are two non-terminals S and A. Rename the non-terminals as A_1 and A_2, respectively. The modified grammar will be

$A1 \rightarrow A_2A_2/\ a$

$A2 \rightarrow A_1A_1/\ b$

Step III: In the grammar $A_2 \rightarrow A_1A_1$ is not in the format $A_i \rightarrow A_jV$ where $i \leq j$. Replace the leftmost A_1 at the right-hand-side of the production $A2 \rightarrow A_1A_1$. After replacing the modified A_2 production will be

$A_2 \rightarrow A_2A_2A_1/\ aA_1/\ b.$

The production $A_2 \rightarrow aA_1/\ b$ is in the format $A \rightarrow \beta_i$, and the production $A_2 \rightarrow A_2A_2A_1$ is in the format of $A \rightarrow A\alpha_j$. Therefore, we can introduce a new non-terminal B_2 and the modified A_2 production will be (According to Lemma II)

$A_2 \rightarrow aA_1/\ b$

$A_2 \rightarrow aA_1B_2$

$A_2 \rightarrow bB_2$

And B_2 productions will be

$B_2 \rightarrow A_2A_1$

$B_2 \rightarrow A_2A_1B_2.$

Step IV: All A_2 productions are in the format of GNF. In the production $A_1 \rightarrow A_2A_2/\ a, A \rightarrow a$ is in the prescribed format. But the production $A_1 \rightarrow A_2A_2$ is not in the format of GNF. Replace the left most A_2, at the right-hand-side of the production by the previous A_2 productions. The modified A_1 productions will be

$A_1 \rightarrow aA_1A_2/\ bA_2/\ aA_1B_2A_2/\ bB_2A_2$

The B_2 productions are not in GNF. Replace left most A_2 at the right-hand-side of the two productions by the A_2 productions. The modified B_2 productions will be

$B_2 \rightarrow aA_1A_1\ /\ bA_1/\ aA_1B_2A_1/\ bB_2\ A_1$

$B_2 \rightarrow aA_1A_1B_2/\ bA_1B_2/\ aA_1B_2A_1B_2/\ bB_2A_1B_2$

For the given CFG the GNF will be.

$A_1 \rightarrow aA_1A_2/bA_2/aA_1B_2A_2/bB_2A_2/a$

$A_2 \rightarrow aA_1/\ b/aA_1B_2/\ bB_2$

$B_2 \rightarrow aA_1A_1$ / bA_1/ $aA_1B_2A_1$/ bB_2A_1
$B_2 \rightarrow aA_1A_1B_2$/ bA_1B_2/ $aA_1B_2A_1B_2$/ $bB_2A_1B_2$.

Q. Convert the following CFG into GNF.

$S \rightarrow XY$
$X \rightarrow YS/ b$
$Y \rightarrow SX/ a$

Ans.

Step I: In the grammar there is no null production and no unit production. The grammar also is in CNF.

Step II: In the grammar there are three non-terminals S, X, Y. Rename the non-terminals as $A1, A2, A_3$, respectively. After renaming the modified grammar will be

$A_1 \rightarrow A_2A_3$
$A_2 \rightarrow A_3A_1$/ b
$A_3 \rightarrow A_1A_2$/ a

Step III: In the grammar the production $A_3 \rightarrow A_1A_2$ is not in the format $A_i \rightarrow A_jV$ where $i \leq j$.
Replace the leftmost A_1 at the right-hand-side of the production $A_3 \rightarrow A_1A_2$ by the production $A_1 \rightarrow A_2A_3$. The production will become $A_3 \rightarrow A_2A_3A_2$, which is not again in the format of $A_i \rightarrow A_jV$ where $i \leq j$. Replace the leftmost A_2 at the right-hand-side of the production $A_3 \rightarrow A_2A_3A_2$ by the production $A_2 \rightarrow A_3A_1$/ b. The modified **A3** production will be

$A_3 \rightarrow A_3A_1A_3A_2$/ bA_3A_2/ a.

The production $A_3 \rightarrow bA_3A_2$/ a is in the format of $A \rightarrow \beta_i$,and the production $A_3 \rightarrow A_3A_1A_3A_2$ is in the format of $A \rightarrow A\alpha_j$ So, we can introduce a new non-terminal B and the modified A_3 production will be (According to Lemma II)

$A_3 \rightarrow bA_3A_2$,
$A_3 \rightarrow a$,
$A_3 \rightarrow bA_3A_2B$,
$A_3 \rightarrow aB$.

And B productions will be

$B \rightarrow A_1A_3A_2$
$B \rightarrow A_1A_3A_2B$.

Step IV: All the A_3 productions are in the specified format of GNF.

The A_2 production is not in the specified format of GNF. Replacing A_3 productions in A_2 productions, the modified A_2 production we get

$A_2 \rightarrow bA_3A_2A_1$/ aA_1/ $bA_3A_2BA_1$/ aBA_1 / b

Now all the A_2 productions are in the prescribed format of GNF.
The A_1 production is not in the prescribed format of GNF. Replacing A_2 productions in A_1 the modified A_1 productions will be

$A_1 \rightarrow bA_3A_2A_1A_3$ / aA_1A_3/ $bA_3A_2BA_1A_3$/ aBA_1A_3/ bA_3

All the A_1 productions are in the prescribed format of GNF.
But the B productions are till not in the prescribed format of GNF. By replacing the left most A_1 at the right-hand-side of the B productions by A_1 productions, the modified B productions will be

$B \rightarrow bA_3A_2A_1A_3A_3A_2 / aA_1A_3A_3A_2 / bA_3A_2BA_1A_3A_3A_2 / aBA_1A_3A_3A_2 / bA_3A_3A_2$
$B \rightarrow bA_3A_2A_1A_3A_3A_2B / aA_1A_3A_3A_2B / bA_3A_2BA_1A_3A_3A_2B / aBA_1A_3A_3A_2B / bA_3A_3A_2B$

Now all the *B* productions of the grammar are in the prescribed format of GNF.

So for the given CFG the GNF will be.

$A_1 \rightarrow bA_3A_2A_1A_3 / aA_1A_3 / bA_3A_2BA_1A_3 / aBA_1A_3 / bA_3$
$A_2 \rightarrow bA_3A_2A_1 / aA_1 / bA_3A_2BA_1 / aBA_1 / b$
$B \rightarrow bA_3A_2A_1A_3A_3A_2 / aA_1A_3A_3A_2 / bA_3A_2BA_1A_3A_3A_2 / aBA_1A_3A_3A_2 / bA_3A_3A_2$
$B \rightarrow bA_3A_2A_1A_3A_3A_2B / aA_1A_3A_3A_2B / bA_3A_2BA_1A_3A_3A_2B / aBA_1A_3A_3A_2B / bA_3A_3A_2B$

Q. Convert the following CFG into GNF.

$S \rightarrow AB/BC$
$A \rightarrow aB/bA/a$
$B \rightarrow bB/cC/b$
$C \rightarrow c$

Ans.

Step I: In the previous grammar there is no unit production and no null production. However, all productions are not in CNF. Let take two non-terminals D_a and D_b which will be placed in the place of '*a*' and '*b*', respectively. Therefore, two new productions $D_a \rightarrow a$ and $D_b \rightarrow b$ will be added to the grammar.

$S \rightarrow AB / BC$
$A \rightarrow D_aB / D_bA / a$
$B \rightarrow D_bB / CC / b$
$C \rightarrow c$
$D_a \rightarrow a$
$D_b \rightarrow b$

Now all the productions are in CNF.

Step II: There are six non-terminals in the grammar. Rename the non-terminals as $A_1, A_2, \ldots, A_6$. After replacing the modified productions will be

$A_1 \rightarrow A_2A_3 / A_3A_4$
$A_2 \rightarrow A_5A_3 / A_6A_2 / a$
$A_3 \rightarrow A_6A_3 / A_4A_4 / b$
$A_4 \rightarrow c$
$A_5 \rightarrow a$
$A_6 \rightarrow b.$

The productions for A_1, A_2, A_3 are all in the format $A_i \rightarrow A_jV$, where $i \leq j$. Replace A_6 and A_4 in the productions $A_3 \rightarrow A_6A_3$ and $A_3 \rightarrow A_4A_4$ by $A_6 \rightarrow b$ and $A_4 \rightarrow c$, respectively. The modified A_3 productions will be

$A_3 \rightarrow bA_3 / cA_4 / b$ All the productions are now in the format of GNF.

Replace A_5 and A_6 in the productions $A_2 \rightarrow A_5A_3$ and $A_2 \rightarrow A_6A_2$ by $A_5 \rightarrow a$ and $A_6 \rightarrow b$, respectively. The modified A_2 productions will be

$A_2 \rightarrow aA_3 / bA_2 / a$ All the productions are now in the format of GNF.

The A_1 productions $A_1 \rightarrow A_2A_3 / A_3A_4$ are not in the format of GNF. Replace A_2 at the right-hand-side of the production $A_1 \rightarrow A_2A_3$. The modified production will be

$A_1 \rightarrow aA_3A_3 / bA_2A_3 / aA_3.$

Replace A_3 at the right-hand-side of the production $A_1 \rightarrow A_3A_4$. The modified production will be $A_1 \rightarrow bA_3A_4/ cA_4A_4/bA_4$.

Therefore for the given CFG the GNF will be.

$A_1 \rightarrow aA_3A_3/ bA_2A_3/ aA_3/ bA_3A_4/ cA_4A_4/ bA_4$,
$A_2 \rightarrow aA_3/ bA_2/ a$,
$A_3 \rightarrow bA_3/ cA_4 / b$,
$A_4 \rightarrow c$,
$A_5 \rightarrow a$,
$A_6 \rightarrow b$.

5.7 CONSTRUCTING FA FROM REGULAR GRAMMAR

Q. What is the process of constructing finite automata directly from a regular grammar?

Ans.

Step I:

(a) If the grammar does not produce any null string then, number of states of the finite automata will be equal to the number of non-terminals of the Regular Grammar + 1. Each state of the finite automata represents each non-terminal and the extra state is the final state of the FA. If it produce null string then number of states is same as number of non-terminals.

(b) The initial state of the finite automata is the start symbol of the Regular Grammar.

(c) If the Language generated by the Regular Grammar contains null string then the initial state will also be the final state of the constructing finite automata.

Step II:

(a) For a production in the form $A \rightarrow aB$, make a δ function $\delta(A, a) \rightarrow B$. There will be an arc from state A to state B with label *a*.

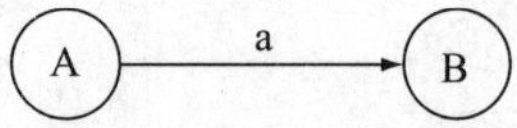

(b) For a production in the form $A \rightarrow a$, make a δ function $\delta(A, a) \rightarrow$ Final state.

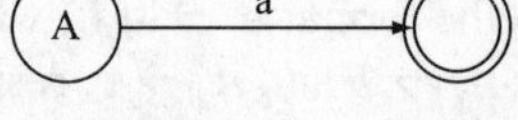

(c) For a production $A \rightarrow \epsilon$, make a δ function $\delta(A, \epsilon) \rightarrow$ A, and A will be final state.

Q. Convert the following Regular grammar into finite automata.

S → aA/ bB/ a/ b
A → aS/ bB/ b
B → aA/ bS

Ans. In the grammar there are three non-terminals S, A, and B. Therefore, number of states of the finite automata will be four. Let name the final state as C.

(i) For the production S → aA/ bB the transitional diagram will be

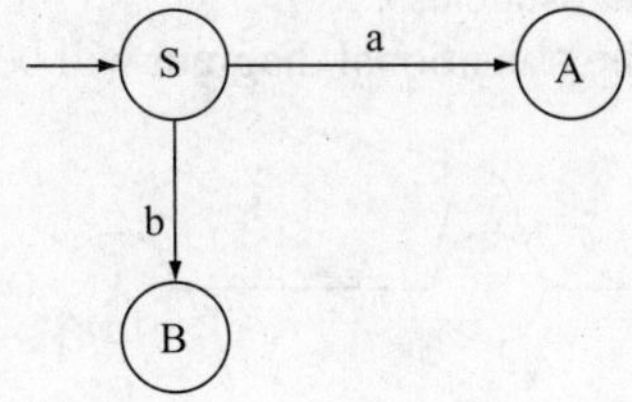

(ii) For the production S → *a*/*b* the transitional diagram including the previous will be

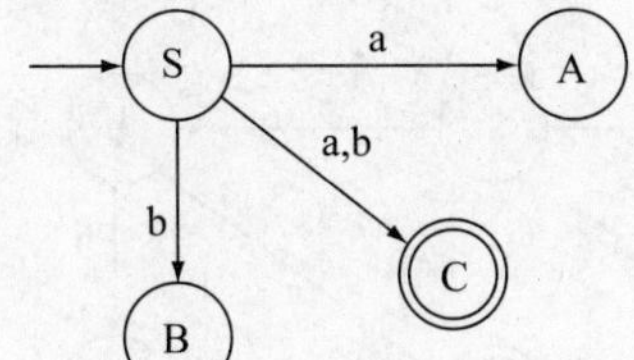

(iii) For the production *A* → *aS*/*bB*/*b* the transitional diagram including the previous will be

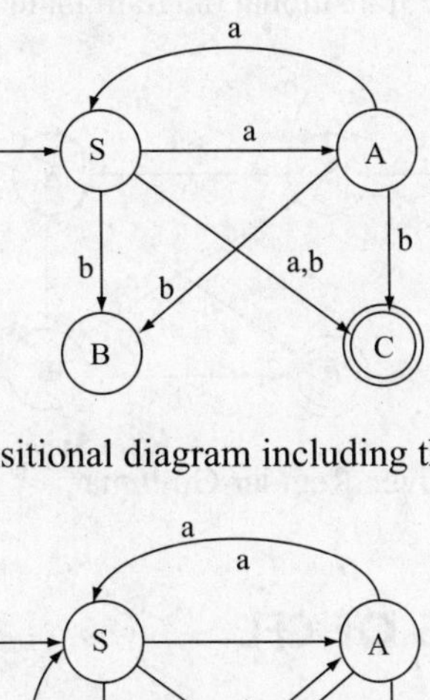

For the production *B* → *aA*/*bS* transitional diagram including the previous will be

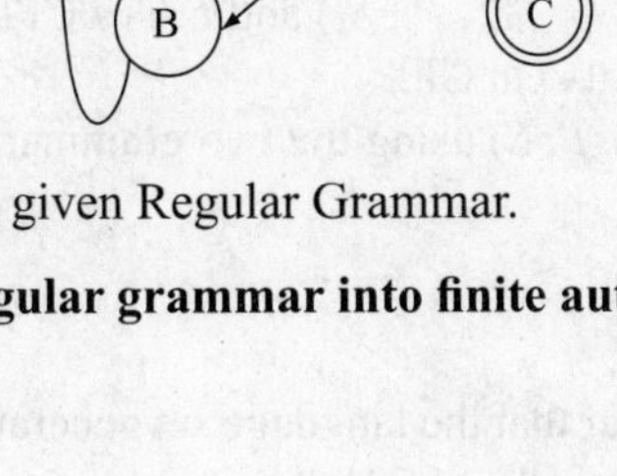

This is the finite automata for the given Regular Grammar.

Q. Convert the following Regular grammar into finite automata.

S → *a*A/bS

A → *b*B/*a*

B → *a*S/*b*

Ans. In the grammar there are three non-terminals S, A and B. So, number of states of the finite automata will be four. Let name the final state as C.

(i) For the production $S \rightarrow aA/bS$, the transitional diagram will be

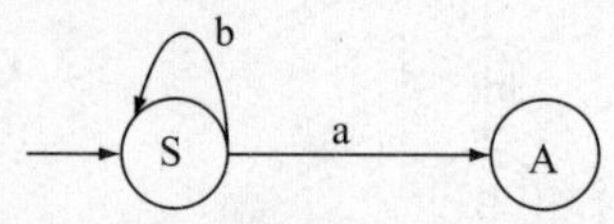

(ii) For the production $A \rightarrow bB/a$, the transitional diagram including the previous one will be.

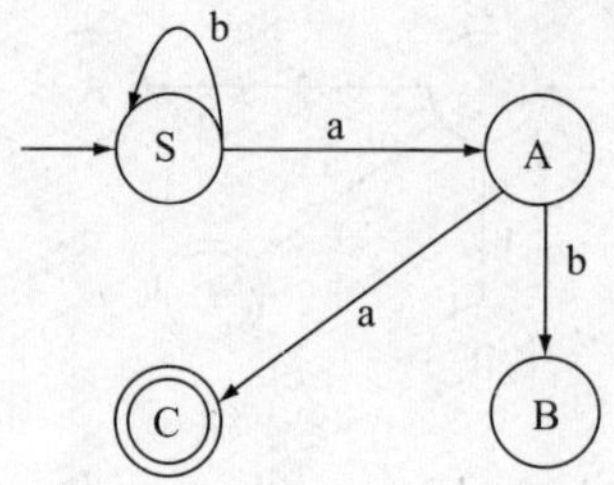

(iii) For the production $B \rightarrow aS/b$, the transitional diagram including the previous one will be

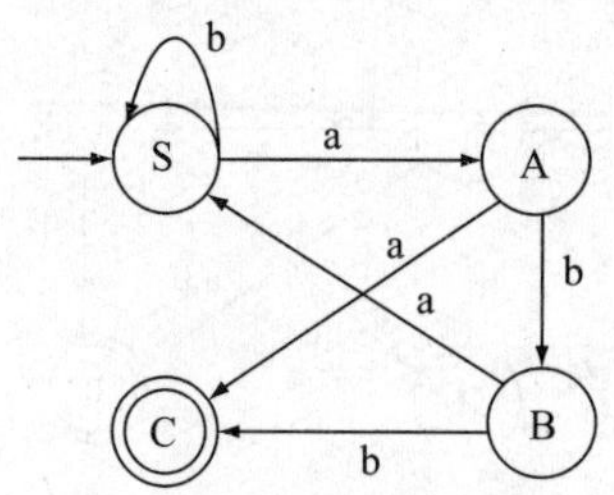

This is the finite automata for the given Regular Grammar.

5.8 CLOSURE PROPERTIES OF CFL

Q. Prove that CFLs are closed under union, concatenation and star-closure.

Ans. Union:

Let L_1 is a CFL for the CFG $G_1 = (V_{N1}, \Sigma_1, P_1, S_1)$ and L_2 is a CFL for the CFG $G_2 = (V_{N2}, \Sigma_2, P_2, S_2)$. We have to prove that $L = L_1 \cup L_2$ is also in CFL.

Let us construct a CFG $G = (V_N, \Sigma, P, S)$ using the two grammars G_1 and G_2 as follows:

$$V_N = V_{N1} \cup V_{N2} \cup \{S\}$$
$$\Sigma = \Sigma_1 \cup \Sigma_2$$
$$P = P_1 \cup P_2 \cup \{S \rightarrow S_1 / S_2\}.$$

From the above discussion it is clear that the language set generated from the grammar G contains all the strings that are derived from S_1 as well as S_2. Hence it is proved that $L = L_1 \cup L_2$.

Concatenation:

Let L_1 is a CFL for the CFG $G_1 = (V_{N1}, \Sigma_1, P_1, S_1)$ and L_2 is a CFL for the CFG $G_2 = (V_{N2}, \Sigma_2, P_2, S_2)$. We have to prove that $L = L_1L_2$ is also in CFL.

Let us construct a Grammar $G = (V_N, \Sigma, P, S)$ using the two grammars G_1 and G_2 as follows.

$V_N = V_{N1} \cup V_{N2} \cup \{S\}$,
$\Sigma = \Sigma_1 \cup \Sigma_2$,
$P = P_1 \cup P_2 \cup \{S \rightarrow S_1S_2\}$.

From the above discussion it is clear that the language set generated from the grammar G contains all the strings that are derived from S_1 as well as S_2. Hence it is proved that $L = L_1L_2$.

Star Closure:

Let L is a CFL for the CFG $G_1 = (V_{N1}, \Sigma_1, P_1, S_1)$. We have to prove that L^* is also in CFL.

Let us construct a Grammar $G = (V_N, \Sigma, P, S)$ using the grammar G_1 as follows

$V_N = V_{N1} \cup \{S\}$,
$P = \{S \rightarrow S_1S / \epsilon\} \cup P_1$.

Obviously, G is a CFG. It is easy to see that $L(G) = L^*$

Q. Prove that CFL are not closed under intersection and complementation.

Ans.

Intersection:

Consider two languages

$L_1 = \{a^nb^mc^n$, where $n, m \geq 0\}$ and
$L_2 = \{a^nb^nc^m$, where $n, m \geq 0\}$.

We can easily show that the two languages L_1 and L_2 are context free. (By constructing grammar)

Consider $L = L_1 \cap L_2$.

Hence $L = a^nb^mc^n \cap a^nb^nc^m = a^nb^n c^n$, where $n \geq 0$.

The $a^nb^nc^n$ is a Context sensitive language not a Context free. From here we can conclude that CFLs are not closed under intersection.

Complementation:

From set theory we can prove $L_1 \cap L_2 = \overline{L}_1 \cup \overline{L}_2$ (D'Morgan's Law.)

If the union of the complements of L_1 and L_2 are closed, i.e. also context free, then the LHS will also be context free. But we have proved that $L_1 \cap L_2$ is not context free. We are getting contradiction here. Hence CFLs are not closed under complementation.

Q. Prove that every regular language is a CFL.

Ans. From recursive definition of Regular set we know Ø and ϵ are regular expression. If R is regular expression, then $R + R$ (Union), $R.R$ (Concatenation) and R^* (Kleene Star) are also regular expressions. A regular expression R is a string of terminal symbols. The Ø and ϵ are also CFL, and we know CFL are closed under Union, concatenation and Kleene star. Therefore, every regular language is a CFL.

5.9 PUMPING LEMMA FOR CFL

Q. What is the application of Pumping Lemma for CFL?

Ans. Pumping lemma for CFL is used to prove that certain sets are not context free. Every CFL fulfils some general properties. But if a set of language fulfils all the properties of Pumping Lemma for

CFL, it cannot be said that the language is context free. But the reverse, i.e. if a language breaks the properties it can be said confirm that the language is not context free.

Q. Prove the following lemma.

"If *G* be a CFG in CNF and *T* be a derivation tree belongs to *G*. If the length of the longest path in *T* is less than or equal to *k*, then the yield of *T* is of length less than or equal to 2^{K-1}"

Ans. We will prove this by method of induction on *k*. The *k* is the longest path for all trees with root label A. (Called A-Tree). When the length of the longest path of an A-tree is of length 1, the root has only one son and that is terminal symbol. When the root has two sons, the labels are variable (The CFG is in CNF). So the yield of *T* is of length 1. We have got a base for induction.

Let $K > 1$, let *T* be an A-tree with the longest path of length less than or equal to *k*. The grammar is in CNF, so the root of *T* that is *A* has exactly two sons with labels A_1 and A_2. The length of the longest path of the two sub trees with the two sons as root, is less than or equal to *k*-1.

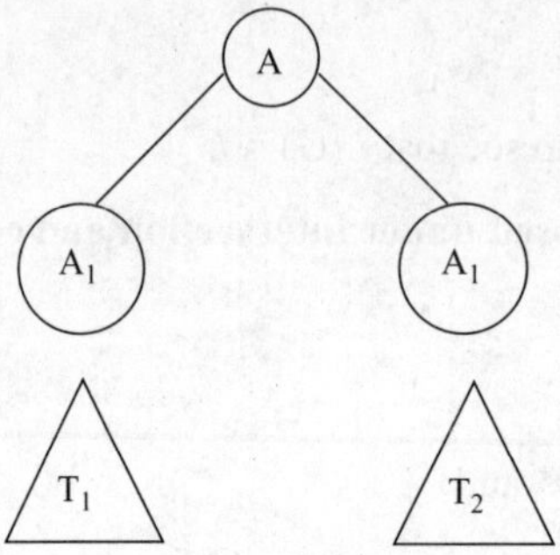

If w_1 and w_2 are the yields of T_1 and T_2, respectively, by induction
$|w_1| \leq 2^{k-2}$ and $|w_2| \leq 2^{k-2}$.
Let w is the yield of T, so $w = w_1w_2$.
$|w| = |w_1w_2| \leq 2^{k-2} + 2^{k-2} = 2^{k-1}$
The yield of *T* is of length less than or equal to 2^{K-1}. **(Proved)**

Q. State and prove Pumping Lemma for CFL.

Ans. Statement: Let *L* be a CFL. Then we can find a natural number *n* such that

(a) Every $z \in$ L with $z \geq n$ can be written as $w = uvwxy$, for some strings u,v,w,x,y.
(b) $|vx| \geq 1$
(c) $|vwx| \leq n$
(d) $uv^kwx^ky \in L$ for all $k \geq 0$.

Proof: We can prove it that if *G* is a context free grammar, then we can find a context free grammar G_1 having no null productions such that $L(G_1) = L(G) - \{\Lambda\}$.

If null string (Λ) belongs to the language set *L*, we will consider $L - \{\Lambda\}$ and will construct CNF of the grammar *G* generating $L - \{\Lambda\}$ [If null string does not belong to L, we will construct CNF of *G* generating *L*].

Let number of non-terminals (V_N) of the grammar is *m*. $|V_N| = m$ and $n = 2^m$. To prove that *n* is the required number, we start with a string *z* where $z \in L$, $|z| \geq 2^m$. Construct a derivation tree or parse treeT of the string *z*. If the length of the longest path in *T* is almost *m*, then we can write the length of the yield of *T*, i.e. $|z| \leq 2^{m-1}$. But $|z| \geq 2^m > 2^{m-1}$. So *T* has a path, say Γ of length greater than or equal to $m + 1$.

Path length of greater than or equal to $m + 1$ needs atleast $m + 2$ vertices, where the last vertex is the leaf. Thus in Γ all the labels except the last one are variables. As $|N| = m$, in $m + 1$ labels of the parse tree T, some labels are repeated.

Choose the repeated label as follows. We start with the leaf of Γ and travel upwards. We stop when we get some label repeated (Let we have got label A as repeated, first).

Let v_1 and v_2 be the vertices with repeated label (Let A) obtained at the time of upward traversal from leaf of Γ. Between v_1 and v_2 let v_1 is nearer to root. In Γ, the portion of the path from v_1 to leaf has only one label repeated (Let A), so its length is almost $m + 1$.

Let T_1 and T_2 are two subtrees taking root as v_1 and v_2, respectively. Let z_1 and w are the yields of T_1 and T_2, respectively. As Γ is the longest path in T, v_1 to leaf is the longest path of T_1 and its length is almost $m + 1$. So the length of z_1 (yield of T_1), i.e. $|z_1| \leq 2^m$

As z is the yield of T and T_1 is a proper subtree of T. Yield of T_1 is z_1. So yield of T, i.e. z can be written as $z = uz_1y$.

As z_1 is the yield of T_1 and T_2 is a proper subtree of T_1. Yield of T_2 is w. So yield of T_1, i.e. z_1 can be written as $z_1 = vwx$. T_2 is a proper subtree of T_1 so $|vwx| > |w|$. So $|vx| \geq 1$. Thus we can write $z = uvwxy$ with $|vwx| \leq n$ and $|vx| \geq 1$. This proves from (i) to (iii) of the pumping lemma theorem.

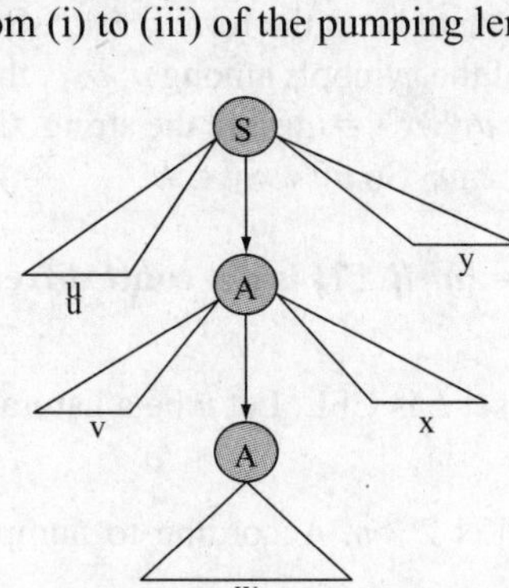

As T is tree with root S (S tree) and T_1, T_2 are tree with root B (B tree), we can write $S \overset{*}{\Rightarrow} uAy, A \overset{*}{\Rightarrow} vAx$ and, $A \overset{*}{\Rightarrow} w$.

As $S \overset{*}{\Rightarrow} uAy \Rightarrow uwy$, $uv^0wx^0y \in L$. For $k \geq 1$, $S \overset{*}{\Rightarrow} uAy \overset{*}{\Rightarrow} uv^k Ax^k y \overset{*}{\Rightarrow} uv^k wx^k y \in L$. By this the theorem is proved.

Q. How pumping lemma can be applied to prove that certain sets are not regular?

Ans. We use pumping lemma for CFL to show that certain sets L are not context free. We assume that the set is context free. By applying pumping lemma we get a contradiction.

This prove can be done in the following ways

Step I: Assume L is context free. Find a natural number such that $|z| \geq n$.

Step II: So we can write $z = uvwxy$ for some strings u,v,w,x,y.

Step III: Find a suitable k such that $uv^kwx^ky \geq L$. This is a contradiction, so L is not context free.

Q. Show that $L = \{a^n b^n c^n$, where $n \geq 1\}$ is not context free.

Ans.

Step I: Assume that the language set L is CFL. Let n be a natural number obtained by using pumping lemma.

Step II: Let $z = a^n b^n c^n$. So $|z| = 3n > n$. According to pumping lemma for CFL we can write $z = uvwxy$, where $|vx| \geq 1$.

Step III: $uvwxy = a^n b^n c^n$. As $1 \leq |vx| \leq n$, $[|vwx| \leq n$, so $|vx| \leq n]$ v or x cannot contain all the three symbols a, b and c. So v or x will be in any of the following forms.

(i) Contain only a and b, i.e. in the form $a^i b^j$.
(ii) Or Contain only b and c i.e. in the form $b^i c^j$
(iii) Or contain only the repetition of any of the symbols among a,b,c.

Let take the value of k as 2. v^2 or x^2 will be in the form $a^i b^i a^i b^i$ (As v is a string here aba is not equal to a^2b or ba^2) or $b^i c^j b^i c^j$. So uv^2wx^2y cannot be in the form $a^m b^m c^m$. So $uv^2wx^2y \notin L$.

If v or x contain repetition of any of the symbols among a, b, c, then v or x will be any of the form of a^i, b^i or c^i. Let take the value of k as 0. $uv^0wx^0y = uwy$. In the string, the number of occurrences of one of the other two symbols in uvy is less than n. So $uv^2wx^2y \notin L$.

Q. Prove that the language $L = \{a^{i^2} / i \geq 1\}$ is not context free.

Ans.

Step I: Assume that the language set L is CFL. Let n be a natural number obtained by using pumping lemma.

Step II: Let $z = a^{2^\wedge i}$. So $|z| = 2^i$. Let $2^i > n$. According to pumping lemma for CFL we can write $z = uvwxy$, where $|vx| \geq 1$ and $|vwx| \leq n$.

Step III: The string z contains only 'a', so v and x will be also a string of only 'a'. Let $v = a^p$ and $x = a^q$., where $(p + q) \geq 1$. Since $n \geq 0$, and $uvwxy = 2^i$, so $|uv^n wx^n y| = |uvwxy| + |v^{n-1} x^{n-1}| = 2^i + (p + q)$ (n–1). As $uv^n wx^n y \in L$, $|uv^n wx^n y|$ is also a power of 2, say 2^j

$$(p + q)(n-1) = 2^j - 2^i$$
$$\Rightarrow (p + q)(n-1) + 2^i = 2^j$$
$$\Rightarrow (p + q)2^{i+1} + 2^i = 2^j$$
$$\Rightarrow 2^i\,(2(p + q) + 1) = 2^j.$$

Here, $(p + q)$ may be even or odd, but $2(p + q)$ is always even. Whereas $2(p + q) + 1$ is odd, which cannot be a power of 2. Thus L is not context free.

Q. Prove that $L = \{0^p$/where p is prime$\}$ is not a CFL.

Ans.

Step I: Suppose $L = L(G)$ is context free. Let n be a natural number obtained from the pumping lemma for CFL.

Step II: Let p is a number $> n$, $z = 0^p \in L$. By using Pumping Lemma for CFL we can write z = $uvwxy$, where $|vx \geq 1$ and $|vwx| \leq n$.

Step III: Let $k = 0$. From the pumping lemma for CFL we can write uv^0wx^0y, i.e. $uwy \in$ L. As uvy is in the form 0^p, where p is prime; so $|uwy|$ is also a prime number. Let take it as q. Let $|vx| = r$. Then $|uv^qwx^qy| = q + qr = q(1 + r)$. This is not prime as it has factors q, $(1 + r)$ including 1 and $q(1 + r)$. So $uv^qwx^qy \notin L$. This is a contradiction. Therefore L is not context free.

5.10 OGDEN'S LEMMA FOR CFL

Q. State Ogden's lemma for CFL. What is its superiority over pumping lemma?

Ans. Ogden's lemma states that if a language L is context-free, then there exists some number $p > 0$ (where p may or may not be a pumping length) such that for any string w of length at least p in L and every way of "marking" p or more of the positions in w, w can be written as

$w = uvxyz$,

with strings u, v, x, y, and z, such that

1. x has at least one marked position,
2. either u and v both have marked positions or y and z both have marked positions,
3. vxy has at most p marked positions, and
4. uv^ixy^iz is in L for every $i \geq 0$.

Ogden's lemma can be used to show that certain languages are not context-free, in cases where the pumping lemma for CFLs is not sufficient. An example is the language $\{a^ib^jc^kd^l: i = 0 \text{ or } j = k = l\}$. It is also useful to prove the inherent ambiguity of some languages.

5.11 DECISION ALGORITHMS

Q. What are the decision algorithms for CFLs?

Ans. From a CFL we can decide either it is empty, finite or infinite by using decision algorithms for CFL.

Emptiness: In a CFG $\{V_N, \Sigma, P, S\}$ if S is nothing but only start symbol then it is non-empty, otherwise the language is empty.

(We have already learnt the process of removing useless symbols from a given CFG. There we did not remove the start symbol if it is found Non-generating. According to decision algorithm if S is found to be useless, L(G) is empty, if not- L(G) contain atleast one element, i.e. L(G) is non-empty.)

Finiteness: A language L generated from a given CFG is finite if there are no cycles in the directed graph generated from the production rules of the given CFG. The longest string generated by the grammar is 2 (length of the longest path in the directed graph).

(Number of vertices of the directed graph is same as number of non-terminals in the grammar. If there is a production rule S →AB the directed graph will be in the form.

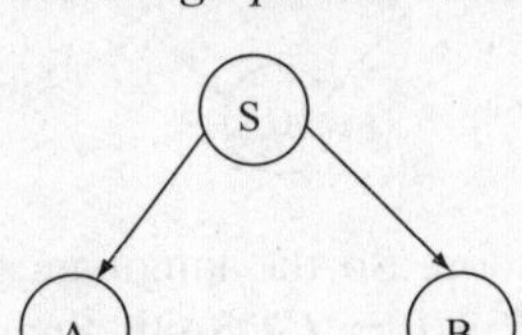

]

Infiniteness: A language L generated from a given CFG is infinite if there is atleast one cycle in the directed graph generated from the production rules of the given CFG.

Q. Verify the following grammars are empty or not.

a) $S \rightarrow AB$
$A \rightarrow aB$
$B \rightarrow bC$

b) $S \rightarrow AB$
$A \rightarrow BC/a$
$B \rightarrow AC/b$

Ans. (a) In the grammar S is not generating any terminal symbol. In the language set generated by the grammar there exist only null. So the CFG is empty.

(b)

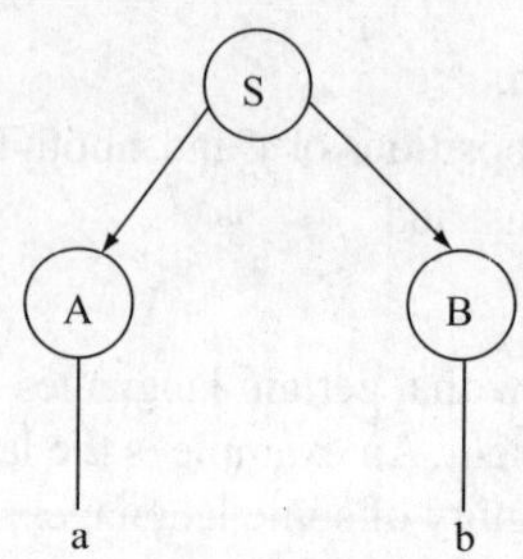

In the grammar S is generating terminal symbols. Hence the CFG is not empty.

Q. Verify the languages generated by the following grammars are finite or not. If finite find the longest string generated by the grammar.

(a)	**(b)**
$S \rightarrow AB$	$S \rightarrow AB$
$A \rightarrow BC$	$A \rightarrow B$
$B \rightarrow C$	$B \rightarrow SC/a$
$C \rightarrow a$	$C \rightarrow AB/b$

Ans.

(a) The directed graph for the first one is

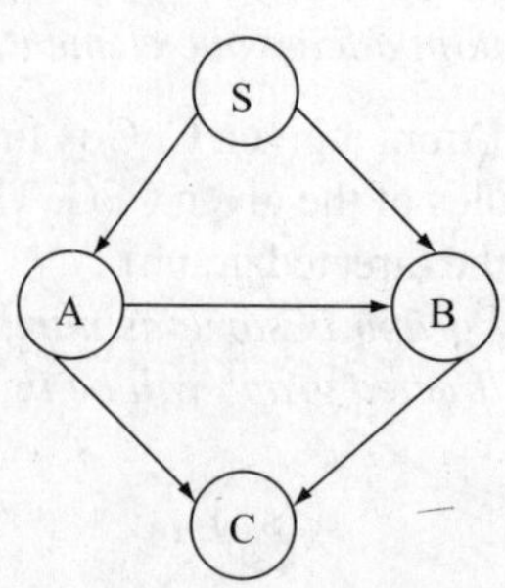

The graph does not contain any loop. So the language generated by the CFG is finite. The length of the longest path is 3 ($S \rightarrow A \rightarrow B \rightarrow C$). So the longest string generated by the grammar is $2^3 = 8$.

(b) The directed graph for the second one is

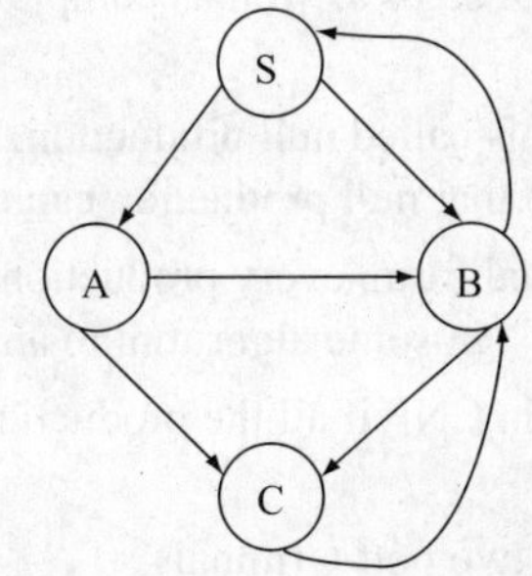

The graph contains two loops. Hence the language generated by the CFG is infinite.

Q. What are the applications of CFL?

Ans. (a) Designing syntax analysis part of a compiler of a language

(b) Development of extensive markup language (XML)

WHAT WE HAVE LEARNED SO FAR

1. According to Chomsky Hierarchy context free grammar (CFG) is Type 2 grammar.
2. In every production of a CFG at the left-hand-side there is a single non-terminal.
3. A derivation is called a Left Most Derivation if only the leftmost non-terminal is replaced by some production rule at each step of the generating process of the language from the grammar.
4. A derivation is called a right most derivation if only the rightmost non-terminal is replaced by some production rule at each step of the generating process of the language from the grammar.
5. Parsing a string is finding a derivation for that string from a given grammar.
6. A parse tree is an ordered tree in which left-hand-side of a production represents a parent node and children nodes are represented by the production's right-hand-side.
7. A grammar of a language is called ambiguous, if any of the cases for generating a particular string; more than one parse tree can be generated.
8. Ambiguity in grammar creates problem at the time of generating languages from the grammar.
9. There is no hard and fast rule for removing ambiguity from a CFG. Some ambiguity can be removed by hand. Some CFG are always ambiguous. Those are called inherently ambiguous.
10. CFG may contain different types of useless symbols, unit productions, and null productions. These types of symbols and productions increase number of steps in generating a language from a CFG.
11. Reduced grammar contains less number of non-terminals and productions, so the time complexity for language generating process becomes less from reduced grammar.
12. Useless symbols are of two types, Non-generating symbol and non-reachable symbol.
13. Non-generating symbols are those symbols, which do not produce any terminal string.
14. Non-reachable symbols are those symbols, which cannot be reached at any time starting from the start symbol.

15. Production in the form **non-terminal → Single non-terminal** is called unit production. Unit production increases the number of steps as well as complexity at the time of generating language from the grammar.
16. A production in the form NT → ϵ is called null production. If **Λ** (null string) is in the language set generated from the grammar, then that null production cannot be removed.
17. When a grammar is made in normal form, every production of the grammar is converted in some specific form. These help us to design some algorithm to answer certain questions.
18. A context free grammar is called in CNF if all the productions of the grammar are in the following form

    non-terminal → String of exactly two non-terminals,

    non-terminal → Single terminal.
19. A grammar is said to be in Greibach Normal Form (GNF) if every productions of the grammar is of the form

    non-terminal → (single terminal)(String of non-terminals)

    non-terminal → single terminal
20. CFLs are closed under union, concatenation and star–closure.
21. CFLs are not closed under intersection and complementation.
22. Pumping lemma and Ogden's lemma for CFL is used to prove that certain sets are not context free.
23. A language L generated from a given CFG is finite if there are no cycles in the directed graph generated from the production rules of the given CFG.
24. A language L generated from a given CFG is infinite if there is atleast one cycle in the directed graph generated from the production rules of the given CFG.

SOLVED PROBLEMS

1. Construct CFG for the following
(a) Set of string of 0 and 1 where consecutive 0 can occur but no consecutive 1 can occur.
(b) Set of all (positive and negative) odd integers.
(c) Set of all (positive and negative) even integers.

Ans.

(a) There will be two non-terminals - S and A. S will produce production $S \rightarrow 0S$. As two consecutive 0 can appear, so there will be a production $S \rightarrow 0$. In the language set 01 can appear. Hence there will be production $S \rightarrow 1$.

The string can start with 1, so there may be a production $S \rightarrow 1S$. But consecutive 1 will not appear, so the production will be $S \rightarrow 1A$. 'A' can produce 0 but not 1. So there will be production $A \rightarrow 0$.

If the string start with 1, then the production rule $S \rightarrow 1A$ is applied. As in the language set there will be no consecutive 1, so A may produce $A \rightarrow 0A$. But if this is the production then there will be no chance of occurring 1 in the string except at last. Hence the production will be $A \rightarrow 0S$.

Hence the grammar is

$$S \rightarrow 0S,\ S \rightarrow 1A,\ S \rightarrow 0,\ S \rightarrow 1,\ A \rightarrow 0S,\ A \rightarrow 0.$$

(b) An integer is odd if its rightmost entry contains any one of '1', '3', '5', '7' or '9'. If the integer is positive then its leftmost entry contains ' + ' sign, if negative then its leftmost entry contains '–' sign. The production rules are

$S \rightarrow$ <sign><integer>
<integer> → <integer1><digit1>
<integer1> → <integer1><digit>/ $\in$
<sign> → + / –
<digit> → 0/ 1/ 2/ 3/ 4/ 5/ 6/ 7/ 8/ 9
<digit1> → 1/ 3/ 5/ 7/ 9

Set of non-terminals V_N are **{S, <sign>, <integer>, <integer1>, <digit>, <digit1>}**

(c) An integer is odd if its rightmost entry contains any one of '2', '4', '6', '8' or '0'. If the integer is positive then its left most entry contains ' + ' sign, if negative then its left most entry contains '–' sign. The production rules are

$S \rightarrow$ <sign><integer>
<integer> → <integer1><digit1>
<integer1> → <integer1><digit>/ $\in$
<sign> → + / –
<digit> → 0/ 1/ 2/ 3/ 4/ 5/ 6/ 7/ 8/ 9
<digit1> → 0/ 2/ 4/ 6/ 8

Set of non-terminals V_N are **{S, <sign>, <integer>, <integer1>, <digit>, <digit1>}**

2.

(a) Construct the string aaabbabbba from the Grammar

S →aB/ bA
A → a/ aS/ bAA
B → b/ bS/ aBB by using

(i) Left Most Derivation
(ii) Right Most Derivation

Ans.

Left Most Derivation:

$S \rightarrow a\underline{B}$
$\rightarrow aa\underline{B}B \quad (B \rightarrow aBB)$
$\rightarrow aaa\underline{B}BB \quad (B \rightarrow aBB)$
$\rightarrow aaab\underline{B}B \quad (B \rightarrow b)$
$\rightarrow aaabb\underline{B} \quad (B \rightarrow b)$
$\rightarrow aaabba\underline{B}B \quad (B \rightarrow aBB)$
$\rightarrow aaabbab\underline{B} \quad (B \rightarrow b)$
$\rightarrow aaabbabb\underline{S} \quad (B \rightarrow bS)$
$\rightarrow aaabbabbb\underline{A} \quad (S \rightarrow bA)$
$\rightarrow aaabbabbba \quad (A \rightarrow a).$

Right Most Derivation:

$S \rightarrow a\underline{B}$
$\rightarrow aaB\underline{B}$ $(B \rightarrow aBB)$
$\rightarrow aaBb\underline{S}$ $(B \rightarrow bS)$
$\rightarrow aaBbb\underline{A}$ $(S \rightarrow bA)$
$\rightarrow aa\underline{B}bba$ $(A \rightarrow a)$
$\rightarrow aaaBBbba$ $(B \rightarrow aBB)$
$\rightarrow aaaBbbba$ $(B \rightarrow b)$
$\rightarrow aaabSbbba$ $(B \rightarrow bS)$
$\rightarrow aaabbAbbba$ $(S \rightarrow bA)$
$\rightarrow aaabbabbba$ $(A \rightarrow a)$

3. Check whether the following grammar is ambiguous or not.

$S \rightarrow a/ Sa/ bSS/ SSb/ SbS$

Ans. Lets take a string ***baababaa.*** Lets try to generate the string by deriving from the given CFG.

Derivation 1:

The string is derived by left most derivation, i.e. only the leftmost non-terminal is replaced by suitable non-terminal.

$S \rightarrow b\underline{S}S \rightarrow ba\underline{S} \rightarrow baSbS \rightarrow baab\underline{S}$
$\rightarrow baab\underline{S}bS \rightarrow baabab\underline{S} \rightarrow baabab\underline{S}a \rightarrow baababaa$

Derivation 2:

The string is derived by right most derivation, i.e. only the rightmost non-terminal is replaced by suitable non-terminal.

$S \rightarrow Sb\underline{S} \rightarrow Sb\underline{S}a \rightarrow \underline{S}baa \rightarrow bS\underline{S}baa \rightarrow bSSb\underline{S}baa$
$\rightarrow bS\underline{S}babaa \rightarrow b\underline{S}ababaa \rightarrow baababaa$

The parse tree for the first derivation:

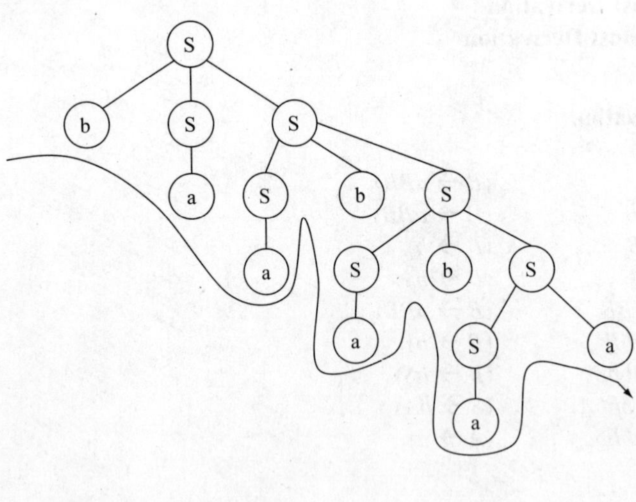

The parse tree for the second derivation

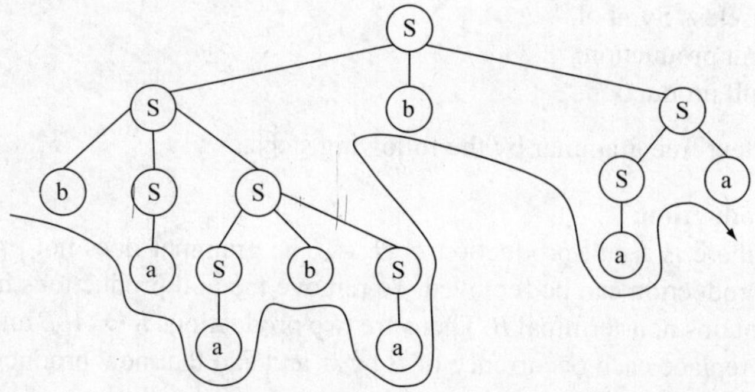

For the string *baababaa* two different parse trees are constructed. Therefore, the given context free grammar is ambiguous.

4. Check whether the following grammar is ambiguous or not.

S → SS/a/b

Ans. Let take a string ***abba.*** Lets try to generate the string by deriving from the given CFG.

Derivation 1:

The string is derived by left most derivation, i.e. only the leftmost non-terminal is replaced by suitable non-terminal.

S → S<u>S</u> → Sa → S<u>S</u>a → <u>S</u>ba → S<u>S</u>ba → <u>S</u>bba → abba

Derivation 2:

The string is derived by left most derivation, i.e. only the leftmost non-terminal is replaced by suitable non-terminal.

S → <u>S</u>S → a<u>S</u> → a<u>S</u>S → ab<u>S</u> → ab<u>S</u>S → abb<u>S</u> → abba

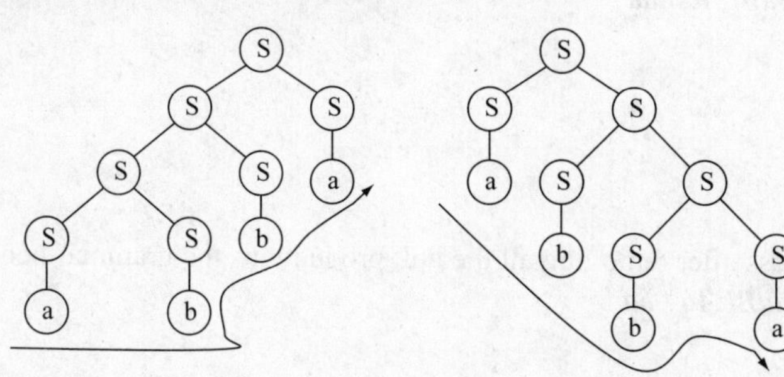

For the string ***abba*** two different parse trees are constructed. So, the given context free grammar is ambiguous.

5. Simplify the following CFG.

S → AaB/aaB

A → D

B → bbA/∈

D → E

E → F

F → aS

Ans. Simplifying a CFG means

(a) Removing Useless Symbol.
(b) Removing unit production.
(c) Removing null production.

Simplify the context free grammar by the following steps.

Remove null production:
In the grammar there is a null production $B \rightarrow \in$. The grammar does not produce any null string Therefore the null production can be removed. To remove the null productions find all the production whose right side contains non-terminal B. There are two productions $S \rightarrow AbB$ and $S \rightarrow aaB$. To remov the null production replace each occurrence of B by $\in$ and add that new production to the grammar t keep the language generating power same.

The grammar after removing the null production become

$S \rightarrow AaB/\ aaB/\ Aa\ /\ aa$
$A \rightarrow D$
$B \rightarrow bbA$
$D \rightarrow E$
$E \rightarrow F$
$F \rightarrow aS$

Remove unit production:
In the grammar, there are three unit productions: $A \rightarrow D$, $D \rightarrow E$ and $E \rightarrow F$. To remove the un production $E \rightarrow F$, we have to find a non-unit production $F \rightarrow$ {Some string of terminal or non terminal or both}. There is such a production $F \rightarrow aS$. Remove $E \rightarrow$ by that non-unit productio $F \rightarrow aS$

After removing the unit production $E \rightarrow F$, the grammar become

$S \rightarrow AaB/\ aaB/\ Aa\ /\ aa$
$A \rightarrow D$
$B \rightarrow bbA$
$D \rightarrow E$
$E \rightarrow aS$
$F \rightarrow aS$

By the same process after removing all the unit productions the grammar become.

$S \rightarrow AaB/\ aaB/\ Aa\ /\ aa$
$A \rightarrow aS$
$B \rightarrow bbA$
$D \rightarrow aS$
$E \rightarrow aS$
$F \rightarrow aS$

Remove useless symbol:
In a grammar there are two types of useless symbols.

(a) Non-generating symbol and (b) non-reachable symbol
In the grammar all are generating symbols, so we have to find non-reachable symbol.

In the grammar D, E, and F are non-reachable symbol because they are not reached any way starting from the start symbol. After removing useless symbols the grammar become

$S \rightarrow AaB/ aaB/ Aa / aa$
$A \rightarrow aS$
$B \rightarrow bbA$

6. Convert the following grammar into CNF.

$S \rightarrow aA/bB$
$A \rightarrow aBB/bS/b$
$B \rightarrow bAA/aS/a$

Ans.

A Context free grammar is called in CNF if all the productions of the grammar are in the following form

non-terminal → String of exactly two non-terminals
non-terminal → Single Terminal

The previous grammar does not contain any useless symbol, unit production or null production. So, the grammar can be directly converted to CNF.

In the previous grammar **$S \rightarrow bA$, $S \rightarrow aB$, $B \rightarrow bAA$, $B \rightarrow aS$, $A \rightarrow aBB$, $B \rightarrow bS$** are not in CNF. So, these productions are needed to be converted into CNF. But the productions $A \rightarrow b$ and $B \rightarrow a$ are in CNF.

Consider two extra non-terminals C_a and C_b and two production rules $C_a \rightarrow a$ and $C_b \rightarrow b$. Replace '*a*' by C_a and '*b*' by C_b in the above productions. The modified production rule become

$S \rightarrow C_aA/ C_bB$
$A \rightarrow C_aBB/ C_bS/ b$
$B \rightarrow C_bAA/ C_aS/ a$
$C_a \rightarrow a$
$C_b \rightarrow b$

In the grammar $A \rightarrow C_aBB$ and $B \rightarrow C_bAA$ are not in CNF as they contain string of three non-terminals at the right-hand-side of the production. Introduce two production rules $X \rightarrow BB$ and $Y \rightarrow AA$ and replace *BB* by *X* and *AA* by *Y*. The modified production rule becomes.

$S \rightarrow C_aA/C_bB$
$A \rightarrow C_aX/ C_bS/ b$
$B \rightarrow C_bY/ C_aS/ a$
$C_a \rightarrow a$
$C_b \rightarrow b$
$X \rightarrow BB$
$Y \rightarrow AA$

Here all the productions are in the specified format of CNF. The CFG is converted to CNF.

7. Convert the following grammar into CNF.

$S \rightarrow aA/ B/ C/ a$
$A \rightarrow aB/ E$
$B \rightarrow aA$
$C \rightarrow cCD$
$D \rightarrow abd.$

Ans. The context free grammar is not simplified as it contains useless symbols and unit productions. First we have to simplify the CFG then it can be converted into CNF.

In the grammar E is the useless symbol (non-generating symbol) as it does not produce any terminal symbol. So the production $A \rightarrow E$ is removed. The modified grammar becomes

$S \rightarrow aA / B / C / a$
$A \rightarrow aB$
$B \rightarrow aA$
$C \rightarrow cCD$
$D \rightarrow abd.$

There are two unit productions in the grammar. After removing the unit productions the grammar become

$S \rightarrow aA / cCD / a$
$A \rightarrow aB$
$B \rightarrow aA$
$C \rightarrow cCD$
$D \rightarrow abd.$

In the grammar except $S \rightarrow a$, all other productions are not in CNF.

Consider four extra non-terminals C_a, C_b, C_c, C_d and two production rules $C_a \rightarrow a$ and $C_b \rightarrow b$, $C_c \rightarrow c$ and $C_d \rightarrow d$. Replace 'a' by C_a and 'b' by C_b, c by C_c and d by C_d in the above productions. The modified production rule become

$S \rightarrow C_aA / C_cCD / a$
$A \rightarrow C_aB$
$B \rightarrow C_aA$
$C \rightarrow C_cCD$
$D \rightarrow C_aC_bC_d$
$C_a \rightarrow a$
$C_b \rightarrow b$
$C_c \rightarrow c$
$C_d \rightarrow d.$

Here $S \rightarrow C_cCD$, $C \rightarrow C_cCD$ and $D \rightarrow C_aC_bC_d$ are not in CNF. Introduce two production rules $X \rightarrow CD$ and $Y \rightarrow C_bC_d$ and replace CD by X and C_bC_d by Y. The modified production rule becomes.

$S \rightarrow C_aA / C_cX / a$
$A \rightarrow C_aB$
$B \rightarrow C_aA$
$C \rightarrow C_cX$
$D \rightarrow C_aY$
$C_a \rightarrow a$
$C_b \rightarrow b$
$C_c \rightarrow c$
$C_d \rightarrow d$
$X \rightarrow CD$
$Y \rightarrow C_bC_d.$

Here all the productions are in the specified format of CNF. The CFG is converted to CNF.

8. Convert the following grammar into CNF.

$E \rightarrow E + T / T$
$T \rightarrow (E) / a$

Ans. The grammar contains two non-terminal symbols E and T and four terminal symbols +, (,), *a*. The grammar contains a unit production $E \rightarrow T$. First the unit production has to be removed. After removing the unit production $E \rightarrow T$ the modified grammar becomes

$E \rightarrow E + T / (E) / a$
$T \rightarrow (E) / a.$

In the above grammar except $E \rightarrow a$ and $T \rightarrow a$ all the other productions are not in CNF.

Introduce three non-terminals *A*, *B*, *C* and three production rules $A \rightarrow +$, $B \rightarrow ($ and $C \rightarrow)$ and appropriate terminal by appropriate non-terminals. The modified production rules become.

$E \rightarrow EAT / BEC / a$
$T \rightarrow BEC / a$
$A \rightarrow +$
$B \rightarrow ($
$C \rightarrow).$

In the above grammar, $E \rightarrow EAT$, $E \rightarrow BEC$ and $T \rightarrow BEC$ are not in CNF. Consider two non-terminals *X* and *Y* and two production rules $X \rightarrow AT$ and $Y \rightarrow EC$. The modified production rules become.

$E \rightarrow EX / BY / a$
$T \rightarrow BY / a$
$A \rightarrow +$
$B \rightarrow ($
$C \rightarrow)$
$X \rightarrow AT$
$Y \rightarrow EC.$

Here all the productions are in the specified format of CNF. The CFG is converted to CNF.

9. Convert the following grammar into CNF.

$S \rightarrow ABb / a$
$A \rightarrow aaA / B$
$B \rightarrow bAb / b$

Ans. The grammar contains unit production $A \rightarrow B$. After removing the unit production the grammar is

$S \rightarrow ABb / a$
$A \rightarrow aaA / bAb / b$
$B \rightarrow bAb / b$

Except $S \rightarrow a$ and $B \rightarrow b$ the productions of the grammar are not in CNF.

Consider two non-terminals C_a and C_b and two production rules $C_a \rightarrow a$ and $C_b \rightarrow b$ and replace '*a*' by C_a and '*b*' by C_b in appropriate production. The modified production rules become

$S \rightarrow ABC_b / a$
$A \rightarrow C_aC_aA / C_bAC_b / b$
$B \rightarrow C_bAC_b / b$
$C_a \rightarrow a$
$C_b \rightarrow b.$

Consider three non-terminals X, Y, and Z. and three production rules $X \rightarrow BC_b$, $Y \rightarrow AC_b$, $Z \rightarrow C_aA$. Replace appropriate group of non-terminals in the production by appropriate new non-terminal. The production rule become

$S \rightarrow AX / a$
$A \rightarrow C_aZ / C_bY / b$
$B \rightarrow C_bY / b$
$C_a \rightarrow a$
$C_b \rightarrow b$
$X \rightarrow BC_b$
$Y \rightarrow AC_b$
$Z \rightarrow C_aA$.

10. Convert the following grammar into GNF.

$S \rightarrow A$
$A \rightarrow aBa / a$
$B \rightarrow bAb / b$

Ans. The grammar is not in CNF. So it has to be converted into CNF. Introduce two non-terminals C_a, C_b and two production rule **$Ca \rightarrow a$, $Cb \rightarrow b$.**

$S \rightarrow A$
$A \rightarrow C_aBC_a / a$
$B \rightarrow C_bAC_b / b$
$Ca \rightarrow a$
$Cb \rightarrow b$.

Introduce two non-terminals *X* and *Y* and two production rules **$X \rightarrow BC_a$** and **$Y \rightarrow AC_b$**
The production rule become

$S \rightarrow A$
$A \rightarrow C_aX / a$
$B \rightarrow C_bY / b$
$C_a \rightarrow a$
$C_b \rightarrow b$
$X \rightarrow BC_a$
$Y \rightarrow AC_b$.

Step I: In the grammar there is no null production and no unit production. The grammar also is in CNF.

Step II: In the grammar there are seven non-terminals *S, A, B,* C_a, C_b, *X, Y.* Rename the non-terminals as A_1, A_2, A_3, A_4, A_5, A_6, and A_7, respectively. After renaming the non-terminals the modified grammar will be

$A_1 \rightarrow A_2$
$A_2 \rightarrow A_4A_6 / a$
$A_3 \rightarrow A_5A_7 / b$
$A_4 \rightarrow a$
$A_5 \rightarrow b$
$A_6 \rightarrow A_3A_4$
$A_7 \rightarrow A_2A_5$

Step III: In the above production $A_6 \rightarrow A_3A_4$ **and** $A_7 \rightarrow A_2A_5$ are not in the form $A_i \rightarrow A_jV$ where $i \le j$. Using Lemma 1 replace $A_3 \rightarrow A_5A_7/\ b$ in the production $A_6 \rightarrow A_3A_4$. The rule becomes

$A_6 \rightarrow A_5A_7A_4 \ /\ bA_4$

Till $A_6 \rightarrow A_5A_7A_4$ is not in the form $A_i \rightarrow A_jV$ where $i \le j$. Using Lemma I replace $A_5 \rightarrow b$ in the production. The modified production is $A_6 \rightarrow bA_7A_4 \ /\ bA_4$, which is in GNF

Step IV: Using Lemma 1 replace $A_2 \rightarrow A_4A_6/\ a$ in the production $A_7 \rightarrow A_2A_5$. The production rule becomes $A_7 \rightarrow A_4A_6A_5/\ aA_5$.

Till $A_7 \rightarrow A_4A_6A_5$ is not in the form $A_i \rightarrow A_jV$ where $i \le j$. Using Lemma I replace $A_4 \rightarrow a$ in the production.

The modified production is $A_7 \rightarrow aA_6A_5/\ aA_5$, which is in GNF

Lemma II can be applied on the productions $A_2 \rightarrow A_4A_6/\ a$ **and** $A_3 \rightarrow A_5A_7/\ b$

Applying Lemma II on $A_2 \rightarrow A_4A_6/\ a$ we get

$A_2 \rightarrow a/\ aX$

$X \rightarrow A_6/\ A_6X$

$X \rightarrow A_6/\ A_6X$ are not in GNF. Replacing $A_6 \rightarrow bA_7A_4 \ /\ bA_4$ in the production, the productions $X \rightarrow bA_7A_4/\ bA_7A_4X \ /\ bA_4/\ bA_4X$ are in GNF.

Applying Lemma II on $A_3 \rightarrow A_5A_7/\ b$ **we get**

$A_3 \rightarrow b/\ bY$

$Y \rightarrow A_7/\ A_7Y$

$Y \rightarrow A_7/\ A_7Y$ are not in GNF. Replacing $A_7 \rightarrow aA_6A_5/\ aA_5$ in the production, the productions $Y \rightarrow aA_6A_5/\ aA_6A_5Y \ /\ aA_5/\ aA_5Y$ are in GNF

$A_1 \rightarrow A_2$ is not in GNF. Replacing $A_2 \rightarrow a/\ aX$ in the production we get $A_1 \rightarrow a/\ aX$, which is in GNF.

The grammar converted into GNF is

$A_1 \rightarrow aX/\ a$

$A_2 \rightarrow aX/\ a$

$A_3 \rightarrow bY/\ b$

$A_4 \rightarrow a$

$A_5 \rightarrow b$

$A_6 \rightarrow bA_7A_4 \ /\ bA_4$

$A_7 \rightarrow aA_6A_5/\ aA_5$

$X \rightarrow bA_7A_4/\ bA_7A_4X \ /\ bA_4/\ bA_4X$

$Y \rightarrow aA_6A_5/\ aA_6A_5Y \ /\ aA_5/\ aA_5Y.$

11. Remove left recursion from the given grammar

$A \rightarrow Ba/\ b$

$B \rightarrow Bc/\ Ad/\ e$

Ans. The grammar has indirect left recursion. To remove the left recursion rename A as A_1 and B as A_2. The modified production rules becomes

$A_1 \rightarrow A_2a/\ b$

$A_2 \rightarrow A_2c/\ A_1d/\ e.$

For $i = 1, j = 1$, there is no production in the form $A_1 \rightarrow A_1\alpha$.

For $i = 2, j = 1$, there is a production in the form $A_2 \rightarrow A_1\alpha$. The production is $A_2 \rightarrow A_1d$. According to the algorithm for removal of indirect left recursion the production becomes

$\boldsymbol{A_2 \rightarrow A_2ad/bd.}$

Now the A_2 production is $\boldsymbol{A_2 \rightarrow A_2c/ A_2ad/ bd/ e}$

$\boldsymbol{A_2 \rightarrow A_2c}$ has immediate left recursion. After removing the left recursion the production becomes

$\boldsymbol{A_2 \rightarrow bdA_2' / eA_2'}$

$A_2/ \rightarrow cA_2' / \in$

$\boldsymbol{A_2 \rightarrow A_2ad}$ has immediate left recursion. After removing the left recursion the production becomes

$\boldsymbol{A_2 \rightarrow bdA_2'' / eA2''}$

$\boldsymbol{A2'' \rightarrow adA2'' / \in.}$

The actual non-left recursive grammar is

$\boldsymbol{A \rightarrow Ba/ b}$

$\boldsymbol{B \rightarrow bdB' / eB' / bdB'' / eB''}$

$\boldsymbol{B' \rightarrow cB' / \in}$

$\boldsymbol{B'' \rightarrow adB'' / \in}$

12. Construct equivalent finite automata from the following regular grammar.

$\boldsymbol{S \rightarrow aS/ bA/ b}$

$\boldsymbol{A \rightarrow aA/ bS/ a}$

Ans. In the grammar there are two non-terminals S and *A*. So, in the finite automata there are three states. For the production $S \rightarrow aS$ the transitional diagram:

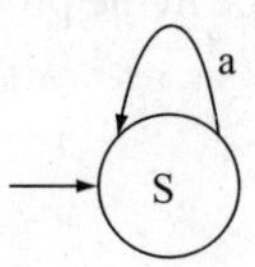

For the production $S \rightarrow bA$ the transitional diagram:

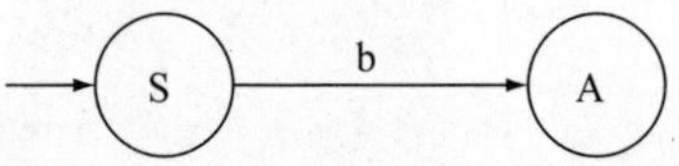

For the production $S \rightarrow b$ the transitional diagram:

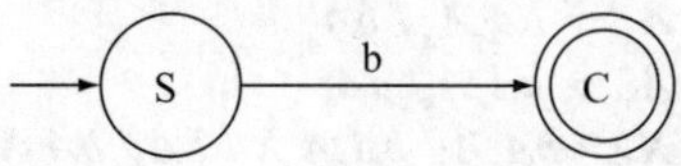

For the 'S' production the complete transitional diagram

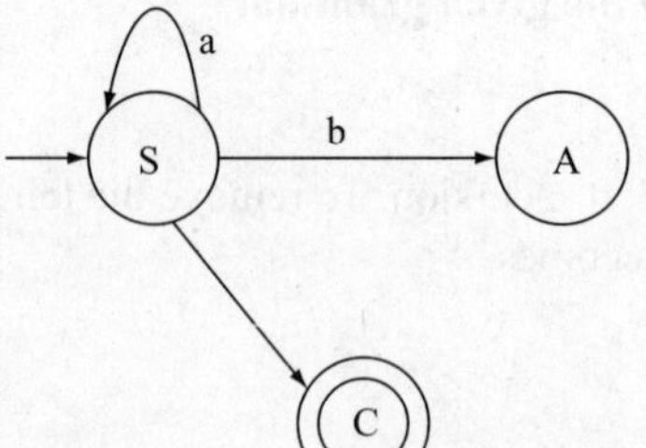

For '*A*' production the transitional diagram:

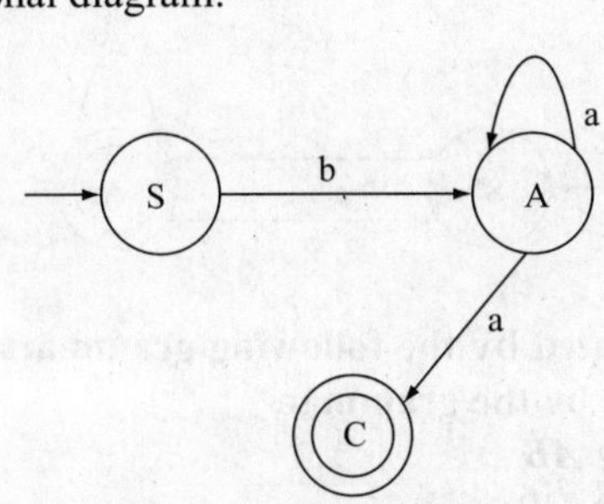

The complete transitional diagram for the above grammar is

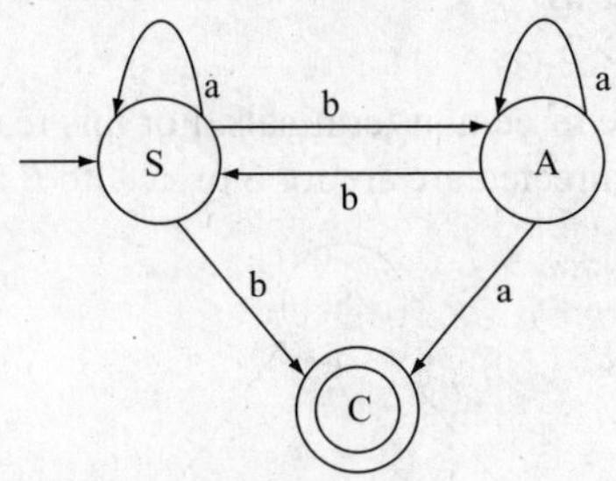

13. **Construct equivalent finite automata from the following regular grammar.**
    S* → *Aa
    ***A* → *Sb*/ *Ab*/ ∈.**

Ans. The grammar accepts null string. So *A* is the final state. For the production rule $A \rightarrow \in$ the transitional diagram is

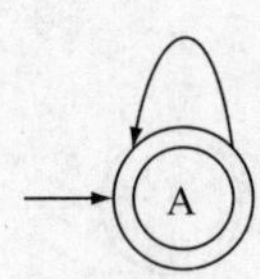

For the production ***S*→*Aa*** the transitional diagram:

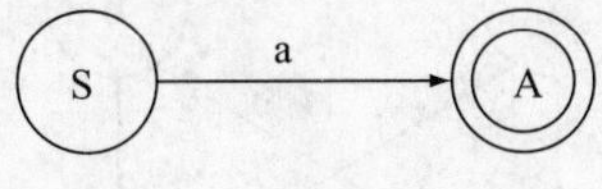

For the production *A* → *Sb*/*Ab* the transitional diagram:

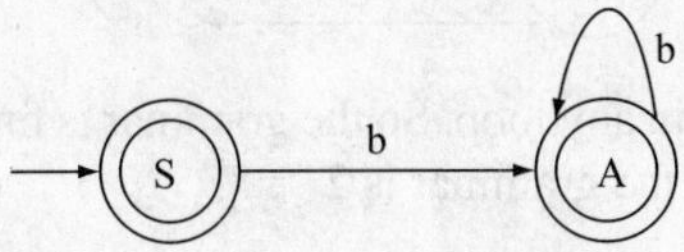

The complete transitional diagram:

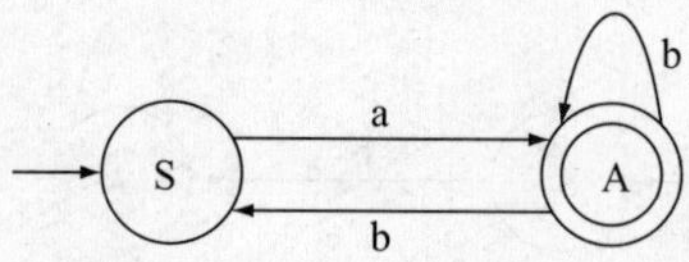

14. Verify the languages generated by the following grammars are finite or not. If finite find the longest string generated by the grammar.

(a) $S \to Ab$
$A \to aB/\ a$
$B \to bS$

(b) $S \to AB$
$A \to CD$
$B \to CD$
$C \to aD$
$D \to b$

Ans. (a) In the grammar there are three non-terminals. For this reason in the directed graph for the grammar there are three nodes. The directed arc are for *S* to *A*, *A* to *B* and *B* to *S*.

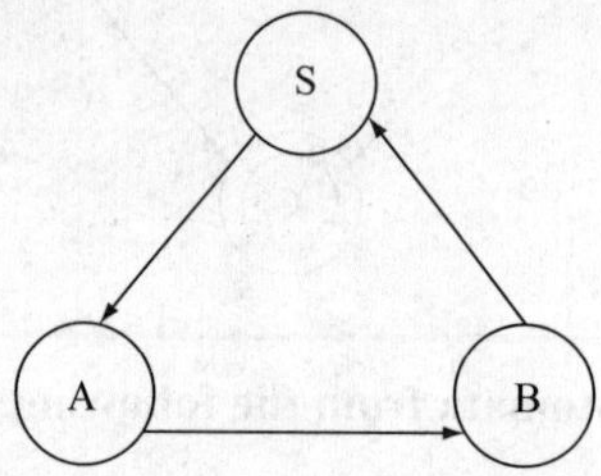

The graph contains loop. So the language generated by the CFG is infinite.

(b) In the grammar there are five non-terminals. For this reason in the directed graph for the grammar there are three nodes.

The directed graph for the grammar:

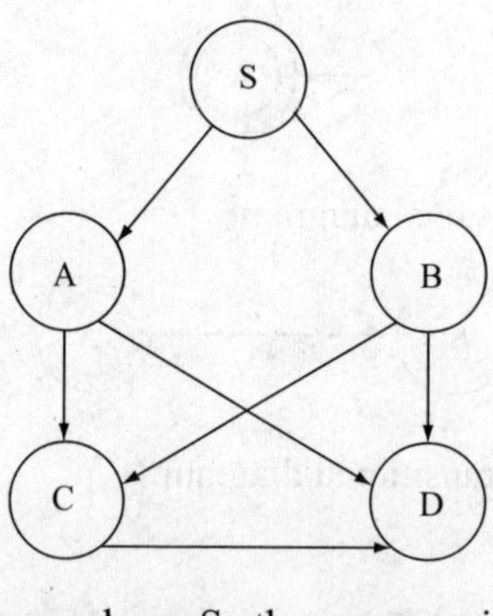

The directed graph does not contain any loop. So the grammar is finite. The length of the longest path is 3. The longest string generated by the grammar is $2^3 = 8$.

MULTIPLE CHOICE QUESTIONS

1. CFL is _____ language.

   (a) Type 0, (b) Type 1, (c) Type 2, (d) Type 3.

2. Parsing a string from a given grammar means.

   (a) Finding a derivation.
   (b) Finding a Left most derivation.
   (c) Finding a Right most derivation.
   (d) Finding a derivation tree.

3. A grammar is called ambiguous if

   (a) it generates more than one string.
   (b) it generates both Left most and Right most derivation for a given string.
   (c) it generates more than one parse tree for a given string.
   (d) it fulfills both (b) and (c).

4. Which is not true for ambiguous grammar?

   (a) Ambiguity creates problem in generating language from a given grammar
   (b) All Ambiguity can be removed.
   (c) Inherent ambiguity cannot be removed.
   (d) Some ambiguity can be removed by hand.

5. Non-generating symbols are those symbols which

   (a) does not generate any string of non-terminals
   (b) does not generate any null string
   (c) does not generate any string of terminal and non-terminals
   (d) does not generate any string of terminals.

6. Useless symbols in CFG are

   (a) Non generating Symbol and non-reachable symbols
   (b) Null alphabets and null string
   (c) Non-terminal symbols
   (d) All of these.

7. Which of the followings is unit production?

   (a) (String of NT) → (String of NT)
   (b) (Single NT) → (String of NT)
   (c) (Single NT) → (Single NT)
   (d) (String of NT) → (Single NT).

8. Which is true for the following CFG?

   $S \rightarrow aA / \in$
   $A \rightarrow bA / a.$

   (a) Null production can be removed,
   (b) Null production cannot be removed,
   (c) As A does not produce null so null cannot be removed,
   (d) Both (b) and (c).

9. Which of the following production is in CNF? (More Specific)

   (a) (NT) → (String of NT),
   (b) (NT) → (String of terminal and non-terminal),
   (c) (NT) → (String of Terminal),
   (d) (NT) → (String of exactly two NT).

10. Which of the following production is in GNF? (More Specific)
 (a) (NT) → (Single T)(String of NT), (b) (NT) → (Single NT)(String of T),
 (c) (NT) → (String of terminal and non-terminal), (d) (NT) → (String of NT).
11. Which of the following common in both CNF and GNF?
 (a) (NT) → (Single T)(String of NT), (b) (NT) → (String of exactly two NT),
 (c) (NT) → (String of NT), (d) (NT) → (Single T).
12. CFL are not closed under
 (a) Union (b) Concatenation (c) Complementation (d) Star closure.
13. The intersection of CFL and RE is always
 (a) CFL, (b) RE, (c) CSL, (d) CFL or CSL.
14. Which of the following is in GNF?
 (a) $A \to BC$, (b) $A \to a$, (c) $A \to Ba$, (d) $A \to aaB$.

Ans. 1.c, 2.a, 3.c, 4.b, 5.d, 6.a, 7.c, 8.b, 9.d, 10.a, 11.d, 12.c, 13.a, 14.b.

EXERCISES

1. Construct CFG for the followings
 (a) $a^n a^m$, where $n > 0$ and $m = n + 1$
 (b) $a^n b a^m$, where $m, n > 0$
 (c) $a^n b^n c^m$, where $n > 0$ and $m = n + 1$
 (d) $L = (011 + 1)^*(01)^*$
 (e) $L = \{$Set of all integers$\}$.
2.
 (a) Construct the string 0110001 from the Grammar
 $S \to AB$
 $A \to 0A/1B/0$
 $B \to 1A/0B/1$ by using
 (i) Left most derivation
 (ii) Right most derivation

 (b) Construct the string *baaabbba* from the Grammar
 $S \to AaB/\ AbB$
 $A \to Sa/\ b$
 $B \to Sb/\ a$ by using
 (i) Left most derivation
 (ii) Right most derivation
3.
 (a) Find the parse tree for generating the string *abaabaa* from the grammar given below
 $S \to aAS/a$
 $A \to bS$

(b) Find the parse tree for generating the string *aabbaa* from the grammar given below

$S \rightarrow aAS / a$

$A \rightarrow SbA / SS / ba$

4. Show that the following grammars are ambiguous.

(a) $S \rightarrow abSb / aAb / a$

$A \rightarrow bS / aAAb$

(b) $E \rightarrow E + E / E{*}E /$ id

(c) $S \rightarrow aB / bA$

$A \rightarrow aS / bAA / a$

$B \rightarrow bS / aBB / b$

5. Remove useless productions from the following grammars

(a) $S \rightarrow AB / a$

$A \rightarrow b$

(b) $S \rightarrow AB / AC$

$A \rightarrow 0A1 / 1A0 / 0$

$B \rightarrow 11A / 00B / AB$

$C \rightarrow 01C0 / 0D1$

$D \rightarrow 1D / 0C$

6. Remove unit production from the following grammars

I. $S \rightarrow SaA$

$A \rightarrow aB / B / b$

$B \rightarrow bC / C / a$

$C \rightarrow ab$

II. $S \rightarrow Aa / B$

$B \rightarrow A / bb$

$A \rightarrow a / bc / B$

7. Remove null production from the following grammars

I. $S \rightarrow aAB$

$A \rightarrow Bb$

$B \rightarrow \in$

II. $S \rightarrow aA$

$A \rightarrow bB$

$B \rightarrow b$

$B \rightarrow \in$

8. Simplify the following context free grammar.

$S \rightarrow AB / aB$

$A \rightarrow BC / B / a$

$B \rightarrow C$

$C \rightarrow b / \in$

9. Convert the following grammars into CNF.

(a) $S \rightarrow AB$

$A \rightarrow aA / a$

$B \rightarrow ab / bB / b$

(b) $S \rightarrow aSa / SSa / a$

10. Convert the following grammar into GNF.

(a) $S \rightarrow Abb / a$

$A \rightarrow aaA / B$

$B \rightarrow bAb$

(b) $S \rightarrow aSb / bSa / a / b$

11. Construct DFA equivalent to the Regular Grammar

 (a) $S \rightarrow aS/ bA/ b$

 $A \rightarrow aA/ bS/ a$

 (b) $S \rightarrow bA/ aB$

 $A \rightarrow bA/ aS/ a$

 $B \rightarrow aB/ bS/ b$

12. Prove that $L = a^n b^n c^{2n}$ is not context free by using Pumping Lemma for CFL.

13. Verify the languages generated by the following grammars are finite or not.

 (a) $S \rightarrow aA$

 $A \rightarrow BC$

 $B \rightarrow SC/ b$

 $C \rightarrow B/a$

 (b) $S \rightarrow AB$

 $A \rightarrow C/ a$

 $B \rightarrow AC/ b$

14. Remove left recursion from the following grammar and then perform left factoring.

 $E \rightarrow E + T \mid T$

 $T \rightarrow T{*}F \mid F$

 $F \rightarrow G\hat{}F \mid G$

 $G \rightarrow id \mid (E)$

15. Generate the string $id + id{*}id$ from the grammar

 $E \rightarrow E + E$

 $E \rightarrow E{*}E$

 $E \rightarrow id$

 Where precedence of operator is given below

	+	*
+	>	<
*	>	>

 Are you getting any ambiguity in the grammar?

FILL IN THE BLANKS

1. According to Chomsky Hierarchy Context Free Grammar is Type ____________ grammar.
2. The grammar where production rules are in the format of

 {A string consists of at least one Non-Terminal} → {A string of terminals and/ or non terminals} is ____________ grammar in particular.
3. The grammar S → aSb/bSb/C produces the string ____________
4. Finding a derivation for a string from a given grammar is called ____________.

5. The Tree representation of deriving a Context free language from a given Context grammar is called ____________
6. Parse Tree construction is only possible for ____________ Grammar
7. The root of the parse tree of a given context free language is represented by the ________ of the corresponding Context Free Grammar.
8. A CFG G is said to be ____________ if there exists some w C L(G) that has at least two distinct parse trees.
9. A CFL L is said to be ____________ if all its grammars are ambiguous.
10. The Context Free grammar where a non-terminal 'A as a left-most symbol appears alternatively at the time of derivation either immediately or through some other non terminal definitions is called ____________ grammar.
11. To avoid the problem of backtracking we need to perform ____________
12. In a context free grammar the symbols which do not produce any terminal string is called ____________.
13. In a Context Free Grammar, the symbols which can not be reached at any time starting from the start symbol are called ____________.
14. In a Context Free Grammar Non-Generating Symbol and Non-Reachable Symbol both are called ____________ symbol.
15. In a Context Free Grammar the production in the form Non Terminal -> Single Non Terminal is called ____________.
16. In a Context Free Grammar a production in the form NT → 6 is called ____________.
17. Normalizing a Context Free Grammar should not hamper the ____________ power of the grammar.
18. A Context free grammar where all the productions of the grammar are in the form
    Non Terminal → String of exactly two Non Terminals
    Non Terminal → Single Terminal
    is called ____________ Normal Form
19. A Context free grammar where all the productions of the grammar are in the form
    Non Terminal → (Single Terminal)(String of Non Terminals)
    Non Terminal → Single Terminal
    is called ____________ Normal Form
20. Context Free Languages are not closed under ____________ and ____________.
21. ____________ is used to prove that certain sets are not Context free
22. $a^n b^n c^n$ where $n > 1$ is not ____________ language but ____________ language.
23. If the length of the longest path of the directed graph generated from a Context Free Grammar is n, then the longest string generated by the grammar is ____________.

24. A language L generated from a given CFG is finite if there are no ____________ in the directed graph generated from the production rules of the given CFG.

ANSWERS

1. Two
2. Context Free
3. WCW^R | We (a,b)*
4. Parsing
5. Parse Tree
6. Context Free
7. Start Symbol
8. Ambiguous
9. inherently ambiguous
10. Left Recursive
11. Left Factoring
12. Non-Generating Symbols
13. Non-Reachable Symbols
14. Useless
15. unit production
16. null production
17. language generating
18. Chomsky
19. Greibach
20. Intersection, complementation
21. Pumping lemma for CFL
22. Context Free, Context Sensitive
23. 2^n
24. cycles

6

Pushdown Automata

6.1 BASICS OF PUSHDOWN AUTOMATA

Q. What is Pushdown Automata? Describe the Block diagram or Mechanical diagram of Pushdown Automata. Why is it so named 'Pushdown'?

Ans. Pushdown Automata (PDA) is the machine format of context free language (CFL). It is one type of finite state machine (FSM) which is used to accept only CFLs.

Mechanical diagram:

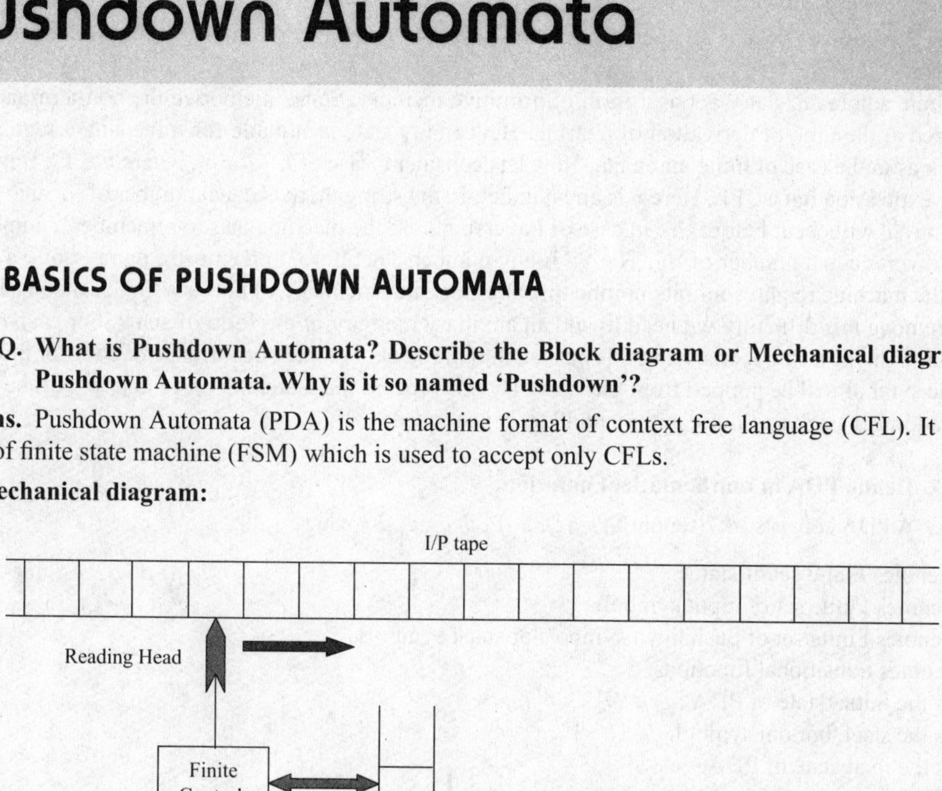

(a) Input Tape: Input tape contains the input symbols. The tape is divided into a number of squares. Each square contains a single input character. The string placed in the input tape is traversed from left to right. Two end sides of the input string contain infinite number of blank symbol.

(b) Reading Head: The head scans each square in the input tape and reads the input from the tape. The head moves from left to right. The input scanned by the reading head is sent to the finite control of the PDA.

(c) Finite Control: Finite control can be considered as a control unit of a PDA. An automaton always resides in a state. The reading head scans the input from the input tape and sends it to finite control. One two way head is also added with the finite control to the stack top. Depending on the input taken from input tape and input from stack top, finite control decides in which state the PDA will move and which stack symbol it will push to the stack or pop from the stack or do nothing on the stack.

(d) Stack: A stack is a temporary storage of stack symbols. Every move of PDA indicates one of the followings to the stack
  (i) One stack symbol may be added to the stack [Push]
  (ii) One stack symbol may be deleted from the top of the stack [Pop]

Stack is the component of PDA which differentiates it from finite automata. In stack there is always a symbol z_0 which denotes the bottom of the stack.

Why Pushdown: Push is an operation related to stack. By this operation one symbol is added to the stack top.

In finite automata, states act as a form of primitive memory. States memorize the non-terminals encountered at the time of derivation of a string. Hence only state is suitable for traversing a regular expression as in the case of finite automata. Now lets consider a case of $L = \{a^n b^n, \text{ where } n \geq 1\}$. It is not a regular expression but a CFL. Here n is any number. In the string there is equal number of 'a' and 'b'. In the string 'a' will occur before 'b'. In case of traversing $a^n b^n$, the machine has to remember n number of a's to traverse equal number of 'b'. The 'n' is any number. Therefore, to memorize number of a's in the string the machine requires infinite number of states, i.e. the machine will not be a finite state machine.

To remove this difficulty we need to add an auxiliary memory in the form of stack. For each occurrence of 'a' in the string L one symbol is pushed into the stack. For each occurrence of b (After finishing 'a') one symbol will be popped from the stack. By this process the matching of 'a' and 'b' will be done.

By adding a stack to a finite automata, PDA is generated.

Q. Define PDA in mathematical notation.

Ans. A PDA consists of 7-touple $M = (Q, \Sigma, \Gamma, \delta, q_0, z_0, F)$ where

Q denotes Finite set of states.
Σ denotes Finite set of input symbols
Γ denotes Finite set of pushdown symbols or stack symbols.
δ denotes transitional functions.
q_0 is the initial state of PDA $[q_0 \in Q]$
z_0 is the stack bottom symbol.
F is the final state of PDA.
In PDA transitional function δ is in the form
$Q \text{ X } (\Sigma \cup \{\lambda\}) \text{ X } \Gamma \rightarrow (Q, \Gamma)$,

(From one state with an input symbol on the tape and with the stack top symbol, the PDA moves to one right, may change its state, and push some symbol in the stack or pop symbol from the stack top.)

Q. Define Instantaneous Description (ID) in the respect of PDA.

Ans. Instantaneous Description (ID) describes the configuration of PDA at a given instant. Instantaneous Description remembers the information of state and stack content at a given instance of time.

An ID is a format of triple (q,w,κ), where $q \in Q$ (finite set of states), $w \in \Sigma$ (Finite set of input alphabets) and $\kappa \in \Gamma$ (Finite set of stack symbols).

6.2 ACCEPTANCE BY A PDA

Q. What are the conditions to declare a string accepted by PDA?

Ans. There are two ways to declare a string accepted by a PDA (a) Accepted by empty stack (store) (b) Accepted by final state.

(a) **Accepted by empty stack (store):** We know in each PDA there is a stack attached. In the stack at the bottom there is a symbol called stack bottom symbol. In each move of the PDA one symbol called stack symbol is either pushed in or popped from the stack. But the symbol z_0 still remains in the stack.

A string w may be declared accepted by empty stack after processing all the symbols of w, if the stack is empty after reading the rightmost input character of the string w. In mathematical notation we can say $M = \{Q, \Sigma, \Gamma, \delta, q_0, z_0, F\}$ be a PDA, the string w is declared accepted by empty stack if

$$\{w \in \Sigma^* / (q_0, w, z_0) \ {}^*\!\rightarrow (q, \lambda, \lambda) \text{ for some } q \in Q\}.$$

In general we can say that a string is accepted by a PDA by empty stack if both the following conditions are fulfilled.

(i) The string is finished (Totally Traversed)
(ii) The stack is empty.

(b) Accepted by final state: A string w may be declared accepted by Final state if after total traversal of the string w the PDA enters into its Final state. In Mathematical notation we can say $M = \{Q, \Sigma, \Gamma, \delta, q_0, z_0, F\}$ be a PDA, the string w is declared accepted by Final State if

$$\{w \in \Sigma^* / (q_0, w, z_0) \ {}^*\!\rightarrow (q_f, \lambda, z_0) \text{ for } q_f \in F \text{ and } z_0 \text{ is the stack bottom symbol}\}.$$

In general we can say that a string is accepted by a PDA by Final State if both the following conditions are fulfilled

(i) The string is finished (totally traversed)
(ii) The PDA enters into its final state.

(Though there are two way to declare a string accepted by a PDA, but it can be proved that both the ways are equivalent. In general for both the cases all the steps are same, except the last step. In the last step it is differentiated whether the string is accepted by empty stack or by final state.

if in the last step $\delta(q_i, \lambda, z_0) \rightarrow (qi, \lambda)$, it is accepted by empty stack
if $\delta(q_i, \lambda, z_0) \rightarrow (q_f, z_0)$, it is accepted by final state.)

Q. Prove that a Language is accepted by a PDA by empty stack if and only if the language is accepted by a PDA by final state.

Ans. Let $M_1 = \{Q, \Sigma, \Gamma, \delta, q_0, z_0, F\}$ is a PDA. Let it accept a language L by final state. Let there exist another PDA M_2, which accepts the same language L by empty stack.

Let $M_2 = \{Q', \Sigma', \Gamma', \delta', q'_0, z_0', F'\}$.

Where $Q' = Q \cup \{q_0', q_e\}$, where $q_0', q_e \notin Q$.
$\Sigma' = \Sigma$
$\Gamma' = \Gamma \cup \{z_0'\}$, where $z_0' \notin \Gamma$

The transitional function δ' is defined as follows

(a) $\delta'(q_0', \lambda, z_0')$ contains $(q_0, z_0 z_0')$
(b) $\delta'(q_i, a, z)$ is the same as $\delta(q_i, a, z)$ for all $q_i \in Q, a \in \Sigma \cup \{\lambda\}$ and $z \in \Gamma$.
(c) $\delta'(q_i, \lambda, z)$ contains (q_e, λ) for $q_i \in F$ and for all $z \in \Gamma \cup \{z'_0\}$
(d) $\delta'(q_e, \lambda, z)$ contains (q_e, λ) for all $z \in \Gamma \cup \{z'_0\}$.

(Here (a) describes that M_2 enters in the initial configuration of M_1 with z'_0 as the leftmost push down symbol.

(b) describes to make M_2 to simulate the behavior of M_1, thus reading an input word w if M_1 reads w and enters a final state. Once w is read and M_2 enter a final state of M_1, the effect of 3 and 4 are to empty the pushdown store.)

Here $w \in M_1$ if and only if

$$(q_0, w, z_0) \overset{*}{\Rightarrow} (q_f, \lambda, z_0)$$

where q_f is the final state of machine M_1.
By rule (a) we can write

$$\begin{aligned}(q_0', w, z_0') &\Rightarrow (q_0, w, z_0'z_0)\\ &\Rightarrow (q_f \lambda, z_0'z_0) \text{ --- by rule (b), where } q_f \text{ is the final state}\\ &\overset{*}{\Rightarrow} (q_e, \lambda, \lambda) \text{ --- by rule (c) and (d),}\end{aligned}$$

i.e. $w \in M_2$, i.e. L is accepted by empty store by M_2.

Conversely, let $M_2 = (Q', \Sigma', \Gamma', \delta', q'_0, z'_0, \phi)$ be a PDA accepting L by empty store

Then $M_1 = \{Q, \Sigma, \Gamma, \delta, q_0, z_0, F\}$.

Where $Q = Q' \cup \{q_0, q_j\}$, where $q_0, q_j \notin Q'$
$\Gamma = \Gamma' \cup \{z_0\}$, where $z_0 \notin \Gamma'$
$F = \{q_j\}$ and δ is defined as follows:

1. $\delta(q_0, \lambda, z_0)$ contains (q'_0, z_0, z'_0),
2. $\delta(q_i, a, z)$ is the same as $\delta'(q_i, a, z)$ for all $q_i \in Q', a \in \Sigma \cup \{\lambda\}$ and $z \in \Gamma'$,
3. $\delta(q_i, \lambda, z_0)$ contains (q_j, z_0) for all $q_i \in Q'$.

From these two it can be proved that a language is accepted by a PDA by empty stack if and only if the language is accepted by a PDA by final state.

6.3 EXAMPLES

Q. Construct a PDA to accept a given language L by empty stack and final state both where $L = (a^n b^n$, where $n \geq 1)$

Ans. The string is $a^n b^n$ where $n \geq 1$. The remarks we can draw from seeing the string $a^n b^n$ where $n \geq 1$ are the following.

(a) The string consists of two alphabets '*a*' and '*b*'.
(b) '*a*' will occur before '*b*'.
(c) Number of '*a*' are equal to number of '*b*'.
(d) There will be at least one '*a*' and one '*b*' in the string.

We have to check equal number of '*a*' and '*b*'. Let take a stack symbol z_1, which is pushed into the stack as an '*a*' is traversed from the input tape. At the beginning, the PDA is in state q_0 and stack top is z_0 as at the beginning there is no other symbol in the stack. In this state it will get an input '*a*' from the input tape (*the string starts with 'a'*). So a stack symbol z_1 will be pushed to the stack. The δ function will be

$$\delta(q_0, a, z_0) \rightarrow (q_0, z_1z_0).$$

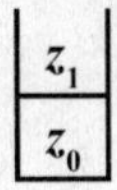

(*At the right-hand-side the stack denotes the placement of the symbols.* z_1z_0 *denotes that there was* z_0 *in the stack. Now the symbol* z_1 *is pushed into the stack. It is given for better understanding of the placement of stack symbols*)

From the next input '*a*' from the input tape, the PDA is in state q_0 and stack top is z_1, so another z_1 will be pushed into the stack. The δ function will be

$$\delta(q_0, a, z_1) \rightarrow (q_0, z_1z_1).$$

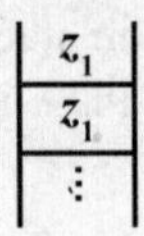

By this δ function all the remaining '*a*'s will be traversed. After the end of '*a*' in the input tape, '*b*' will occur. When first '*b*' will occur on the input tape at that time the PDA is in state q_0 with stack top z_1 (*Just before it 'a's are traversed*). When '*b*' will traversed the stack top z_1 will be popped and the PDA will change its state to q_1. (*So that there will be no chance to push* z_1 *in the stack if any 'a' occur. The PDA is designed only for string* a^nb^n*, but the input string may not be in the form of* a^nb^n*. In that case the string will not be accepted by the PDA.*) The δ function will be

$$\delta(q_0, b, z_1) \rightarrow (q_1, \lambda).$$

When next '*b*' will occur, the PDA is in state q_1 with stack top z_1. That z_1 will be popped. The δ function will be

$$\delta(q_1, b, z_1) \rightarrow (q_1, \lambda).$$

By this δ function all the remaining '*b*' will be traversed.

If the input string is in the form of a^nb^n where $n \geq 1$ then after traversing the last '*b*' the PDA will be in state q_1 with stack top z_0 (*All other stack symbols are removed*).

If we have to design the PDA accepted by Empty stack the δ function will be

$$\delta(q_1, \lambda, z_0) \rightarrow (q_1, \lambda).$$

If we have to design the PDA accepted by Final State the δ function will be

$$\delta(q_1, \lambda, z_0) \rightarrow (q_f, z_0).$$

So the PDA for $L = (\mathbf{a^nb^n}$**, where** $\mathbf{n \geq 1}$**)** is

$Q = \{q_0, q_1, q_f\}$
$\Sigma = \{a,b\}$
$\Gamma = \{z_0, z_1\}$
$q_0 = \{q_0\}$
$z_0 = \{z_0\}$
$F = \{q_f\}$

δ is defined as follows:

$$\delta(q_0, a, z_0) \rightarrow (q_0, z_1z_0)$$
$$\delta(q_0, a, z_1) \rightarrow (q_0, z_1z_1)$$
$$\delta(q_0, b, z_1) \rightarrow (q_1, \lambda)$$
$$\delta(q_1, b, z_1) \rightarrow (q_1, \lambda)$$
$$\delta(q_1, \lambda, z_0) \rightarrow (q_1, \lambda) \text{ accepted by empty stack}$$
$$\delta(q_1, \lambda, z_0) \rightarrow (q_f, z_0) \text{ accepted by final state.}$$

Q. Construct a PDA to accept $L = (a,b)^*$ with equal number of 'a' and 'b', i.e. $n_a(L) = n_b(L)$ by empty stack and final state.

Ans. The string is any combination of '*a*' and '*b*' including null and number of '*a*' is equal to number of '*b*'. In the language set a string may start with '*a*' or a string may start with '*b*'. An '*a*' can come after '*a*' or '*b*' can come after '*a*', same like '*a*' can come after '*b*' or '*b*' can come after '*b*'. If a string start with '*a*' then push a stack symbol z_1 in the stack. If a string start with '*b*' then push a stack symbol z_2 in the stack. For these two cases the PDA is in state q_0. The δ function for these two cases will be

$$\delta(q_0, a, z_0) \rightarrow (q_0, z_1z_0).$$

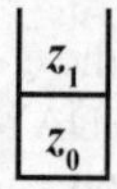

$$\delta(q_0, b, z_0) \rightarrow (q_0, z_2z_0).$$

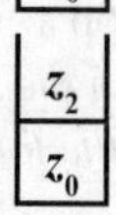

If the string starts with '*a*' and '*a*' comes after '*a*' then the PDA is in state q_0 with stack top z_1. Another z_1 will be pushed to the stack. The δ function will be

$$\delta(q_0, a, z_1) \rightarrow (q_0, z_1z_1).$$

If the string starts with '*a*', and '*b*' comes after '*a*' then the PDA is in state q_0 with stack top z_1. The stack top will be popped from the stack as one 'b' is found after one 'a'. The δ function will be

$$\delta(q_0, b, z_1) \rightarrow (q_0, \lambda).$$

If the string starts with '*b*' and '*b*' comes after '*b*' then the PDA is in state q_0 with stack top z_2. Another z_2 will be pushed to the stack. The δ function will be

$$\delta(q_0, b, z_2) \rightarrow (q_0, z_2z_2).$$

If the string starts with '*b*', and '*a*' comes after '*b*' then the PDA is in state q_0 with stack top z_2. The stack top will be popped from the stack as one 'a' is found after one 'b'. The δ function will be

$$\delta(q_0, a, z_2) \rightarrow (q_0, \lambda).$$

By these δ functions all the input symbols of the input tape will be traversed. The PDA will be in state q_0 with stack top z_0.

If we have to design the PDA accepted by empty stack the δ function will be

$$\delta(q_0, \lambda, z_0) \rightarrow (q_0, \lambda),$$

If we have to design the PDA accepted by Final State the δ function will be

$$\delta(q_0, \lambda, z_0) \rightarrow (q_f, z_0).$$

(In the Language set null string can occur. If null string occurs in the language set, then it will also be accepted by the last two δ functions directly.)

So the PDA for $L = (a,b)^*$ with equal number of 'a' and 'b', i.e. $n_a(L) = n_b(L)$ is

$$Q = \{q_0, q_f\}$$
$$\Sigma = \{a,b\}$$
$$\Gamma = \{z_0, z_1, z_2\}$$
$$q_0 = \{q_0\}$$
$$z_0 = \{z_0\}$$
$$F = \{q_f\}$$

δ is defined as follows:

$\delta(q_0, a, z_0) \rightarrow (q_0, z_1z_0)$
$\delta(q_0, b, z_0) \rightarrow (q_0, z_2z_0)$
$\delta(q_0, a, z_1) \rightarrow (q_0, z_1z_1)$
$\delta(q_0, b, z_1) \rightarrow (q_0, \lambda)$
$\delta(q_0, b, z_2) \rightarrow (q_0, z_2z_2)$
$\delta(q_0, a, z_2) \rightarrow (q_0, \lambda)$
$\delta(q_0, \lambda, z_0) \rightarrow (q_0, \lambda)$ accepted by empty stack
$\delta(q_0, \lambda, z_0) \rightarrow (q_f, z_0)$ accepted by final state.

Q. Construct a PDA to accept $L = (a,b)^+$ with equal number of 'a' and 'b', i.e. $n_a(L) = n_b(L)$ by empty stack and final state.

In the string $(a,b)^+$ there will be at least one 'a' and one 'b' with equal number of 'a', and 'b'. So the δ functions of the PDA will be made such that null string will not be accepted. All the conditions are same like $(a,b)^*$ but to avoid null occurrence the transitions will be like this

By getting 'a' at the beginning, change the state from q_0 to q_1 and push z_1 in the stack. From the next input all the transitions will be on state q_1.

Same like, if the string start with 'b', change the state from q_0 to q_1 and push z_2 in the stack. From the next input all the transitions will be on state q_1.

The transitional functions (δ) will be

$\delta(q_0, a, z_0) \rightarrow (q_1, z_1z_0)$
$\delta(q_0, b, z_0) \rightarrow (q_1, z_2z_0)$
$\delta(q_1, a, z_1) \rightarrow (q_1, z_1z_1)$
$\delta(q_1, b, z_1) \rightarrow (q_1, \lambda)$
$\delta(q_1, b, z_2) \rightarrow (q_1, z_2z_2)$
$\delta(q_1, a, z_2) \rightarrow (q_1, \lambda)$
$\delta(q_1, \lambda, z_0) \rightarrow (q_1, \lambda)$ accepted by empty stack,
$\delta(q_1, \lambda, z_0) \rightarrow (q_f, z_0)$ accepted by final state.

.(If in the language set there is a null string, there exists no transitional function in the PDA, because the null string will only be traversed if the machine in state q_1*. For coming to* q_1*, it needs to traverse atleast one* 'a' *or one* 'b'*. It is clear from the discussion that the PDA will not accept null string, i.e. it is for L =* $(a,b)^+$ *with equal number of* 'a' *and* 'b'*.)*

Q. Construct a PDA to accept the language $L = \{WCW^R$, where $W \in (a,b)^+$ and W^R is the reverse of $W\}$ by empty stack and by final state.

Ans. The W is a string consists of any combination of 'a' and 'b' not including null. The string W may start with 'a' or may start with 'b'. In the string, 'a' may come after 'a' (E.g. *aa*) or 'b' may come after 'a' (E.g. *ab*). Or 'a' may come after 'b' [*ba*] or 'b' may come after 'b' (E.g. *bb*).

The W^R is the reverse of W. It means if 'a' appears at the ith place from the beginning in W^R, then 'a' must appeared at the ith place from the end in W. The C is the marker which denotes the end of W and beginning of W^R.

The PDA will be designed as follows:

The PDA is in state q_0 with stack top $z_{0.}$ In the string W if 'a' is traversed as start symbol, a stack symbol z_1 will be pushed and the PDA will change its state to q_1 (To avoid accepting null string). If 'b' is traversed, a stack symbol z_2 will be pushed and the PDA will change its state to q_1 (To avoid accepting null string) .The δ function will be

$\delta(q_0, a, z_0) \rightarrow (q_1, z_1z_0)$.

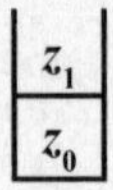

$\delta(q_0, b, z_0) \rightarrow (q_1, z_2z_0)$.

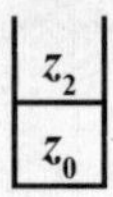

If in W, 'a' occurs after 'a', then state is q_1 and stack top is z_1. One z_1 will be pushed to the stack. If 'b' occurs after 'a', then state is q_1 and stack top is z_1. One z_2 will be pushed to the stack. The δ function will be

$\delta(q_1, a, z_1) \rightarrow (q_1, z_1z_1)$.

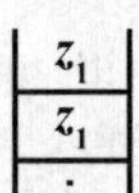

$\delta(q_1, b, z_1) \rightarrow (q_1, z_2z_1)$.

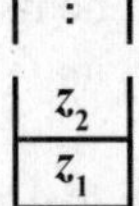

If in W, 'a' occurs after 'b', then state is q_1 and stack top is z_2. One z_1 will be pushed to the stack. If 'b' occurs after 'b', then state is q_1 and stack top is z_2. One z_2 will be pushed to the stack. The δ function will be

$\delta(q_1, a, z_2) \rightarrow (q_1, z_1z_2)$.

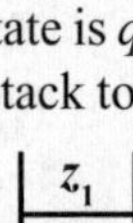

$\delta(q_1, b, z_2) \rightarrow (q_1, z_2z_2)$.

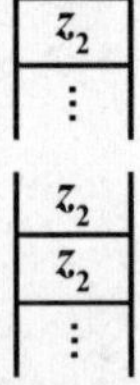

By the already given transitional functions the string W will be traversed.

At the end of W the input head will come to the symbol C to traverse it. The C indicates that the string W is finished and W^R will start. Before traversing C, either 'a' or 'b' is traversed. When C is going to be traversed, at the stack top there will be either z_1 (if just before '*a*' is traversed) or z_2 (if just before 'b' is traversed). Upon traversing C only there will be a state change from q_1 to q_2 but no operation will be done on stack. The δ function will be

$$\delta(q_1, C, z_1) \rightarrow (q_2, z_1),$$
$$\delta(q_1, C, z_2) \rightarrow (q_2, z_2).$$

After traversing *C* the reverse string of *W*, i.e. W^R will come. If '*a*' comes at the ith place from the beginning then '*a*' will come at the ith place from the end in *W*. If for the string W^R as an input '*a*' comes, the stack top will be z_1 and state will be q_2. If for the string W^R as an input '*b*' comes, the stack top will be z_2 and state will be q_2. This stack top will be popped from the stack. The δ function will be

$$\delta(q_2, a, z_1) \rightarrow (q_2, \lambda),$$
$$\delta(q_2, b, z_2) \rightarrow (q_2, \lambda).$$

By these δ functions all the input symbols of the input tape will be traversed. The PDA will be in state q_2 with stack top z_0.

If we have to design the PDA accepted by Empty stack the δ function will be

$$\delta(q_2, \lambda, z_0) \rightarrow (q_2, \lambda).$$

If we have to design the PDA accepted by Final State the δ function will be

$$\delta(q_2, \lambda, z_0) \rightarrow (q_f, z_0).$$

The PDA for $L = \{WCW^R$, where $W \in (a,b)^+$ and W^R is the reverse of $W\}$ is

$Q = \{q_0, q_1, q_2, q_f\}$
$\Sigma = \{a,b,C\}$
$\Gamma = \{z_0, z_1, z_2\}$
$q_0 = \{q_0\}$
$z_0 = \{z_0\}$
$F = \{q_f\}$

δ is defined as follows:

$\delta(q_0, a, z_0) \rightarrow (q_1, z_1z_0)$
$\delta(q_0, b, z_0) \rightarrow (q_1, z_2z_0)$
$\delta(q_1, a, z_1) \rightarrow (q_1, z_1z_1)$
$\delta(q_1, b, z_1) \rightarrow (q_1, z_2z_1)$
$\delta(q_1, a, z_2) \rightarrow (q_1, z_1z_2)$
$\delta(q_1, b, z_2) \rightarrow (q_1, z_2z_2)$
$\delta(q_1, C, z_1) \rightarrow (q_2, z_1)$
$\delta(q_1, C, z_2) \rightarrow (q_2, z_2)$
$\delta(q_2, a, z_1) \rightarrow (q_2, \lambda)$
$\delta(q_2, b, z_2) \rightarrow (q_2, \lambda)$
$\delta(q_2, \lambda, z_0) \rightarrow (q_2, \lambda)$ **accepted by empty stack,**
$\delta(q_2, \lambda, z_0) \rightarrow (q_f, z_0)$ **accepted by final state.**

Q. Construct a PDA to accept the language $L = \{WCW^R$, where $W \in (a, b)^*$ and W^R is the reverse of $W\}$ by Empty stack and by Final state.

Ans. The string W may contain null string. If W is null then W^R is null. It means in the language set there will be only C if W is null. The PDA will always be in state q_0 at the time of traversing the string W. The δ functions for traversing W will be

$$\delta(q_0, a, z_0) \rightarrow (q_0, z_1z_0)$$
$$\delta(q_0, b, z_0) \rightarrow (q_0, z_2z_0)$$
$$\delta(q_0, a, z_1) \rightarrow (q_0, z_1z_1)$$
$$\delta(q_0, b, z_1) \rightarrow (q_0, z_2z_1)$$
$$\delta(q_0, a, z_2) \rightarrow (q_0, z_1z_2)$$
$$\delta(q_0, b, z_2) \rightarrow (q_0, z_2z_2).$$

Here C indicates the end of W and beginning of W^R. When C will be traversed a state change from q_0 to q_1 will occur. The string W may be null. The set L may contain only C. So, stack top will one of the followings at the time of traversing C

May be z_1 (if just before 'a' is traversed)

May be z_2 (if just before 'b' is traversed)

May be z_0 (if no input alphabet is traversed, i.e. W is null).

The δ function for traversing C will be

$$\delta(q_0, C, z_1) \rightarrow (q_1, z_1),$$
$$\delta(q_0, C, z_2) \rightarrow (q_1, z_2),$$
$$\delta(q_0, C, z_0) \rightarrow (q_1, z_0).$$

By the previous given δ functions all the input symbols of the input tape will be traversed. The PDA will be in state q_1 with stack top z_0.

If we have to design the PDA accepted by Empty stack the δ function will be

$$\delta(q_1, \lambda, z_0) \rightarrow (q_1, \lambda).$$

If we have to design the PDA accepted by Final State the δ function will be

$$\delta(q_1, \lambda, z_0) \rightarrow (q_f, z_0).$$

Q. Construct a PDA to accept the language $L = \{a^nb^mc^md^n$, where $m,n \geq 1\}$ by empty stack and by final state.

Ans. The string is $a^nb^mc^md^n$, **where $m,n \geq 1$.** The remarks we can draw from the string are as follows

(a) The string consists of a, b, c and d.

(b) 'b' will follow 'a', 'c' will follow 'b' and 'd' will follow 'c'.

(c) Number of 'a' is equal to number of 'd' and number of 'b' is equal to number of 'c'.

(d) In all the strings of the language set there will be at least one 'a', one 'b', one 'c' and one 'd'.

We need to check equal number of 'a' and 'd' and equal number of 'b' and 'c'. The string starts with 'a', so in the input tape 'a' will come first with state q_0 and stack top z_0. A stack symbol z_1 will be pushed to the stack. From the next appearance of 'a' in the input tape, stack top will be z_1. Another z_1 will be pushed to the stack. The δ function for traversing 'a' will be

$\boldsymbol{\delta(q_0, a, z_0) \rightarrow (q_0, z_1z_0),}$
$\boldsymbol{\delta(q_0, a, z_1) \rightarrow (q_0, z_1z_1).}$

After complete traversal of '*a*' in the input tape, '*b*' will come to be traversed. At the time of traversal of first '*b*' in the input tape, the PDA will be in state q_0 with stack top z_1 (Before it all '*a*'s are traversed). A state change from q_0 to q_1 will occur and a stack symbol z_2 will be added to the stack. From the next appearance of 'b' in the input tape, the state will be q_1 and stack top will be z_2. Another z_2 will be pushed to the stack. The δ function for traversing '*b*' will be

$\boldsymbol{\delta(q_0, b, z_1) \rightarrow (q_1, z_2z_1),}$
$\boldsymbol{\delta(q_1, b, z_2) \rightarrow (q_1, z_2z_2).}$

After complete traversal of '*b*' in the input tape, '*c*' will come to be traversed. The number of '*b*' and number of '*c*' are equal in all strings belongs to the Language set *L*. At the time of traversal of first '*c*' in the input tape, the PDA will be in state q_1 with stack top z_2 (Before it all '*b*'s are traversed). A state change from q_1 to q_2 will occur and stack top symbol z_2 will be popped from the stack. From the next appearance of '*b*' in the input tape, the state will be q_2 and stack top will be z_2.The symbol z_2 will be popped from the stack. The δ function for traversing '*b*' will be

$\boldsymbol{\delta(q_1, c, z_2) \rightarrow (q_2, \lambda),}$
$\boldsymbol{\delta(q_2, c, z_2) \rightarrow (q_2, \lambda).}$

When all the '*c*' will be traversed, the stack top will be z_1, which was added at the time of traversal of '*a*' and the PDA will be in state q_2. At the time of traversal of first '*d*' in the input tape, the PDA will be in state q_2 with stack top z_1. A state change from q_2 to q_3 will occur and stack top symbol z_1 will be popped from the stack. From the next appearance of '*d*' in the input tape, the state will be q_3 and stack top will be z_1. The symbol z_1 will be popped from the stack. The δ function for traversing '*b*' will be

$\boldsymbol{\delta(q_2, d, z_1) \rightarrow (q_3, \lambda),}$
$\boldsymbol{\delta(q_3, d, z_1) \rightarrow (q_3, \lambda).}$

By the previous given δ functions all the input symbols of the input tape will be traversed. The PDA will be in state q_3 with stack top z_0.

If we have to design the PDA accepted by Empty stack the δ function will be

$\boldsymbol{\delta(q_3, \lambda, z_0) \rightarrow (q_3, \lambda)}$

If we have to design the PDA accepted by Final State the δ function will be

$\boldsymbol{\delta(q_3, \lambda, z_0) \rightarrow (q_f, z_0)}$

The PDA for $L = \{a^nb^mc^md^n, \text{where } m,n \geq 1\}$ is

$Q = \{q_0, q_1, q_2, q_3, q_f\}$
$\Sigma = \{a, b, c, d\}$
$\Gamma = \{z_0, z_1, z_2\}$
$q_0 = \{q_0\}$
$z_0 = \{z_0\}$
$F = \{q_f\}$

δ is defined as follows:

$\delta(q_0, a, z_0) \rightarrow (q_0, z_1z_0)$
$\delta(q_0, a, z_1) \rightarrow (q_0, z_1z_1)$
$\delta(q_0, b, z_1) \rightarrow (q_1, z_2z_1)$
$\delta(q_1, b, z_2) \rightarrow (q_1, z_2z_2)$
$\delta(q_1, c, z_2) \rightarrow (q_2, \lambda)$
$\delta(q_2, c, z_2) \rightarrow (q_2, \lambda)$
$\delta(q_2, d, z_1) \rightarrow (q_3, \lambda)$
$\delta(q_3, d, z_1) \rightarrow (q_3, \lambda)$
$\delta(q_3, \lambda, z_0) \rightarrow (q_3, \lambda)$ **Accepted by empty stack,**
$\delta(q_3, \lambda, z_0) \rightarrow (q_f, z_0)$ **Accepted by final state.**

Q. Construct a PDA to accept the language $L = \{a^nb^nc^md^m$, where $m,n \geq 1\}$ by Empty Stack and by Final State.

Ans. Here number of '*a*' and number of '*b*' are same and number of '*c*' and number of '*d*' are same. State change will occur in transition from '*a*' to '*b*', '*b*' to '*c*' and '*c*' to '*d*'. Upon traversing '*a*', stack symbol z_1 will be pushed to the stack. Number of '*b*' are same as number of '*a*'. Number of z_1 pushed to the stack will be equal to number of '*a*,' i.e. number of '*b*'. For traversal of each '*b*' in the input tape one z_1 will be popped from the stack.

When first '*c*' will be traversed the stack top will be z_0.Upon traversing '*c*', stack symbol z_2 will be pushed to the stack. Upon traversing '*d*' those z_2's will be popped from the stack.

By these process all the string will be traversed. The PDA for accepting the string $a^nb^nc^md^m/m,n \geq 1$ will be

$Q = \{q_0, q_1, q_2, q_3, q_f\}$
$\Sigma = \{a, b, c, d\}$
$\Gamma = \{z_0, z_1, z_2\}$
$q_0 = \{q_0\}$
$z_0 = \{z_0\}$
$F = \{q_f\}$

The transition function for constructing PDA for the string $a^nb^nc^md^m/m,n \geq 1$ will be

$\delta(q_0, a, z_0) \rightarrow (q_0, z_1z_0)$

$\delta(q_0, a, z_1) \rightarrow (q_0, z_1z_1)$
$\delta(q_0, b, z_1) \rightarrow (q_1, \lambda)$
$\delta(q_1, b, z_1) \rightarrow (q_1, \lambda)$
$\delta(q_1, c, z_0) \rightarrow (q_2, z_2z_0)$
$\delta(q_2, c, z_2) \rightarrow (q_2, z_2z_2)$
$\delta(q_2, d, z_2) \rightarrow (q_3, \lambda)$
$\delta(q_3, d, z_2) \rightarrow (q_3, \lambda)$
$\delta(q_3, \lambda, z_0) \rightarrow (q_3, \lambda)$ **Accepted by empty stack,**
$\delta(q_3, \lambda, z_0) \rightarrow (q_f, z_0)$ **Accepted by final state.**

Q. Construct a PDA to accept the language $L = \{a^n b^{2n}$, where $n \geq 1\}$ by empty stack and by final state.

Ans. In the language set L each string is in the form $a^n b^{2n}$ where $n \geq 1$. Number of 'b' is double to number of 'a'. At the time of traversing a single 'a' from the input tape two z_1 as stack symbol will be pushed to the stack.

$\delta(q_0, a, z_0) \rightarrow (q_0, z_1z_1z_0)$.

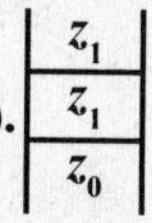

$\delta(q_0, a, z_1) \rightarrow (q_0, z_1z_1z_1)$.

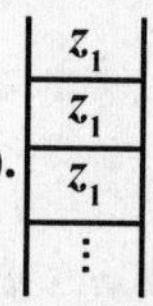

These two z_1 will be popped at the time of traversing two 'b'. [Single 'a' is equal to two 'b'].

The δ function for traversing 'b' will be

$\delta(q_0, b, z_1) \rightarrow (q_1, \lambda)$,
$\delta(q_1, b, z_1) \rightarrow (q_1, \lambda)$.

By the previous given δ functions all the input symbols of the input tape will be traversed. The PDA will be in state q_1 with stack top z_0.

If we have to design the PDA accepted by Empty stack the δ function will be

$\delta(q_1, \lambda, z_0) \rightarrow (q_1, \lambda)$.

If we have to design the PDA accepted by Final State the δ function will be

$\delta(q_1, \lambda, z_0) \rightarrow (q_f, z_0)$.

The PDA will be as follows:

$Q = \{q_0, q_1, q_f\}$
$\Sigma = \{a, b\}$
$\Gamma = \{z_0, z_1\}$
$q_0 = \{q_0\}$
$z_0 = \{z_0\}$
$F = \{q_f\}$.

The transitional function will be

$\delta(q_0, a, z_0) \rightarrow (q_0, z_1z_1z_0)$,
$\delta(q_0, a, z_1) \rightarrow (q_0, z_1z_1z_1)$,
$\delta(q_0, b, z_1) \rightarrow (q_1, \lambda)$,
$\delta(q_1, b, z_1) \rightarrow (q_1, \lambda)$,
$\delta(q_1, \lambda, z_0) \rightarrow (q_1, \lambda)$,
$\delta(q_1, \lambda, z_0) \rightarrow (q_f, z_0)$.

Q. Construct a PDA for the language $L = \{a^nCb^{2n}$, where $n \geq 1\}$.

Ans. In the language set number of 'b' is twice of 'a'. The 'C' is the middle element, which indicates the end of 'a' and beginning of 'b'. For each 'a', two z_1 are inserted in the stack, for each 'b', one z_1 is popped from the stack.

The transitional functions are

$\delta(q_0, a, z_0) \rightarrow (q_1, z_1z_1z_0)$,
$\delta(q_1, a, z_1) \rightarrow (q_1, z_1z_1z_1)$,
$\delta(q_1, C, z_1) \rightarrow (q_2, z_1)$,
$\delta(q_2, b, z_1) \rightarrow (q_2, \lambda)$,
$\delta(q_2, \lambda, z_0) \rightarrow (q_f, z_0)$ **accepted by final state,**
$\delta(q_2, \lambda, z_0) \rightarrow (q_2, \lambda)$ **accepted by empty stack.**

Q. Construct a PDA for the language $L = \{a^mb^n$ where $m \leq n$ and $m,n \geq 1\}$

Ans. In the language set number of 'a' is less than number of 'b'. At the time of traversing 'a', one z_1 is added to the stack. For m number of 'a', m number of z_1 are added to the stack. At the time of traversing m number of 'b', stack top is z_1, which is popped. If $n > m$, then at the time of traversing last $(n–m)$ number of 'b', stack top is z_0.

The transitional functions are

$\delta(q_0, a, z_0) \rightarrow (q_1, z_1z_0)$,
$\delta(q_1, a, z_1) \rightarrow (q_1, z_1z_1)$,
$\delta(q_1, b, z_1) \rightarrow (q_2, \lambda)$,
$\delta(q_2, b, z_1) \rightarrow (q_2, \lambda)$,
$\delta(q_2, b, z_0) \rightarrow (q_2, z_0)$,
$\delta(q_2, \lambda, z_0) \rightarrow (q_f, z_0)$ **accepted by final state,**
$\delta(q_2, \lambda, z_0) \rightarrow (q_2, \lambda)$ **accepted by empty stack.**

Q. Construct a PDA to accept the language $L = \{a^nb^mc^{n+m}$, where $n > 0$, $m > 0\}$

Ans. In the language set total number of 'c' is equal total number of 'a' and 'b'. The PDA can be designed in the following way, at the time of traversing n number of 'a', n number of 'z_1' are added to the stack and for traversing m number of 'b', m number of z_1 are added to the stack. At the time of traversing $(n + m)$ number of c all the z_1 are popped from the stack.

The transitional functions are:

$\delta(q_0, a, z_0) \rightarrow (q_1, z_1z_0)$,
$\delta(q_1, a, z_1) \rightarrow (q_1, z_1z_1)$,
$\delta(q_1, b, z_1) \rightarrow (q_2, z_1z_1)$,
$\delta(q_2, b, z_1) \rightarrow (q_2, z_1z_1)$,
$\delta(q_2, c, z_1) \rightarrow (q_3, \lambda)$,
$\delta(q_3, c, z_1) \rightarrow (q_3, \lambda)$,
$\delta(q_3, \lambda, z_0) \rightarrow (q_f, z_0)$ **accepted by final state,**
$\delta(q_3, \lambda, z_0) \rightarrow (q_3, \lambda)$ **accepted by empty stack.**

Q. Construct a PDA to accept the language $L = \{a^n b^m c^{n+m}$, where $n \geq 0, m > 0\}$

Ans. The string is same as the previous but in the language set number of 'a' may be zero. In the case when number of 'a' is zero, then the string starts from 'b'.

The transitional functions are

$\delta(q_0, a, z_0) \rightarrow (q_1, z_1z_0)$
$\delta(q_1, a, z_1) \rightarrow (q_1, z_1z_1)$
$\delta(q_1, b, z_1) \rightarrow (q_2, z_1z_1)$
$\delta(q_2, b, z_1) \rightarrow (q_2, z_1z_1)$
$\delta(q_0, b, z_0) \rightarrow (q_2, z_1z_0)$ **// If the string starts with b, i.e. there is no 'a'**
$\delta(q_2, c, z_1) \rightarrow (q_3, \lambda)$
$\delta(q_3, c, z_1) \rightarrow (q_3, \lambda)$
$\delta(q_3, \lambda, z_0) \rightarrow (q_f, z_0)$ **Accepted by final state.**
$\delta(q_3, \lambda, z_0) \rightarrow (q_3, \lambda)$ **Accepted by empty stack.**

Q. Construct a PDA to accept the language $L = \{a^n b^{n+m} c^m$, where $n,m > 0\}$

Ans. In the language set number of 'b' is total number of 'a' and 'c'. At the time of traversal of n number of 'a', n number of z_1 are pushed in the stack, at the time of traversal of n number of 'b', n number of z_1 are popped from the stack. At the time of traversal of rest m number of 'b', m number of z_2 are pushed into the stack, which are popped at the time of traversal of m number of 'c'.

The transitional functions are

$\delta(q_0, a, z_0) \rightarrow (q_1, z_1z_0)$,
$\delta(q_1, a, z_1) \rightarrow (q_1, z_1z_1)$,
$\delta(q_1, b, z_1) \rightarrow (q_2, \lambda)$,
$\delta(q_2, b, z_1) \rightarrow (q_2, \lambda)$,
$\delta(q_2, b, z_0) \rightarrow (q_3, z_2z_0)$,
$\delta(q_3, b, z_2) \rightarrow (q_3, z_2z_2)$,
$\delta(q_3, c, z_2) \rightarrow (q_4, \lambda)$,
$\delta(q_4, c, z_2) \rightarrow (q_4, \lambda)$,
$\delta(q_4, \lambda, z_0) \rightarrow (q_f, z_0)$ **accepted by final state,**
$\delta(q_4, \lambda, z_0) \rightarrow (q_4, \lambda)$ **accepted by empty stack.**

Q. Construct a PDA to accept the language $L = \{a^n b^{n+m} c^m$, where $n \geq 0, m > 0\}$

Ans. The string is same as the previous but in the language set number of 'a' may be zero. In the case when number of 'a' is zero, then the string starts from 'b'.

The transitional functions are

$\delta(q_0, a, z_0) \rightarrow (q_1, z_1z_0)$
$\delta(q_1, a, z_1) \rightarrow (q_1, z_1z_1)$,
$\delta(q_1, b, z_1) \rightarrow (q_2, \lambda)$,
$\delta(q_2, b, z_1) \rightarrow (q_2, \lambda)$,
$\delta(q_2, b, z_0) \rightarrow (q_3, z_2z_0)$,

$\delta(q_0, b, z_0) \rightarrow (q_3, z_2z_0)$ **// If the string starts with *b*, i.e. there is no '*a*',**
$\delta(q_3, b, z_2) \rightarrow (q_3, z_2z_2)$,
$\delta(q_3, c, z_2) \rightarrow (q_4, \lambda)$,
$\delta(q_4, c, z_2) \rightarrow (q_4, \lambda)$,
$\delta(q_4, \lambda, z_0) \rightarrow (q_f, z_0)$ **accepted by final state,**
$\delta(q_4, \lambda, z_0) \rightarrow (q_4, \lambda)$ **Accepted by empty stack.**

Q. Construct a PDA to accept the following language $L = \{a^{2n}b^n$, where $n > 0\}$

Ans. In the language set number of $2n$ number of '*a*' and *n* number of '*b*'. The PDA can be designed as follows – at the time of traversing first '*a*', two z_1 are added to the stack with a state changed from q_0 to q_1. At the time of traversing second '*a*' one z_1 is popped from the stack with a state change from q_1 to q_0. By this process after traversing $2n$ number of '*a*' only *n* number of z_1 exist in the stack. At the time of traversing first '*b*' stack top is z_1 and state q_0. Those z_1 are popped at the time of traversing *n* number of '*b*'.

The transitional functions are

$\delta(q_0, a, z_0) \rightarrow (q_1, z_1z_1z_0)$
$\delta(q_1, a, z_1) \rightarrow (q_0, \lambda)$
$\delta(q_0, a, z_1) \rightarrow (q_1, z_1z_1z_1)$
$\delta(q_0, b, z_1) \rightarrow (q_2, \lambda)$
$\delta(q_2, b, z_1) \rightarrow (q_2, \lambda)$
$\delta(q_2, \lambda, z_0) \rightarrow (q_f, z_0)$ **// accepted by final state,**
$\delta(q_2, \lambda, z_0) \rightarrow (q_2, \lambda)$ **// accepted by empty stack.**

Q. Construct a PDA to accept the language $L = \{a^nb^nc^m$, where $n,m \geq 1\}$ by empty stack and by final state.

Ans. The language is in the form $a^nb^nc^m$, **where $n,m \geq 1$.** In the language set number of '*a*' and number of '*b*' are same, but number of '*c*' is different. All the strings in the language set starts with *n* number of '*a*'s followed by *n* number of '*b*'s and ends with *m* number of '*c*'s. Here *m* and *n* both $\geq$ **1**, null string does not belongs to the language set.

The PDA for the language can be designed in the following way.

When traversing '*a*'s from the input tape, one by one z_1 are pushed in the stack. At the time of traversing '*b*'s, all the z_1's which were pushed into the stack are popped one by one. When first '*c*' will be traversed, at that time the machine is in state q_1 and stack top z_0. At the time of traversal of *m* number of 'c's, no operation is done on stack.

The transition function for constructing PDA for the string $a^nb^nc^m$ **where $m,n \geq 1$** are

$\delta(q_0, a, z_0) \rightarrow (q_0, z_1z_0)$
$\delta(q_0, a, z_1) \rightarrow (q_0, z_1z_1)$
$\delta(q_0, b, z_1) \rightarrow (q_1, \lambda)$
$\delta(q_1, b, z_1) \rightarrow (q_1, \lambda)$
$\delta(q_1, c, z_0) \rightarrow (q_1, z_0)$
$\delta(q_1, \lambda, z_0) \rightarrow (q_1, \lambda)$ **Accepted by empty stack,**
$\delta(q_1, \lambda, z_0) \rightarrow (q_f, z_0)$ **Accepted by final state.**

Q. Construct a PDA to accept the language $L = \{a^n b^m c^n$, where $n,m \geq 1\}$ by empty stack and by final state.

Ans: The language is in the form $a^n b^m c^n$, **where** $n,m \geq 1$. In the language set, number of '*a*'s are equal to number of '*c*'s. In the language set, '*a*'s are separate with '*c*'s by *m* number of '*b*'s. As $m,n \geq 1$, null string does not belong to the language set. In the language set number of '*a*' are equal to number of '*c*' but not with number of '*b*'.

The PDA can be designed in the following way:

When traversing '*a*'s from the input tape, one by one z_1 are pushed in the stack. When the first '*b*' is read by the input head, the machine is in state q_0 and stack top z_1. One state change has occurred. (If after '*b*' again '*a*' comes as input, the language is in wrong format. But that '*a*' will also be traversed as there will be a function $\delta(q_0, a, z_1) \rightarrow (q_0, z_1z_1)$.

to traverse that '*a*'. To avoid this mismatch and to guarantee that the PDA is only for accepting $a^n b^m c^n$, **where** $n,m \geq 1$, the state change is required.) At the time of traversing '*b*', no operation is done on the stack.

When '*c*' will going to be traversed, the machine is in state q_1, with stack top z_1. The stack top is popped and a state change has occurred. (To avoid appearance of '*b*' after '*c*').

The transition function for constructing PDA for the string $a^n b^n c^m$ **where** $m,n \geq 1$ will be

$\delta(q_0, a, z_0) \rightarrow (q_0, z_1z_0)$,
$\delta(q_0, a, z_1) \rightarrow (q_0, z_1z_1)$,
$\delta(q_0, b, z_1) \rightarrow (q_1, z_1)$,
$\delta(q_1, b, z_1) \rightarrow (q_1, z_1)$,
$\delta(q_1, c, z_1) \rightarrow (q_2, \lambda)$,
$\delta(q_2, c, z_1) \rightarrow (q_2, \lambda)$,
$\delta(q_2, \lambda, z_0) \rightarrow (q_2, \lambda)$ **accepted by empty stack,**
$\delta(q_2, \lambda, z_0) \rightarrow (q_f, z_0)$ **accepted by final state.**

Q. Construct a PDA to accept the language $L = \{w$, where number of 'a' + number of 'b' = number of 'c'$\}$

Ans. According to the given specification any string belong to the language set consists of any combination of '*a*', '*b*' and '*c*' and number of '*c*' is equal to number of '*a*' and number of '*b*'. In the string '*a*', '*b*' and '*c*' can occur in any sequence with fulfilling the given condition.

The transitional functions are

$\delta(q_0, a, z_0) \rightarrow (q_0, z_1z_0)$ **// 'a' traversed first or when the stack contain only z_0**
$\delta(q_0, b, z_0) \rightarrow (q_0, z_1z_0)$ **// 'b' traversed first or when the stack contain only z_0**
$\delta(q_0, c, z_0) \rightarrow (q_0, z_2z_0)$ **// 'c' traversed first or when the stack contain only z_0**
$\delta(q_0, c, z_2) \rightarrow (q_0, z_2z_2)$ **// 'c' traversed after 'c'**
$\delta(q_0, a, z_1) \rightarrow (q_0, z_1z_1)$ **// 'a' traversed after 'a' or 'b'**
$\delta(q_0, b, z_1) \rightarrow (q_0, z_1z_1)$ **// 'b' traversed after 'a' or 'b'**
$\delta(q_0, c, z_1) \rightarrow (q_0, \lambda)$ **// 'c' traversed after 'a' or 'b'**
$\delta(q_0, a, z_2) \rightarrow (q_0, \lambda)$ **// 'a' traversed after 'c'**
$\delta(q_0, b, z_2) \rightarrow (q_0, \lambda)$ **// 'b' traversed after 'c'**
$\delta(q_0, \lambda, z_0) \rightarrow (q_f, z_0)$ **// accepted by final state,**
$\delta(q_0, \lambda, z_0) \rightarrow (q_0, \lambda)$ **// accepted by empty stack.**

6.4 DETERMINISTIC PDA AND NON-DETERMINISTIC PDA

Q. How many types of PDA are there? Describe each of them by suitable example.

Ans: There are two types of PDA:

(a) Deterministic PDA (DPDA)
(b) Non-Deterministic PDA (NPDA)

(a) Deterministic PDA (DPDA): A PDA is said to be a DPDA if all derivations in the design give only single move.

If a PDA being in a state with a single input and single stack symbol gives a single move, then the PDA is called Deterministic PDA.

As an example for $L = \{a^n b^n$, where $n \geq 1\}$ can be designed a DPDA if the transitional functions are as following.

$$\delta(q_0, a, z_0) \rightarrow (q_0, z_1z_0),$$
$$\delta(q_0, a, z_1) \rightarrow (q_0, z_1z_1),$$
$$\delta(q_0, b, z_1) \rightarrow (q_1, \lambda),$$
$$\delta(q_1, b, z_1) \rightarrow (q_1, \lambda),$$
$$\delta(q_1, \lambda, z_0) \rightarrow (q_1, \lambda) \text{ accepted by empty stack,}$$
$$\delta(q_1, \lambda, z_0) \rightarrow (q_f, z_0) \text{ accepted by final state.}$$

In the previous PDA, in a single state with a single input and single stack symbol there is only one move. So the PDA is deterministic.

(b) Non-Deterministic PDA (NPDA): A PDA is called non-deterministic if one of the derivations generates more than one move.

If a PDA being in a state with a single input and single stack symbol gives more than one move for any of its transitional functions, then the PDA is called Non-Deterministic PDA.

Q. Design a non-deterministic PDA for accepting the string $\{WW^R$ where $W \in (a,b)^+$ and W^R is the reverse of $W\}$ by empty stack and by final state.

Ans. The W is a string consists of 'a' and 'b'. The W^R is the reverse string of W. Let $W = abaa$, then W^R will be *aaba*. WW^R will be *abaaaaba*. Traversing input symbol 'a' from the input tape, z_1 will be pushed into the stack and traversing input symbol 'b' from the input tape, z_2 will be pushed into the stack. When W^R will start, for the traversal of first symbol the state of the PDA will be changed and the stack top will be popped. From the next input symbols belong to W^R the stack top will be popped.

But here is a problem. In the PDA it is not assigned where W is ended and W^R is started. The PDA will traverse the total string assuming it as W. Some attempt has been done to differentiate W and W^R by traversing a λ symbol and changing the state in between W and W^R. But this is also wrong, as all the input symbols are placed on the input tape from left to right in a continuous fashion. There is no gap in between two input symbols, as they are placed one by one in each square from left to right on the input tape.

From the above discussion it is clear that a Deterministic PDA cannot be designed for WW^R.

But this is possible for Non-deterministic PDA. Our problem is to find the middle of the string where W ends and W^R starts. In the string where consecutive two 'a' and two 'b' appear, that may be the middle of the string, because the last alphabet of W is the first alphabet of W^R. Make two transitional functions when stack top is z_1 and 'a' is traversed as input and stack top is z_2 and 'b' is traversed as input. (All the other δ functions are same as WCW^R). The PDA for accepting the string $WW^R/W \in (a,b)^+$ and W^R is the reverse of W is

$$Q = \{q_0, q_1, q_2, q_f\}$$
$$\Sigma = \{a, b\}$$
$$\Gamma = \{z_0, z_1, z_2\}$$
$$q_0 = \{q_0\}$$
$$z_0 = \{z_0\}$$
$$F = \{q_f\}.$$

The transitional function will be

$\boldsymbol{\delta(q_0, a, z_0) \rightarrow (q_1, z_1z_0)}$
$\boldsymbol{\delta(q_0, b, z_0) \rightarrow (q_1, z_2z_0)}$
$\boldsymbol{\delta(q_1, a, z_1) \rightarrow (q_1, z_1z_1), (q_2, \lambda)}$
$\boldsymbol{\delta(q_1, b, z_1) \rightarrow (q_1, z_2z_1)}$
$\boldsymbol{\delta(q_1, a, z_2) \rightarrow (q_1, z_1z_2)}$
$\boldsymbol{\delta(q_1, b, z_2) \rightarrow (q_1, z_2z_2), (q_2, \lambda)}$
$\boldsymbol{\delta(q_2, a, z_1) \rightarrow (q_2, \lambda)}$
$\boldsymbol{\delta(q_2, b, z_2) \rightarrow (q_2, \lambda)}$
$\boldsymbol{\delta(q_2, \lambda, z_0) \rightarrow (q_2, \lambda)}$ **accepted by empty stack,**
$\boldsymbol{\delta(q_2, \lambda, z_0) \rightarrow (q_f, z_0)}$ **accepted by final state.**

Consider a string abbbba. The string is in the form WW^R, where W = abb.

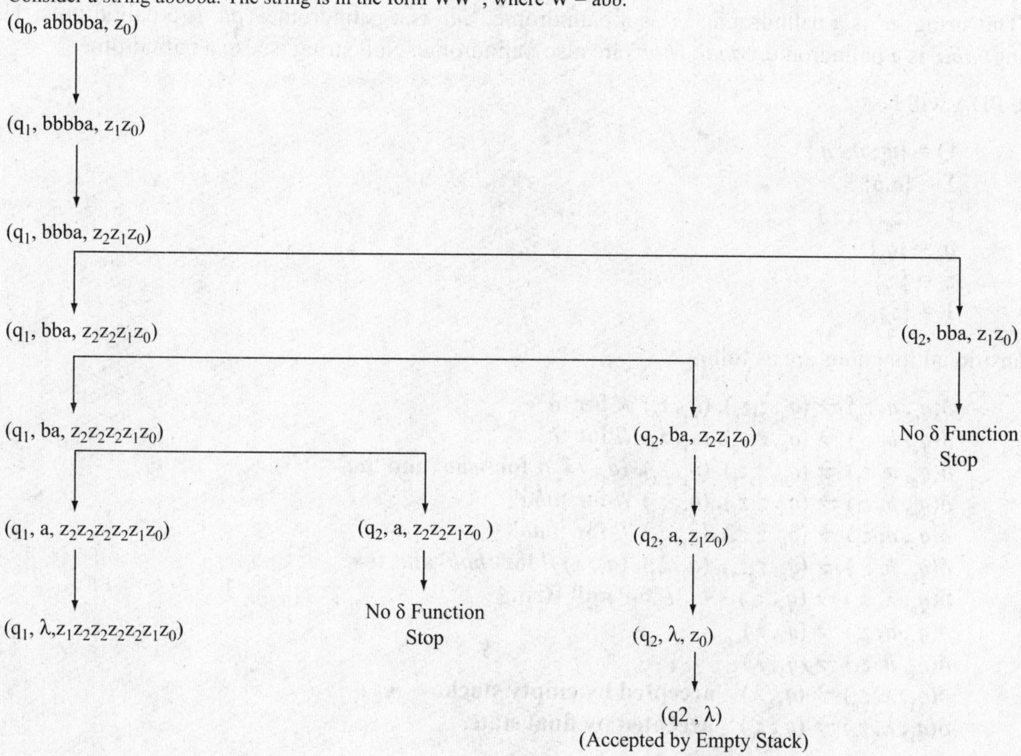

Q. Design a non-deterministic PDA for accepting the string $\{WW^R$ where $W \in (a,b)^*$ and W^R is the reverse of $W\}$ by empty stack and by final state.

Ans. Null string may belong to the Language set. The PDA will be designed in such a way that null string can be accepted by the PDA. The transitional functions will be:

$\delta(q_0, a, z_0) \rightarrow (q_0, z_1z_0)$,
$\delta(q_0, b, z_0) \rightarrow (q_0, z_2z_0)$,
$\delta(q_0, a, z_1) \rightarrow (q_0, z_1z_1), (q_1, \lambda)$,
$\delta(q_0, b, z_1) \rightarrow (q_0, z_2z_1)$,
$\delta(q_0, a, z_2) \rightarrow (q_0, z_1z_2)$,
$\delta(q_0, b, z_2) \rightarrow (q_0, z_2z_2), (q_1, \lambda)$,
$\delta(q_1, a, z_1) \rightarrow (q_1, \lambda)$,
$\delta(q_1, b, z_2) \rightarrow (q_1, \lambda)$,
$\delta(q_0, \lambda, z_0) \rightarrow (q_1, \lambda)$ **// this function is for accepting null string,**
$\delta(q_1, \lambda, z_0) \rightarrow (q_1, \lambda)$ **accepted by empty stack,**
$\delta(q_1, \lambda, z_0) \rightarrow (q_f, z_0)$ **accepted by final state.**

Q. Design a Non-Deterministic PDA for accepting the string L = {(Set of all palindromes over a, b)} by empty stack and by final state.

Ans. A string read from left to right and right to left gives the same result is called palindrome. Palindrome can be of two types (a) Odd Palindrome (b) Even Palindrome. Odd palindromes are those where number of characters is odd and even palindromes are those where number of characters is even.

The string '*a*' is a palindrome, '*b*' is a palindrome. '*aa*' is a palindrome, '*bb*' is a palindrome. The string '*aba*' is a palindrome, '*aaa*', '*bbb*' are also palindrome. Null string is also a palindrome.

The PDA will be

$Q = \{q_0, q_1, q_f\}$
$\Sigma = \{a,b\}$
$\Gamma = \{z_0, z_1, z_2\}$
$q_0 = \{q_0\}$
$z_0 = \{z_0\}$
$F = \{z_f\}$.

Transitional functions are as follows

$\delta(q_0, a, z_0) \rightarrow (q_0, z_1z_0), (q_1, z_0)$ **// for '*a*'**
$\delta(q_0, b, z_0) \rightarrow (q_0, z_2z_0), (q_1, z_0)$ **// for '*b*'**
$\delta(q_0, a, z_1) \rightarrow (q_0, z_1z_1), (q_1, z_1), (q_1, \lambda)$ **// for '*aaa*' and '*aa*'**
$\delta(q_0, b, z_1) \rightarrow (q_0, z_2z_1), (q_1, z_1)$ **// for '*aba*'**
$\delta(q_0, a, z_2) \rightarrow (q_0, z_1z_2), (q_1, z_2)$ **// for '*bab*'**
$\delta(q_0, b, z_2) \rightarrow (q_0, z_2z_2), (q_1, z_2), (q_1, \lambda)$ **// for '*bbb*' and '*bb*'**
$\delta(q_0, \lambda, z_0) \rightarrow (q_1, z_0)$ **// for null string**
$\delta(q_1, a, z_1) \rightarrow (q_1, \lambda)$
$\delta(q_1, b, z_2) \rightarrow (q_1, \lambda)$
$\delta(q_1, \lambda, z_0) \rightarrow (q_1, \lambda)$ **accepted by empty stack,**
$\delta(q_1, \lambda, z_0) \rightarrow (q_f, z_0)$ **accepted by final state.**

6.5 PUSHDOWN AUTOMATA FROM CONTEXT FREE GRAMMAR

Q. How to construct an equivalent PDA of a context free grammar.

Ans.

Step I: Convert the PDA into Greibach Normal Form (GNF).

Step II: First the start symbol S of the CFG is put to the stack by transition function

$\delta(q_0, \epsilon, z_0) \rightarrow (q_1, Sz_0)$

Step III: For a production in the form $\{NT_1\} \rightarrow \{\text{Single T}\}\{\text{String of NT}\}$, the transitional function will be

$\delta(q_1, \text{T}, \text{NT}_1) \rightarrow (q_1, \text{String of NT})$.

Step IV: For a production in the form $\{NT_1\} \rightarrow \{\text{Single T}\}$, the transitional function will be $\delta(q_1, \text{T}, \text{NT}_1) \rightarrow (q_1, \lambda)$.

Step V: For accepting a string two transitional functions are added, one for accepted by empty stack and one for accepted by final state.

Q. Construct a PDA that accept the language generated by the following grammar

$S \rightarrow aB$

$B \rightarrow bA/\ b$

$A \rightarrow aB$

Show an ID for the string *abab* for the PDA generated.

Ans.

The Context Free Grammar is in GNF.

First the start symbol S is pushed into the stack by the following production

$\delta(q_0, \epsilon, z_0) \rightarrow (q_1, Sz_0)$.

For the production $S \rightarrow aB$ the transitional function is

$\delta(q_1, a, S) \rightarrow (q_1, B)$.

For the production $A \rightarrow aB$ the transitional function is

$\delta(q_1, a, A) \rightarrow (q_1, B)$.

For the production $B \rightarrow bA/b$ the transitional function is

$\delta(q_1, b, B) \rightarrow (q_1, A), (q_1, \lambda)$.

So, the PDA for the above CFG is

$Q = \{q_0, q_1\}$

$\Sigma = \{a, b\}$

$\Gamma = \{z_0, S, A, B\}$

$q_0 = \{q_0\}$

$z_0 = \{z_0\}$

$F = \{\varnothing\}$

δ functions are defined as follows:

$\delta(q_0, \epsilon, z_0) \rightarrow (q_1, Sz_0)$
$\delta(q_1, a, S) \rightarrow (q_1, B)$
$\delta(q_1, a, A) \rightarrow (q_1, B)$
$\delta(q_1, a, A) \rightarrow (q_1, B)$
$\delta(q_1, b, B) \rightarrow (q_1, A), (q_1, \lambda)$
$\delta(q_1, \lambda, z_0) \rightarrow (q_f, z_0)$ **// accepted by final state**
$\delta(q_1, \lambda, z_0) \rightarrow (q_1, \lambda)$ **// accepted by empty stack**

Id for the string *abab*.

$\delta(q_0, \varepsilon, z_0) \rightarrow (q_1, Sz_0)$
$\delta(q_1, abab, S) \rightarrow (q_1, Bz_0)$
$\delta(q_1, bab, B) \rightarrow (q_1, Az_0)$
$\delta(q_1, ab, A) \rightarrow (q_1, Bz_0)$
$\delta(q_1, b, B) \rightarrow (q_1, z_0)$
$\delta(q_1, \lambda, z_0) \rightarrow (q_f, z_0)$ // accepted by final state,
$\delta(q_1, \lambda, z_0) \rightarrow (q_1, \lambda)$ // accepted by empty stack.

(*The process is very easy. First try to generate the string from the given grammar by left most derivation. Then according to the non terminal symbols replaced use the particular transitional function to give the ID*

For the previous case the string 'abab' *is generated like the derivation(Left Most) given below* S → a<u>B</u> → ab<u>A</u> → aba<u>B</u> → abab

First transitional function is adding S *in the stack. After that* S *is replaced by* B *for the input* 'a' *using the transitional function* $\delta(q_1, a, S) \rightarrow (q_1, B)$

The process continues like this till the end of the string.)

Q. Construct an equivalent PDA for the following Context Free Grammar.
$S \rightarrow aAB/bBA$,
$A \rightarrow bS/a$
$B \rightarrow aS/b$.

Show an ID for the string *abbaaabbbbab* for the PDA generated with stack description.

Ans. The CFG is in GNF.
First the start symbol *S* is pushed into the stack by the following production

$\delta(q_0, \epsilon, z_0) \rightarrow (q_1, Sz_0)$.

For the production $S \rightarrow aAB$, the transitional function is

$\delta(q_1, a, S) \rightarrow (q_1, AB)$.

For the production $S \rightarrow bBA$, the transitional function is

$\delta(q_1, b, S) \rightarrow (q_1, BA)$.

For the production $A \rightarrow bS$, the transitional function is

$\delta(q_1, b, A) \rightarrow (q_1, S)$.

For the production $B \rightarrow aS$, the transitional function is

$$\delta(q_1, a, B) \rightarrow (q_1, S).$$

For the production $A \rightarrow a$, the transitional function is

$$\delta(q_1, a, A) \rightarrow (q_1, \lambda).$$

For the production $B \rightarrow b$, the transitional function is

$$\delta(q_1, b, B) \rightarrow (q_1, \lambda).$$

For acceptance transitional function is

$\delta(q_1, \lambda, z_0) \rightarrow (q_f, z_0)$ **//accepted by final state,**
$\delta(q_1, \lambda, z_0) \rightarrow (q_1, \lambda)$ **//accepted by empty stack.**

Id for the string *abbaaabbbbab*

Transition	Stack
$\delta(q_0, \epsilon, z_0) \rightarrow (q_1, Sz_0)$	S, z_0
$\delta(q_1, abbaaabbbbab, S) \rightarrow (q_1, AB)$	A, B, z_0
$\delta(q_1, bbaaabbbbab, A) \rightarrow (q_1, S)$	S, B, z_0
$\delta(q_1, baaabbbbab, S) \rightarrow (q_1, BA)$	B, A, B, z_0
$\delta(q_1, aaabbbbab, B) \rightarrow (q_1, S)$	S, A, B, z_0
$\delta(q_1, aabbbbab, S) \rightarrow (q_1, AB)$	A, B, A, B, z_0
$\delta(q_1, abbbbab, A) \rightarrow (q_1, \lambda)$	B, A, B, z_0
$\delta(q_1, bbbbab, B) \rightarrow (q_1, \lambda)$	A, B, z_0
$\delta(q_1, bbbab, A) \rightarrow (q_1, S)$	S, B, z_0
$\delta(q_1, bbab, S) \rightarrow (q_1, BA)$	B, A, B, z_0
$\delta(q_1, bab, B) \rightarrow (q_1, \lambda)$	A, B, z_0
$\delta(q_1, ab, A) \rightarrow (q_1, \lambda)$	B, z_0
$\delta(q_1, b, B) \rightarrow (q_1, \lambda)$	z_0

$\delta(q_1, \lambda, z_0) \rightarrow (q_f, z_0)$ **//accepted by final state,**
$\delta(q_1, \lambda, z_0) \rightarrow (q_1, \lambda)$ **//accepted by empty stack.**

Q. Construct an equivalent PDA for the following CFG.

$S \rightarrow 0BB$

$B \rightarrow$ 0S/1S/0

Show an ID for the string 010000 for the PDA generated.

Ans. First the start symbol S is pushed into the stack by the following production

$\delta(q_0, \in, z_0) \rightarrow (q_1, Sz_0)$.

For the production $S \rightarrow 0BB$, the transitional function is

$\delta(q_1, 0, S) \rightarrow (q_1, BB)$.

For the production $B \rightarrow 0S$, the transitional function is

$\delta(q_1, 0, B) \rightarrow (q_1, S)$.

For the production $B \rightarrow 1S$, the transitional function is

$\delta(q_1, 1, B) \rightarrow (q_1, S)$.

For the production B $\rightarrow$ 0, the transitional function is

$\delta(q_1, 0, B) \rightarrow (q_1, \lambda)$.

For acceptance transitional function is

$\delta(q_1, \lambda, z_0) \rightarrow (q_f, z_0)$ **//accepted by final state,**
$\delta(q_1, \lambda, z_0) \rightarrow (q_1, \lambda)$ **//accepted by empty stack.**

Id for the string 010000

$(q_0, 010000, z_0) \rightarrow (q_1, 010000, Sz_0) \rightarrow (q_1, 10000, BBz_0) \rightarrow (q_1, 0000, SBz_0) \rightarrow$
$(q_1, 000, BBBz_0) \rightarrow (q_1, 00, BBz_0) \rightarrow (q_1, 0, Bz_0) \rightarrow (q_1, \lambda, z_0) \rightarrow (q_1, \lambda)$ //By empty stack.

Q. Construct an equivalent PDA for the following CFG.

$S \rightarrow aA$

$A \rightarrow aABC/bB/a$

$C \rightarrow c$

Show an ID for the string *aabbbc* for the PDA generated.

Ans.

First the start symbol S is pushed into the stack by the following production

$\delta(q_0, \in, z_0) \rightarrow (q_1, Sz_0)$

For the production $S \rightarrow aA$, the transitional function is

$\delta(q_1, a, S) \rightarrow (q_1, A)$.

For the production A $\rightarrow$ aABC, the transitional function is

$\delta(q_1, a, A) \rightarrow (q_1, ABC)$.

For the production $A \rightarrow bB$, the transitional function is

$\boldsymbol{\delta(q_1, b, A) \rightarrow (q_1, B)}$.

For the production $A \rightarrow a$, the transitional function is

$\boldsymbol{\delta(q_1, a, A) \rightarrow (q_1, \lambda)}$.

For the production $C \rightarrow c$, the transitional function is

$\boldsymbol{\delta(q_1, c, C) \rightarrow (q_1, \lambda)}$.

For acceptance transitional function is

$\boldsymbol{\delta(q_1, \lambda, z_0) \rightarrow (q_f, z_0)}$ **//accepted by final state,**
$\boldsymbol{\delta(q_1, \lambda, z_0) \rightarrow (q_1, \lambda)}$ **//accepted by empty stack.**

Id for the string *aabbbc*

$(q_0, aabbbc, z_0) \rightarrow (q_1, aabbbc, Sz_0) \rightarrow (q_1, abbbc, Az_0) \rightarrow (q_1, bbbc, ABCz_0) \rightarrow (q_1, bbc, BBC) \rightarrow (q_1, bc, BC) \rightarrow (q_1, c, C) \rightarrow (q_1, \lambda, z_0) \rightarrow (q_f, z_0)$ // Accepted by final state

Q. Construct an equivalent PDA for the following CFG.
$\boldsymbol{S \rightarrow aSbb/aab}$

Show an ID for the string *aaabbb* for the PDA generated.

Ans. The given grammar is not in GNF. First we need to convert the grammar into GNF. Replace '*b*' by *B* and '*a*' by *A*. The converted grammar in GNF is

$S \rightarrow aSBB/aAB$
$A \rightarrow a$
$B \rightarrow b$

Now the grammar can be easily converted into PDA.

The transitional functions for the PDA accepted by the language generated by the grammar are

$\boldsymbol{\delta(q_0, \epsilon, z_0) \rightarrow (q_1, Sz_0)}$
$\boldsymbol{\delta(q_1, a, S) \rightarrow (q_1, SBB)}$
$\boldsymbol{\delta(q_1, a, S) \rightarrow (q_1, AB)}$
$\boldsymbol{\delta(q_1, a, A) \rightarrow (q_1, \lambda)}$
$\boldsymbol{\delta(q_1, a, B) \rightarrow (q_1, \lambda)}$
$\boldsymbol{\delta(q_1, \lambda, z_0) \rightarrow (q_f, z_0)}$ **//accepted by final state**
$\boldsymbol{\delta(q_1, \lambda, z_0) \rightarrow (q_1, \lambda)}$ **//accepted by empty stack.**

ID for the string *aaabbb*

$\delta(q_0, aaabbb, z_0) \rightarrow (q_1, aaabbb, Sz_0) \rightarrow (q_1, aabbb, SBBz_0) \rightarrow (q_1, abbb, ABBBz_0) \rightarrow (q_1, bbb, BBBz_0) \rightarrow (q_1, bb, BBz_0) \rightarrow (q_1, b, Bz_0) \rightarrow (q_1, \lambda, z_0) \rightarrow (q_f, z_0)$ //accepted by final state

6.6 GRAPHICAL NOTATION FOR PDA

Q. How a PDA can be denoted by graphical notation?

Ans. The mathematical notation for a PDA is (Q, Σ, Γ, δ, q_0, z_0, F). In a PDA the transitional function δ consists of three touples, first is a present state, second is present input and the third is stack top symbol; which generates one next state and stack symbol(s) if a symbol is pushed into the stack or ε, if the top most symbol is popped from the stack.

In the graphical notation of PDA there are states. Among them a circle with an arrow indicates a beginning state and a state with double circle indicates a final state. The state transitions are denoted by arrow. The labels of the state transitions consists of input symbol, stack top symbol and the stack top symbol which is added after the transitions or null is a symbol is popped.

Q. Construct a PDA with graphical notation to accept $L = (a, b)^*$ with equal number of '*a*' and '*b*', i.e. $n_a(L) = n_b(L)$ by final state.

Ans. At the beginning of transition the PDA is in state q_0 with stack to z_0. The string may start with '*a*' or '*b*'. If the string start with '*a*', one z_1 is pushed into the stack. If the string start with '*b*', one z_2 is pushed into the stack. If '*b*' is traversed after '*a*', and stack top is z_1, and that stack top is popped. If '*a*' is traversed after '*b*', and stack top is z_2, and that stack top is popped. If '*a*' is traversed after '*a*', and stack top is z_1, and one 'z_1' is pushed into the stack. If '*b*' is traversed after '*b*', and stack top is z_2, and one 'z_2' is pushed into the stack.

The PDA in graphical notation is

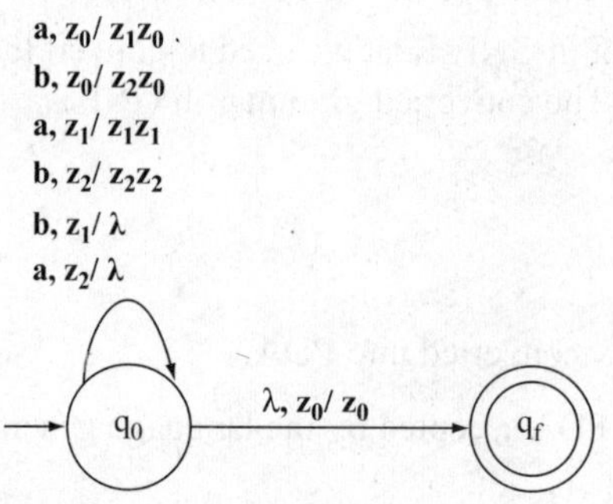

Q. Construct a PDA with graphical notation to accept the language L = {WCW^R, where $W \in$ (a,b)$^+$ and W^R is the reverse of W} by Final state.

Ans. At the beginning of the transition the machine is in state q_0 and stack top symbol z_0. If it gets input symbol '*a*', one z_1 is pushed into the stack, if it gets input symbol '*b*', one z_2 is pushed into the stack and state is changed from q_0 to q_1. In state q_1 if it gets input '*a*' and stack top z_1 or z_2 another z_1 or z_2 is pushed into the stack, respectively. In state q_1 if it gets input '*b*' with stack top z_2 or z_1, another z_2 or z_1 is pushed into the stack, respectively.

The C is the symbol which differentiate W with W^R. Before C, W is traversed. Therefore, at the time of traversing C, stack top symbol may be z_1 or z_2. In state q_1 if the PDA gets C as input and stack top

z_1 or z_2, no operation is done on the stack, only state is changed from q_1 to q_2. After C the string W^R is traversed. If the machine gets 'a' as input, stack top must be z_1. And that z_1 is popped from the stack top. If the machine gets 'b' as input, stack top must be z_2. And that z_2 is popped from the stack top. The state is not changed. By this process the whole string WCW^R is traversed. In state q_2 if the machine gets no input but stack top z_0, the machine goes to its final state q_f.

The graphical notation for the PDA is

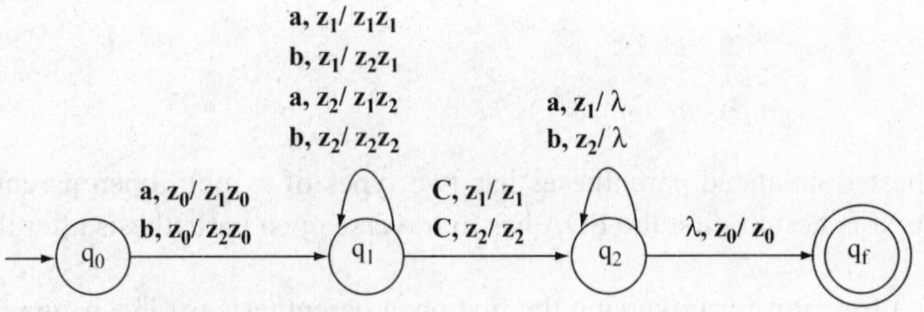

WHAT WE HAVE LEARNED SO FAR

1. PDA (in short PDA) is the machine format of CFL.
2. The mechanical diagram of a PDA contains Input tape, Reading head, Finite control and a stack.
3. A PDA consists of 7-touple M = (Q, Σ, Γ, δ, q_0, z_0, F), where Q, Σ, q_0 and F has their original meaning, Γ is finite set of stack symbols and z_0 is the stack bottom symbol.
4. In PDA transitional function δ is in the form $Q \times (\Sigma \cup \{\lambda\}) \times \Gamma \rightarrow (Q, \Gamma)$.
5. Instantaneous Description (ID) remembers the information of state and stack content at a given instance of time.
6. There are two ways to declare a string accepted by a PDA (a) accepted by empty stack (store) (b) accepted by final state.
7. A string is declared accepted by a PDA by empty stack if the string is totally traversed and the stack is empty.
8. A string is declared accepted by a PDA by Final state if the string is totally traversed and the machine reaches to its final state.
9. A string accepted by a PDA by empty stack if and only if the language is accepted by that PDA by final state.
10. If a PDA being in a state with a single input and single stack symbol gives a single move, then the PDA is called Deterministic PDA.
11. If a PDA being in a state with a single input and single stack symbol gives more than one move for any of its transitional functions, then the PDA is called Non Deterministic PDA.
12. From Context free grammar NPDA can be directly constructed.

SOLVED PROBLEMS

1. Design a PDA to accept the language of nested balanced parentheses.[Where number of opening and close parenthesis is greater than 0]

Ans. Nested balanced parenthesis is in the form ((())). More precisely

(
  (
    (
)
)
)

This type of nested balanced parentheses has two types of symbol open parenthesis '(' and close parenthesis ')'. As it is nested, first the PDA has to traverse open parenthesis after that the close parenthesis.

The transitional function for traversing the first open parenthesis is (The beginning state is q_0, input symbol is '(' and stack top is z_0.)

$$\delta(q_0, (, z_0) \rightarrow (q_0, z_1z_0).$$

From then on the state is q_0, input symbol is '(' [if number of open parenthesis is > 1] and stack top is z_0. The transitional function for traversing the next open parenthesis is

$$\delta(q_0, (, z_1) \rightarrow (q_0, z_1z_1).$$

By using the previous transitional function all the remaining open parenthesis will be traversed.

After traversing all open parentheses the PDA will get the first close parenthesis. At that time the state is q_0, input symbol is ')', and stack top is z_1. After getting the ')' as an input symbol the stack top [here z_1] will be popped from the stack and state will be changed to q_1. The transitional function is

$$\delta(q_0,), z_1) \rightarrow (q_1, \lambda).$$

After that the state is q_1, input symbol is ')' and stack top is z_1. (If the string contain multiple open and close parentheses). The transitional function is

$$\delta(q_1,), z_1) \rightarrow (q_1, \lambda).$$

When all input symbols are traversed the PDA is in state q_1, input symbol is λ and stack top is z_0.

If we have to design the PDA accepted by empty stack the δ function will be

$$\delta(q_1, \lambda, z_0) \rightarrow (q_1, \lambda).$$

If we have to design the PDA accepted by final State the δ function will be

$$\delta(q_1, \lambda, z_0) \rightarrow (q_f, z_0).$$

The transitional functions for the PDA is

$$\delta(q_0, (, z_0) \rightarrow (q_0, z_1z_0)$$
$$\delta(q_0, (, z_1) \rightarrow (q_0, z_1z_1)$$
$$\delta(q_0,), z_1) \rightarrow (q_1, \lambda)$$
$$\delta(q_1,), z_1) \rightarrow (q_1, \lambda)$$

$\boldsymbol{\delta(q_1, \lambda, z_0) \rightarrow (q_1, \lambda)}$ **// accepted by empty stack,**
$\boldsymbol{\delta(q_1, \lambda, z_0) \rightarrow (q_f, z_0)}$ **// accepted by final state.**

2. Design a PDA to accept the language of balanced parentheses. (Where number of opening and close parenthesis is greater than 0.)

Ans. There are two types of parentheses – open parentheses and close parentheses. Balanced parenthesis means for each open parenthesis there is a close parenthesis. It may be nested like **((( )))** or may be non nested like **(( ) ( ))** or **( )( )( )** or any other form. But for each open parenthesis there is a close parenthesis. (The definition that balanced parenthesis means equal number of open and close parentheses is wrong. As an example, **) ( )( ) (** is not a balanced parenthesis). The string must start with an open parenthesis and after that open parenthesis or close parenthesis can appear, but for any position of the string, number of open parenthesis is greater than or equal to number of close parenthesis.

The transitional function for traversing the first open parenthesis is (The beginning state is q_0, input symbol is '(' and stack top is z_0.)

$$\delta(q_0, (, z_0) \rightarrow (q_1, z_1z_0) \text{ (As null string is not accepted by the PDA).}$$

After the first open parenthesis, there may be open parenthesis or close parenthesis. If open parenthesis is to be traversed then a z_1 is added at the stack top. The transitional function is

$$\delta(q_1, (, z_1) \rightarrow (q_1, z_1z_1).$$

If close parenthesis is to be traversed then one z_1 is popped from the stack top. The transitional function is

$$\delta(q_1,), z_1) \rightarrow (q_1, \lambda).$$

It may happen that the state is q_1, and stack top is z_0 and the input symbol is '('. [As an example for the case (())()] The transitional function for the case is

$$\delta(q_1, (, z_0) \rightarrow (q_1, z_1z_0).$$

(But this type of case can not appear –where the state is q_1, and stack top is z_0 and the input symbol is ')'.)

If we have to design the PDA accepted by empty stack the δ function is

$$\delta(q_1, \lambda, z_0) \rightarrow (q_1, \lambda).$$

If we have to design the PDA accepted by final state the δ function is

$$\delta(q_1, \lambda, z_0) \rightarrow (q_f, z_0).$$

The transitional functions for the entire PDA is

$$\delta(q_0, (, z_0) \rightarrow (q_1, z_1z_0)$$

$$\delta(q_1, (, z_1) \rightarrow (q_1, z_1z_1)$$
$$\delta(q_1,), z_1) \rightarrow (q_1, \lambda)$$

$$\delta(q_1, (, z_0) \rightarrow (q_1, z_1z_0)$$

$\boldsymbol{\delta(q_1, \lambda, z_0) \rightarrow (q_1, \lambda)}$ **// accepted by empty stack,**
$\boldsymbol{\delta(q_1, \lambda, z_0) \rightarrow (q_f, z_0)}$ **// accepted by final state.**

3. Design a PDA to accept the language $L = a^m b^n c^{m-n}$, where $m >= n$ and $m, n > 0$

Ans. The language consists of '*a*', '*b*' and '*c*'. Here in every string all '*a*' will appear before '*b*' and after '*b*', '*c*' will appear. Number of '*c*' is the subtraction of number of '*a*' and number of '*b*'. At the beginning the machine is in state q_0 with stack top z_0 and input is '*a*'. After traversing, the machine will add z_1 in the stack. The transitional function is

$$\delta(q_0, a, z_0) \rightarrow (q_0, z_1z_0).$$

If number of '*a*' is greater than one then the machine have to traverse '*a*' with state q_0 and stack top z_1. Another z_1 is added to the stack top. The transitional function is

$$\delta(q_0, a, z_1) \rightarrow (q_0, z_1z_1).$$

After traversal of all '*a*', '*b*' will appear. When '*b*' will come at that time state is q_0, stack top is z_1 .The stack top is popped from the top. The transitional function is.

$$\delta(q_0, b, z_1) \rightarrow (q_1, \lambda).$$

If number of '*b*' is greater than one then the machine has to traverse '*b*' with state q_1 and stack top z_1. (Number of '*b*' greater than one means number of '*a*' was greater than one.) The stack top is popped from the top. The transitional function is.

$$\delta(q_1, b, z_1) \rightarrow (q_1, \lambda).$$

If number of '*b*' is less than number of '*a*', then '*c*' will appear after fully traversal of all '*b*'s. At that time the state is q_1, and stack top is z_1. After traversal of '*c*', the stack top is popped. The transitional function is.

$$\delta(q_1, c, z_1) \rightarrow (q_2, \lambda).$$

If number of '*c*' is greater than one then the machine have to traverse '*c*' with state q_2 and stack top z_1. (Number of '*c*' greater than one means number of '*a*' was greater than one.) The stack top is popped. The transitional function is.

$$\delta(q_2, c, z_1) \rightarrow (q_2, \lambda).$$

If we have to design the PDA accepted by empty stack the δ function is

$$\delta(q_2, \lambda, z_0) \rightarrow (q_2, \lambda).$$

If we have to design the PDA accepted by Final State the δ function is

$$\delta(q_2, \lambda, z_0) \rightarrow (q_f, \lambda).$$

It may also happen that $m = n$, i.e. number of '*a*' is equal to number of '*b*'. At that case there is no '*c*' in the language. The string ends after fully traversal of all '*b*'. After traversal of all '*b*' s the state of the machine is q_1. If we have to design the PDA accepted by empty stack the δ function is

$$\delta(q_1, \lambda, z_0) \rightarrow (q_1, \lambda).$$

If we have to design the PDA accepted by final state the δ function is

$$\delta(q_1, \lambda, z_0) \rightarrow (q_f, \lambda).$$

The transitional functions for the entire PDA is

$\delta(q_0, a, z_0) \rightarrow (q_0, z_1z_0)$
$\delta(q_0, a, z_1) \rightarrow (q_0, z_1z_1)$
$\delta(q_0, b, z_1) \rightarrow (q_1, \lambda)$
$\delta(q_1, b, z_1) \rightarrow (q_1, \lambda)$
$\delta(q_1, c, z_1) \rightarrow (q_2, \lambda)$
$\delta(q_2, c, z_1) \rightarrow (q_2, \lambda)$
$\delta(q_2, \lambda, z_0) \rightarrow (q_2, \lambda)$ **//accepted by empty stack if $m > n$**
$\delta(q_2, \lambda, z_0) \rightarrow (q_f, \lambda)$ **//accepted by final state if $m > n$**
$\delta(q_1, \lambda, z_0) \rightarrow (q_1, \lambda)$ **//accepted by empty stack if $m = n$**
$\delta(q_1, \lambda, z_0) \rightarrow (q_f, \lambda)$ **//accepted by final state if $m = n$.**

4. Design a PDA to accept the language $L = a^nb^mc^{m-n,}$ where $m > n$ and $m, n > 0$.

Show an ID for the string *aabbbbcc*.

Ans. The language consists of '*a*', '*b*' and '*c*'. Here in every string all '*a*' will appear before '*b*' and after '*b*', '*c*' will appear. Number of '*c*' is the subtraction of number of '*b*' and number of '*a*'. In the string number of '*b*' is the sum of number of '*a*' and number of '*c*'. It can be designed as follows: For *n* number of '*a*', *n* number of z_1 are added to the stack. For next *n* number of *b*, those z_1 are popped from the stack and z_0 becomes the stack top. For the remaining $(m–n)$ number of '*b*', $(m–n)$ number of z_2 are added to the stack. For $(m–n)$ number of '*c*', $(m–n)$ number of z_2 are popped from the stack.

The transitional functions are designed as follows.

At the beginning the machine is in state q_0 with stack top z_0 and input is '*a*'. After traversing, the machine will add z_1 in the stack. The transitional function is

$\delta(q_0, a, z_0) \rightarrow (q_0, z_1z_0)$.

If number of '*a*' is greater than one then the machine have to traverse '*a*' with state q_0 and stack top z_1. Another z_1 is added to the stack top. The transitional function is

$\delta(q_0, a, z_1) \rightarrow (q_0, z_1z_1)$.

After traversal of all '*a*', '*b*' will appear. When '*b*' will come at that time state is q_0, stack top is z_1. The stack top is popped from the top. The transitional function is.

$\delta(q_0, b, z_1) \rightarrow (q_1, \lambda)$.

If number of '*a*' is greater than one then number of '*b*' is also greater than one because $m = (m–n) + n$. The machine has to traverse '*b*' with state q_1 and stack top z_1. The stack top is popped from the top. The transitional function is.

$\delta(q_1, b, z_1) \rightarrow (q_1, \lambda)$

After some time all z_1 s are popped from the stack. The stack top becomes z_0. As *m* is greater than *n*, till the input symbol is '*b*' with machine state q_1. In this situation z_2 is pushed into the stack. The transitional function is

$\delta(q_1, b, z_0) \rightarrow (q_1, z_2z_0)$

If $m–n$ is greater that one, i.e. number of 'c' is more than one then machine state q_1, input symbol 'b' and stack top z_2. Another z_2 is pushed into the stack. The transitional function is

$$\delta(q_1, b, z_2) \rightarrow (q_1, z_2z_2).$$

After fully traversal of all 'b's,'c' appears in the string. When 'c' appears machine state is q_1 and stack top is z_2. The stack top z_2 is popped from the stack. The transitional function is.

$$\delta(q_1, c, z_2) \rightarrow (q_2, \lambda)$$

If $m–n$ is greater that one, i.e. number of 'c' is more than one the machine has to traverse 'c' with state q_2 and stack top z_2. The stack top z_2 is popped from the stack. The transitional function is

$$\delta(q_2, c, z_2) \rightarrow (q_2, \lambda).$$

If we have to design the PDA accepted by empty stack the δ function is

$$\delta(q_2, \lambda, z_0) \rightarrow (q_2, \lambda).$$

If we have to design the PDA accepted by final State the δ function is

$$\delta(q_2, \lambda, z_0) \rightarrow (q_f, \lambda).$$

The transitional functions for the entire PDA is

$$\delta(q_0, a, z_0) \rightarrow (q_0, z_1z_0)$$
$$\delta(q_0, a, z_1) \rightarrow (q_0, z_1z_1)$$
$$\delta(q_0, b, z_1) \rightarrow (q_1, \lambda)$$
$$\delta(q_1, b, z_1) \rightarrow (q_1, \lambda)$$
$$\delta(q_1, b, z_0) \rightarrow (q_1, z_2z_0)$$
$$\delta(q_1, b, z_2) \rightarrow (q_1, z_2z_2)$$
$$\delta(q_1, c, z_2) \rightarrow (q_2, \lambda)$$
$$\delta(q_2, c, z_2) \rightarrow (q_2, \lambda)$$
$$\delta(q_2, \lambda, z_0) \rightarrow (q_2, \lambda) \text{ //accepted by empty stack,}$$
$$\delta(q_2, \lambda, z_0) \rightarrow (q_f, \lambda) \text{ //accepted by final state.}$$

ID for the string *aabbbc*

$$\delta(q_0, aabbbbcc, z_0) \rightarrow (q_0, abbbbcc, z_1z_0) \rightarrow (q_0, bbbbcc, z_1z_1z_0) \rightarrow (q_1, bbbcc, z_1z_0)$$
$$\rightarrow (q_1, bbcc, z_0) \rightarrow (q_1, bcc, z_2z_0) \rightarrow (q_1, cc, z_2z_2z_0) \rightarrow (q_2, c, z_2z_0) \rightarrow (q_2, \lambda, z_0)$$
$$\rightarrow (q_2, \lambda) \text{ // Accepted by empty stack.}$$

5. **Design a PDA for Hypertext Markup Language (HTML) consisting of all tags having immediate closing tags within the <BODY></BODY> tag.**

Show an ID for the following language

<HTML>
<HEAD>
<TITLE>
My First Web Page
</TITLE>
</HEAD>

<BODY>

<B> First Web Page</B>

<P> <B>HTML </B> is an <I>interpreted language.</I> No error is produced in HTML. </P>

</BODY>

</HTML>

Ans. Hypertext Markup Language (HTML) is a language used for webpage designing. This language is an interpreted language and produces no error. The language has a basic structure in the following form

<HTML>

<HEAD>

<TITLE>

</TITLE>

</HEAD>

<BODY>

Some other tags with closing tags

</BODY>

<HTML>

The tags can be of capital letter, small letter or mixture of both. The tags within <> is called open tag and the tags within </> is called closing tags. Most of the tags in HTML has closing tags, but some of the tags like <BR>, <HR> has no closing tags.

In <BODY> </BODY> tag all the other tags appear. The tags may appear in any order. But for all the opening tags there is a closing tag except the tags which do not have any closing tag. For the line **<B>HTML </B> is an <I>interpreted language.</I>, the output is**

HTML is an *interpreted language.*

If the line is in the form **<B>HTML is an <I>interpreted </B>language.</I>,** the output:

HTML is an *interpreted* *language.*

In this section we are interested in tags with immediate closing tags like the first example, i.e., the tag within the body which has opened first will close at last.

Every HTML file starts with <HTML> tag. At state q_0, when the machine gets <HTML> as input it pushes $Z_{<HTML>}$ in the stack. The transitional function is

$$\delta(q_0, <HTML>, Z_0) \rightarrow (q_1, Z_{<HTML>}Z_0)$$

In every HTML document after <HTML>, <HEAD> tag comes. The transitional function for traversing <HEAD> is

$$\delta(q_1, <HEAD>, Z_{<HTML>}) \rightarrow (q_2, Z_{<HEAD>} Z_{<HTML>}).$$

In every HTML document after <HEAD>, <TITLE> tag comes. The transitional function for traversing <TITLE> is

$$\delta(q_2, <TITLE>, Z_{<HEAD>}) \rightarrow (q_3, Z_{<TITLE>} Z_{<HEAD>}).$$

When the machine gets closing </TITLE> tag it pops the stack top symbol $Z_{<TITLE>}$. The transitional function

$$\delta(q_3, </TITLE>, Z_{<title>}) \rightarrow (q_3, \lambda).$$

When the machine gets closing </HEAD> tag it pops the stack top symbol $Z_{<HEAD>}$. The transitional function is

$$\delta(q_3, </HEAD>, Z_{<HEAD>}) \rightarrow (q_3, \lambda).$$

Now the stack top is $Z_{<HTML>}$. The next symbol is <BODY>. The transitional function for traversing <BODY> tag is

$$\delta(q_3, <BODY>, Z_{<HTML>}) \rightarrow (q_4, Z_{<BODY>} Z_{<HTML>})$$

Within <BODY> tag any tag can come. Let a tag named <tag j> has come. Let the state of the PDA is q_i, where i is greater than or equal to 4. For traversing that tag the transition function is

$$\delta(q_i, <tag\ j>, Z_{<tag\ j/>}) \rightarrow (q_{i+1,} Z_{<tag\ j>} Z_{<tag\ j/>})$$

If <tag j> appears with immediate closing tags then its closing tag will get the symbol $Z_{<'ag\ j>}$ as stack top. That stack top is popped.

$$\delta(q_i, </tag\ j>, Z_{<tag\ j>}) \rightarrow (q_{i,} \lambda).$$

The last two tags are </BODY> and </HTML>. When </BODY> is traversed the stack top is $Z_{<BODY>}$. The stack top is popped by the following transitional function.

$$\delta(q_i, </BODY>, Z_{<BODY>}) \rightarrow (q_{i,} \lambda).$$

When </HTML> is traversed the stack top is $Z_{<HTML>}$. The stack top is popped by the following transitional function.

$$\delta(q_i, </HTML>, Z_{<HTML>}) \rightarrow (q_{i,} \lambda).$$

If we have to design the PDA accepted by empty stack the δ function is

$$\delta(q_i, \lambda, z_0) \rightarrow (q_i, \lambda).$$

If we have to design the PDA accepted by final state the δ function is

$$\delta(q_i, \lambda, z_0) \rightarrow (q_f, \lambda).$$

ID for the given HTML document:

It is not possible to show the string in each phase. Only the state and the stack condition is shown in the description.

$$\delta(q_0, <HTML>, Z_0) \rightarrow (q_1, Z_{<HTML>} Z_0)$$
$$\delta(q_1, <HEAD>, Z_{<HTML>}) \rightarrow (q_2, Z_{<HEAD>} Z_{<HTML>} Z_0)$$
$$\delta(q_2, <TITLE>, Z_{<HEAD>}) \rightarrow (q_3, Z_{<TITLE>} Z_{<HEAD>} Z_{<HTML>} Z_0)$$
$$\delta(q_3, </TITLE>, Z_{<title>}) \rightarrow (q_3, Z_{<HEAD>} Z_{<HTML>} Z_0)$$
$$\delta(q_3, </HEAD>, Z_{<HEAD>}) \rightarrow (q_3, Z_{<HTML>} Z_0)$$
$$\delta(q_3, <BODY>, Z_{<HTML>}) \rightarrow (q_4, Z_{<BODY>} Z_{<HTML>} Z_0)$$
$$\delta(q_4, <B>, Z_{<BODY>}) \rightarrow (q_5, Z_{<B>} Z_{<BODY>} Z_{<HTML>} Z_0)$$
$$\delta(q_5, </B>, Z_{<B>}) \rightarrow (q_5, Z_{<BODY>} Z_{<HTML>} Z_0)$$

$\delta(q_5, \text{<P>}, Z_{\text{<Body>}}) \rightarrow (q_6, Z_{\text{<P>}} Z_{\text{<BODY>}} Z_{\text{<HTML>}} Z_0)$
$\delta(q_6, \text{<B>}, Z_{\text{<P>}}) \rightarrow (q_7, Z_{\text{<B>}} Z_{\text{<P>}} Z_{\text{<BODY>}} Z_{\text{<HTML>}} Z_0)$
$\delta(q_7, \text{</B>}, Z_{\text{<B>}}) \rightarrow (q_7, Z_{\text{<P>}} Z_{\text{<BODY>}} Z_{\text{<HTML>}} Z_0)$
$\delta(q_7, \text{<I>}, Z_{\text{<P>}}) \rightarrow (q_8, Z_{\text{<I>}} Z_{\text{<P>}} Z_{\text{<BODY>}} Z_{\text{<HTML>}} Z_0)$
$\delta(q_8, \text{</I>}, Z_{\text{<P>}}) \rightarrow (q_8, Z_{\text{<P>}} Z_{\text{<BODY>}} Z_{\text{<HTML>}} Z_0)$
$\delta(q_8, \text{</P>}, Z_{\text{<P>}}) \rightarrow (q_8, Z_{\text{<BODY>}} Z_{\text{<HTML>}} Z_0)$
$\delta(q_8, \text{</BODY>}, Z_{\text{<BODY>}}) \rightarrow (q_8, Z_{\text{<HTML>}} Z_0)$
$\delta(q_8, \text{</HTML>}, Z_{\text{<HTML>}}) \rightarrow (q_8, Z_0)$
$\delta(q_8, \lambda, Z_0) \rightarrow (q_8, \lambda)$ **// Accepted by empty stack.**

6. Design a PDA for the language $L = \{a^n b^m a^m b^n$, where m, n $\geq 1\}$

Ans. The language is a CFL. The CFG for the language is $S \rightarrow aSb / aAb$

$A \rightarrow bAa / ba$

The grammar is not in GNF. So, first we need to convert the grammar into GNF. Take two non-terminals C_a and C_b and two productions $C_a \rightarrow a$ and $C_b \rightarrow b$. Replacing in appropriate positions the modified context free grammar is

$S \rightarrow aSC_b$
$S \rightarrow aAC_b$
$A \rightarrow bAC_a$
$A \rightarrow bC_a$
$C_a \rightarrow a$
$C_b \rightarrow b$

The CFG is in GNF.

First the start symbol S is pushed into the stack by the following production

$\delta(q_0, \epsilon, z_0) \rightarrow (q_1, Sz_0)$.

For the production $S \rightarrow aSC_b$ the transitional function is

$\delta(q_1, a, S) \rightarrow (q_1, SC_b)$.

For the production $S \rightarrow aAC_b$ the transitional function is

$\delta(q_1, a, S) \rightarrow (q_1, AC_b)$.

For the production $A \rightarrow bAC_a$ the transitional function is

$\delta(q_1, b, A) \rightarrow (q_1, AC_a)$.

For the production $A \rightarrow bC_a$ the transitional function is

$\delta(q_1, b, A) \rightarrow (q_1, C_a)$.

For the production $C_a \rightarrow a$ the transitional function is

$\delta(q_1, a, C_a) \rightarrow (q_1, \lambda)$.

For the production $C_b \rightarrow b$ the transitional function is

$\delta(q_1, b, C_b) \rightarrow (q_1, \lambda)$.

If we have to design the PDA accepted by empty stack the δ function is

$\delta(q_1, \lambda, z_0) \rightarrow (q_1, \lambda)$.

If we have to design the PDA accepted by final state the δ function is

$$\delta(q_1, \lambda, z_0) \rightarrow (q_f, \lambda).$$

7. Construct PDA for the language $L = \{(ab)^n\} \cup \{(ba)^n\}\ n \geq 1$.

Ans. The given language is the union of two languages $(ab)^n$ and $(ba)^n$. The grammar for the first language is $S_1 \rightarrow abS_1/ab$. Grammar for the second language is $S_2 \rightarrow baS_2/ba$. Here we have considered two start symbols S_1 and S_2, respectively. As two languages are connected with union symbol, consider another start symbol for the entire language as S. Make a production rule $S \rightarrow S_1/S_2$. The production rule for the grammar satisfying the language is

$$S \rightarrow S_1/S_2$$
$$S_1 \rightarrow ab/abS_1$$
$$S_2 \rightarrow ba/baS_2$$

The production rule after removing unit productions and useless symbol is

$$S \rightarrow ab/ba/abS_1/baS_2$$
$$S_1 \rightarrow ab/abS_1$$
$$S_2 \rightarrow ba/baS_2$$

The grammar is not in GNF. Consider two non-terminals C_a and C_b and two productions $C_a \rightarrow a$ and $C_b \rightarrow b$. The modified production rule become

$$S \rightarrow aC_b/bC_a/aC_bS_1/bC_aS_2$$
$$S_1 \rightarrow aC_b/aC_bS_1$$
$$S_2 \rightarrow bC_a/bC_aS_2$$
$$C_a \rightarrow a$$
$$C_b \rightarrow b.$$

The CFG is in GNF.

First the start symbol S is pushed into the stack by the following production

$$\delta(q_0, \epsilon, z_0) \rightarrow (q_1, Sz_0).$$

For the production $S \rightarrow aC_b$ the transitional function is

$$\delta(q_1, a, S) \rightarrow (q_1, C_b).$$

For the production $S \rightarrow bC_a$ the transitional function is

$$\delta(q_1, b, S) \rightarrow (q_1, C_a).$$

For the production $S \rightarrow aC_bS_1$ the transitional function is

$$\delta(q_1, a, S) \rightarrow (q_1, C_bS_1).$$

For the production $S \rightarrow bC_aS_2$ the transitional function is

$$\delta(q_1, b, S) \rightarrow (q_1, C_aS_2).$$

For the production $S_1 \rightarrow aC_b$ the transitional function is

$$\delta(q_1, a, S_1) \rightarrow (q_1, C_b).$$

For the production $S_1 \rightarrow aC_bS_1$ the transitional function is

$$\delta(q_1, a, S_1) \rightarrow (q_1, C_bS_1).$$

For the production $S_2 \rightarrow bC_a$ the transitional function is

$$\delta(q_1, b, S_2) \rightarrow (q_1, C_a).$$

For the production $S_2 \rightarrow bC_aS_2$ the transitional function is

$$\delta(q_1, b, S_2) \rightarrow (q_1, C_aS_2).$$

For the production $C_a \rightarrow a$ the transitional function is

$$\delta(q_1, a, C_a) \rightarrow (q_1, \lambda).$$

For the production $C_b \rightarrow b$ the transitional function is

$$\delta(q_1, b, C_b) \rightarrow (q_1, \lambda).$$

If we have to design the PDA accepted by Empty stack the δ function is

$$\delta(q_1, \lambda, z_0) \rightarrow (q_1, \lambda).$$

If we have to design the PDA accepted by final state the δ function is

$$\delta(q_1, \lambda, z_0) \rightarrow (q_f, \lambda).$$

8. Construct PDA for the language $L = \{a^nb^n\} \cup \{a^mb^{2m}\}\ m, n > 0$

Ans. The given language is the union of two languages a^nb^n and a^mb^{2m}. The grammar for the first language is $A \rightarrow aAb$ and $A \rightarrow ab$.

Grammar for the second language is $B \rightarrow aBbb$ and $B \rightarrow abb$. Here we have considered two start symbols A and B, respectively. As two languages are connected with union symbol, consider another start symbol for the entire language as S. Make a production rule $S \rightarrow A/ B$. The production rule for the grammar satisfying the language is

$S \rightarrow A/ B$
$A \rightarrow aAb/ ab$
$B \rightarrow aBbb/ abb$

The grammar contains two unit productions $S \rightarrow A$ and $S \rightarrow B$. After removing the unit productions the production rules become

$S \rightarrow aAb/ aBbb / abb /ab$
$A \rightarrow aAb/ ab$
$B \rightarrow aBbb/ abb$

The CFG is not in GNF. Consider two non-terminals S_a and S_b and two extra production rules $S_a \rightarrow a$ and $S_b \rightarrow b$. Replacing a and b by S_a and S_b, respectively in suitable places, the modified production rules become.

$S \rightarrow aAS_b / aBS_bS_b/ aS_bS_b/ aS_b$
$A \rightarrow aAS_b/ aS_b$
$B \rightarrow aBS_bS_b/ aS_bS_b$

The CFG is in GNF.

First the start symbol S is pushed into the stack by the following production

$$\delta(q_0, \in, z_0) \rightarrow (q_1, Sz_0).$$

For the production $S \rightarrow aAS_b$ the transitional function is

$$\delta(q_1, a, S) \rightarrow (q_1, AS_b).$$

For the production $S \rightarrow aBS_bS_b$ the transitional function is

$$\delta(q_1, a, S) \rightarrow (q_1, BS_bS_b).$$

For the production $S \rightarrow aS_bS_b$ the transitional function is

$$\delta(q_1, a, S) \rightarrow (q_1, S_bS_b).$$

For the production $S \rightarrow aS_b$ the transitional function is

$$\delta(q_1, a, S) \rightarrow (q_1, S_b).$$

For the production $A \rightarrow aAS_b$ the transitional function is

$$\delta(q_1, a, A) \rightarrow (q_1, AS_b).$$

For the production $A \rightarrow aS_b$ the transitional function is

$$\delta(q_1, a, A) \rightarrow (q_1, S_b).$$

For the production $B \rightarrow aBS_bS_b$ the transitional function is

$$\delta(q_1, a, B) \rightarrow (q_1, BS_bS_b).$$

For the production $B \rightarrow aS_bS_b$ the transitional function is

$$\delta(q_1, a, B) \rightarrow (q_1, S_bS_b).$$

If we have to design the PDA accepted by empty stack the δ function is

$$\delta(q_1, \lambda, z_0) \rightarrow (q_1, \lambda).$$

If we have to design the PDA accepted by final state the δ function is

$$\delta(q_1, \lambda, z_0) \rightarrow (q_f, \lambda).$$

MULTIPLE CHOICE QUESTIONS

1. PDA is the machine format of
   (a) Type 0 language (b) Type 1 language (c) Type 2 language (d) Type 3 language.
2. Which is not true for mechanical diagram of PDA?
   (a) PDA contains a stack
   (b) The head reads as well as writes
   (c) The head moves from left to right
   (d) Input string is surrounded by infinite number of blank in both side.

3. The difference between finite automata and PDA is in _____.

   (a) Reading Head (b) Input tape (c) Finite Control (d) Stack

4. In PDA transitional function δ is in the form

   (a) $Q \times (\Sigma \cup \{\lambda\}) \times \Gamma \rightarrow (Q, \Gamma)$. (b) $Q \times \Sigma \rightarrow Q$ (c) $Q \times \Sigma \times \Gamma \rightarrow Q$
   (d) $Q \times \Gamma \rightarrow Q \times \Sigma$. (Where Q is the finite set of states, Σ is the set of input alphabets, Γ is the stack symbols.)

5. Instantaneous Description remembers

   (a) the information of state and input tape content at a given instance of time.
   (b) the information of state and stack content at a given instance of time.
   (c) the information of input tape and stack content at a given instance of time.
   (d) the information of state, input tape and stack content at a given instance of time

6. Which of the following is not possible algorithmically?

   (a) RE to CFG (b) NFA to DFA (c) CFG to PDA (d) NPDA to DPDA

7. Which of the following is not accepted by DPDA but accepted by NPDA?

   (a) $L = a^n b^n$, where $n > 0$ (b) $L = WCW^R$, where $W \in (a, b)^*$
   (c) $L = WW^R$, where $W \in (a, b)^+$ (d) $L = a^n b^m c^m d^n$, where $m,n > 0$

8. Which of the followings cannot be designed by PDA?

   (a) $a^n b^n c^i$, where $n, i > 0$ (b) $a^n b^n c^n$, where $n > 0$,
   (c) $a^n c^i b^n$, where $n, i > 0$ (d) $c^i a^n b^n$, where $n, i > 0$.

Ans. 1. c, 2.b, 3.d, 4. a, 5. b, 6. d, 7. c, 8. b.

EXERCISES

1. Construct PDA to accept the following languages by empty store and final state.

   (a) $L = \{a^n$, where $n > 0\}$
   (b) $L = \{a^n$, where $n \geq 0\}$
   (c) $L = \{a^n b c^n$, where $n > 0\}$
   (d) $L = \{a^n b^{2n}$, where $n > 0\}$
   (e) $L = \{a^n b^m c^{m+n}$, where $m, n > 0\}$
   (f) $L = \{a^n b a^n$, where $n > 0\}$
   (g) $L = \{a^n b^n c^i$, where $n, i > 0\}$
   (h) $L = \{a^m b^{m+n} c^n$, where $m, n > 0\}$.

(Hints: For m number of 'a', m number of Z_1 are pushed into the stack. For first m number of 'b', m number of Z_1 are popped from the stack. For next n number of 'b', n number of Z_2 are pushed into the stack, which will be popped for next n number of 'c'.)

   (i) $L = \{a^m b^{m+n} a^n$, where $m, n > 0\}$
   (j) $L = \{WCW$, where $W \in (a, b)^+\}$
   (k) $L = \{WCW$, where $W \in (a, b)^*\}$.

2. Construct an equivalent PDA for the following Context Free Grammars.

   (a) $S \rightarrow aB/bA$
   $A \rightarrow aS/bAA/a$
   $B \rightarrow bS/aBB/b$

(b) $S \rightarrow bA/aB$
$A \rightarrow bA/aS/a$
$B \rightarrow aB/bS/b$

(c) $S \rightarrow Abb/a$
$A \rightarrow aaA/B$
$B \rightarrow bAb$

3. Construct PDA with graphical notation to accept the following languages by graphical notation
   (a) $L = \{a^n b^n c^m d^m$, where $m,n \geq 1\}$
   (b) $L = \{a^n b^n c^m$, where $n,m \geq 1\}$.

FILL IN THE BLANKS

1. Full form of PDA is ____________.
2. ____________ is the machine format of Context Free Language.
3. The mechanical diagram of Pushdown Automata is similar to Finite Automata but difference is in ____________.
4. ____________ of PDA describes the configuration of PDA at a given instant.
5. There are two ways to declare a string accepted by a Pushdown Automata a) ____________ and b) ____________.
6. For directly constructing PDA from a given grammar we first need to convert the grammar into ____________ normal form.
7. If a PDA being in a state with a single input and single stack symbol gives a single move, then the PDA is called ____________ -Pushdown automata.
8. If a PDA being in a state with a single input and single stack symbol gives more than one move for any of its transitional functions, then the PDA is called ____________ Pushdown automata.
9. The PDA for the string L = {(Set of all palindromes over a, b)} can be designed by ____________ Pushdown automata not by ____________ Pushdown automata.

ANSWERS

1. Pushdown Automata
2. Pushdown Automata
3. stack
4. Instantaneous Description (ID)
5. Accepted By Empty Stack, Accepted by Final State
6. Greibach
7. Deterministic
8. Non Deterministic
9. Non Deterministic Deterministic

7

Turing Machine

7.1 BASIC OF TURING MACHINE

Q. What is Turing Machine? What is the significance of it?

Ans. Turing Machine is the machine format of unrestricted language, i.e. all types of languages are accepted by Turing Machine. In 1936, this machine was proposed by A.M.Turing as a model of any possible combination. Any computational process carried out by present days computer can be done on Turing machine.

Based on Turing machine a new theory called "Theory of undecidable problems" is developed. These types of problems can not be solved by any computer. Turing machine is a model of present days' computer. We can say that is any problem is not solved by Turing Machine, that problem can not be solved by computer, i.e. there does not exist any program or algorithm to solve it.

Q. Define Turing Machine. Give a block diagram with specified functions of each parts of it. What is the difference with Turing machine and Two way Finite Automata?

Ans. Turing machine in short TM is defined by 7 touples (Q, Σ, Γ, δ, q_0, B, F), where

Q: Finite set of states

Σ: Finite set of input alplabets.

Γ: Finite set of allowable tape symbol.

δ: Transitional function

q_0: Initial state

B: Is a symbol of Γ called blank

F: Final states.

Where δ is a mapping from $Q \text{ X } \Gamma \rightarrow (Q \text{ X } \Gamma \text{ X } \{L, R, H\})$

That is from one state by getting one input from the input tape the machine moves to a state, writing a symbol on the tape and moves to left, right or halts.

Mechanical Diagram:

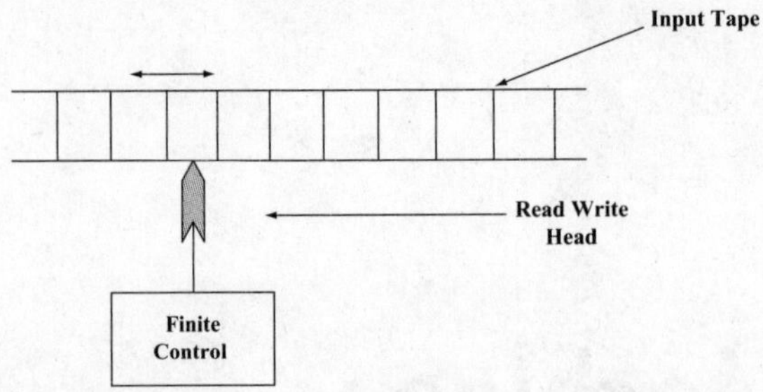

A Turing machine consists of an input tape, read-write head and finite control. The input tape contains input alphabets with infinite number of blanks at the left and right hand-side of the input symbols. The read-write head reads an input symbol from the input tape and send it to finite control. The machine must be in some state. In Finite control transitional functions are written. According to the present state and present input suitable transitional function is executed. Upon execution of a suitable transitional function the following operations are performed

(a) The machine goes into some state

(b) Writes a symbol in the cell of the input tape from where the input symbol was scanned

(c) Moves the reading head in left or right or halts.

Two way finite automata has a movement in both left and right-side like Turing machine. But, in Turing machine both read and write operations are done from and on the input tape, but for Two way Finite Automata only read operation is done, no write operation is done. A string is accepted by a Turing machine if the string is totally traversed and the machine halts. A string is accepted by a Two way finite automata is the string is totally traversed and the machine reaches to a final state.

Q. Define instantaneous description in the respect of Turing Machine.

Ans. The Instantaneous Description (ID) of Turing machine remembers

(a) The contents of all the cells of the tape, starting from the right most cell upto atleast the last cell, containing a non-blank symbol and containing all cells upto the cell being scanned.

(b) The cell currently being scanned by the read write head and

(c) The state of the machine.

at a given instance of time.

Q. Show the movement of the read-write head and the contain of the input tape for the string '*abba*' traversed by the following Turing Machine

$\delta(q_0, a) \rightarrow (q_0, X, R)$

$\delta(q_0, b) \rightarrow (q_0, b, R)$

$\delta(q_0, B) \rightarrow (q_1, B, L)$

$\delta(q_1, b) \rightarrow (q_1, Y, L)$

$\delta(q_1, X) \rightarrow (q_1, X, L)$

$\delta(q_1, B) \rightarrow (q_1, B, H)$

Ans.

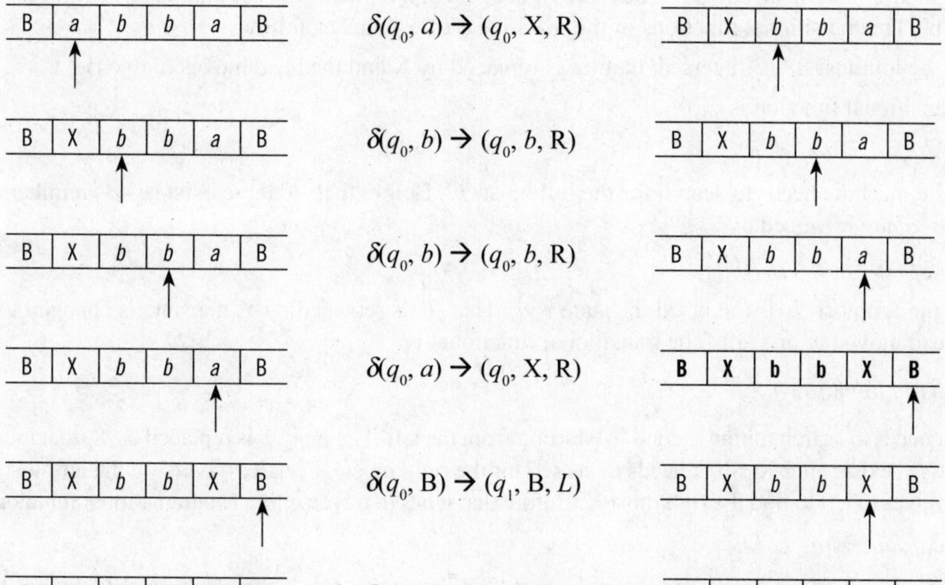

7.2 EXAMPLES

Q. Design a Turing Machine to accept the language $L = \{a^nb^n, n \geq 1\}$. Show an ID for the string '*aaabbb*' with tape symbols.

Ans. The string consists of two types of input alphabets, '*a*' and '*b*'. Number of '*a*' is equal to number of '*b*'. All the '*a*'s will come before '*b*'. In the language set there is at least one '*a*' and one '*b*'. Traverse the leftmost 'a' and replace this by X, then traverse right to find the leftmost 'b'. When it is found, replace 'b' by Y and traverse left to find the next 'a'. When traversing left if 'X' is found, the next 'a' is the 'a' after the traversed X. So, traverse right again and replace 'a' by X and traverse right to find the next 'b'. The transitional functions of the machine are designed as follows

When the leftmost '*a*' is traversed, that '*a*' is replaced by X and the head moves to one right. The transitional function is

$$\delta(q_0, a) \rightarrow (q_1, X, R)$$

Then the machine needs to search for the left most '*b*'. Before that '*b*' there exist (*n* - 1) numbers of '*a*'. Those '*a*' are traversed by

$$\delta(q_1, a) \rightarrow (q1, a, R).$$

When the leftmost '*b*' is traversed the state is q_1. That '*b*' is replaced by Y, the state is changed to q_2 and the head moved to one left. The transitional functional is

$$\delta (q_1, b) \rightarrow (q_2, Y, L).$$

Then it needs to search for the second '*a*' starting from the left. The first '*a*' is replaced by X, that means the second '*a*' exists after X. So, it needs to search for the right most 'X'. After traversing the leftmost '*b*' the head moves to left to find the rightmost X. Before that it has to traverse '*a*'. The transitional function is

$$\delta(q_2, a) \rightarrow (q_2, a, L).$$

After traversing all the '*a*' we get the rightmost 'X'. Traversing the X the machine changes its state from q_2 to q_0 and the head moves to one right. The transitional function is

$$\delta(q_2, X) \rightarrow (q_0, X, R).$$

From the traversal of second '*b*' onwards the machine has to traverse 'Y'. The transitional function is $\delta(q_1, Y) \rightarrow (q_1, Y, R)$

Like the same, after traversing '*b*' the machine has to traverse some Y to get the right most 'X'.

$$\delta(q_2, Y) \rightarrow (q_2, Y, L).$$

When all the '*a*'s are traversed the state is q_0, because before that state was q_2 and the input was X. The head moves to one right and gets a Y. Getting a Y means all '*a*'s are traversed and same number of '*b*'s are traversed. Traversing right if at last the machine gets no '*b*' but blank 'B' then the machine halts. The transitional functions are

$$\delta (q_0, Y) \rightarrow (q_3, Y, R),$$
$$\delta (q_3, Y) \rightarrow (q_3, Y, R),$$
$$\delta (q_3, B) \rightarrow (q_4, B, H).$$

ID for the string '*aaabbb*'

First the tape symbols are

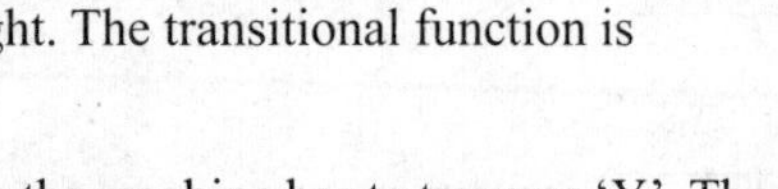

$\delta(q_0, a) \rightarrow (q_1, Xaabbb, R)$

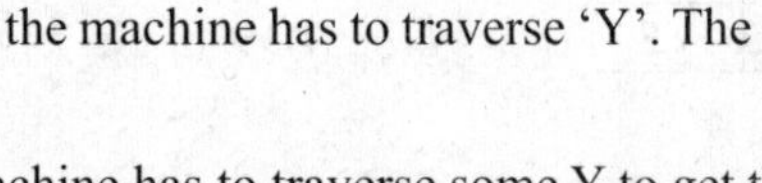

$\delta(q_1, a) \rightarrow (q_1, Xaabbb, R)$

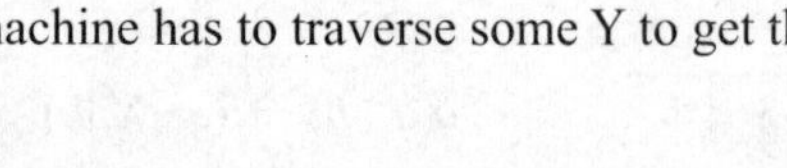

$\delta(q_1, a) \rightarrow (q_1, \mathrm{X}aabbb, \mathrm{R})$

$\delta(q_1, b) \rightarrow (q_2, \mathrm{X}aa\mathrm{Y}bb, L)$

$\delta(q_2, a) \rightarrow (q_2, \mathrm{X}aa\mathrm{Y}bb, L)$

$\delta(q_2, a) \rightarrow (q_2, \mathrm{X}aa\mathrm{Y}bb, L)$

$\delta(q_2, \mathrm{X}) \rightarrow (q_0, \mathrm{X}aa\mathrm{Y}bb, \mathrm{R})$

$\delta(q_0, a) \rightarrow (q_1, \mathrm{XX}a\mathrm{Y}bb, \mathrm{R})$

$\delta(q_1, a) \rightarrow (q_1, \mathrm{XX}a\mathrm{Y}bb, \mathrm{R})$

$\delta(q_1, \mathrm{Y}) \rightarrow (q_1, \mathrm{XX}a\mathrm{Y}bb, \mathrm{R})$

$\delta(q_1, b) \rightarrow (q_2, \mathrm{XX}a\mathrm{YY}b, L)$

$\delta(q_2, \mathrm{Y}) \rightarrow (q_2, \mathrm{XX}a\mathrm{YY}b, L)$

$\delta(q_2, a) \rightarrow (q_2, \mathrm{XX}a\mathrm{YY}b, L)$

$\delta(q_2, \mathrm{X}) \rightarrow (q_0, \mathrm{XX}a\mathrm{YY}b, \mathrm{R})$

$d(q_0, a) \rightarrow (q_1, \mathrm{XXXYY}b, \mathrm{R})$

$\delta(q_1, \mathrm{Y}) \rightarrow (q_1, \mathrm{XXXYY}b, \mathrm{R})$

$\delta(q_1, \mathrm{Y}) \rightarrow (q_1, \mathrm{XXXYY}b, \mathrm{R})$

$\delta(q_1, \mathrm{b}) \rightarrow (q_2, \mathrm{XXXYYY}, L)$

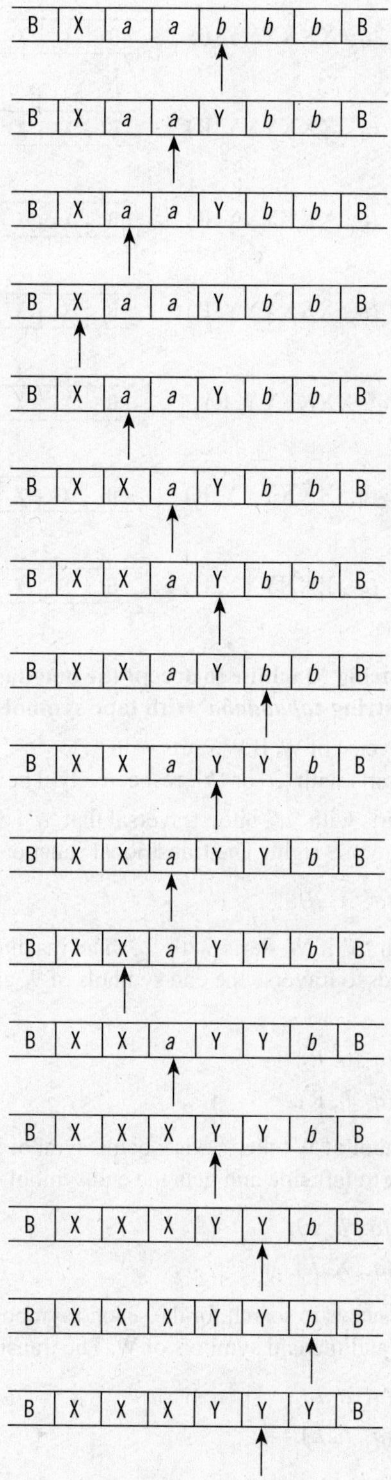

$\delta(q_2, Y) \rightarrow (q_2, XXXYYY, L)$

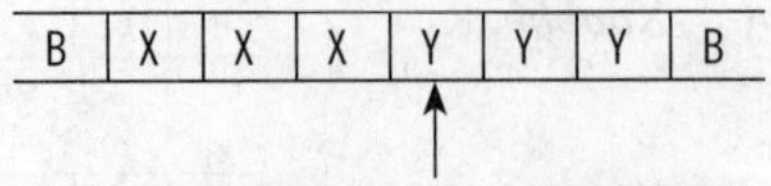

$\delta(q_2, Y) \rightarrow (q_0, XXXYYY, R)$

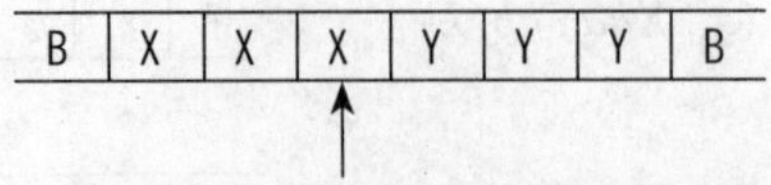

$\delta(q_0, Y) \rightarrow (q_3, XXXYYY, R)$

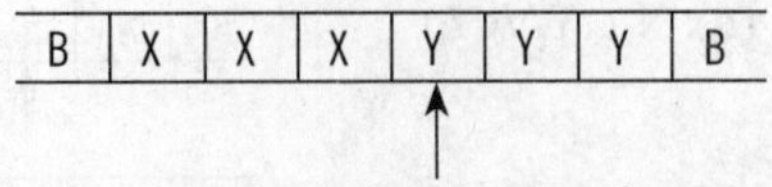

$\delta(q_3, Y) \rightarrow (q_3, XXXYYY, R)$

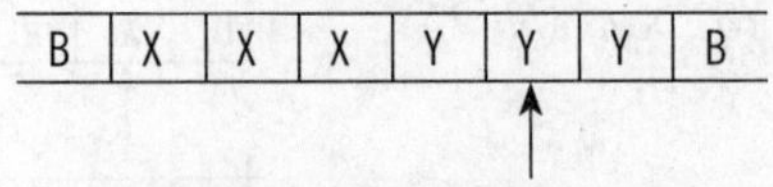

$(q_3, Y) \rightarrow (q_3, XXXYYY, R)$

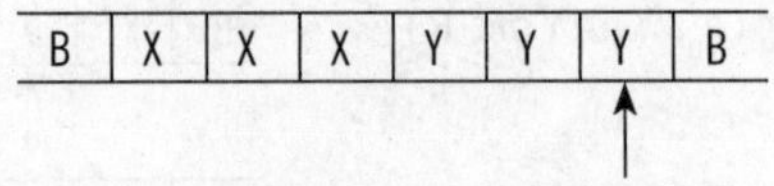

$\delta(q_3, Y) \rightarrow (q_3, XXXYYY, R)$

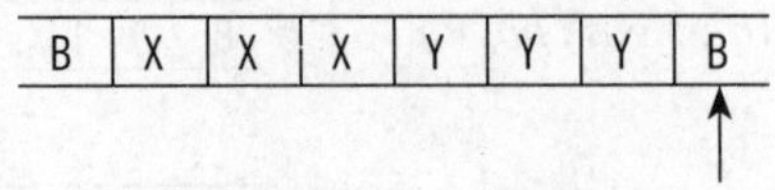

$\delta(q_3, B) \rightarrow (q_3, XXXYYY, H)$

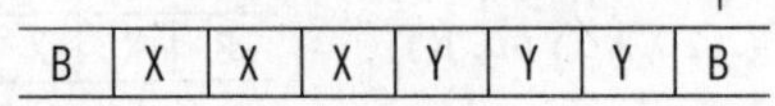

Q. Design a Turing Machine to accept the language $L = \{WW^R$, where $W \in (a, b)^+\}$. Show an ID for the string '*abaaaaba*' with tape symbols.

Ans. W^R is the reverse of W. If W starts with '*a*' or '*b*', W^R ends with '*a*' or '*b*' respectively. If W ends with '*a*' or '*b*', W^R starts with '*a*' or '*b*', respectively. The Turing Machine can be designed as follows:

If the string W starts with '*a*', upon traversal that '*a*' is replaced by X with state change from q_0 to q_1 and the head moves to one right. The transitional function:

$\delta(q_0, a) \rightarrow (q_1, X, R)$.

The W^R ends with '*a*' if W starts with '*a*'. The machine needs to search the end 'a' of W^R. Before that the machine needs to traverse the end symbols of W and beginning symbols of W^R. The transitional functions are

$\delta(q_1, a) \rightarrow (q_1, a, R)$,
$\delta(q_1, b) \rightarrow (q_1, b, R)$.

After the end symbol of W^R there exists blank symbol B. In the traversal process if the machine gets a B, it traverses back to left side and gets the end symbol of W^R. The transitional functions are

$\delta(q_1, B) \rightarrow (q_2, B, L)$,
$\delta(q_2, a) \rightarrow (q_3, X, L)$.

Now the machine needs to search for the second symbol of W. Before that it has to traverse the beginning symbols of W^R and the end symbols of W. The transitional functions are

$\delta(q_3, a) \rightarrow (q_3, a, L)$,
$\delta(q_3, b) \rightarrow (q_3, b, L)$.

When the machine gets the right most X, it recognizes that the next symbol of W exists after that 'X'. The transitional function:

$\delta(q_3, X) \rightarrow (q_0, X, R)$.

If the string W starts with 'b' the transitions are same as the previous but with some states changed. The transitional functions are

$\delta(q_0, b) \rightarrow (q_4, Y, R)$,
$\delta(q_4, a) \rightarrow (q_4, a, R)$,
$\delta(q_4, b) \rightarrow (q_4, b, R)$,
$\delta(q_4, B) \rightarrow (q_5, B, L)$,
$\delta(q_5, b) \rightarrow (q_6, Y, L)$,
$\delta(q_6, a) \rightarrow (q_6, a, L)$,
$\delta(q_6, b) \rightarrow (q_6, b, L)$,
$\delta(q_6, Y) \rightarrow (q_0, Y, R)$.

From second traversal onwards the machine needs not to traverse upto the end of W^R. In state q_1 (W starts with 'a') or q_4 (W starts with 'b') if the machine gets X or Y it traverses back to left to point the rightmost 'a' or 'b'. The transitional functions are

$\delta(q_1, X) \rightarrow (q_2, X, L)$,
$\delta(q_1, Y) \rightarrow (q_2, Y, L)$,
$\delta(q_4, X) \rightarrow (q_5, X, L)$,
$\delta(q_4, Y) \rightarrow (q_5, Y, L)$.

When all the symbols of W and W^R are traversed, the machine gets X or Y in the state q_0. The machine halts if in state q_0 it gets X or Y. The transitional functions are

$\delta(q_0, X) \rightarrow (q_f, X, H)$,
$\delta(q_0, Y) \rightarrow (q_f, Y, H)$.

The transitional functions can be given in a tabular format like this

State	a	b	B	X	Y
q_0	(q_1, X, R)	(q_4, Y, R)	-	(qf, X, H)	(qf, Y, H)
q_1	(q_1, a, R)	(q_1, b, R)	(q_2, B, L)	(q_2, X, L)	(q_2, Y, L)
q_2	(q_3, X, L)	–	–	–	–
q_3	(q_3, a, L)	(q_3, b, L)	–	(q_0, X, R)	–
q_4	(q_4, a, R)	(q_4, b, R)	(q_5, B, L)	(q_5, X, L)	(q_5, Y, L)
q_5		(q_6, Y, L)	–	–	–
q_6	(q_6, a, L)	(q_6, b, L)	–	–	(q_0, Y, R)

ID for the string '*abaaaaba*'

(Here the symbol is bold represents the read write-head position)

(q_0, ***a***baaaaba) → (q_1, X***b***aaaaba) → (q_1, Xb***a***aaaba) → (q_1, Xba***a***aaba) → (q_1, Xbaa***a***aba)
→ (q_1, Xbaaa***a***ba)→(q_1, Xbaaaa***b***a)→(q_1, Xbaaaab***a***)→(q_1, Xbaaaaba**B**) → (q_2, Xbaaaab***a***B)
→(q_3, Xbaaaa***b***X)→(q_3, Xbaaaa***b***X)→(q_3, Xbaaa***a***bX)→(q_3, Xbaa***a***abX)→ (q_3, Xba***a***aabX)
→(q_3, Xb***a***aaabX)→(q_3, X***b***aaaabXB)→(q_3, **X**baaaabX)→(q_0, X***b***aaaabX)→(q_4, XY***a***aaabX)
→(q_4, XYa***a***aabX)→(q_4, XYaa***a***abX)→(q_4, XYaaa***a***bX)→(q_4, XYaaaa***b***X)→(q_4, XYaaaab**X**)
→(q_5, XYaaaa***b***X)→(q_6, XYaaa***a***YX)→(q_6, XYaa***a***aYX)→ (q_6, XYa***a***aaYX)→(q_6, XY***a***aaaYX)
→(q_0, XY***a***aaaYX)→(q_1, XYX***a***aaYX)→(q_1, XYXa***a***aYX)→(q_1, XYXaa***a***YX)→(q_1, XYXaaa**Y**X
→(q_2, XYXaa***a***YX)→(q_3, XYXa***a***XYX)→(q_3, XYX***a***aXYX)→(q_3, XY**X**aaXYX)→(q_0, XYX***a***aXY
→(q_1, XYXX***a***XYX)→(q_1, XYXXa**X**YX)→ (q_2, XYXX***a***XYX)→(q_3, XYX**X**XXYX)
→(q_0, XYXX**X**XYX) →(*qf*, XYXXXXYX) (Halt)

Q. Design a Turing Machine to accept the language *L* = {set of all palindrome over *a*,
Show IDs for null string, '*a*', '*aba*' and '*baab*'.

Ans. Palindrome are of two types (a) Odd palindrome, where number of characters are odd and
Even palindrome, where number of characters are even. Null string is also a palindrome.

A string starts with '*a*' or '*b*' must ends with '*a*' or '*b*', respectively if the string is a palindrome.

If a string starts with '*a*' that '*a*' is replaced by blank symbol 'B' upon traversal with a state chan
from q_1 to q_2 and right shift of the read-write head. The transitional function:

$\delta(q_1, a) \rightarrow (q_2, B, R)$.

Then the machine needs to search for the end of the string. The string must ends with '*a*' and that exists before blank symbol B at the right-hand-side. Before getting that blank symbol the machine nee to traverse all the remaining '*a*' and '*b*' of the string. The transitional functions are

$\delta(q_2, a) \rightarrow (q_2, a, R)$,
$\delta(q_2, b) \rightarrow (q_2, b, \text{R})$,
$\delta(q_2, \text{B}) \rightarrow (q_3, \text{B}, L)$,
$\delta(q_3, a) \rightarrow (q_4, \text{B}, L)$.

The machine now needs to search for the second symbol (from the starting) of the string. Th
symbol exists after the blank symbol B, which is replaced at the first. Before that the machine needs
traverse the remaining '*a*' and '*b*' of the string. The transitional functions are

$\delta(q_4, a) \rightarrow (q_4, a, L)$,
$\delta(q_4, b) \rightarrow (q_4, b, L)$,
$\delta(q_4, \text{B}) \rightarrow (q_1, \text{B}, \text{R})$.

If the string starts with '*b*' the transitional functions are same as '*a*' but some states changed. T
transitional functions are

$\delta(q_1, b) \rightarrow (q_5, B, R)$
$\delta(q_5, a) \rightarrow (q_5, a, \text{R})$

$\delta(q_5, b) \rightarrow (q_5, b, \text{R})$
$\delta(q_5, \text{B}) \rightarrow (q_6, \text{B}, L)$
$\delta(q_6, b) \rightarrow (q_4, \text{B}, L)$.

When all '*a*' and '*b*' are traversed and replaced by B, the states may be one of q_3 or q_6, if the last mbol traversed is '*a*' or '*b*', respectively. Transitional functions for acceptance are

$\delta(q_3, B) \rightarrow (q_7, B, H)$,
$\delta(q_6, \text{B}) \rightarrow (q_7, \text{B}, \text{H})$.

Null string is also a palindrome. On the tape null symbol means blank B. In state q_1 the machine gets e symbol. The transitional function is

$\delta(q_1, B) \rightarrow (q_7, B, H)$.

The transitional functions in tabular form are represented as

State	*a*	*b*	B
q_1	$(q_2, \text{B}, \text{R})$	$(q_5, \text{B}, \text{R})$	$(q_7, \text{B}, \text{H})$
q_2	(q_2, a, R)	(q_2, b, R)	(q_3, B, L)
q_3	(q_4, B, L)	—	$(q_7, \text{B}, \text{H})$
q_4	(q_4, a, L)	(q_4, b, L)	$(q_1, \text{B}, \text{R})$
q_5	(q_5, a, R)	(q_5, b, R)	(q_6, B, L)
q_6	—	(q_4, B, L)	$(q_7, \text{B}, \text{H})$

ID for null string

$(q_1, B) \rightarrow (q_7, B)$ *(Halt)*

ID for the string '*a*'

$(q_1, \mathbf{a}B) \rightarrow (q_2, B\mathbf{B}) \rightarrow (q_3, \mathbf{B}B) \rightarrow (q_7, BB)$ *(Halt)*

ID for the string '*aba*'

$(q_1, \mathbf{a}baB) \rightarrow (q_2, B\mathbf{b}aB) \rightarrow (q_2, Bb\mathbf{a}B) \rightarrow (q_2, Bba\mathbf{B}) \rightarrow (q_3, Bb\mathbf{a}B) \rightarrow (q_4, B\mathbf{b}BB) \rightarrow (q_4, \mathbf{B}bBB)$
$\rightarrow (q_1, \text{B}\mathbf{b}\text{BB}) \rightarrow (q_1, \text{BB}\mathbf{B}\text{B}) \rightarrow (q_7, \text{BBBB})$ (Halt)

ID for the string '*baab*'

$(q_1, \mathbf{b}aabB) \rightarrow (q_5, B\mathbf{a}abB) \rightarrow (q_5, Ba\mathbf{a}bB) \rightarrow (q_5, Baa\mathbf{b}B) \rightarrow (q_5, Baab\mathbf{B}) \rightarrow (q_6, Baa\mathbf{b}B)$
$\rightarrow (q_4, \text{Ba}\mathbf{a}\text{BB}) \rightarrow (q_4, \text{B}\mathbf{a}\text{aBB}) \rightarrow (q_4, \mathbf{B}\text{aaBB}) \rightarrow (q_1, \text{B}\mathbf{a}\text{aBB}) \rightarrow (q_2, \text{BB}\mathbf{a}\text{BB}) \rightarrow (q_2, \text{BBa}\mathbf{B}\text{B})$
$\rightarrow (q_3, \text{BB}\mathbf{a}\text{BB}) \rightarrow (q_3, \text{B}\mathbf{B}\text{BBB}) \rightarrow (q_7, \text{BBBBB})$ (Halt).

Q. Design a Turing Machine to accept the language $L = a^n b^n c^n$, where $n \geq 1$.

Ans. This is a context sensitive language. The language consists of *a*, *b*, *c*. Here number of '*a*' is ual to number of '*b*' which is equal to number of '*c*'. The *n* number of '*c*' are followed by *n* number of 'b' which are followed by n number of 'a'. The Turing machine is designed as follows. For each 'a', search for 'b' and 'c' and again traverse back to left to search for the leftmost 'a'. The 'a' is replaced by 'X', 'b' is replaced by 'Y' and 'c' is replaced by 'Z'.

When all 'a' are traversed and replaced by 'X' the machine traverses right side to find if any untraversed 'b' or 'c' left or not. If not the machine gets Y and Z and at last Blank. Upon getting Blank symbol the machine halts.

The transitional functions are

$\delta(q_1, a) \rightarrow (q_2, X, R)$ // '*a' is traversed.*

$\delta(q_2, a) \rightarrow (q_2, a, R)$ // Remaining 'a's are traversed.

$\delta(q_2, b) \rightarrow (q_3, Y, R)$ // 'b' is traversed.

$\delta(q_3, b) \rightarrow (q_3, b, R)$ // Remaining 'b's are traversed.

$\delta(q_3, c) \rightarrow (q_4, Z, L)$ // 'c' is traversed.

$\delta(q_4, b) \rightarrow (q_4, b, L)$ // Remaining 'b's are traversed from right to left.

$\delta(q_4, Y) \rightarrow (q_4, Y, L)$// Y, replacement for '$b$' is traversed.

$\delta(q_4, a) \rightarrow (q_4, a, L)$ // Remaining 'a' s are traversed from right to left.

$\delta(q_4, X) \rightarrow (q_1, X, R)$ //Rightmost X, replacement of 'a' is traversed.

$\delta(q_2, Y) \rightarrow (q_2, Y, R)$ //This is used from second time onwards.

$\delta(q_3, Z) \rightarrow (q_3, Z, R)$ //This is used from second time onwards.

$\delta(q_4, Z) \rightarrow (q_4, Z, L)$ //This is used from second time onwards.

$\delta(q_1, Y) \rightarrow (q_5, Y, R)$ // This is used when all 'a' are traversed.

$\delta(q_5, Y) \rightarrow (q_5, Y, R)$ //This is used when all 'a' are traversed and machine traversing right.

$\delta(q_5, Z) \rightarrow (q_6, Z, R)$ // This is used when all 'a' and 'b' are traversed.

$\delta(q_6, Z) \rightarrow (q_6, Z, R)$ //This is used when all 'a' and 'b are traversed and machine traversing right to search for remaining 'c'.

$\delta(q_6, B) \rightarrow (q_f, B, H)$ // This is used when all 'a', 'b' and 'c' are traversed.

Upon executing the last transitional function the machine halts.

The transitional functions in tabular form are represented as

State	a	b	c	B	X	Y	Z
q_1	(q_2, X, R)	–	–	–	–	(q_5, Y, R)	–
q_2	(q_2, a, R)	(q_3, Y, R)	–	–	–	(q_2, Y, R)	–
q_3	–	(q_3, b, R)	(q_4, Z, L)	–	–	–	(q_3, Z, R)
q_4	(q_4, a, L)	(q_4, b, L)	–	–	(q_1, X, R)	(q_4, Y, L)	(q_4, Z, L)
q_5	–	–	–	–	–	(q_5, Y, R)	(q_6, Z, R)
q_6	–	–	–	(q_f, B, H)	–	–	(q_6, Z, R)

Q. Design a Turing Machine to perform the concatenation operation on string of '1' Show an ID for *w*1= 111 and *w*2 = 1111.

Ans.: The Turing machine does the concatenation operation on two strings w_1 and w_2. These two strings are placed on tape of the Turing Machine separated by Blank symbol B. After traversal the blank symbol is removed and the two strings are concatenated.

The transitional functions are

$\delta(q_1, 1) \rightarrow (q_1, 1, R)$ *// Traversing '1' of first string.*

$\delta(q_1, B) \rightarrow (q_2, 1, R)$ //Traversing the separating blank symbol and convert it to '1'.

$\delta(q_2, 1) \rightarrow (q_2, 1, R)$ // Traversing '1' of second string.

$\delta(q_2, B) \rightarrow (q_3, B, L)$ // Blank symbol traversal means end of second string.

$\delta(q_3, 1) \rightarrow (q_4, B, L)$ //Last'1' of second string is converted to 'B' to keep number of'1' same.

$\delta(q_4, 1) \rightarrow (q_4, 1, L)$ // Traversing the remaining '1' at the left side.

$\delta(q_4, B) \rightarrow (q_5, B, H)$ // halts.

(*This machine is also applicable for performing Z = X+Y, where X = |w1| and Y = |w2|*)

ID for w1= 111 and w2 = 1111 resulting 1111111

$(q_1,$**1**$11B1111B)$ $\rightarrow(q_1,1$**1**$1B1111B)\rightarrow(q_1,11$**1**$B1111)$ $\rightarrow(q_1,111$**B**$1111B)\rightarrow(q_2,1111$**1**$11B)$
$\rightarrow(q_2,11111$**1**$1B)$ $\rightarrow(q_2,111111$**1**$B)$ $\rightarrow(q_2,1111111$**B**$)$ $\rightarrow(q_2,1111111$**B**$)\rightarrow(q_3,111111$**1**$B)$
$\rightarrow(q_4,11111$**1**$1BB)$ $\rightarrow(q_4,1111$**1**$1BB)$ $\rightarrow(q_4,111$**1**$111BB)\rightarrow(q_4,11$**1**$1111BB)$
$\rightarrow (q_4,B1$**1**$11111BB)\rightarrow (q_4,B$**1**$111111BB)\rightarrow (q_4,$**B**$1111111BB) \rightarrow (q_4,$**B**$1111111BB)$
$\rightarrow (q_5,B1111111BB)$ (Halt)

Q. Design a Turing machine to perform the following operation *f*(*x*,*y*) = *x*-*y*, where *x* > *y*

Show an ID for 4 –2 =2.

Ans.

This performs subtraction operation. Here *x* and *y* both are integer number. Let $x = |W_1|$ and $y = |W_2|$. Where W_1 and W_2 are strings of '1'. The two strings are placed on the input tape separated by B.

Starting traversal from left-hand-side '1' the machine moves towards right. It traversed B with a state changed from q_0 to q_1. In state q_1 it again traverses right to find B, that is end of second string. It changes its state and traverses left and changes the rightmost '1' by B(With state change and traversing left). It traverses the separating 'B' symbol and all '1's of the first string and find the beginning of first string, which starts after B at the left hand side. It changes the first '1' by B and again traverses right. This process continues till all '1's of the second string are replaced by 'B'.

The transitional functions are

$\delta(q_0, 1) \rightarrow (q_0, 1, R)$ *// All '1' of first string are traversed.*

$\delta(q_0, B) \rightarrow (q_1, B, R)$ // separating B is traversed.

$\delta(q_1, 1) \rightarrow (q_1, 1, R)$ // All '1' of second string are traversed.
$\delta(q_1, B) \rightarrow (q_2, B, L)$ // To signify end of second string.
$\delta(q_2, 1) \rightarrow (q_3, B, L)$ // Right most '1' of second string is converted to B.
$\delta(q_3, 1) \rightarrow (q_3, 1, L)$ // Remaining '1' of second string are traversed.
$\delta(q_3, B) \rightarrow (q_4, B, L)$ // Separating Blank symbol is traversed.
$\delta(q_4, 1) \rightarrow (q_4, 1, L)$ // All '1's of first string is traversed.
$\delta(q_4, B) \rightarrow (q_5, B, R)$ // Blank symbol before the first string is traversed.
$\delta(q_5, 1) \rightarrow (q_0, B, R)$ // Left most '1' of first string is converted to blank symbol.
$\delta(q_2, B) \rightarrow (qf, B, H)$ // Halts.

ID for 4 –2 = 2:

$(q_0$, **1**111B11) →(q_0, 1**1**11B11)→ (q_0, 11**1**1B11) → (q_0, 111**1**B11) → (q_0, 1111**B**11)
→ (q_1, 1111B**1**1) → (q_1, 1111B1**1**B) → (q_1, 1111B11**B**) → (q_2, 1111B1**1**B)
→ (q_3, 1111B**1**BB) → (q_3, 1111**B**1BB) → (q_4, 111**1**B1BB) → (q_4, 11**1**1B1BB)
→ (q_4, 1**1**11B1BB) → (q_4, **B**1111B1BB) → (q_4, **B**1111B1BB) → (q_5, B**1**111B1BB)
→ (q_5, B**1**111B1BB)→(q_0,BB**1**11B1BB) →(q_0,BB1**1**1B1BB) → (q_0,BB11**1**B1BB)
→ (q_0,BB111**B**1BB) → (q_0,BB111**B1**BB) → (q_1,BB111B**1**BB) → (q_1,BB111B1**B**B)
→ (q_2,BB111B**1**BB) → (q_3,BB111**B**BBB) → (q_4,BB11**1**BBBB) → (q_4,BB1**1**1BBBB)
→ (q_4,BB**1**11BBBB) → (q_4,B**B**111BBBB) → (q_5,BB**1**11BBBB)→ (q_0,BBB**1**1BBBB)
→ (q_0,BBB1**1**BBBB) → (q_0,BBB11**B**BBB) → (q_1,BBB11B**B**BB) → (q_2,BBB11**B**BBB)
→ (q_f,BBB11BBBB).

Q. Design a Turing Machine to accept string $L = (a,b)^*$, where N(a) + N(b) = even.

Ans. The string consists of any combination of 'a' and 'b'. In the string total number of characters is even. The Turing machine is designed as follows. If the machine gets 'a' or 'b' it moves right with state changed from q_0 to q_1. In state q_1 if the machine gets 'a' or 'b', it moves right with state changed from q_1 to q_0. In state q_0 if the machine gets blank symbol it halts.

The transitional functions are:

$\delta(q_0, a) \rightarrow (q_1, a, R)$,
$\delta(q_0, b) \rightarrow (q_1, b, R)$,
$\delta(q_1, a) \rightarrow (q_0, a, R)$,
$\delta(q_1, b) \rightarrow (q_0, b, R)$,
$\delta(q_0, B) \rightarrow (q_f, B, H)$.

Q. Design a Turing machine for infinite loop.

Ans. Infinite loop means the machine does not halts. It can be designed in the following way.

Let the string consists of only 'a'. If 'a' is traversed in state q_1, the machine moves right. After all 'a' of the string are traversed B is traversed and the machine moves left and changes state to q_2. Getting 'a' in state q_2 the machine moves left again to find the beginning of the string.

When the machine gets 'B', it moves right again with changed state from q_2 to q_1. This process continues and the machine falls in an infinite loop.

The transitional functions are:

$\delta(q_1, a) \rightarrow (q_1, a, R)$,
$\delta(q_1, B) \rightarrow (q_2, B, L)$,
$\delta(q_2, a) \rightarrow (q_2, a, L)$,
$\delta(q_2, B) \rightarrow (q_1, a, R)$.

Q. Design a Turing Machine to perform the function *f*(*x*) = *x*+1.

Ans. The function adds a '1' with the value of *x*. If one blank symbol at the right-hand-side is replaced by '1' then the machine can be easily designed.

The transitional functions are:

$\delta(q_1, 1) \rightarrow (q_1, 1, R)$,
$\delta(q_1, B) \rightarrow (q_2, 1, L)$,
$\delta(q_2, 1) \rightarrow (q_2, 1, L)$,
$\delta(q_2, B) \rightarrow (q_f, B, H)$.

Q. Design a Turing machine which copies a string of '0' and paste it just after the string. Show an ID for the string 00.

Ans. We have to design a Turing Machine which performs copy paste operation

The machine is designed in the following way.

(a) Replace each '0' of the given string by X.
(b) Go to right and find the blank and traverse left and replace the right most X by 0 again.
(c) Then traverse to right and replace the first 'B' after the right most '0' by '0' and traverse left. Repeat the last two steps until there are no more X.

The transitional functions are:

$\delta(q_0, 0) \rightarrow (q_0, X, R)$,
$\delta(q_0, B) \rightarrow (q_1, B, L)$,
$\delta(q_1, X) \rightarrow (q_2, 0, R)$,
$\delta(q_2, 0) \rightarrow (q_2, 0, R)$,
$\delta(q_2, B) \rightarrow (q_1, 0, L)$,
$\delta(q_1, 0) \rightarrow (q_1, 0, L)$,
$\delta(q_1, B) \rightarrow (q_f, B, H)$.

ID for the string 00

(q_0, **0**0BB)→(q_0, X**0**BB)→(q_0, XX**B**B)→(q_1, X**X**BB)→(q_2, X0**B**B)→(q_1, X**0**0B)→(q_1, **X**00B) → (q_2, 0**0**0B)→(q_2, 00**0**B)→(q_2, 000**B**)→(q_1, 00**0**0)→(q_1, 0**0**00)→(q_1, **0**000)→ (q_1,**B**0000) → (q_f,B0000) (Halt)

Q. Design a Turing Machine which performs 1's complement operation on binary string.

Ans. Complement operation means '0' is converted to '1' and '1' is converted to '0'.

The transitional functions for the Turing Machine are:

$\delta(q_0, 0) \rightarrow (q_0, 1, R)$,

$\delta(q_0, 1) \rightarrow (q_0, 0, R)$,

$\delta(q_0, B) \rightarrow (q_f, B, H)$.

Q. Design a Turing Machine to perform 2's Complement operation on binary string. Show IDs for the string 010 and 101

Ans. To calculate 2's complement, first a binary string is converted into 1's complement then with that 1's complement 1 is added to get 2's complement. If in the 1's complement the rightmost bit is '0', that '0' is converted into '1'. If the rightmost bit is '1',that '1' is converted into '0' and traverses left to find a '0'. If it gets '1' that '1' is converted into '0' again. If it gets '0' that '0' is converted into '1' and traverses left to find the leftmost symbol of the string.

	1 0 0 1	
	0 1 1 0	(1's Complement)
+	1	
	0 1 1 1	(2's Complement)

	0 1 0 0	
	1 0 1 1	(1's Complement)
+	1	
	1 1 0 0	(2's Complement)

The Turing Machine is designed in the following way.

Starting from state q_1 if the machine gets '1' or '0' that is converted into '0' or '1', respectively and the machine traverses right. When the machine gets B, it changes its state from q_1 to q_2 and traverse left. If it gets '0', that is converted into '1' with state changed from q_2 to q_3 and traverses left to find the leftmost symbol.

$\delta(q_1, 0) \rightarrow (q_1, 1, R)$ // *'0' is converted into '1'.*

$\delta(q_1, 1) \rightarrow (q_1, 0, R)$ // '1' is converted into '0'.

$\delta(q_1, B) \rightarrow (q_2, B, L)$ // Getting 'B' traverses left.

$\delta(q_2, 0) \rightarrow (q_3, 1, L)$ // If the rightmost bit in 1's complement is '0'.

$\delta(q_2, 1) \rightarrow (q_2, 0, L)$ // If the rightmost bit in 1's complement is '1' and search for '0'.

$\delta(q_3, 0) \rightarrow (q_3, 0, L)$ // Left traversal to find the left end.

$\delta(q_3, 1) \rightarrow (q_3, 1, L)$ // Left traversal to find the left end.

$\delta(q_3, B) \rightarrow (qf, B, H)$ //If 'B' then halts.

$\delta(q_2, B) \rightarrow (qf, B, H)$ // If in 1's complement all bits are 1's in state q_2 machine gets B.

ID for 010

(q_1, *B***0***10B*) → (q_1, *B1***1***0B*) → (q_1, *B10***0***B*) → (q_1, *B101***B**) → (q_2, *B10***1***B*) → (q_2, *B1***0***0B*) → (q_3, B**1**10B) → (*qf*, B110B) (Halt)

ID for 101

$(q_1, B101B) \rightarrow (q_1, B001B) \rightarrow (q_1, B011B) \rightarrow (q_1, B010B) \rightarrow (q_2, B010B) \rightarrow (q_3, B011B)$
$\rightarrow (q_3, B011B) \rightarrow (q_3, B011B) \rightarrow (qf, B011B)$ (Halt)

Q. Design a Turing Machine for set of all strings with *e*qual number of 'a' and '*b*'.

Ans. The machine is designed as follows.

The machine first finds an '*a*', replace this by X and moves left. When it gets blank again moves right to search for '*b*' and replace it by Y. Again traverse left to search for '*a*'. The process continues till right side Blank symbol is traversed in state q_0

The transitional functions are:

$\delta(q_0, a) \rightarrow (q_1, X, R)$,
$\delta(q_0, b) \rightarrow (q_0, b, R)$,
$\delta(q_0, X) \rightarrow (q_0, X, R)$,
$\delta(q_0, Y) \rightarrow (q_0, Y, R)$,
$\delta(q_1, B) \rightarrow (q_2, B, R)$,
$\delta(q_1, X) \rightarrow (q_1, X, R)$,
$\delta(q_1, Y) \rightarrow (q_1, Y, L)$,
$\delta(q_1, b) \rightarrow (q_1, b, L)$,
$\delta(q_2, a) \rightarrow (q_1, a, R)$,
$\delta(q_2, X) \rightarrow (q_2, X, R)$,
$\delta(q_2, Y) \rightarrow (q_2, Y, R)$,
$\delta(q_2, b) \rightarrow (q_3, Y, L)$,
$\delta(q_3, a) \rightarrow (q_3, a, L)$,
$\delta(q_3, X) \rightarrow (q_3, X, L)$,
$\delta(q_3, Y) \rightarrow (q_3, Y, L)$,
$\delta(q_3, B) \rightarrow (q_0, B, R)$,
$\delta(q_0, B) \rightarrow (q_f, B, H)$.

Q. Design a Turing Machine to accept the language $L = a^n b^{2n}$ $n > 0$

Ans. Number of '*b*' is equal to twice the number of '*a*'. In the language, all '*a*' appear before '*b*'. The Turing machine is designed as follows.

Replace one '*a*' by X and traverse right to search for the end of the string. After getting 'B' traverse left and replace two '*b*'s by Y. In the state q_0 if the machine gets Y as input it halts.

The transitional functions are.

$\delta(q_0, a) \rightarrow (q_1, X, R)$,
$\delta(q_1, a) \rightarrow (q_1, a, R)$,
$\delta(q_1, b) \rightarrow (q_1, b, R)$,
$\delta(q_1, B) \rightarrow (q_2, B, L)$,

$\delta(q_2, b) \rightarrow (q_3, Y, L)$,
$\delta(q_3, b) \rightarrow (q_4, Y, L)$,
$\delta(q_4, b) \rightarrow (q_4, b, L)$,
$\delta(q_4, a) \rightarrow (q_4, a, L)$,
$\delta(q_4, X) \rightarrow (q_0, X, R)$,
$\delta(q_0, Y) \rightarrow (qf, Y, H)$.

7.3 TRANSITIONAL REPRESENTATION OF TURING MACHINE

Q. How a Turing Machine can be denoted by graphical notation?

Ans. The mathematical notation for a Turing Machine is (Q, Σ, Γ, δ, q_0, B, F). In a Turing Machine the transitional function δ consists is in the form Q X Γ → (Q X Γ X {L, R, H}), where first is a present state, second is present input (Single character ∈ Γ). The transition produces a state, a symbol ∈ G written on the input tape and the head moves either left or right or halts.

In the graphical notation of Turing Machine there are states. Among them a circle with an arrow indicates a beginning state and a state with double circle indicates a final state, where the machine halts finally. The state transitions are denoted by arrow. The labels of the state transitions consists of input symbol, symbol written on the tape after traversal and the direction of movement of the read-write heaδ (Left, Right or Halt).

Q. Design a Turing Machine by transitional notation for the language

$L = a^n b^n$, where $n > 0$.

Ans. When the machine traverses '*a*', replace that '*a*' by X and traverse right to find the leftmost '*b*'. Replace that '*b*' by 'Y' and traverse left to find the second '*a*'. The second '*a*' exists after 'X', which was replaced first for the first '*a*'. By this process when *n* number of '*a*' and *n* number of '*b*' are traversed and replaced by X and Y, respectively then by getting a blank (B) the machine halts.

The transitional representation of the Turing machine:

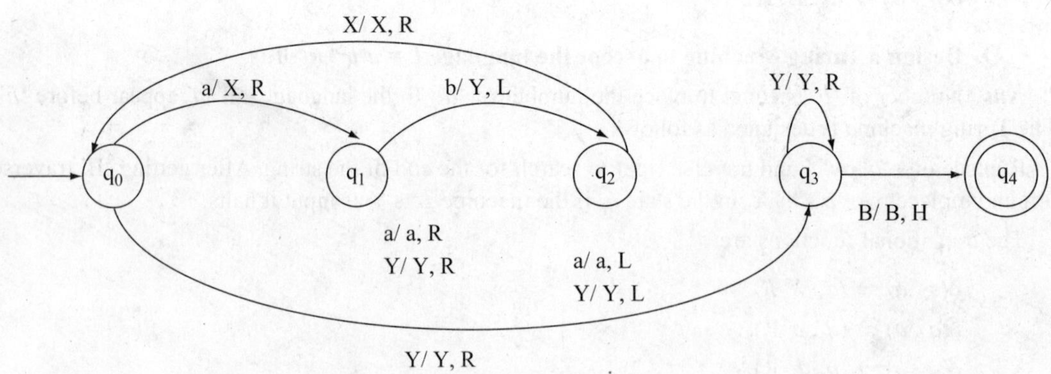

Q. Design a Turing Machine by transitional notation for the language L = {set of all palindrome over a,b}.

Ans. Palindrome can be of two types Odd palindrome and Even palindrome. Null string is also a palindrome. There are three paths to reach to the final state with Halt from q_1, the beginning state.

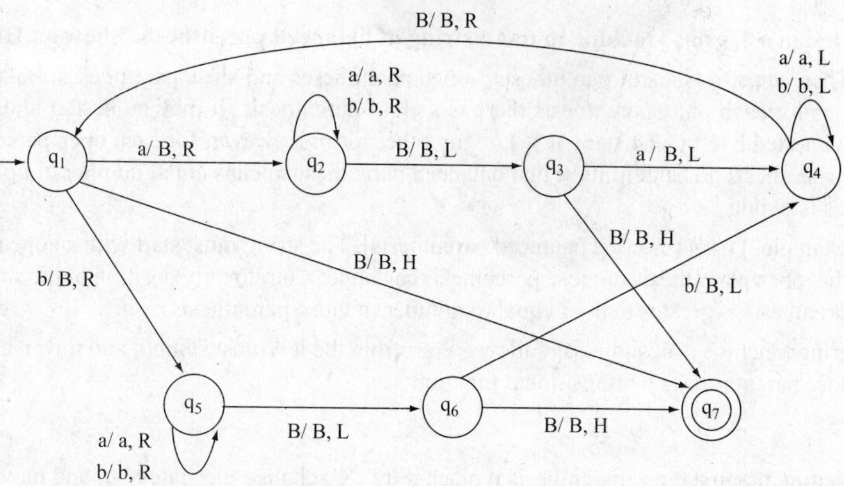

WHAT WE HAVE LEARNED SO FAR

1. Turing Machine was proposed by A.M. Turing in 1936 as a model of any possible combination. Any computational process carried out by present day's computer can be done on Turing machine.
2. Turing Machine is the machine format of unrestricted language, i.e. all types of languages are accepted by Turing Machine.
3. Indecisive problems are not solved by computer as no Turing machine can be developed for these problems.
4. Mathematical description of Turing Machine consists of 7 touples (Q, Σ, Γ, δ, q_0, B, F), where Q: Finite set of states, Σ: Finite set of input alplabets, Γ: Finite set of allowable tape symbol, δ: Transitional function, q_0: Initial state, B: is blank symbol, and F: Final state.
5. The transitional functions of Turing Machine is in the form $Q \text{ X } \Gamma \rightarrow (Q \text{ X } \Gamma \text{ X } \{L, R, H\})$, i.e. from one state by getting one input from the input tape the machine moves to a state, writing a symbol on the tape and moves to left, right, or halts.
6. The mechanical diagram of Turing machine consists of input tape, finite control and read-write head.
7. Upon execution of a transitional function the machine goes to some state, writes a symbol in the cell of the input tape from where the input symbol was scanned and moves the reading head in left or right or halts.

8. The ID of a Turing Machine remembers the contents of all cells from right most to atleast left-most, the cell currently being scanned by the read write head and the state of the machine at a given instance of time.

SOLVED PROBLEMS

1. Design a Turing Machine to test a string of balanced parenthesis. Show an ID for ( )(( )).

Ans. There are two types of parentheses –open parentheses and close parentheses. Balanced parenthesis means for each open parenthesis there is a close parenthesis. It may be nested like **((( )))** or may be non nested like **(( ) ( ))** or **( )( )( )** or any other form. However, for each open parenthesis there is a close parenthesis. [The definition that balanced parenthesis means equal number of open and close parentheses is wrong.

As an example, **) ( )( ) (** is not a balanced parenthesis]. The string must start with an open parenthesis and after that open parenthesis or close parenthesis can appear, but for any position of the string, number of open parenthesis is greater than or equal to number of close parenthesis.

The Turing Machine is designed as follows. Start from the left most symbol and traverse right to find the first close parenthesis. The transitional function:

$$\delta(q_0, \text{`('}) \rightarrow (q_0, (, R).$$

Upon getting the first close parenthesis replace it by 'X', change the state to q_1 and move left to find the open parenthesis for the replaced close parenthesis. The transitional function:

$$\delta(q_0, \text{`)'}) \rightarrow (q_1, X, L).$$

Getting the open parenthesis replace it by 'X' and change the state to q_0. The transitional function

$$\delta(q_1, \text{`('}) \rightarrow (q_0, X, R).$$

Then traverse towards right to find the close parenthesis. Here the machine may have to traverse X, which is the replaced symbol of close parenthesis. The transitional function for traversing this is

$$\delta(q_0, \text{`X'}) \rightarrow (q_0, X, R).$$

For a nested parenthesis like (( )), the machine have to traverse X, which is the replaced symbol of open parenthesis at the time of finding open parenthesis. The transitional function for traversing this is

$$\delta(q_1, \text{`X'}) \rightarrow (q_1, X, L).$$

Traversing right if B appears as input then there is no parenthesis (Open or close) left at the right side. Then traverse left to find if any parenthesis left at the left side or not. The transitional function is

$$\delta(q_0, \text{`B'}) \rightarrow (q_2, B, L).$$

At the time of left traversing the machine have to traverse X by the following transitional function

$$\delta(q_2, \text{`X'}) \rightarrow (q_2, B, L).$$

At the left hand side if it gets B, the machine halts.

$$\delta(q_2, \text{`B'}) \rightarrow (q_3, B, H).$$

ID for ( ) (( ))

$(q0, B()(())B) \rightarrow (q0, B()(())B) \rightarrow (q1, B(X(())B) \rightarrow (q0, BXX(())B) \rightarrow (q0, BXX(())B)$
$\rightarrow (q0, BXX(())B) \rightarrow (q0, BXX(())B) \rightarrow (q0, BXX(())B) \rightarrow (q1, BXX((X)B)$
$\rightarrow (q0, BXX(XX)B) \rightarrow (q0, BXX(XX)B) \rightarrow (q1, BXX(XXXB) \rightarrow (q1, BXX(XXXB)$
$\rightarrow (q1, BXX(XXXB) \rightarrow (q0, BXXXXXXB) \rightarrow (q0, BXXXXXXB) \rightarrow (q0, BXXXXXXB)$
$\rightarrow (q0, BXXXXXXB) \rightarrow (q2, BXXXXXXB) \rightarrow (q2, BXXXXXXB) \rightarrow (q3, BXXXXXXB)$ (Halt)

2. **Design a Turing Machine to perform n mod 2 (Or checking whether a number is odd or even) From here by instantaneous description check whether the number 5 is odd or even.**

Ans. An n is any number of same input alphabets. Let take n number of '0's. The machine is in state q_0 and the read-write head is on the beginning input symbol of the input tape. Getting input '0' it moves towards right replacing '0' by 'B' and changes state to q_1. The transitional function:

$\delta(q_0, 0) \rightarrow (q_1, B, R)$.

In state q_1 by getting input '0' it moves towards right replacing '0' by 'B' and changes state to q_0. The transitional function

$\delta(q_1, 0) \rightarrow (q_0, B, R)$.

By the previous two transitional functions all the '0's are replaced by 'B'. If number of '0' is even then the machine will reach to the end of the string with state q_0. At the end it will get 'B' and traversing that the machine will halt. (Means the number is even)

The transitional function

$\delta(q_0, B) \rightarrow (q_2, B, H)$.

If number of '0' is even then the machine will reach to the end of the string with state q_1. With getting input symbol 'B' it will traverse left by changing state to q_3. The transitional function:

$\delta(q_1, B) \rightarrow (q_3, B, L)$.

In state q_3 by getting input B the machine halts by replacing 'B' to '0'. (Means the number is odd). The transitional function

$\delta(q_3, B) \rightarrow (q_2, 0, H)$.

ID for $n = 5$: The string is 00000

$(q0, 00000B) \rightarrow (q1, B0000B) \rightarrow (q0, BB000B) \rightarrow (q1, BBB00B) \rightarrow (q0, BBBB0B)$
$\rightarrow (q1, BBBBBB) \rightarrow (q3, BBBBBB) \rightarrow (q2, BBBB0B)$ (Halt)

3. **Design a Turing Machine to perform reverse of a string, where the string $\in (a, b)^*$.**

Ans. The string consists of 'a' and 'b'. The string may start with 'a' or may start with 'b'. If the string starts with 'a', the reverse of the string will ends with 'a'. Same for 'b' also.

If the beginning state is q_1 and if the string starts with 'a', the TM will traverse right replacing 'a' by 'X' and changing state to q_2. (This q_2 specifies that the symbol was 'a'). The transitional function:

$\delta(q_1, a) \rightarrow (q_2, X, R)$.

At the time of traversing right the machine can get 'a' or 'b'. The transitional functions for traversing 'a' and 'b' are

$\delta(q_2, a) \rightarrow (q_2, a, R)$,

$\delta(q_2, b) \rightarrow (q_2, b, R)$.

If it gets 'B', means the string is end. The TM changes the state to q_3 and traverses left by the transitional function

$\delta(q_2, B) \rightarrow (q_3, B, L)$.

The string may ends with 'a' or may ends with 'b'. As the beginning symbol was 'a' (Which is memorized by the machine by state q_2, then q_3) the end symbol will be replaced by X, whatever it may be. However, the end symbol will be the beginning symbol. So, what the end symbol is – it will be memorized by different states. In this case if the end symbol is 'a', it will be memorized by changing state q_3 to q_6 and if the end symbol is 'b', it will be memorized by changing q_3 to q_7. The transitional functions are:

$\delta(q_3, a) \rightarrow (q_6, X, L)$.

$\delta(q_3, b) \rightarrow (q_7, X, L)$.

Traversing left the TM has to traverse 'a' or 'b'. It the state is q_6, the transitional functions are:

$\delta(q_6, a) \rightarrow (q_6, a, L)$,

$\delta(q_6, b) \rightarrow (q_6, b, L)$.

At the time of traversing left the TM may get 'X' or 'Y', the replaced symbols of 'a' or 'b'. The machine is in state q_6, which means the right most symbol of the string was 'a'. Upon getting 'X' or 'Y' at the left end the TM replaces it by 'X' and changes the state to q_1. The transitional functions are:

$\delta(q_6, X) \rightarrow (q_1, X, R)$,

$\delta(q_6, Y) \rightarrow (q_1, X, R)$.

If the string starts with 'b' the transitions are same as the string starts with 'a', but only some changes of states. The transitional functions are:

$\delta(q_1, b) \rightarrow (q_4, Y, R)$

$\delta(q_4, a) \rightarrow (q_4, a, R)$ // traversing right in search of end of string,

$\delta(q_4, b) \rightarrow (q_4, b, R)$,

$\delta(q_4, B) \rightarrow (q_5, B, L)$ // End of the string and traversing left

$\delta(q_5, a) \rightarrow (q_6, Y, L)$ // If the end symbol is 'a'

$\delta(q_5, b) \rightarrow (q_7, Y, L)$ // // If the end symbol is 'b'.

If the end symbol is 'b' at the time of traversing left the transitional functions are:

$\delta(q_7, a) \rightarrow (q_7, a, L)$,

$\delta(q_7, b) \rightarrow (q_7, b, L)$,

$\delta(q_7, X) \rightarrow (q_1, Y, R)$,

$\delta(q_7, Y) \rightarrow (q_1, Y, R)$.

By the above mentioned transitional functions the total string is traversed and reversed but in the place of '*a*' and '*b*' there are 'X' and 'Y'.

From the second time of traversing the string, the TM needs not to find the symbol 'B' to mark the right end of the string. In the state q_2 or q_5, it will get 'X' or 'Y', which are representations of already traversed symbol. The transitional functions are

$\delta(q_2, X) \rightarrow (q_3, X, L)$,
$\delta(q_2, Y) \rightarrow (q_3, Y, L)$,
$\delta(q_4 X) \rightarrow (q_5, X, L)$,
$\delta(q_4 Y) \rightarrow (q_5, Y, L)$.

The string may be of even length or odd length. For odd length string the middle element may be '*a*' or '*b*'. If the middle element is '*a*', then after replacing the middle element by 'X' the TM moves right but it finds either 'X' or 'Y' (Because all the other symbols are already replaced). It backs left by changing the state to q_3 or q_5 using the transitional functions mentioned above. At the left again it gets either 'X' or 'Y'. The TM changes the state to q_8 and moves right by the following transitional functions:

$\delta(q_3, X) \rightarrow (q_8, X, R)$,
$\delta(q_3, Y) \rightarrow (q_8, Y, R)$,
$\delta(q_5, X) \rightarrow (q_8, X, R)$,
$\delta(q_5, Y) \rightarrow (q_8, Y, R)$.

If the string is of even length then the machine gets 'X' or 'Y' in the state q_1 after replacing all the '*a*' and '*b*'. The transitional functions are:

$\delta(q_1, X) \rightarrow (q_8, X, R)$,
$\delta(q_1, Y) \rightarrow (q_8, Y, R)$.

The machine traverses right to find the end of the string consists of 'X' and 'Y'. When it gets 'B', it traverses left by changing the state from q_8 to q_9.

$\delta(q_8, X) \rightarrow (q_8, X, R)$,
$\delta(q_8, Y) \rightarrow (q_8, Y, R)$,
$\delta(q_8, B) \rightarrow (q_9, B, L)$.

In the state q_9 at the time of traversing left the TM replaces all 'X's by '*a*' and all 'Y's by '*b*'.

$\delta(q_9, X) \rightarrow (q_9, a, L)$,
$\delta(q_9, Y) \rightarrow (q_9, b, L)$.

By this process when it gets the symbol 'B at the left it halts.

$\delta(q_9, B) \rightarrow (q_{10}, B, H)$.

If the string is a blank string (No 'a' and/or 'b'), the machine gets 'B' in the state q_1 and halts.

$\delta(q_1, B) \rightarrow (q_{10}, B, H)$.

The transitional functions are represented in the tabular format.

State	A	b	X	Y	B
q_1	(q_2, X, R)	(q_4, Y, R)	(q_8, X, R)	(q_8, Y, R)	(q_{10}, B, H)
q_2	(q_2, a, R)	(q_2, b, R)	(q_3, X, L)	(q_3, Y, L)	(q_3, B, L)
q_3	(q_6, X, L)	(q_7, X, L)	(q_8, X, R)	(q_8, Y, R)	–
q_4	(q_4, a, R)	(q_4, b, R)	(q_5, X, L)	$(q_5, Y L)$	(q_5, B, L)
q_5	(q_6, Y, L)	(q_7, Y, L)	(q_8, X, R)	(q_8, Y, R)	–
q_6	(q_6, a, L)	(q_6, b, L)	(q_1, X, R)	(q_1, X, R)	–
q_7	(q_7, a, L)	(q_7, b, L)	(q_1, Y, R)	(q_1, Y, R)	–
q_8	–	–	(q_8, X, R)	(q_8, Y, R)	(q_9, B, L)
q_9			(q_9, a, L)	(q_9, b, L)	(q_{10}, B, H)

MULTIPLE CHOICE QUESTIONS

1. Turing Machine is the machine format of ____ language
   (a) Type 0, (b) Type 1, (c) Type 2, (d) Type 3.
2. Which is not a part of the mechanical diagram of Turing Machine?
   (a) Input tape, (b) Read-write head, (c) Finite Control, (d) Stack.
3. Difference between Turing Machine and Two way FA is in
   (a) Input Tape, (b) Read-write head, (c) Finite Control, (d) All of these.
4. Difference between Turing Machine & Push down automata is in
   (a) Input Tape, (b) Finite Control, (c) Stack, (d) All of these.
5. Which is not true for mechanical diagram of Turing Machine
   The head moves in both directions.
   The head reads as well as writes.
   Input string is surrounded by infinite number of blank in both side.
   Some symbols are pushed into the stack.
6. In Turing Machine transitional function δ is in the form
   (a) $Q \text{ X } \Gamma \rightarrow (Q \text{ X } \Gamma \text{ X } \{L, R, H\})$, (b) $Q \text{ X } \Sigma \rightarrow (Q \text{ X } \{L, R, H\})$,
   (c) $Q \text{ X } \Sigma \rightarrow (Q \text{ X } \Sigma \{L, R, H\})$, (d) $Q \text{ X } \Gamma \rightarrow (Q \text{ X } \Sigma \text{ X } \{L, R, H\})$.
   (where Q is the finite set of states, Σ is the finite set of input alphabets, Γ is the allowable tape symbol, L means left, R means right and H means halt)
7. Which of the strings is accepted by Turing Machine?
   (a) $L = a^n c^m b^n$, where $m, n > 0$, (b) $L = a^n b^n c^i$, where $n, i > 0$,
   (c) $L = a^n b^n c^n$, where $n > 0$, (d) All of the above.

8. Which is not true for Instantaneous Description (ID) of Turing Machine.
   (a) It remembers the state of the machine
   (b) It remembers the cell currently being scanned by the read write head
   (c) The contents of all the cells of the tape.
   (d) The content of the cell on which the head previously be in.

Ans: 1. a 2. d 3. b 4. c 5. d 6. a 7. d 8. d

EXERCISES

1. Construct a Turing machine for the followings
   $L = \{a,b\}^+$,
   L = WW, where W $\in (a, b)^+$,
   L = WW^R, where W $\in (a, b)^+$,
   L = {all even palindromes over (a, b)},
   $L = a^n b^n c^n$, $n > 0$,
   $L = n$ -1, where $n > 0$.
2. Design a Turing Machine which acts as a eraser.
   [*Hints: Starts from left-hand-side, scan each symbol from left to right and replace it of these by blank. Halts if gets blank.*]
3. Design a Turing Machine which replaces '0' by '1' and '1' by '0' of the string traversed.
4. Design a Turing Machine to accept the string $L = \{a^n b^m c^{n+m}$, where $n > 0$, $m > 0\}$
   [*Hints: Traverse an 'a', replace it by X and moves right to find the first 'c' and replace it by Y. Then traverse left to find the second 'a'. By this process replace n number of 'a' by X and n number of 'b' by Y. By the same process replace m number of 'b' by Z and last m number of 'c' by Z'*]
5. Design a Turing Machine to accept the string $L = \{a^m b^{m+n} c^n$, where $m, n > 0\}$
6. Design a Turing Machine by transitional notation for the following languages
   (a) $L = a^n b^n$, $n > 0$,
   (b) $L = \{a^n b^n c^m d^m$, where $m,n \geq 1\}$,
   (c) $L = \{a^n b^n c^m$, where $n,m \geq 1\}$.

FILL IN THE BLANKS

1. All types of languages are accepted by ____________.
2. According to Chomsky hierarchy Type 0 language is called ____________.
3. Diagram of Turing Machine is like Finite Automata but here the head moves ____________.
4. The head of Turing machine is called ____________.
5. The string $a^n b^n c^n$, $n > 0$ is accepted by ____________.
6. Turing Machine is called ____________.

ANSWERS

1. Turing Machine
2. Unrestricted Language
3. In both direction
4. Read Write Head
5. Turing Machine
6. Universal Machine

References

Aho, Hopcroft and Ullman, *The Design and Analysis of Computer Algorithms,* Addison-Wesley.

Aho, Sethi, Ullman, *Compilers Principles, Techniques and Tools,* Pearson Education, 2003.

Hopcroft and Ullman, *Introduction to Automata Theory, Languages and Computation,* Addison-Wesley.

Kohavi, ZVI, *Switching And Finite Automata Theory*, Tata McGraw-Hill, 2006.

Lewis and Papadimitriou, *Elements of the Theory of Computation,* Prentice-Hall.

Martin, *Introduction to Languages and the Theory of Computation,* McGraw-Hill, Second Edition, 1996.

Mishra, KLP, Chandrasekaran, N. *Theory of Computer Science,* (Automata, Languages and Computation) PHI, 2002.

Pandey, *An Introduction to Automata Theory & Formal Languages*, S. K. Kataria & Sons, 2010.

Pandey, *Concept of Compiler Design*, S. K. Kataria & Sons, 2010.

Index

S

T

U

V